Understanding Violent R

This is the first book to address in depth the interplay between radicalisation and political violence in Europe, as well as the effectiveness of counter-measures.

As evidenced from the multitude of intercepted plots across several European cities since 2001, the threat level and the intensity of the desire to perpetrate mass-casualty attacks within Europe is not diminishing. While violent radicalisation has gradually moved to the top of the EU counterterrorism agenda, it has been accompanied by a relatively embryonic understanding about the processes and interplay of factors that contribute to radicalisations, which are played out differently in cities like Paris, Rome, London and Copenhagen. Undoubtedly, there are common factors at the global and regional levels that facilitate radicalisation, but it is also clear that radicalisation is very context dependent. This book provides crucial insights into different ways to understand violent radicalisation within national contexts and the challenges addressing the many pathways into terrorism inspired by Al-Qaeda and other forms of Islamic extremism.

This book will be of great interest to students of terrorism studies and political violence, counterterrorism, EU politics, security studies and international relations in general.

Magnus Ranstorp is Research Director of the Center for Asymmetric Threat Studies at the Swedish National Defence College and a Member of EU Expert Groups on (Violent) Radicalisation. He has twenty years of experience in research on counterterrorism issues and testified at the 9/11 Commission Hearing.

Series: Political Violence
Series Editors: Paul Wilkinson and David Rapoport

This book series contains sober, thoughtful and authoritative academic accounts of terrorism and political violence. Its aim is to produce a useful taxonomy of terror and violence through comparative and historical analysis in both national and international spheres. Each book discusses origins, organisational dynamics and outcomes of particular forms and expressions of political violence.

Aviation Terrorism and Security
Edited by Paul Wilkinson and Brian M. Jenkins

Counter-Terrorist Law and Emergency Powers in the United Kingdom, 1922–2000
Laura K. Donohue

The Democratic Experience and Political Violence
Edited by David C. Rapoport and Leonard Weinberg

Inside Terrorist Organizations
Edited by David C. Rapoport

The Future of Terrorism
Edited by Max Taylor and John Horgan

The IRA, 1968–2000
An analysis of a secret army
J. Bowyer Bell

Millennial Violence
Past, present and future
Edited by Jeffrey Kaplan

Right-Wing Extremism in the Twenty-First Century
Edited by Peter H. Merkl and Leonard Weinberg

Terrorism Today
Christopher C. Harmon

The Psychology of Terrorism
John Horgan

Research on Terrorism
Trends, achievements and failures
Edited by Andrew Silke

A War of Words
Political violence and public debate in Israel
Gerald Cromer

Root Causes of Suicide Terrorism
Globalization of martyrdom
Edited by Ami Pedahzur

Terrorism versus Democracy
The liberal state response, 2nd edition
Paul Wilkinson

Countering Terrorism and WMD
Creating a global counter-terrorism network
Edited by Peter Katona, Michael Intriligator and John Sullivan

Mapping Terrorism Research
State of the art, gaps and future direction
Edited by Magnus Ranstorp

The Ideological War on Terror
World-wide strategies for counter-terrorism
Edited by Anne Aldis and Graeme P. Herd

The IRA and Armed Struggle
Rogelio Alonso

Homeland Security in the UK
Future preparedness for terrorist attack since 9/11
Edited by Paul Wilkinson et al.

Terrorism Today, 2nd Edition
Christopher C. Harmon

Understanding Terrorism and Political Violence
The life cycle of birth, growth, transformation, and demise
Dipak K. Gupta

Global Jihadism
Theory and practice
Jarret M. Brachman

Combating Terrorism in Northern Ireland
Edited by James Dingley

Leaving Terrorism Behind
Individual and collective disengagement
Edited by Tore Bjørgo and John Horgan

Unconventional Weapons and International Terrorism
Threat convergence in the twenty-first century
Edited by Magnus Ranstorp and Magnus Normark

International Aviation and Terrorism
Evolving threats, evolving security
John Harrison

Walking Away from Terrorism
John Horgan

Understanding Violent Radicalisation
Terrorist and Jihadist Movements in Europe
Edited by Magnus Ranstorp

Understanding Violent Radicalisation

Terrorist and Jihadist Movements in Europe

Edited by Magnus Ranstorp

Routledge
Taylor & Francis Group

LONDON AND NEW YORK

First published 2010
by Routledge
2 Park Square, Milton Park, Abingdon, Oxon OX14 4RN

Simultaneously published in the USA and Canada
by Routledge
711 Third Avenue, New York, NY 10017, USA

Routledge is an imprint of the Taylor & Francis Group, an informa business

© 2010 selection and editorial matter, Magnus Ranstorp; individual chapters, the contributors

Typeset in Times New Roman by Wearset Ltd, Boldon, Tyne and Wear

All rights reserved. No part of this book may be reprinted or reproduced or utilised in any form or by any electronic, mechanical, or other means, now known or hereafter invented, including photocopying and recording, or in any information storage or retrieval system, without permission in writing from the publishers.

British Library Cataloguing in Publication Data
A catalogue record for this book is available from the British Library

Library of Congress Cataloging-in-Publication Data
Understanding violent radicalisation: terrorist and jihadist movements in Europe/edited by Magnus Ranstorp.
p. cm.
Includes bibliographical references.
1. Radicalism–Europe. 2. Political violence–Europe. 3. Terrorism–Europe. 4. Jihad. 5. Islamic fundementalism–Europe. 6. Europe–Politics and government. 7. Europe–Race relations. 8. Europe–Foreign relations. I. Ranstorp, Magnus.
HN380.5.Z9R39 2009
363.325094–dc22   2009024399

ISBN10: 0-415-55629-5 (hbk)
ISBN10: 0-415-55630-9 (pbk)
ISBN10: 0-203-86574-X (ebk)

ISBN13: 978-0-415-55629-3 (hbk)
ISBN13: 978-0-415-55630-9 (pbk)
ISBN13: 978-0-203-86574-3 (ebk)

Contents

Notes on contributors ix

Introduction 1

MAGNUS RANSTORP

PART I
Understanding radicalisation as a process 19

1 **Background contributing factors to terrorism: radicalization and recruitment** 21

   REM KORTEWEG WITH SAJJAN GOHEL, FRANCOIS HEISBOURG, MAGNUS RANSTORP AND ROB DE WIJK

2 **Where does the radicalisation process lead? Radical community, radical networks and radical subcultures** 50

   PETER WALDMANN, MATENIA SIRSELOUDI AND STEFAN MALTHANER

3 **The physiology of Al-Qaeda: from ideology to participation** 68

   CHRISTINA HELLMICH

4 **Joining jihadi terrorist cells in Europe: exploring motivational aspects of recruitment and radicalization** 87

   PETTER NESSER

PART II
Understanding radicalisation in context   115

5   Radicalisation and recruitment in Europe: the UK case   117

      MARK HUBAND

6   An overview of violent jihad in the UK: radicalisation and the state response   144

      LINDSAY CLUTTERBUCK

7   Islamism, radicalisation and jihadism in the Netherlands: main developments and counter-measures   168

      EDWIN BAKKER

8   The Jihadists and anti-terrorist challenges in France: an overview   191

      JEAN-LUC MARRET

9   Radicalisation and recruitment among jihadist terrorists in Spain: main patterns and subsequent counter-terrorist measures   207

      ROGELIO ALONSO

10   Salafi–Jihadi terrorism in Italy   231

      CARL BJÖRKMAN

Index   256

Contributors

Editor

Magnus Ranstorp is Research Director of the Center for Asymmetric Threat Studies at the Swedish National Defence College and an invited Member of EU Expert Groups on (Violent) Radicalisation. He has 20 years of experience in research on terrorism and counter-terrorism issues and testified at the 9/11 Commission Hearing.

Contributors

Rogelio Alonso is Associate Professor in Politics and Security Studies at Rey Juan Carlos University, Madrid. From 1994 to 2004 he held various positions in UK academic institutions at the University of Ulster in Belfast and as a Research Fellow at the Institute of Governance, Public Policy and Social Research, as well as at the Institute of Irish Studies, both at the Queen's University of Belfast. His most recent book, *The IRA and Armed Struggle*, which is based on the widest sample of personal interviews with former IRA members ever carried out, was published by Routledge in 2007. He is book review editor for the journal *Democracy and Security* and is a member of the editorial board of *Studies in Conflict and Terrorism* and *Terrorism and Political Violence*. He is a member of the European Commission's Expert Group on Violent Radicalisation.

Edwin Bakker is the Head of Clingendael Security and Conflict Programme in the Netherlands where he leads research into non-conventional threats to international security, including terrorism and the proliferation of WMD. Edwin is on the editorial board of the Dutch journal *Vrede & Veiligheid* and is a member of the executive committee of the Netherlands Helsinki Committee.

Carl Björkman is Regional Manager for Europe and Central Asia at the World Economic Forum where he is responsible for developing the government engagement strategy, carrying out research on selected themes affecting the European economic, political and social agenda, and participates in the creation and coordination of the Forum's initiatives for and in the region. He is also managing the Global Agenda Council on the Future of Europe. Carl has previously worked as a terrorism analyst with the United Nations and a programme officer for the European Commission where he focused on aid effectiveness, good governance and human rights issues.

Lindsay Clutterbuck is Research Leader at RAND Europe focusing on research into terrorism and counter-terrorism. He served for 22 years as a detective officer in the Specialist Operations Department at New Scotland Yard. During that period he was involved at all levels of counter-terrorism; from covert operations to the development of strategy and policy at a national level, and from contingency planning to the planning and delivery of multi-agency exercises. He has contributed articles to academic journals and chapters to books, encompassing both historical and contemporary aspects of terrorism and counter-terrorism.

Christina Hellmich is Lecturer in International Relations at the University of Reading with teaching experience in Oxford and the United States. She is a specialist in Middle East politics with a particular research interest in Political Islam, International Security and Global Health. During fieldwork in Iraq and the Yemen she has conducted extensive research into the role of Islamic preaching in the process of radicalisation as well as gender relations and women's health. Her recent publications focus on the ideology of Al-Qaeda and the image of the Pan-Islamic ideal.

Mark Huband co-founder of *Livingstone & Company* in 2008, which provides high-quality business intelligence and country research, with a primary focus on Africa and the Middle East. Previously he was the Security Correspondent of the *Financial Times* with responsibility to cover Al-Qaeda and terrorism-related issues after the 9/11 attacks. He is the author of numerous books on Africa, Islam and intelligence issues.

Rem Korteweg is a policy analyst at The Hague Centre for Strategic Studies (HCSS) in the Netherlands. From 2004 to 2008 he was a doctoral candidate at Leiden University, researching the dynamic of defence transformation in response to changes in the international security environment. He has been a Fulbright scholar in Washington DC, a visiting fellow at the Center for Transatlantic Relations at Johns Hopkins University's School of Advanced International Studies (SAIS) and a visiting fellow at the European Union Institute for Security Studies in Paris. He has published, amongst others, on the link between ungoverned territories and terrorism, as well as co-authored projects on radicalisation, counter-terrorism and counterinsurgency doctrine.

Stefan Malthaner is a researcher at Institut für interdisziplinäre Konflikt- und Gewaltforschung, University of Bielefeld, Germany.

Jean-Luc Marret is a Visiting Fellow at the Center for Transatlantic Relations at John Hopkins University and a Research Fellow at the Fondation pour la

Recherche Stratégique, the leading think tank on international security issues in France. Prior to that, he was an Associate Professor of US Foreign Policy, Counter-Terrorism, and the Middle East at the Special Military School of Saint-Cyr (the French West-Point).

Petter Nesser is Research Fellow at FFI's Terrorism Research Group in Norway. He has conducted extensive research on Jihadi terrorism in Western Europe (2003 onwards) while focusing on motivational factors, recruitment and radicalisation processes.

Matenia Sirseloudi is Research Fellow at the Institute for Peace Research and Security Policy, IFSH, at the University of Hamburg. She graduated in sociology, psychology and communication science and earned her doctorate at the University of Augsburg with a dissertation on the topic "The strategy of early warning on violent escalations". From 2005 to 2006 she was Marie Curie Fellow of INCORE, International Conflict Research, Centre of Excellence, at Londonderry, Northern Ireland. She has conducted independent research on terrorism and radicalisation, among others for the United Nations and the European Commission.

Peter Waldmann is Professor Emeritus of Sociology at the University of Augsburg, Germany, and a long time member of the advisory board of the German Ministry of Development.

Introduction

Magnus Ranstorp

In 2003 I happened to share a unique speaking platform with Sir David Omand, Tony Blair's Cabinet Intelligence and Security Coordinator, at the British Defence Academy in Shrivenham. At this event Sir David presented for the first time a concept of a cohesive UK counterterrorism strategy that he called CONTEST and which rested on the four "P's": Prevent, Pursue, Protect and Prepare. This strategy would later become formalized as an official British strategy and would serve to influence not only other individual states but also the entire EU counterterrorism strategy. The end state of this strategy was to minimize the threat and the risk of terrorism so that citizens in democracies could go about their daily business with confidence and security. The aim was to create and maintain resilience within society in order for it to bounce back as quickly as possible when assaulted by terrorism. The strategy was surrounded by integrated intelligence as a critical factor (creating the ideas of terrorism intelligence fusion centres) and a robust communication policy (to limit societal polarization and divisions in the aftermath of a terrorist event). As such, Sir David was the first among equals as he sharply recognized that the al-Qaeda forces and its exclusionary ideology that was unleashed by 9/11 required essentially both a strategy to confront its many strands and that preventative approaches would be crucial to contain its global contagion effect and ideological appeal for a next generation of recruits and militants.

For Sir David, myself and others present at the Defence Academy that day it was clear that preventing violent radicalization had to be an overarching priority to complement the tactical intelligence, law enforcement and military firefighting efforts occurring across different theatres around the world. Despite this foresight it was equally clear that none were really intellectually capable of predicting the scope, contours and velocity of the appeal of this Al-Qaeda narrative and associated radicalization and so-called homegrown terrorism that would become such an issue of strategic importance and urgency. Understanding violent radicalization was critical but an enigma to most experts whether in government or in academia.

The terrorist attacks in Madrid in March 2004 and in London in July 2005 brought starkly home the fact that terrorism was no longer an imported, foreign phenomenon but rather homegrown. As evidenced from the multitude of intercepted plots across several European cities since 2001, the emerging regionalization of Al-Qaeda inspired terror cells in regions adjacent to Europe combined with the corrosive and explosive nature of the Danish Muhammed cartoon crisis, the threat level and the intensity of the desire to perpetrate mass-casualty attacks within Europe is not diminishing – rather the complexity of the security environment is increasing with the advance of the Internet and new technologies; the global influencing the local – with a range of adversaries better organized, more clever, more connected with conflict zones than we previously thought. It is also clear that the radicalization processes are becoming more challenging to address as it is simply not just a linear progression, a complex combination of push–pull factors or that people move in and out of roles and functions. While violent radicalization has gradually emerged at the top of the EU counterterrorism agenda, it has been accompanied by a relatively embryonic understanding about the processes and interplay of factors that contribute to radicalization that are playing out differently in Paris, Rome, London or Copenhagen in terms of the underlying causes, nature and direction of the radicalization forces. While there are commonalities, there are also stark differences between contexts. Undoubtedly there are common factors at the global and regional levels that facilitate radicalization, but it is simultaneously clear that radicalization is very context dependent. This book is an effort to explore the different ways in which radicalization is understood as a phenomenon while it is being played out in varying ways or degrees across different EU states.

Understanding violent radicalization

To date, there exist few serious scholarly or practitioner-orientated literatures addressing the *interplay* between radicalization leading to violence and the consequential impact as well as effectiveness of countermeasures. Some cursory academic studies have examined recruitment processes and patterns within Europe, mostly through cursory empirical case-studies in efforts to understand sociopsychological profiles of recruits and the extremist milieus.[1] Others, as exemplified by Peter Nesser, have sought to generically categorize the different functions according to specific roles played within the terrorist cells.[2] Some academic work, spearheaded by John Horgan and Jeff Victoroff, has critiqued psychological approaches and engagement as well as group dynamics within terrorist groups.[3] A few academics have focused on the religious components and content analysis.[4] More theoretically orientated academic work has prioritized the processes of radicalization and recruitment using social movement theory in unlocking the mobilization potential of extremist Salafist movements, especially in understanding the role and function of so-called "gateway" organizations as a vehicle for extremism.[5] Some researchers have also sought to provide useful comparative theoretical exploration as to different casual mechanisms explaining radicalization as a complex social and behavioural phenomenon.

Some academic contributions have argued the central importance of foreign policy (the Iraq war, regional conflicts, etc.) but few studies offer a deeper understanding of its relationship with domestic radicalization.[6] This demonstrates the complexities involved in understanding the processes of violent radicalization since globalization has meant the simultaneous conflation of global and local contexts. In this sense, the deterritorialization of Islam and a sense of "global grievance" are woven together with local and individual contexts.[7] Deconstruction of the so-called "Single narrative" involves simultaneous local and global parts which are not easily separated in efforts to understand causality or relative weighting as to their role as "tipping points" into violence. This naturally complicates efforts to devise community-based counter-radicalization measures and to gauge their overall effectiveness.

Some academic contributions have addressed specific extremist milieus, focusing on the role of prisons in the radicalization and recruitment processes as well as the increased and expanding role of the Internet. For example, Farhad Khosrokhavar has spearheaded research into understanding these processes in prisons[8] while Fernando Reinares has conducted mapping of social characteristics of 188 Muslim extremist prisoners arrested in 2001–2005 and the resultant policy implications within a Spanish context.[9] Ranstorp has surveyed the interplay between ideological content as psychological warfare and operational functionality provided by the Internet[10] whilst others have addressed the Internet as a new forum for discourse and relationships among extremists.[11] While exploring the processes of radicalization, *few of these studies have focused on identifying potential intervention points or specific counter-radicalization measures.*

Government reports do exist that focus on elements and processes of violent radicalization, most notably those by the Dutch domestic intelligence and security service (Algemene Inlichtingen en Veiligheidsdienst – AIVD).[12] Similarly, various national classified and unclassified studies exist that have been developed by the joint national intelligence assessment centres (JTAC, NcTB, etc.), as well as internal EU SITCEN documents which explore primarily the multivariate causality of radicalization, most notably in the United Kingdom, the Netherlands and Canada. A number of studies have been commissioned within the United Kingdom following the July 2005 bombing, most notably the May 2006 report by the House of Commons Intelligence and Security Committee (*Report into the London terrorist attacks on July 2005*) and the Home Office-commissioned report *Preventing Extremism Together (PET)*. However, few (if any) policy documents exist comparing these violent radicalization processes across the European Union, nor has any identifiable research been conducted identifying and collating so-called "best practice" within community-based approaches towards preventing or responding to violent radicalization. This research lacuna is problematic as "the most important battle in the war for the Muslim minds during the next decades", writes Gilles Kepel, "will be fought not in Palestine or Iraq but in (the) communities of believers on the outskirts of London, Paris, and other European cities, where Islam is already a growing part of the West".[13]

Understanding the processes of radicalization and recruitment is a complex task as there are no single causes or mechanisms that are transferable from case-to-case.[14] Rather it is the complex interplay between these factors being played out simultaneously across the global and local levels and across different geographic contexts down to the individual level. This is the very core as to why finding decisive factors has proven so difficult, if not almost futile. It is instead the combination of different factors that facilitate the journey towards radicalization.

Nevertheless, analytical efforts have been made to try to isolate contributing factors across different contexts which can be broadly divided into an internal and external dimension. In many ways it is a kaleidoscope of factors, much like vectors, that push individuals towards radicalization and enable their recruitment.

Some of the internal factors relate to: a prevailing lack of public Muslim debate about the justification of violence; polarizing public rhetoric and stigmatization and political polarization; identity crisis; alienation from society; the presence of radical imams; glorification of jihad and martyrdom; youths trapped in a downward spiral of discrimination, stigmatization and criminalization – making them susceptible to recruitment efforts; etc.

On the external dimension, Western policy is a source of radicalization of individuals in Muslim communities. Some of these external factors are related to the perceived injustice suffered by Muslims across several key regional conflicts (such as Chechnya, Iraq, Kashmir, Somalia and the Palestinian territories) that exposes Western double-standards and leads to passive and active contributions to these struggles by Muslim communities within Europe; military interventions by Western states; the changing role of global media and cyberspace; and perception of injustice among a multitude of other factors.

Both the internal and external factors emphasize the primacy of grievances and discontent with almost inexhaustible lists of precipitating factors. Moreover, these two dimensions are interchangeable; personal grievances are transformed into global ones and vice versa; and the public and private spheres become inextricably intertwined.

An alternative approach to deal with this kaleidoscope of factors relating to radicalization of individuals within Muslim communities in Europe is to apply, in a systematic and rigorous fashion, the generic framework developed by Tore Bjørgø *et al.* (2005) on the root causes of terrorism. According to this study, there are four main categories that cause terrorism:

1 *Structural causes* (demographic imbalances, globalization, rapid modernization, transitional societies, increased individualism with rootlessness and atomization, relative deprivation, class structure);
2 *Facilitating (or accelerator) causes* make terrorism possible and attractive (these include mobility, technology, transport, publicity, etc.);
3 *Motivational causes*; and
4 *Triggering causes.*

It is important to note that the structural causes and the facilitating causes by themselves do not cause terrorism per se; rather a combination of interaction between the different factors across the categories is necessary. Towards this end, the study identified a further 14 specific factors causing terrorism and four factors sustaining it.[15] This of course does not take into account the motivational factors embedded in a now vast literature on the socio-psychological profiles of different terrorists; work principally spearheaded by Jerrold Post and John Horgan.[16]

In addition, Marc Sageman in his groundbreaking book *Understanding Terror Networks* (2004) indicated that people join terrorist groups predominantly on the basis of friendship and kinship bonds. Understanding these social and kinship-based relationships becomes important in adding another layer to the complex mechanisms of radicalization and recruitment.[17] The role of cultural studies in this endeavour is absolutely critical. From a constructivist perspective, the work by Michael Vlahos on the cultural anatomy of terrorism and its symbolic framework is a useful approach in this respect.[18] The relevance here lay in the links between recognizing cultural and social frameworks which could be used in order to figure out how to break negative patterns of uprisings of radicalization. This becomes particularly relevant when considering how to best penetrate these cultural and social frameworks when combating radicalization via teamwork between authorities and civil society and via helpful legislation on the Member state and EU levels.

As urged by David Leheny,[19] the vast literature on social movements may also have a lot to offer the study of terrorism. In particular, this framework may be the most relevant to our understanding of radicalization and recruitment. The groundbreaking theoretical framework developed by Quintan Wiktorowicz of using social movement theory in relation to religious mobilization and radicalization is ideally suitable for deepening our understanding of these processes across diverse contexts.[20] According to Wiktorowicz, there are three broad parallel processes that explain how and why Muslims in Western liberal democracies are drawn to radical Islamic groups: through cognitive openings, religious seeking, and constructing sacred authority.

First, a cognitive opening (a willingness to be receptive to the message) is a prerequisite given the extremist views espoused by radical movements. A crisis (moral shock) or outreach activism (to germinate a sense of crisis through interaction and discussion) can achieve this. A principal ingredient in the West acting as a catalyst towards a cognitive opening is a profound identity crisis, beginning with a series of questions about what it means to be Muslim in a non-Muslim land.[21]

Second, an individual experiencing a cognitive opening may lead to "religious seeking" – "a process in which an individual searches for some satisfactory system of religious meaning to interpret and resolve his discontent". It is in this process of seeking that those that are drawn to militant groups complain about the failure of mainstream religious leaders to address pressing issues, including politics, and they complain that these mainstream leaders represent an archaic, non-intellectual approach to a religion failing often to engage university-educated second- and third-generation Muslims. These disaffected seekers are vulnerable to the message and mechanism of engagement (through intense debate and dialogue) by more extremists groups, providing them with a vehicle for an intellectual and spiritual voyage. Many of these radicals use personal social networks to facilitate religious seeking.[22]

Third, the role of charismatic leadership is crucial as radical groups attempt to promote their spiritual leadership as a reputable religious authority. The issue of (Weberian) charismatic leadership has been explored exhaustively in Scott Appleby's excellent biographies of fundamentalist leaders in *Spokesmen for the Despised* (1996).

The fusion of social movement studies and Islamic extremism can be further explored through social network analysis to understand how the underlying nature of trust and influence shape and are shaped by underground social networks. This would explore the theoretical foundation of trust and influence and their application in networks, specifically how trust and influence are established, maintained, exploited and (even) lost and the functions they serve for individuals, organizations and societies.[23] Some analysts, like John Horgan, have argued that there is a disproportionate focus on looking at the onset of radicalization as there is much to be learned from why individuals actually disengage or de-radicalize from terrorist groups and violence. Radicalization occurs through different pathways, at different speeds and in different facilitating environments. There is no simple trajectory into radicalization.

Much of contemporary efforts to improve our understanding of violent radicalization processes focus either on law enforcement profiling efforts (personality profiling and vulnerability assessments according to the individual's respective function and role in a group setting) or on a more granulated understanding of group dynamics in clandestine milieus. Understanding the interplay between leaders and followers and the requisite group dynamic processes may provide possibly the most fruitful avenues to understand the tipping points into violence. Understanding group dynamics is seemingly the radicalization engine that propels recruits towards embracing violent Salafist jihadism.

Understanding radicalization processes is complex as there are multiple pathways and speeds of progression, devotion and functions within groups. It is simply a multifaceted combination of push–pull factors involving a combination of socio-psychological factors, political grievance, religious motivation and discourse, identity politics and triggering mechanisms that collectively move individuals towards extremism. A number of different factors that interplay are at the heart of radicalization which is highly individualized – it differs from person to person: from Muslim identity crisis standing in between two cultures and societies and not belonging anywhere; personal crisis and traumas; discrimination; alienation and perceived injustices and a relative absence of critical Muslim debates about terrorism to the myth of the jihadi mission; charismatic leadership to Western foreign policy and interventions. Facilitating meeting places – like the Internet, school or universities, youth clubs, prison and sports clubs have often played a crucial role. Often the engine of radicalization leading to violence is group dynamics and charismatic leadership channelling anger and frustration.

Each case study of radicalization contributes to the overall understanding of the processes at work and what it will take to contain and reverse the phenomenon that either prevents or facilitates radicals from tipping over towards violence.

In February 2008 I visited detention camps in Riyadh where Al-Qaeda detainees, who had fought in Iraq before capture, and Saudi Guantanamo detainees were being imprisoned while efforts were made for their rehabilitation. Similarly as I sat through court hearings in terrorist trials in Denmark it was becoming evident that in some cases *recruitment precedes radicalization* and not the other way around. The Saudi rehabilitation or re-education programme brought up two things that also apply in Europe: first, the fact that radicals are generally ignorant about Islam (and Islamic history); second, that family members are often the first to ask authorities for help in reaching the straying son/daughter. Radicals often embrace *takfiri* Islam as a rebellion against family members and as a justification for rejecting various norms. As such, we need to pay attention to the counter-cultural aspects of the radical belief-system. At the same time it illustrates we need to focus on the so-called radicalization brokers as the key targets. In thinking about the radicalization dilemma in Europe, this volume brings out starkly that we still need to recognize the diversity of our Muslim communities and which are at greater risk of being influenced by radicalization forces. We still do not possess adequate data on the dynamics within our Muslim communities and how these impact on the different measures we apply. It requires high-resolution pictures of diverse dynamics within cities and even down to neighbourhood levels. As such, it will require (terrorism) researchers to talk to different stakeholders and pursue research agendas in a broader academic mode and manner in the future, beyond focusing on terrorists themselves and wresting clarity of motivation out of violent backgrounds forensically mined for deviance and other clues in a *post-hoc* fashion.

Structure of the book

This book originates from a conference organized by the Swedish National Defence College in late 2006 that brought together disparate academic and practitioner expertise to examine radicalization as a process and how radicalization manifests itself in select EU states. There are two principal parts to this book: the first deals with radicalization as a broad-based phenomenon; the second deals with radicalization in the United Kingdom, France, Spain, Italy and the Netherlands.

The first chapter is collectively authored under the skilful stewardship of Rem Korteweg together with Sajjan Gohel, Francois Heisbourg, Magnus Ranstorp and Rob de Wijk. It provides a contextual background to the broad radicalization phenomenon that occurred after 11 September 2001. It investigates the various layers of radicalization and the underlying causes of the phenomenon, marrying both the internal and external dimensions before offering some general recommendations.

The second chapter is written by Peter Waldmann, Matenia Sirseloudi and Stefan Malthaner and explores the various facets of the journey towards extremism undertaken by individuals towards radical subcultures. It argues that the combination of "social and cultural uprootedness of migrants and their offspring, discrimination and social marginalization and identity and orientation problems typical for young Muslims in the West" are possible contributing factors for susceptibility to more extremist messages.

The third chapter, authored by Christina Hellmich, explores the multiple dimensions surrounding the way in which ideology is translated into participation and collective mobilization. It then proceeds to apply social movement theory outlines to how the ideology of Al-Qaeda translates into popular support and overcomes barriers to participation. The concept of "recruitment of the toughest" explains the limited number of participants.

The fourth chapter is written by Petter Nesser and focuses on the motivational aspects behind radicalization and recruitment into jihadi extremist terror cells. It provides three main motivational paths to the jihad in Europe with different roles and functions and it argues that more "systematic, micro-level, empirical studies of the various roads into militant milieus and terrorist networks" are needed to understand the similarities and differences of pathways into terrorism.

Part II provides a country-by-country assessment on the drivers of radicalization as well as various efforts by governments to counter radicalization leading to violence. It begins with two chapters on the radicalization situation in the United Kingdom. The fifth chapter is authored by the former *Financial Times* correspondent Mark Huband who shares his vast insight into the mindset of radicalization at work within the United Kingdom. Huband provides a personal account of the mindset and discourse of those extremists he encountered and the challenges posed to security in the United Kingdom. The next chapter by Lindsay Clutterbuck, who worked for many years in the antiterrorism branch SO-13 within New Scotland Yard, explores the various ways jihadism has manifested itself in the United Kingdom and what principles the British approach has been based on to effectively contain and reverse radicalization.

The seventh chapter, written by Edwin Bakker, focuses on developments in the Netherlands and explores the concern of Dutch authorities over Salafist trends and manifestations and the way in which authorities have approached the issue of countering radicalization through various measures.

The eighth chapter focuses on the situation in France with Jean-Luc Marret's analysis on the challenge of its discontent migrant communities and the experience with Salafist jihadi terrorist cells. The ninth chapter deals with the Spanish experience as Rogelio Alonso explores the legacy of the Madrid experience and the particular challenge of the spread of Salafist jihadi extremism within the prison population. The last chapter, authored by Carl Björkman, deals with the array of challenges within Italy as it confronts a full spectrum of illicit activities by different terrorist cells and networks. In particular it highlights the role of mosques and prison as well as the Internet in facilitating radicalization.

All these chapters provide different insights into the complexity of the radicalization challenge within Europe. Together they paint a rather stark picture as to the nature, scope and extent of radicalization within an array of different

European states and the future challenges in providing effective measures to prevent and respond to violent radicalization. It is clear the road is rather long ahead.

The road ahead: challenges of preventing and responding to violent radicalization

T.E. Lawrence once famously wrote that "fighting a rebellion is messy and slow it is like eating soup with a knife".[24] This likeness can probably be extended to counter-radicalization as the instruments necessarily need to be multidisciplinary in approach and extend beyond the traditional counterterrorism toolbox. More importantly, they are necessarily long term in their nature, they will have to sustain crisis events and it is very difficult to measure their effectiveness. Above being a politically sensitive issue, the key is to identify and calibrate appropriate policies and practices which do not themselves have a detrimental effect and lead to increased alienation of some vulnerable religious and ethnic minorities.

This last point is important to bring to the forefront as was done by a recent study co-authored by Frank Buijs, Atef Hamdy and Froukje Demant on the political orientation of young Dutch Muslims embracing Salafist tendencies.[25] In essence it persuasively argued that the cumulative negative and critical climate towards Islam in the Netherlands significantly contributed to the degree to which Dutch Muslim youth embrace radicalization. It forcefully pointed out that young "second generation" Moroccans often felt misunderstood by their parents and simultaneously felt rejected by Dutch society. This conclusion is worthwhile to underscore as we sometimes forget the close-knit continuity between opposite poles of extremism (right-wing and Islamic extremism) that constantly feed off each other. This connectivity also reminds us that government policies need to be cognizant of the necessity constantly to calibrate and adjust policies so as not to inadvertently play into supporting one or the other poles of extremism. It is often blatantly obvious that politicians can greatly contribute in pouring petrol onto flames by divisive comments towards ethnic or religious minorities, especially in the aftermath of a violent incident, only leading to further polarization.

This book is not about counter-radicalization policies and the effects of countermeasures, as most of the EU has a long way to travel before it begins to understand the nature of the problem of radicalization within each Member state and before it is in a position to evaluate credibly the effects of its various countermeasures. However, there are a number of different guiding principles that could serve to guide and educate our thinking of how to prevent and counter violent radicalization in efforts to constrict the space of extremists and in enhancing the resilience and robustness of society. A half-dozen or so guiding principles are necessary to think about as we approach different and varyingly effective strategies to counter radicalization within Europe.

First, at the core of any counter-radicalization approach it is absolutely essential to have benchmarking – a clearly delineated vision of the end-game. What exactly do governments and society want to achieve; is it realistic and achievable;

and what are the most optimum means through which some or all goals are to be achieved? Moreover, where should the centre of gravity of efforts be? Where should the balance lie between government interference and support and for more grassroots initiatives and bottom-up community-based approaches?

Second, in this concerted effort, which government agency should take the "lead"? Is the coordination architecture adequate for the task? It may be useful to consider having a publicly communicated strategy to articulate the vision of this end-game and, more importantly, to ensure that the various strands of efforts and government departments know their place in the greater scheme and pull in the same direction. The Dutch Empowerment project and the British PET (Preventing Extremism Together) are prominent projects and visions that illustrate this point. They also demonstrate that the centre of gravity of these efforts should be prioritized at the community-based levels. There may be very sensible reasons to avoid labelling integration measures as countering terrorism, because it would obviously be counterproductive to do so. Here the language employed in these efforts is critically important. It may also be advisable to focus on extremism rather than singling out particular ethnic and religious minority communities to avoid stigmatization. It is very clear that there are major advantages in having a clearly crafted strategic document to emphasize the direction and focus of the totality of efforts.

Third, there is still a need to recognize the incredible diversity of Muslim communities and which segments are at greater risk of being influenced by radicalization forces. There is also great diversity within our cities that needs to be further explored, as the radicalization forces differ from city district to neighbourhoods. Engaging city planners or managers becomes critical as they are often best equipped to understand in detail the dynamics within city neighbourhoods. It is abundantly clear that governments do not possess high enough resolution of data on the dynamics within our Muslim communities. Nor do they understand how the nature of the radicalization phenomenon is changing by the different measures that are being applied and the longer term effects. As such, there is a comprehensive need to craft, deploy and evaluate community impact assessment as to how various measures – soft and hard – are perceived by minority ethnic and religious communities. Poorly calibrated policies can actually create problems rather than solve them if they are applied wrongly or at the wrong level.

There is also too much of a divorce between the understanding of radicalization as a process and the impact of measures. This is illustrative of the fact that much of research into the processes of violent radicalization is embryonic at best and often divorced from policy realities. A common complaint is that although research communities are hard at work trying to grapple with radicalization processes, by the time they have come to any meaningful conclusions in a leisurely scholarly fashion, much of its applicability in the real world has lost its relevance and timeliness. Academics, like government bureaucracies, are often fiercely territorial and stove-piped into their disciplines, but interdisciplinary collaboration is necessary given that the problem of radicalization has simultaneously political, social, cultural and religious dimensions. At the other end of the research spectrum there is a disproportionate amount of focus on research into radicalization as a process rather than focusing on the viability of countermeasures.

Fourth, the compression of the global into local politics has complicated our ability to understand and effectively engage with the so-called Single Narrative projected by the so-called "Al-Qaeda project". The enduring appeal of this Single Narrative in striking emotive chords among a sizeable number of Muslims worldwide is incredibly effective and complex to disaggregate. The best description of this complexity is one which was offered by BBC journalist Roger Hardy at a conference on radicalization at St Anthony's College, Oxford in December 2006. According to Hardy,

> the force of the narrative revolves around three distinctive but mutually reinforcing elements, explaining its widespread appeal. It is a narrative of humiliation and one that is painted *in primary colours*. The core of this is that the West is at war with Islam: daily evidence is barraging us of the West's aggressive design from conflict zones: Palestine, Iraq, Afghanistan, Chechnya, Kashmir ... and Somalia, Darfur ... Reinforcing these are the metaphorical wars – disputes over headscarf; Mohammed cartoon and countless other controversies. All these conflicts and controversies, big and small, act like streams feeding a single river. The second theme is redemptive violence offering to transform humiliation into inevitable victory; suffering into self-sacrifice; shame into honour. The third theme is the projection of emotionally powerful imagery ... which provides compelling moral shock to take direct action.[26]

These three themes are extremely potent mobilization instruments and serve collectively to illustrate the interwoven nature of the foreign policy arena, religious and cultural elements, and the way in which different communication arenas serve to influence often young and impressionable minds.

They also underscore the importance of handling crisis events, whether fuelling or defusing the cartoon row, or the balance between security and freedom of expression as illustrated by Danish Prophet Mohammed Cartoons. Investment in crisis management and best practices should be a priority within the EU, especially considering the potential polarization within and between societies as new crises may emerge with, for example, the release of provocative films like Van Gogh's and Hirsha Ali's *Submission* that test our values and democratic rights as well as responsibilities.

Fifth, governments need to be increasingly innovative when engaging with different sectors of Muslim communities through various innovative platforms (such as explaining foreign policy approaches to the Middle East or conflict regions) and the development of new initiatives and delivery vehicles. Two innovative examples – one from Denmark and one from outside the EU – illustrate this point vividly.

In 2007, PET, the Danish Security Service, held a conference on the possibilities of early coordinated measures to confront radicalization in Denmark. What was unique about this forum was that it gathered SSP (School, Social Services and Police) representatives alongside moderate or more radical imams, media representatives and the security service in several parallel collective brainstorming exercises. Instead of being a counterproductive and potentially explosive cocktail, the meeting was a success. One of the results was a forum where voices of concern or dissent over specific policies could be aired and it also produced a so-called "Idea-catalogue" which contained some specific recommendations of action and focus surrounding community-based approaches.

These PET-initiatives have been very useful in laying the groundwork for broader political initiatives; in the Danish case revolving around the role of mentoring – mentor, role models and direct dialogue with young immigrants (voluntary identity-mentors available 24 hours a day). Most notably Denmark has completed a strategy and an action plan for prevention of extremism and violent radicalization among youth in 2008.

Another example of innovation comes from outside the EU: the LibForAll Foundation's approach in Indonesia, which has grown into a countervailing force against extremism, established in 2003 by co-founders Charles Holland Taylor and Kyai Haji Abdurrahman Wahid (Indonesia's first democratically elected president and head of the world's largest Muslim organization – Nadhlatul Ulama with 40 million members. One of the most innovative and also successful high-impact programmes was Launching a Musical Jihad against Religious Hatred and Terrorism by legendary Muslim rock star Ahmad Dhani with an album entitled Laskar Cinta (Warriors of Love). This album confronted tens of millions of Muslims with the stark choice of whether they wanted to be murderous Warriors of Jihad or Warriors of Love. The threatening popularity of Dhani's message produced an extremist reaction which was further deliberately countered by a series of measures that shattered the credibility of what the extremists were arguing, further shrinking their operational and religious space.

The message should not be interpreted that we need a Musical Jihad against Extremism in Europe or that we employ MTV in our effort. It may be useful, however, to examine and collate different knowledge, strategies and programme templates from LibForAll and other regional efforts outside our region to seek new inspiration, innovation and evaluation of how success elsewhere can be replicated in new innovative ways across Europe. These measures emphasize that we need new and creative delivery vehicles and the involvement of new actors: how we harness humour, soap operas and PR-industries in efforts to disarm the extremist message and win over young people. In this area there is much work ahead for us to think-outside-the-box to greater effect.

This last point about innovation serves to illustrate the necessity to share "best practice" not only between countries and regions but also within national boundaries. Creating information hubs within and across the EU with community-based best practice models could provide a useful vehicle to collate otherwise atomized local efforts and models from government and non-governmental sources. Additionally there needs to be wide distribution of ways in which one can benchmark the effectiveness of various initiatives. We need new innovative and interdisciplinary networks of scholars and policymakers within and across national boundaries – learning from different regions and sharing best practice. We need more cohesive strategies applied in context and we need to establish more effective mechanisms sharing best practice across Europe. In reality there are not going to be any quick fixes to this problem.

The road ahead: a future research agenda on radicalization

This volume provides some interesting insights into the mechanisms of radicalization processes and the way in which they play out in specific national contexts. Scientific research into radicalization must be considered fragmentary and embryonic at best. Resources needs to be developed that provide a cohesive focus for existing fragmented research efforts across national boundaries. Some baseline research has been conducted that provides useful direction. The European Commission through its Network of Experts commissioned four studies during 2007–2008 that focused on: (1) triggering factors for violent radicalization; (2) the beliefs, ideologies and narratives of violent radicals; (3) recruitment and mobilization of support; (4) best practices in preventing and countering radicalization.

The following research suggestions build on the work of this volume and provide a cohesive, comprehensive approach for the next wave of research into radicalization.

State-of-the-art research inventory into radicalization

Research into radicalization is fragmentary and often fails to integrate the dynamic interrelationship with countermeasures against the terrorist threat. This dynamic relationship constantly changes the nature of the radicalization challenge. No research exists that captures this evolving complexity.

More research needs to be conducted that encapsulates the existing growing literature, theories and methods into radicalization research, models and existing findings which are critiqued and accumulated to prepare the way for the next wave of research. Much research focuses on the pathways into radicalization and some has emerged on disengagement and exit strategies out of radicalization networks and milieus. There needs to be a critical evaluation of the strengths and weaknesses of existing research and future research priorities. More research needs to focus on the connectivity between radicalization as a phenomenon and the way in which countermeasures affect and change it. More interdisciplinary research agendas are necessary as radicalization simultaneously involves individual socio-psychological factors, social and political factors, religious dimensions, cultural identity and group dynamics. Capturing the dynamics and complexity of these interrelationships in specific national contexts and over time is a prioritized research theme.

Radicalization in education

Research into radicalization has found that education can be considered both as a key influencer and major intervention point. This means that more research needs to focus on: curriculum development that takes into account radicalization; best practices and models how to approach and achieve effective delivery across levels and milieus; strategies for responding to radicalization, especially in higher education; capacity building and intercultural competence development within educational establishments, for teachers and for local public officials. Development of conflict resolution models needs to be considered within education to better build resilience against the forces of radicalization and as a mechanism to handle cultural clashes that occur in identity building among youths. How do youths navigate between different cultural identities; does mentorship work and what are effective mechanisms to engage youths on radicalization issues? What should the role be for civil society in dealing with radicalization?

Best practices in crisis management dealing with terrorism

Terrorism events severely test social cohesion within societies whether it is small events that unleash vast social forces (murder of Theo van Gogh in 2004), a synchronized major event (London bombings 2005) or a metaphorical war (Mohammed Cartoon controversy in Denmark). Research needs to focus across contexts and incidents to compare the best practices and effectiveness of different approaches of how to respond to and communicate most effectively with the public. The end game of these strategies is to assert government control and to limit the effects of the violence and any associated polarization between communities. More research needs to be conducted on best practice models of how best to respond to crisis events from a communication and crisis management perspective. What are the lessons learned from different types of events? What type of message needs to be crafted, how is this credibly delivered and how is this best delivered in a fragmented media environment?

Best practices in community-based approaches to radicalization

Both research and practice have shown that the most effective level of intervention against radicalization occurs at the community-based level. Despite the existence of different community-based approaches, there has been little effort to benchmark and evaluate the effectiveness of various measures according to national context. What works, why and is it possible to evaluate each measure and its effects in the community? More comparative research needs to be conducted as to the merits and effectiveness of various community-based approaches according to context. Where should the balance lie between government interference and support and for more grassroots initiatives, civil society engagement and community-based approaches? In particular, studies on the way in which cities have approached and managed radicalization ought to be encouraged.

Developing effective counter-narratives

Strategically it is necessary to create mechanisms for a counter-narrative against Al-Qaeda and other extremist elements with an exclusionary ideology and global agenda. The so-called Single Narrative is composed of an expanding collage of intertwined foreign policy and domestic issues that are difficult to separate and deconstruct and one that feeds into the grievance and view that the West is at war with Islam. Some have argued that it is foreign policies and regional conflicts that take precedence over domestic causes leading to radicalization; others argue that foreign issues are only legitimating issues and it is the domestic grievances that are the primary causes for radicalization. More research needs to focus on this interrelationship between the foreign and domestic parts of the Single Narrative.

Research needs to focus on: what is the media strategy of Al-Qaeda and other extremist groups? Who are receptive to the extremist message? How can the attractiveness of the extremist message be undermined? What weaknesses of the extremist messages can be utilized and is it possible to build resilience among the target audience?

Are there hierarchies of contested issues and which ones can be affected strategically and during times of crisis? What are the best strategies to deliver effective counter-narrative and who are best placed to deliver what part of this strategy? Is there a role for public–private partnerships? What are effective and credible delivery mechanisms?

The role of the media and Internet

Terrorism is invariably the "propaganda of the deed" and the media has often been charged as being the "oxygen" of terrorism. Competing narratives in a global, fragmented media environment may feed into the radicalization discourse and the projection of grievances. Research needs to be conducted on the role media play in fuelling radicalization and as a countervailing force against it. The role of symbolic discourse and the way it feeds into cultural identity needs to be further understood and studied. Similarly the Internet communities are an important gateway into extremist circles and research needs to focus on understanding the extent to which online discourse and media connects radicalized individuals with each other and how it affects the radicalization phenomenon. On another level, research should be encouraged to study how existing self-regulation in relation to child pornography and racism could be similarly applied to radicalization.

The role of gateway organizations

Extremist groups that espouse an antidemocratic agenda and advocate separation from mainstream society are increasingly difficult to deal with for governments within democratic societies. On the one hand, these extremist groups may be viewed as a potential conveyer belt into further extremism leading to violence. On the other hand, these groups may be considered to absorb violent tendencies rather than promote them. Research needs to be conducted into what avenues are available for engagement by governments. Should governments engage radical elements? If so, what are the best methods and where are the pitfalls? Should these extremist groups be banned? How do Western democracies engage and empower moderate elements as a countervailing force against extremism?

Limits of political activism

Freedom of speech and freedom of assembly and public protest constitute some essential elements of democratic practice and principles. Activism and public protest are part of a vibrant democracy. However, knowledge about where the limits lie is not always widely known among youths and activists. Where are the so-called red lines of social protest? More research needs to focus on how far political activism can and should proceed. Similarly, research should focus on the limits of extremist activist groups, their strategies and behaviour to understand the dilemmas posed for democracies, social cohesion and integration agendas.

Linkages with gangs and youth violence including the study of group dynamics and entry/exit strategies

Radicalization and recruitment occurs through different pathways and at varying speeds. Research has uniformly shown that there is no single trajectory into radicalization. It is the cumulative combination of complex push–pull factors. Trends show a growing connection between gangs and radicalization networks. Studies on gangs constitute a mature scientific literature and there is merit in considering the insights and lessons from gangs in relation to radicalization phenomenon. Similarly, group dynamics constitute the engine of radicalization. More studies need to consider the role of leadership and the specifics of group dynamics in understanding different entry/exit strategies.

Connectivity between extremism

Research shows in some contexts there is a connection between right-wing extremism and radicalization within the Muslim community. Recent EU-commissioned studies on radicalization have concluded that the sense of living in a hostile society that views Islam with suspicion creates pressure for religious communities and they feel under pressure to assess, as Muslims, their relationship to violent radical narratives and the politics of the Muslim world without knowing them or their interrelationship. Similarly, governments need to be cognizant of policies in order to avoid playing into supporting one of the poles of extremism. How is this best done?

Research needs to focus on the dynamics of interrelationship between different forms of extremism and across historical contexts. How do extremist ideologies and behaviour feed other forms of extremism?

Notes

1 See Michael Taarnby, *Recruitment of Islamist Terrorists in Europe: Trends and Repercussions* (submitted 14 January 2005). This 55-page study can be found at: www.washingtoninstitute.org/documents/41ed337225897.
2 For example, see: Petter Nesser, "Profiles of Jihadist Terrorists in Europe", in C. Bernard (ed.), *A Future for the Young, Options for Helping Middle Eastern Youth Escape the Trap of Radicalization* (Washington DC: RAND Corporation, 2006): pp. 31–49.
3 John Horgan, "Understanding Terrorist Motivation: A Socio-Psychological Perspective", in Magnus Ranstorp (ed.), *Mapping Terrorism Research: State of the Art, Gaps and Future Direction* (London: Routledge, 2006): pp. 106–126; Jeff Victoroff, "The Mind of the Terrorist: A Review and Critique of Psychological Approaches", *Journal of Conflict Resolution*, Vol. 49, No. 1 (February 2005): pp. 3–42.
4 For example, see: J.P. Larson, "The Role of Religious Ideology in Modern Terrorist Recruitment", in James J.F. Forest (ed.), *The Making of a Terrorist: Recruitment, Training and Root Causes* (London: Wesport Publishers, 2006): pp. 197–215.
5 See: Quintan Wiktorowitcz, *Radical Islam Rising: Muslim Extremism in the West* (Oxford: Rowman & Littlefield, 2005).
6 See: Paul Wilkinson and Frank Gregory, "Riding Pillion for Tackling Terrorism is a High-Risk Policy", in *Security, Terrorism and the UK*, Chatham House ISP/NSC Briefing Paper 05/01.
7 Oliver Roy, Globalized Islam: the search for a New Ummah (London: Hurst Publishers, 2004).
8 Farhad Khosrokhavar, *L'Islam dans les prisons* (Paris, Balland, 2004). See also: Pascale Combelles Siegel, "Radical Islam and the French Muslim Prison Population", *Terrorism Monitor*, Vol. 4, Issue 15 (Jamestown Foundation, July 2006).
9 Fernando Reinares, "Towards a Social Characterisation of Jihadist Terrorism in Spain: Implications for Domestic Security and Action Abroad", ARI 34/2006 (Madrid: Elcano Institute, 2006).
10 Magnus Ranstorp, "The Virtual Sanctuary of Al-Qaeda and Terrorism in an Age of Globalisation", in Johan Eriksson and Giamiero Giacomello (eds), *International Relations and Security in the Digital Age* (London: Routledge, 2007).
11 Brynjar Lia, "Al-Qaeda on-line: Understanding Jihadist Terrorist Infrastructure", *Jane's Intelligence Review*, 1 January 2006; Gabriel Weimann, *Terrorism on the Internet* (US Institute of Peace Press, 2006).
12 For a summary of reports, see: Menno Steketee, "Dutch Authorities Report Increase in Islamist Radicalisation", *Jane's Intelligence Review* (February 2005).
13 Gilles Kepel, *The War for the Muslim Minds: Islam and the West* (Cambridge: The Belknap Press of Harvard University Press, 2004): p. 8.
14 For example, see: *Global War on Terrorism: Analyzing the Strategic Threat*, Joint Military Intelligence College, Discussion Paper no. 13 (November 2004).
15 Tore Bjørgø, *Root Causes of Terrorism* (Routledge, 2005).
16 Jerrold Post, Ehud Sprinzhak and Laurita M. Denny, "The Terrorists in Their Own Words: Interviews with 35 Incarcerated Middle East Terrorists", *Terrorism & Political Violence*, Vol. 15, No. 1 (Spring 2003): pp. 171–184.
17 For example, see: Lisa Wedeen, "Conceptualising Culture: Possibilities for Political Science", *American Political Science Review*, Vol. 96, No. 4 (December 2002); and Reed L. Wadley, "Treachery and Deceit: Parallels in Tribal and Terrorist Warfare", *Studies in Conflict and Terrorism*, Vol. 26, (2003): pp. 331–345.

18 Michael Vlahos, *Terror's Mask: Insurgency Within Islam*, An occasional paper of the Joint Warfare Analysis Department, Applied Physics Laboratory, John Hopkins University (May 2002).
19 David Leheny, "Symbols, Strategies, and Choices for International Relations Scholarship After September 11", *International Organisation* (Spring 2002): pp. 57–70.
20 For the best studies on Islamic movements and social movement theory, see: Quintan Wiktorowicz, *Islamic Activism: A Social Movement Theory Approach* (Bloomington: Indiana University Press, 2004).
21 Quintan Wiktorowicz, "The Allure of Radical Islam in the West: Al-Muhajiroun in the UK as a Case Study" (unpublished manuscript completed December 2004 – in author's possession). Quintan Wiktorowicz, *Radical Islam Rising*, (London: Rowman & Littlefield, 2005).
22 Ibid.
23 Piotr Sztompka, *Trust* (Cambridge University Press, 1999); and Marc Sageman, *Understanding Terror Networks* (University of Pennsylvania Press, 2004). Also see: John Arquilla and David Ronfeldt (eds), *Networks and Netwars* (RAND, 2001); Mark Duffield, "War as a Network Enterprise", *Cultural Values*, Vol. 6, No. 1&2 (2002): pp. 153–165; and Manuel Castells, *The Rise of Network Society* (Oxford: Blackwell, 1996, 2000).
24 T.E. Lawrence, *Seven Pillars of Wisdom: A Triumph* (New York: Doubleday, 1926, 1935).
25 Frank Buijs, Atef Hamdy and Froukje Demant, *Strijders van eigen bodem: Radicale en democratische moslims in Nederland* (Amsterdam University Press, 2006).
26 Unpublished paper by Roger Hardy, December 2006.

Part I
Understanding radicalisation as a process

1 Background contributing factors to terrorism

Radicalization and recruitment[1]

Rem Korteweg with Sajjan Gohel, Francois Heisbourg, Magnus Ranstorp and Rob de Wijk

Introduction

On 2 November 2004, a 26-year-old Dutch national of Moroccan descent fired a gun six times at, and slit the throat of, Dutch film-maker Theo van Gogh, killing him on the spot. On 22 December 2001, a Jamaican-British man boarded a plane in Paris bound for Miami. During the flight he attempted to ignite an explosive hidden in his shoe with the intention of bringing the plane crashing down to earth. In August 2001, a 34-year-old French national of Moroccan descent was arrested by US federal agents because while taking flying lessons he was neither interested in learning landings or takeoffs. His arrest was later brought in connection with the 9/11 attacks. These three cases are instances of Muslim extremist terrorism or attempts thereof committed by European nationals. This chapter tries to offer an answer to the question of how the European Union can deal with these "home-grown" terrorists and stifle their radicalization and recruitment. Due to the nature of the threat, European states cannot address the root causes of terrorism and solve terrorism altogether, yet instead the European Union needs to develop an effective strategy targeting radicalization and recruitment.

Anti-systemic terrorism

In their study *Political Terrorism*, Alex Schmidt and Berto Jongman identified 109 different definitions of terrorism.[2] In general, terrorism can be defined as the intentional use of, or threat to use, violence against civilians and civilian targets, in order to attain political aims. The EU uses the following definition of terrorism.

Terrorist acts are those that:

> given their nature or context, may seriously damage a country or an international organization where committed with the aim of: seriously intimidating the population; or unduly compelling a Government or international organization to perform or abstain from performing any act; or seriously destabilizing or destroying the fundamental political, constitutional, economic, or social structures of a country or an international organization.[3]

A serious problem is that this definition says little about the nature of the present threat. As a consequence its policy implications are hard to define. Traditionally, terrorists used well-known techniques such as hostage taking, murder, blackmail and terror aimed at specific segments of the population to reach specific, limited political objectives such as the release of prisoners. Their operations could be deadly, but did not affect the lives of many citizens. Nonetheless, a few well armed terrorists could seriously disrupt public order, as violence against citizens results in fear and chaos. Liberal democracies have always been extremely vulnerable to terrorism. The threat of the use of weapons of mass destruction and disruption is however a relatively recent phenomenon.

Since the targets are civilians, terrorism is distinguished from other types of political violence, such as guerrilla operations. The latter is defined as a form of warfare against a state by which the strategically weaker side assumes the tactical offensive in selected forms, times and places. The 9/11 attacks carried out by Osama bin Laden's Al-Qaeda network blurred the traditional distinction between terrorism and war. War is usually associated with combating state actors which pose a threat to international peace and security; terrorism is usually associated with deadly, but small-scale actions and limited objectives.

However, the new threat cannot be considered a tactical or local challenge, requiring cooperation between the national intelligence services and the police. The new threat is strategic and international in nature, which requires international cooperation among intelligence services, armed forces and the traditional law enforcement authorities. Combating terrorists could involve interventions in failed and weak states, especially *black holes*, those areas used by terrorists as sanctuaries. Here terrorists could use small armies to protect their interests. For example in Afghanistan, bin Laden used the 5,000-strong multinational Arabic "055 Brigade" to protect his training camps, other bases and to keep elements of the Taliban in check. Terrorist organizations could possess the military capabilities of small states and turn non-military means, such as airliners, into weapons of mass destruction to achieve strategic objectives.[4]

The new threat is sometimes defined as catastrophic terrorism[5] because it aims to kill people on a large scale. This, however, does not explain the specific nature of the threat. The attacks of 9/11 were directed at outstanding symbols of Western civilization; bin Laden had often spoken of targeting the "Zionist–Crusader Alliance" and of dealing blows to Americans and Jews.

This kind of terrorism is of a cultural and religious nature and aimed at removing alien influences from the Islamic world. Therefore some authors name the new threat cultural or religious terrorism, which is not an accurate description either.[6] Under such a definition, 9/11 and the destruction of two giant Buddha statutes of Bamiyan, Afghanistan by the Taliban in February 2001 fall in the same category. What really distinguishes the events of 9/11 from other terrorist acts is that the terrorists try to change the international system through mass destruction. A better term therefore is *anti-systemic terror*, defined as the unconventional, but worldwide and large-scale use by (state-sponsored) non-state actors against civilian and government targets, with the aim to change the international system.

Three layers

Stopping terrorists implies looking for a limited number of people. Although the numbers are small, the manner in which terrorist organizations organize and manifest themselves dictates substantial policy implications. Besides being spread out internationally, their recruitment activities and operations take place within the fabric of society instead of isolated from it. The operations in modern societies of terrorist organizations such as Al-Qaeda are enabled by three groups, or tiers, which can be represented in a pyramid structure (Figure 1.1).

- The first tier is formed by the "operators/managers"; these individuals often have experience in fighting as a jihadist or *mujahideen*, are generally well-educated and are part of the "staff" or management of the terrorist group.
- Disenfranchised, marginalized young Muslims make up the second tier; the members of this group are, due to political, social and/or socio-ethnic alienation, in search of an identity and are willing to assert themselves in the outside world. This pool of individuals is susceptible to radicalization because of its willingness to act.
- Finally, there are the "blind-eye bystanders", the third tier. This group neither supports nor opposes the operations of terrorists and it is in these communities that disenfranchised youth live and where the operators/managers immerse themselves.[7] This can be conceptualized as similar to Mao Zedong's view that guerrilla soldiers must operate as "fish in the sea", whereby the latter consists of a particular group of the population which offers tacit support, although short of being complicit to the guerrillas' activities.

Because the two bottom tiers are also present within European countries, they are suitable recruitment and radicalization grounds for Islamic extremists.

Causes of terrorism

Anti-systemic terror is associated with Osama bin Laden's Al-Qaeda network. His goal is to unite all Muslims and to establish a government which follows in

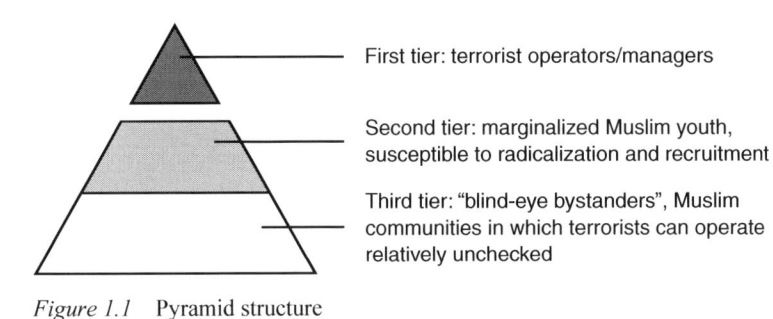

First tier: terrorist operators/managers

Second tier: marginalized Muslim youth, susceptible to radicalization and recruitment

Third tier: "blind-eye bystanders", Muslim communities in which terrorists can operate relatively unchecked

Figure 1.1 Pyramid structure

the footsteps of the Caliphs, the ancient religious rulers. The only way to do so is by the use of force. Muslim governments need to be overthrown because they are corrupt and are influenced by the "Zionist–Crusader Alliance"; an alliance of Jews and Christians, embodied by Israel and the United States and supported by Western liberal democracies in general. In bin Laden's view, this unholy alliance has occupied the land of Islam's holy sites (Mecca, Medina and Jerusalem) and tries to crush Islam altogether. To end this influence, the destruction of Israel and the United States is a prerequisite for reform in Muslim societies. Consequently, in August 1996 bin Laden issued a "Declaration of War" against the United States. While in his March 1997 interview with CNN's Peter Arnett, bin Laden said that he would only target US soldiers, he hardened his line in his *fatwah* issued in February 1998, when he called for attacks on Americans wherever they can be found.

A paradigm supported by history

A brief overview of several historical elements upon which bin Laden justifies Al-Qaeda's actions against the "Zionist–Crusader Alliance" yields insights into the mind of the Muslim extremist and is helpful in unearthing the motivating factors for Al-Qaeda's operations.

The 1998 *fatwa*, the "Declaration of the World Islamic Front for Jihad against the Jews and the Crusaders", described the US presence in the Middle East as a catastrophe that had humiliating and debilitating effects on Muslims. Bin Laden wrote, "Since God laid down the Arabian peninsula, created its desert, and surrounded it with its seas, no calamity has ever befallen it like these Crusader hosts that have spread in it like locusts, crowing its soil, eating its fruits, and destroying its verdure."

A Western power has never occupied the Hijaz (the region of Islam's holy places) in Muslim history. Traditionally, non-Muslims are not permitted to enter Mecca and Medina based on the Prophet's deathbed statement, "Let there not be two religions in Arabia". Bin Laden cites as an example the Crusader, Reynald of Chatillon in 1182, who attacked Muslim caravans in the Hijaz, including those of pilgrims to Mecca. His actions were perceived as a "provocation" and a "challenge directed against Islam's holy places". Historians of the Crusades state that Reynald's motive was primarily economic – desire for loot. However, bin Laden describes this as a campaign of provocation, a challenge directed against Islam's holy places. More than eight hundred years later, bin Laden applies the same principle and interprets the US presence as an equal provocation requiring retribution. Bin Laden conveniently ignores the fact that there is no Western presence in the Hijaz region of Saudi Arabia.

A key historical event in the development of the global jihad movement is one mentioned by bin Laden himself. In a taped message of 7 October 2001 bin Laden spoke about "the tragedy of Andalusia (Al-Andalus)", which refers to the conquering in 1492 of the Muslim Kingdom of Granada by the Catholic monarchs Ferdinand and Isabella. It was a central moment in the Islamic caliphate's quest for political and military power; Muslim expansion was not just checked, it was reversed. Moorish armies from North Africa had conquered the Iberian Peninsula in the eighth century and transformed the region into an integral part of the Muslim *ummah*, or community of believers. The "humiliation" has never been forgotten in parts of the Arab world, especially not by bin Laden and his followers.

Another key moment was the Sykes–Picot agreement (1915), which planned the division of the Arab provinces of the Ottoman Empire between the British and the French after the Second World War. Bin Laden's prime goal is said to be the restoration of the Islamic caliphate, and the Sykes–Picot agreement signalled, to bin Laden, the collapse of Muslim political and military power. The end of the Second World War meant "the destruction of the old order which, for better or for worse, had prevailed for four centuries or more in the Middle East". Throughout all these events bin Laden uses the historical term "crusaders" to describe the West and base that as a platform for war. Bin Laden however ignores that the Ottoman Empire was not a strict religious one and did not impose religion on all its subjects.

Other lesser or unknown groups inspired by Al-Qaeda might have similar perceptions as well. In general, Muslim extremism considers the war against the West a clash of civilizations. They hate everything that represents "decadent" Western civilization: commerce, most notably its banking system, sexual freedom, artistic freedom, secularism, democracy, religious tolerance, scientific pursuits and pluralism. They reject everything that makes Western civilization "modern" and instead strive for a pure, simple and uncorrupted world, one that is based on religious principles, self-denial, tied to the soil and obedient to authority, especially God. Thus, the West and the Islamic world seem opposite civilizations.[8]

In *Jihad vs. McWorld*, Benjamin Barber argues that there is a collision between the forces of Islamic disintegral tribalism along with reactionary fundamentalism ("Jihad") and the forces of integrative modernism and aggressive economic and cultural globalism ("McWorld"). In contrast to Samuel Huntington, Barber does not consider this a "clash of civilizations", but a "dialectic expression of tensions built into a single global civilization as it emerges against the backdrop of traditional ethnic and religious divisions, many of which are actually created by McWorld and its infotainment industries and technological innovations".[9] It's the pre-modern world, using the technologies of the modern and post-modern world to fight McWorld that seeks to overcome sovereignty and make its impact global. Indeed, bin Laden and other Muslim extremists use the things they are supposed to hate to reach their objectives: the media, the global financial system, modern technology and the Internet.

Anti-systemic terrorism finds its roots in the idea that Islam is the solution to political and socio-economic problems that had become manifest during the 1970s. Due to the increasing oil revenues, rapid but uneven modernization, urbanization and economic liberalization occurred which led to social tensions in large parts of the Muslim world, especially the Middle East. Youngsters in the fast growing cities felt betrayed by their rulers, who failed to use the oil revenues to create a civil society based on Islamic values, and used them for their own objectives instead. They also accused their leaders of having become puppets to Western companies and governments.

The resurgence of Islam is both a product of this development as well as the attempt by Muslims to deal with this development by rejecting Western culture and influence, committing to Islam as the guide to life in the modern world. Muslim extremism is closely linked to this resurgence. However, fundamentalism is mainstream and not extremist at all. Extremism is only one aspect of the resurgence which began in the 1970s when Islamic symbols, beliefs, practices and institutions won support throughout the Islamic world. As a product of modernity, the core constituency of Islamic resurgence consists of middle-class students and intellectuals. Indeed, the militants who carried out the 11 September attacks were well-educated, middle-class men.

A significant problem facing the European Union is that the Muslim fundamentalist perception of the world draws support for its actions precisely from the policies of Western states. In their view, from al-Andalus to Iraq, Western nations have been engaged in a crusade against Islam. These historical interpretations have obtained the status of a paradigm. For the European states this leads to the dilemma that whatever they do, their actions will support the views of the radicals. This has significant consequences for the policies pursued under the Common Foreign and Security Policy (CFSP), and the European Security and Defence Policy.

Ideological roots of current terrorism

Understanding the roots of Islamic extremist anti-systemic terrorism requires briefly reviewing two of its most prominent exponents, Sayyid Qutb and Abdullah Azzam. Sayyid Qutb was an important theoretician of the Egyptian Muslim Brotherhood and provided the genesis for Al-Qaeda decades later. Qutb's first major theoretical work of religious social criticism, *Al-'adala al-Ijtima'iyya fi-l-Islam* (Social Justice in Islam), was published in 1949, during his time overseas. In it he describes how corrupt and materialistic Western society is. It is largely through his rejection of Western values that he moved towards radicalism upon returning to Egypt. Resigning from the civil service he became perhaps the most persuasive publicist of the Muslim Brotherhood. The school of thought he inspired has become known as Qutbism.

After the attempted assassination of Gamal Abdel Nasser in 1954, the Egyptian government cracked down on the Muslim Brotherhood, imprisoning Qutb along with many others. While in prison, Qutb wrote his two most important works: a commentary of the Qur'an *Fi zilal al-Qur'an* (In the Shade of the Qu'ran), and a manifesto of political Islam called *Ma'alim fi-l-Tariq* (Milestones). It was Sayyid Qutb who fused together the core elements of modern Islamism. Qutb advocated that the unity of God and his sovereignty implied that democratic and secular governments were illegitimate. One of Qutb's main ideas was applying the term *Jahiliyya*, which originally referred to humanity's state of ignorance before the revelation of Islam, to modern-day Muslim societies. In his view, turning away from Islamic law and Islamic values under the influence of European imperialism had left the Muslim world in a condition of debased ignorance, similar to that of the pre-Islamic era (or *Jahiliyya*). His brother, Muhammad Qutb, moved to Saudi Arabia where he became a Professor of Islamic Studies. One of Muhammad Qutb's students and ardent followers was Ayman Zawahiri, who was to become the mentor of Osama bin Laden. Sayyid Qutb dramatically impacted Zawahiri. In his *Knights under the Prophet's Banner*, Zawahiri calls Qutb "the most prominent theoretician of the fundamentalist movements".

Qutb's argument found its most infamous manifestation in Mohammed al-Faraj's *The Neglected Duty*. Faraj was a member of Egyptian Islamic Jihad and used the book as a kind of internal discussion paper to explain and defend the group's ideology. The book uses several lines of argument that have become key to the development of Islamic terrorist groups. Faraj draws on Taqi al-Din Ibn Taymiyya, the best known medieval Salafi scholar, to argue for the centrality of jihad in faith. He uses an assortment of quotes and hadiths (stories about the Prophet) in an effort to demonstrate that "jihad is second only to belief" in Islam. This is used to elevate the importance of jihad as a "pillar of Islam", a mandatory requirement to be a Muslim. Faraj argues that jihad had become "the neglected duty", something that must be resurrected as a central pillar of the faith. Faraj also reiterates Qutb's argument that rulers who do not implement Islamic law are unbelievers and must be removed from power. This is based on a Qur'anic verse consistently cited by Al-Qaeda: "Whoever does not rule by what God hath sent down – they are unbelievers" (Qur'an 5:48).

But it was Abdullah Azzam who translated Qutb's theory to practice. Azzam had become convinced that only by means of organized military force would the Muslim world be victorious. He became absorbed with religious warfare: "Jihad and the rifle alone: no negotiations, no conferences and no dialogues". It was Azzam, an Arab-Afghan mujahid during the Afghanistan war, who set up the *Mujahideen Services Bureau*, its objective being to recruit, support, train and assist mujahideen in all possible ways. In many ways, this *Bureau* was the frontrunner of Al-Qaeda. During his fighting, he wrote one of his most influential books, *Join the Caravan*. In it he described four main duties of jihadists, the third being that enlightened Muslims pursuing jihadism should take up arms and assist Muslims anywhere in the world where they are faced with injustice and oppression. These struggles where Muslims were under siege were those in Bosnia, Chechnya and Kashmir. *Join the Caravan* appeared among the foreign jihadists fighting in the 7th Muslim brigade of the Bosnian army and these conflict zones created the embryonic jihadist volunteers who would crystallize towards Afghanistan and become Al-Qaeda. This combat experience in these conflict zones created a dedicated vanguard and a sense of brotherhood and unity of purpose in pursuing violence against Islam's enemies.

Challenges to the EU

The extremist variant of Muslim fundamentalism presents Western states with a major challenge. First, both for the West and Muslim extremists vital interests are at stake. For Western states it is about protecting interests in an important region; both geo-strategically in terms of energy resources as well as ideologically, such as basic human rights. For the extremists it is about protecting the Islamic community and its values against Western imperialists.

Second, religion plays a dominant role in the struggle. Especially when comparing Muslim extremism and the United States, both sides see the fight in more or less religious terms. There is a striking similarity between Muslim fundamentalism and US neo-conservatism. Both are guided by strong beliefs about values and the desired world order. Both believe that the other tries to destroy one's society. On the other hand, for European states it is precisely their secular nature which makes it difficult to relate to a phenomenon so overtly religiously motivated.

Third, since Islamic fundamentalism is fundamentally anti-Western, building and maintaining coalitions with Muslim states is not easy. Support for these regimes in itself may become the ground for them being targeted. This gives both a military and a moral advantage to the radicals. The coalition with Muslim states that was built in the aftermath of the 9/11 attacks was basically anti-bin Laden, not pro-Western. As bin Laden seeks to establish a new Caliphate under a political-religious leader, he poses a challenge to most regimes in the Islamic world as well. Most regimes and large parts of the population, however, shared the anti-Western ideas of bin Laden. Many Islamic people, in bin Laden's words, would consider a military campaign against a "Zionist–Crusader alliance", which is being carried out by Western forces. As a consequence, the Muslim component of the coalition has remained fragile and has only been willing to give passive support at best.

Fourth, a number of events led to the idea that "Zionists" and "Crusaders" can be expelled from the Islamic world. In turn this provides a powerful incentive for the extremists to continue their struggle. The Iranian revolution, the Soviet defeat in Afghanistan together with the break up of the Soviet Union in 1991 led to the belief that Islam was so powerful that new states could be created and the infidels expelled from the Islamic world. The Iranian revolution by the Shiite Muslims revived ties with Shiites elsewhere. Shiites in Lebanon began to carry out suicide bombings to drive out US and other foreign forces that had entered the country after the 1982 Israeli invasion. Of crucial importance is that in the eyes of the extremists the West did little to protect its interests. In 1979 the Americans did not act when the Shah was replaced by Ayatollah Khomeini, who founded a fundamentalist Islamist republic. In 1983 the Americans withdrew their forces from Lebanon, after 243 marines were killed. In 1993 bin Laden successfully helped warlord Aideed combating the US during the humanitarian intervention in Somalia. Following the attacks on the Khobar Towers the United States relocated from urbanized areas to Prince Sultan Air Force base in the desert. In August 1998 Al-Qaeda members attacked the US embassies in Kenya and Tanzania killing almost 300 people, including 12 Americans and wounding thousands. The Americans responded to the attacks on the American East-Africa embassies with operation Infinite Reach, aimed at killing Osama bin Laden, who was the main suspect. Operation Infinite Reach turned out to be a symbolic cruise missile volley on targets in Sudan and Afghanistan.[10] Both attacks did not affect the Al-Qaeda network. It later turned out that Operation Infinite Reach was the default option, because it was the only option left after the rejection of other, riskier options, i.e. with Special Operations Forces.[11]

The next attack came in December 2000 when the USS Cole was struck in the harbour of Aden, Yemen. But the United States did not retaliate. Undoubtedly, the first phase of the war against the West, which runs from the early 1990s to 11 September 2001, was won by the Muslim extremists. But also after 9/11 and America's declaration of the War on Terrorism, extremists remained quite successful. Tourism throughout Muslim countries came to a temporary standstill, especially after the October 2002 attack on a night club in Bali, killing 187 people, mostly Westerners. In May 2003 a series of attacks were carried out against Western interests in Riyadh and against Jewish as well in Casablanca, killing dozens. As a result some Western embassies were temporarily closed and their staffs reduced. Only after the events of 9/11 did the Americans embark on operations *Enduring Freedom* and *Iraqi Freedom*. Nevertheless, the Americans decided to withdraw their forces from Saudi Arabia and redeploy them to Qatar and Iraq. This move was again applauded by extremists. Although the war on Iraq was won by the Americans, the insurgencies in Afghanistan and Iraq are far from over and America's withdrawal from countries such as Saudi Arabia has facilitated the extremist's targeting of the "corrupt" Saudi monarchy.

Focusing on radicalization and recruitment: a strategy for Europe

The struggle against terrorism is complex and formulating an effective strategy against the spread of terrorism in the EU a complex undertaking. A fundamental question is how secularized European governments deal with a phenomenon that is so transcendentally religiously motivated? Answering it requires identifying three potential pitfalls concerning Muslim-extremist terrorism that are relevant for developing a coherent European policy. First of all, it is necessary to differentiate between *causes* of terrorism and *background contributing factors*. This concerns both an analytical as well as an important semantic distinction. The *cause* of Muslim extremist terrorism, as illustrated above, is ascribed to the state of persistent political/social/economic/or religious disenfranchisement among a significant part of the population of the Middle East. The background contributing factors that lead to radicalization such as the socio-economic gap among Muslim communities, however, are not *causes* for terrorism in the sense that they are uniquely responsible for terrorist activities. In fact, such an argumentation could lead to over-simplifications along the lines of "all Muslims are terrorists".

Policy based on similar over-simplifications would increase rather than decrease civil strife. European lessons of dealing with regional terrorist groups such as the IRA are not applicable to decisively fight anti-systemic terrorism owing to a difference in scale of operations and a divergence in the terrorist's objectives. While the causes of terrorism are a consequence of events inside Muslim countries, radicalization and recruitment also take place in European states and among their populations. The *causes* of terrorism are mostly of an external, international nature and are supported by an anti-Western historical paradigm; the background contributing factors, however, that lead to and catalyse the radicalization of EU citizens, constitute a topic that EU institutions and member states can inherently confront. It is indeed politically viable to address the factors contributing to radicalization as they lend themselves to political and social treatment.

A consequence of this observation is that it is not possible for EU states to resolve the threat of terrorism completely. Since the sources of the problem lie elsewhere and EU policies in themselves may constitute a source of terrorism, European states can manage the risks of Muslim-extremist terrorism by targeting the factors conducive to radicalization and recruitment. As outlined above, *causes of terrorism* cannot be targeted, those factors contributing to radicalization and recruitment can.

Second, a difference should be made between exogenous and endogenous (*homegrown*) radicalization processes. This chapter focuses on the endogenous variant; those individuals with EU citizenship that have radicalized along Muslim extremist lines and have become susceptible to violence. For instance the focus lies on people such as the "shoe-bomber" Richard Reid and the killer of Theo van Gogh, Mohammed Bouyeri and not with foreign nationals such as 9/11-mastermind Mohammed Atta or Al-Qaeda-operative Khalid Sheikh Mohammed. A substantial challenge facing the European Union member states lies in addressing the extremist re-Islamization of second- or third-generation nationals of Muslim heritage, not to mention the conversion to radical Islam of EU citizens of European stock. These so-called "born-again Muslims" are generally more fanatical in their beliefs than "regular" Muslims. At the same time, this coincides with the observation that disenfranchised Muslim youth are particularly susceptible to radicalization. Alienated from society or even multiple societies and with few socio-economic opportunities, their sense of belonging is lost. A search for identity commences that can lead towards a path of radicalization. Hence, recognizing and addressing this disenfranchisement is key.

Third, it must be made explicit that the EU focuses on behaviour, and not on belief. All those who radicalize are not terrorists, yet all terrorists have gone through a process of radicalization. Radicalization is a necessary stage that a European Muslim extremist terrorist must go through before committing his acts. The issue then that this chapter deals with is the process of radicalization among certain groups within EU societies. What are the factors for radicalization and how does this lead to the recruitment of individuals within the EU-area? How do we prevent European Muslims from "conniving in terror"? The assumption underlying this is that acts of terrorism performed by EU citizens are preceded by a process of radicalization and recruitment; hence there is a discernible chain of cause-and-effect that leads an individual on the road to terrorism. From a policy perspective there is both an internal political dimension relating to, for instance, educational reform and law enforcement, and an external political dimension relating to aspects of foreign and defence policy. Although the two are closely linked, they are analytically and operationally distinct. In this dialectic one dimension affects the other thereby rendering it impossible to assign relative weights to each dimension. Hence it becomes important to understand both sides of the equation. The factors described below are not mutually exclusive and each factor does not constitute a cause in itself for radicalization. Instead it is the kaleidoscope of factors, more like vectors, that push and pull individuals to radicalization and enable their recruitment. In the end, individuals are responsible for their own actions. The aim is to identify background contributing factors to radicalization, how this leads to recruitment of individuals and what policy instruments need to be prioritized either present in the current toolbox or that require development.

Radicalization

What is radicalization? Paraphrased along the lines of a report issued by the Dutch Intelligence Services (AIVD) radicalization is the quest to drastically alter society, possibly through the use of unorthodox means, which can result in a threat to democratic structures and institutions.[12] As has been made apparent, radicalization along Islamic extremist lines is considered here.

Internal dimension

- A primary factor contributing to radicalization is the lack of debate within the Islamic community concerning the interpretation of holy text, which has created a possibility for extremist views to proliferate. There is a necessity to address the violent strains of thought within the Islamic community. One way of doing so without antagonizing the community itself is to stimulate the debate among these different strains. The clash within Islam is a clash of ideas and interpretations. Just as democratic societies are based upon a constant tug-of-war of ideas, perceptions and arguments, so should the alternative voices of Islam be allowed to confront each other.
- Second, stigmatization and political polarization of Muslim communities through public debate contribute to an atmosphere where young Muslims feel detached from society and search for an identity, including in the violent strains of Islam. It is essential that any measures taken by governments receive passive, perhaps even active, support from moderates inside Muslim communities. If policy is perceived to be driven from the "outside" (in this case, government or state institutions) it will merely increase civil strife. It is therefore imperative that a clear distinction is developed and

stimulated between moderates and extremists within these communities and expressions of a stigmatizing nature in the public arena are minimized. It is necessary to gain greater insight into how government policy and political discourse are a source for radicalization.
- The general socio-economic lag of Muslim immigrant populations, and their generally lower level of integration in European society at large, contributes to the search by Muslim youth for new means of development and progress. High levels of unemployment, or lack of opportunity, reinforce the sensation of disenfranchisement and contribute to radicalization. Extremist Islamism offers these people new meaning.
- The presence of radical imams within EU states is conducive to the spread of Muslim extremist thought. The significance of foreign, in particular Wahabbi Saudi, money flows to these imams and orthodox mosques characterizes the internal–external link of radicalization processes.
- Among the jihadists there is a discourse of glorification of the jihad and martyrdom which has made Muslim youths, who are trapped in a cycle of discrimination, stigmatization and criminalization, susceptible to recruitment efforts.
- Various media play a role in catalysing radicalization. Especially the Internet and Internet newsgroups offer access to recruitment broadcasts and can bring "second-tier" youth into contact with gatekeepers and their organizations (see The dynamic of recruitment, below).
- Prisons form a primary ground for both radicalization and recruitment (see The dynamic of recruitment, below). In terms of radicalization, prisons are in themselves environments conducive to the radicalization of alienated individuals who have dismissed society and are in search of a new or higher purpose in life.

External dimension

Western policy abroad can be a source of radicalization for individuals in Muslim communities. Although the problems within Muslim countries that are causes for terrorism are of an internal nature, EU external policies can become catalysing factors for recruitment and radicalization abroad and at home. The dilemma for European states is that due to their membership of the Western civilization they are automatically perceived by jihadists as potential enemies. This underscores the observation that the EU and its member states should focus on managing risks of terrorism instead of wishing to solve it in absolute terms. Radicalization through aspects of European foreign and defence policy is driven by a Muslim-extremist perception of Western policies which may find resonance among "second-tier" young Muslims. Because Muslims in European countries often identify themselves with their "brothers and sisters" in Muslim countries, their plights in turn affect behaviour of their European co-religionists. It should be made explicit, however, that the EU's external policies are not the motivators for radicalization; they are not the objective causes that drive particular people towards terrorism. Instead, the radicalizing individual's *Weltanschau* is the motivator, and EU external policies are "handles" on which the extremist can base his rhetoric. However, the EU should be aware of this. The observation is reflected in the external factors identified below which to a large extent are not objective factual conditions but rather conditions perceived as such by particular groups in the Middle East and are elements in shaping their paradigm.

- The perceived injustice suffered by Muslims across several key conflicts, such as Chechnya, Iraq and in the Palestinian territories contributes to the radicalization of Muslims in EU countries. The perception that Western (in particular US) policy in the Middle East and Muslim countries constitutes veiled colonialism or neo-imperialism stimulates this sense of injustice. Similarly, there is perceived policy of double standards vis-à-vis the Israeli–Palestinian conflict. This is reinforced by a lack of fundamental progress in the Palestinian issue which is attributed to half-hearted measures being taken by Western countries, most notably the United States. It leads to an overall sentiment of humiliation and brotherhood (collective identification) among Muslims.
- Military interventions by Western states contribute to radicalization of Muslims at home. Indiscriminate use of force, (large-scale) Muslim civilian casualties and suffering, as well as "collateral damage" contribute to shaping a perception of injustice suffered by Muslims at the hands of "the West". These instances reinforce the Muslim-extremist's paradigm and support assertions by people like bin Laden who state that the West is out to dominate the Muslim world. Hence, the consequences for Europe's foreign and security policy and the way Europe acts abroad are significant.
- The perception of injustice is also reinforced by the flow of development aid to regimes in the Middle East that are qualified as "corrupt" or "authoritarian" by radicals.
- Besides these perceived grievances, the media and Internet play an important role in shaping perceptions among young Muslims concerning conflicts abroad and the policies pursued by Western states. The access to media and web sites meant to rally individuals for the Muslim-jihadist cause presents a dilemma of free speech. Often radical Islamic sites are based on services in Muslim countries.

Iraqi Jihad veterans

With respect to the interaction of external and internal policies, and radicalization and recruitment, a significant threat is caused by returning European "Iraqi Jihad veterans", the so-called blowback effect. The number of these returning veterans is estimated for Germany at 50, from France "several dozen" have travelled to Iraq and from the Netherlands approximately 30 are active in Iraq.[13] Much as Afghani mujahid-veterans from the Afghan–Soviet war formed the human resource foundation of Al-Qaeda and similar organizations in the 1990s, returning Iraqi jihadists have the potential to function as operators/managers for operations in Europe. They function as an experienced and motivated "first-tier" group able to tap into the pool of "second-tier" Muslim youth and exploit "third-tier" Muslim communities or elements thereof. Their increased experience and knowledge of European societies could lead to new attacks as well as more effective strategies of recruiting youth.

The dynamics of recruitment[14]

Since the 2004 terrorist attack in Madrid, Europe is widely considered to be on the frontline of the global jihad. In reality, however, Europe already was a main jihad recruitment centre and started to form a direct threat to the continent in the late 1990s. Recruitment for jihad is not a new phenomenon in Europe, as European jihad fighters were recruited earlier for the wars in Afghanistan and Bosnia. Various changes have taken place in the recruitment environment. The concept of jihad transformed from a "noble" cause during the 1980s in Afghanistan to all-out large-scale violence against the masses. The war in Iraq is exploited to encourage recruitment. At the same time, recruitment activities have become less visible due to increased counter-terrorism efforts by the European security services. Moreover, military operations in Afghanistan ruined most training camps and meeting places for new recruits, causing a shift towards alternative local training methods. Due to these military operations in Afghanistan and counter-terrorism efforts in Europe, the earlier terrorist networks also suffered serious blows, leaving younger recruits to form looser, more adaptive and dynamic networks. This in turn presents new challenges to law enforcement agencies.

These new networks are formed from the bottom-up. In the absence of a comprehensive recruitment drive, alienated religious youths voluntarily join the jihad movement. Those being recruited are mostly young Muslim men belonging to one of three categories: born-again Muslims, recent immigrants and second- or third-generation immigrants, i.e. "second-tier" youth. These recruits have in common that they each embrace militant Islam unconditionally and are somehow marginalized in their societies. Usually, these groups develop from close friendships made at mosques or other religious centres. The tighter these groups become, the more extreme their views and the more alienated they become from society. Eventually many leave the mosques when they find them not to be radical enough.

In order for these groups to be recruited into the global jihad and become operational, they need a link to the jihad movement, a so-called gatekeeper. Due to current counter-terrorism efforts, these links have been more difficult to establish, causing many groups to adapt and act autonomously. Gatekeepers are individuals that can operate from charitable foundations, mosques or Internet newsgroups, but they can also be imams. Foreign sponsorship of these gatekeepers or the organizations in which they function is common.

The following segment is a description of the recruitment process in the Netherlands according to the Dutch Intelligence Services.

Mujahideen find it easy through the more orthodox mosques to contact a group of second generation Muslim youth that are struggling with their identity and are susceptible to or sympathize with radical-islamist thought. Hence finding potential recruits is relatively straightforward for the mujahideen. They merely need to participate in the prayers, conversations and activities in order to come into contact with the youth. "Spotting" however does not only take place in the mosque. Also Islamic community centers, coffee houses and especially prisons are suitable locations to make first contact and to discuss the Islamic jihad. Integrated Muslim youth tend to be surprisingly susceptible for this radical recruitment. Recruiters have therefore also been remarkably active with regards to the prison population.[15]

Prison recruitment

Several physical locations exist where gatekeepers function, where the recruitment of Muslims for global jihad takes place. These locations are risk areas that require government attention. Prisons in EU member states are among the most disturbing. Regarding inmate recruitment strategies there are four types of individuals identified who are central in recruitment activities.

- Detained jihadist recruiters often continue their operations once inside prison walls.
- There are inmates who have a terrorism-related background or who are convicted for terrorism-related crimes and pursue recruitment activities once in prison.
- Prison-imams can play a role in the recruitment process.
- Islamic extremists who are convicted for "regular" felonies and motivate others to radicalize.[16]

An example is Richard Reid who was apprehended aboard a Miami-bound flight from Paris trying to ignite an explosive device. He radicalized and converted to Islam while in a British jail.[17]

Saudi charity

The factors mentioned above have contributed to radicalization and have mobilized the operations of extremists. At the same time, they have led to money flows originating from Middle Eastern states, mostly through charities, towards terrorist organizations either directly or indirectly which facilitate the recruitment of individuals for the global jihad.[18] The following paragraphs highlight the role of Saudi charities. The European Union needs to grasp the full scope of the reach of these Saudi charities, and develop effective policy to minimize its effect on radicalization and recruitment in the EU.

Several charitable and humanitarian organizations, predominantly based in Saudi Arabia, have not only financed terrorist groups, but actively facilitated terrorist operations. These activities are conducive to radicalizing and recruiting youths in the Middle East, and to the extent that the organizations are active within the EU contribute to radicalization at home. The EU should clamp down on these organizations. Some details of several charities that play an active role in organizing for terrorism are mentioned below.

A key Saudi charity linked to terrorist financing is the al-Wafa Humanitarian Organization. US officials have described al-Wafa as a key component of bin Laden's organization. Several humanitarian organizations such as the Mercy International Relief Organization (Mercy) played central roles in the 1998 US embassy bombings. At the New York trial of four men convicted of involvement in the embassy attacks, a former Al-Qaeda member named several charities as fronts for the terrorist group, including Mercy. Documents presented at the trial demonstrated that Mercy smuggled weapons from Somalia into Kenya, and Abdullah Mohammad, one of the Nairobi bombers, delivered eight boxes of convicted Al-Qaeda operative Wadi el-Hage's belongings – including false documents and passports – to Mercy's Kenya office.

On 2 June 2004, the Saudi government outlined plans to dismantle all international charity organizations operating in the kingdom and place their holdings under a new commission in what officials said is an effort to stop the flow of funds to terrorist groups. The charities to be dissolved include the Al Haramain Islamic Foundation, one of the largest and most influential Saudi charities, whose chairman is the Saudi minister of Islamic affairs.

The Al Haramain charity was identified in a CIA investigation as allegedly dispensing $50 million (£27 million) a year through some 50 offices worldwide. American officials believed that branches in at least ten countries, including Indonesia, Pakistan and Somalia, were providing arms or cash to terrorists. Al Haramain was acting as a key source of funds for Al-Qaeda, while Russian officials suspected it of channelling $1 million to Chechen rebels and helping to purchase 500 "heavy weapons" from the Taliban. Al Haramain created a fund in support of the rebels called "Foundation Regarding Chechnya". In late 1999 a branch of the Foundation begun operating in Azerbaijan. It is believed that the Foundation employs 25 agents in regions bordering Chechnya and more in Chechnya itself. The foundation also has branches in European states, most notably the Netherlands has been identified as being a host to an Al Haramain-affiliated organization.

The United States has long pressured the Saudis to reform oversight of its wealthy charities. Government officials generally agree that in the past year there has been significant progress in the desert kingdom's war on terrorism, including financial oversight as a series of deadly terrorist attacks has been conducted on Saudi soil. However, contrary to Saudi promises, on 7 October 2004, the Al Haramain foundation said in a statement to the English-language Saudi daily newspaper *Arab News* it had not received official notice to shut down. While direct ties to terrorism are one thing, there is also the worry about the intolerant brand of Islam that Saudi charities seek to export. The World Assembly of Moslem Youth, for instance, distributes and publishes books worldwide – some describing a vast Jewish conspiracy to take over the world and destroy Muslims. The EU should be aware of the Saudi charities that function either as gatekeepers or that fund terrorist organizations and support the processes of radicalization and recruitment. These charities are key enablers for the operations of recruiters and gatekeepers.

Dealing with radicalization and recruitment

Doctrine

A fortnight following the Madrid attacks on 11 March 2004 the EU heads of state issued a declaration pledging the Union and its 25 member states "to do everything within their power to combat all forms of terrorism". Its efforts were poised at finding and stopping the fundraisers of terrorism, rooting out the causes of terrorism, facilitating free movement of terror-related intelligence among member states, and managing the consequences of an attack should one occur. Nevertheless a year later, the president of the European Parliament noted that much still needed to be achieved. There has been insufficient cooperation among judicial and police authorities, difficulties in setting up the office of an EU public prosecutor, and delays in adopting a directive against money laundering. The common arrest warrant has encountered trouble being implemented, as does the initiative to create an agency to monitor the EU's external borders. The initiatives that have been decided upon need to be implemented.

The European Union needs to come to grips with the reality that it should not focus on the root causes of terrorism but rather on the factors leading to radicalization and recruitment. These latter factors are malleable. Similarly, the European Union needs to grasp that the current situation is bound to last for a significant length of time. A reactive mode thereby becomes ineffective. Long-term recommendations are required as the European Union organizes itself for the long haul on doctrinal, conceptual and budgetary aspects. With the security of the EU citizen as the principle motivator, the EU and its member states need to rethink and develop a coherent strategy in relation to this new threat. This should occur on conceptual, organizational and doctrinal levels. The leading question should be *how to organize our societies in order to protect citizens over a 10–20 year term*. The analysis should start at a conceptual level and develop understanding of "best practices", following which ideas, tools and in particular a doctrine needs to be developed. The conceptual nature of the problem requires knowledge of doctrine alongside operational expertise. Doctrinal knowledge focuses on the balance between the use of "hard" and "soft" measures and makes full use of the interplay between internal and external policies.

A broad understanding of the various facets of the problem is necessary on which to base a policy-vision. For Ministries of Interior this explicitly implies that they need a more doctrinal and operational approach and this will simultaneously require the development of a proper R&D programme. Because the threat facing European member states is also of a WMD-nature, thinking in R&D terms to ascertain the necessary interoperability, sensors and framework of command and communication is a necessity. As will be made apparent, a central component of an effective doctrine for the European Union is the development of a coherent research programme focusing on aspects of radicalization and recruitment; providing sufficient funding, enabling policy-research interaction by bringing relevant academics, researchers and policymakers together and focusing the diffuse efforts that characterize the current research landscape on these topics. In short, the first step towards shaping a European doctrine is establishing centres of excellence for the study of background contributing factors to terrorism.

The external dimension

Hearts and minds

Regarding the external dimension of dealing with the radicalization and recruitment of terrorists, British experiences with counterinsurgencies warrant a closer look. The British are the founders of "imperial policing"; controlling parts of the empire with a minimal number of forces and a minimal use of force. Due to the span of the British empire and the limited number of available troops, the British concluded that a certain level of consensus was a necessary condition for stability in the empire. Local power structures were preserved, local chiefs and leaders were won for the British cause, and the British troops themselves were required to practise caution and avoid the use of force as much as possible. Most recently, British forces have drawn experience from Northern Ireland.

The British general Sir Gerald Templar coined the term "hearts and minds" during the Malayan Emergency in the 1950s. He concluded that a combination of "minimum force" and a dedicated commitment to the well-being of the population was an absolute necessity for winning the "hearts and minds" of the local population. Military power, it was concluded, needed to be secondary to political process. The use of power instruments – police and army – is required to manage a situation, to create a form of stability and to enable dialogue. The British experience made it clear that the most important objective is to avoid being perceived as the occupier. This would antagonize the local population and be detrimental to establishing stability. Instead it would lead to resistance, a situation which the British armed forces were incapable of countering on a large scale. The coalition in Iraq currently faces a similar dilemma. The US engagement in operations in Iraq and in particular its counterinsurgency operations in Fallujah have fuelled jihadist movements and are a source for radicalization. It demonstrates that doctrine – the correct mix between "hard" and "soft" – is key. Stabilization operations emphasizing "hearts and minds" campaigns are required. Europe's foreign policymakers should take this into account when considering interventions, especially of the military sort. Coming to grips with this is a priority objective for CFSP.

Arab development and democracy

The EU's share of responsibility for the lack of democracy in the Islamic World to date is not down to too much enthusiasm for promoting democracy, but too little. The approach has often been tactical rather than strategic, preferring a known status quo to an unknown process of change, and claiming that the time was never quite right. Democracy involves difficult choices for governments between short-term and long-term aims. However, the European Union cannot go back to the days of supporting unsatisfactory stasis over unpredictable change. For the EU, democracy is the best possible guarantee of sustainable, long-term security. No two full democracies have ever made war on each other. Democracy is not just the holding of regular votes, but also involves the creation of a stable and strong set of institutions and norms to underpin democracy between the general elections. Democracy must be based on the respect for individuals' basic human rights. It requires government to be transparent and fair, adhering to international treaties and institutions, functioning courts, and police and armed forces under civilian control. And it requires open societies, with free media, fair treatment of minorities, equal access to education and opportunity, open markets and free trade unions. The recent Arab Human Development Reports, drafted under the auspices of the United Nations Development Program, offer good starting points for policy goals. An example follows.

The Arab Human Development Report of 2003 sketches the Arab World as an underdeveloped area.[19] This is apparent by the limited number of newspapers in the Arab World (53 per 1000 inhabitants, whereas the figure is 285 per 1000 inhabitants in developed countries), the limited number of computers (18 per 1000 in the Arab world, and 78.3 per 1000 in the developed world) and the limited access of the population to the Internet, only 1.6 per cent. The most dramatic figure consists of the number of books translated yearly: 4.4 per million inhabitants, whereas for example the figure is 519 for Hungary and 920 for Spain. These disappointing figures are conducive to a lack of creativity and development, according to the Report. There is a limited knowledge base which makes innovation nearly impossible. Conspiracy theories and assumptions are the norm. This underdevelopment explains why the population is hardly receptive to modernization and why fundamentalist thought is the answer to processes of globalization. This has been accentuated by the fact that in the Arab World rentier states have been created owing to the economic dependence upon oil and gas revenues. This has stimulated the *braindrain* of the limited numbers of educated people and the results are deep-rooted social and economic obstacles for the development of the Arab World. The conclusions of the Arab Human Development Report support the premises that bin Laden's ideas are supported by a large part of the population, although again fundamentalism should not be equated to extremism. The EU's policies and objectives such as those outlined in the Barcelona Process should be brought in sync with the recommendations in the Arab Human Development Reports. Supporting the emergence of democracy in the Middle East and around the world must be a central part of a progressive EU foreign policy. This is the time to re-affirm the EU commitment to that.

Further priority areas

In relation to the external policy dimension, besides those mentioned above, a number of general policy recommendations follow below. Several priority areas which require further understanding and necessitate EU action are identified.

- The interaction between foreign policy/development aid and internal security with respect to Muslim-extremist radicalization is an understudied area. Within the realm of development aid, the introduction of a *security impact assessment* can aid in maximizing the positive effects of aid policy. This clause can be introduced under the heading of *good governance* criteria for aid. It could become a tool under which Official Development Aid (ODA) is evaluated.;
- Recognize that foreign policy as well as CFSP can be a source of radicalization. This is the case due to three factors:
  1. The (military) operations that European countries pursue abroad. This mostly concerns active involvement in wars within the Muslim world.
  2. The countries that European states support. This includes the United States which is considered the leading state in the "Zionist–Crusader" Alliance.
  3. The rhetoric that European states use in support of their policies.
- Greater awareness is required among military policymakers and among military cultures that particular doctrines in military interventions are grounds for radicalization. Subsequently, the identification of unintended consequences reinforcing radicalization at home resulting from military doctrines/standard operating procedures/operations abroad is required. The prevalence of "hearts and minds" campaigns in defence policy needs to be enhanced.
- Stimulate the development of European knowledge hubs, possibly in cooperation with North-African/Middle Eastern counterparts. The academic dimension of the study of radicalization and recruitment requires strengthening. The dynamic of these activities needs to be studied in greater detail. At the same time there is no suitable forum to discuss the topics at hand. There is a lack of ability to operationalize strategies to deal with radicalization caused by a knowledge gap between the subject matter experts on the one hand and the policymakers on the other.
- The possibility of merging the Barcelona Process and recommendations of the Arab Human Development Report or coalescing aspects thereof.
- Pursue coherent strategies for dealing with the financing of terrorist operations. Due to the relatively small costs associated with non-WMD-related terrorist operations, tracking their money flows is exceedingly difficult. Nevertheless dealing with the "charities" is imperative. Money flow meas-

ures can most likely focus more effectively on the more costly WMD-related expenditures, such as those related to AQ Khan's network.

Several specific policy recommendations follow for the EU's dealings with Pakistan, Morocco and Indonesia. With regards to Pakistan, a strong emphasis is placed on the role that madrasas play.

Pakistan

The EU needs to promote civil society in Pakistan to encourage the reduction of the role that the armed forces play, particularly as it has been the military in the past that has hindered democracy. The military intelligence establishment has not been effective in monitoring the activities of European citizens who have entered Pakistan and then joined the madrasas, from which some of them have become radicalized. A fully functional democratic Pakistan which has a strong civil society would be the best way to hinder fundamentalism from taking root inside Pakistan. There is a also a concern that the military has control over Pakistan's nuclear programme. This should really be in the hands of the civilian establishment, particularly as the military has a significant presence of individuals that are sympathetic towards fundamentalists. By accepting the status quo in Pakistan the EU puts at risk its own security with European citizens becoming potential terrorists as well as allowing fundamentalism to grow, as also the prospect of nuclear proliferation to rogue regimes and anti-Western elements.

It is believed that Al-Qaeda's underground network in Pakistan is functioning with the complicity and assistance of several clergymen and individuals in the intelligence services in preparing recruits from cradle to grave. These two elements cultivate and sustain the terrorist groups that operate inside and outside Pakistan. They are their lifeline, the umbilical cord. Life for the terrorist would be much harder without these supporters.

A number of Pakistan's madrasas are the recruiting grounds for terrorists. The jihadi leaders who practise and teach fundamentalist doctrines control many of these religious schools and militant Islam is at the core of the curriculum. Since the 1980s, Pakistan has been the epicentre for the global jihad movement. There are between 8,000 and 10,000 registered madrasas and between 40,000 and 50,000 unregistered ones in Pakistan. Currently there are some 1 million to 1.7 million students enrolled in the registered madrasas alone. These madrasas receive about 64 per cent of their funding from Muslim countries like Saudi Arabia and Libya, and Pakistan provides the rest by the "zakat", a 2.5 per cent tax collected by the Pakistani government from the bank accounts of Sunni Muslims once a year. The tax draws in millions of dollars every year. Unlike elitist and very selective schools in the West, the madrasas are more than willing to educate anyone and are open to all, class and colour are irrelevant. Students are from all strata of society – innocent village boys, sons of urban middle-class families, highly qualified expatriates and those who did not even have any link with Pakistan in the past.

Radical madrasas often receive financial support from abroad. An example of such a madrasa network is the one funded by the Al Rashid Trust, a charitable organization. The Al Rashid Trust, another group that funded Al-Qaeda and the Taliban, is closely associated with the Al-Qaeda-associated Pakistani terror group the Jaish-e-Mohammed (JeM). Al Rashid has been directly linked to the 23 January 2002 abduction and subsequent brutal murder of Wall Street Journal reporter Daniel Pearl in Pakistan. It is believed that Pearl had uncovered a link to both bin Laden and the Pakistani intelligence agency the ISI, through the Al Rashid Trust. The attackers, linked to a motley crew of domestic Pakistani radical Islamic fundamentalist groups (including JeM) operating in cooperation with, and on behalf of, Al-Qaeda, held Pearl in a two-room hut in the compound of a commercial nursery owned by Al Rashid. Several madrasas under construction dominate the immediate area around the nursery, the largest and closest of which is owned by Al Rashid.

The students in these radical extremist madrasas are indoctrinated to remove all doubts; the only truth is divine truth and the only code of conduct is that written in the Qur'an and the Hadiths (life and sayings of the holy prophet on various issues) as selected by the clerics. The teachings cannot be questioned; there is no debate and only one answer permissible. Virtue lies in unthinking obedience. Anyone who rebels against the clerics rebels against god. "The madrasas indulge in brainwashing on a large scope, of the young children and those in their early teens", said Arasiab Khattak, chairman of the Human Rights Commission of Pakistan. The aim is clear. These madrasas have a single function. They are nurseries engineered to produce fanatics. Many of those who have been recruited by the terrorist groups from the madrasas are then given "field experience" by sending these jihadis to launch attacks against civilians in Indian-administered Kashmir.

One Pakistani terror group that has relied heavily on the madrasas is the Lashkar-e-Toiba (LeT). The group along with being active in Kashmir has a large and developed recruiting system not only in Pakistan but also the UK, France, Australia and the US. The LeT was formed in 1990 as the military wing of the Markaz-ud-Dawa-wal-Irshad (MDI). The MDI recruited volunteers to fight as mujahideen against the Soviet occupation in Afghanistan during the 1980s, and many of its members trace their military expertise to this campaign. The group had close ties with the Taliban regime in Afghanistan, where it continued to train and educate its members until the US-led Operation *Enduring Freedom* forced them to relocate. The LeT doctrine is heavily influenced by Wahhabism and is actively promoted by the MDI's radical Islamist views. The group advocates pan-Islamic rule in South Asia and beyond. Its leaders and publications encourage greater ambitions, calling for a worldwide jihad.

Pakistan needs to recognize the terror groups for what they are; dangerous institutions whose resources and reach have continued to grow over the years and which now are threatening to destabilize and bleed not just Pakistan but the entire region and beyond. Pakistan's continued support to terror groups that are particularly aligned to Al-Qaeda suggests that it does not recognize its own susceptibility to the culture of violence it has helped to nurture and maintain. Therein lays the problem. The various groups that exist in Pakistan have paralysed the nation and held it hostage for developing into a modern secular state like Turkey. The terror groups have created an environment ripe for Al-Qaeda to sustain its activities and conduct its global agenda. Without compliance from official elements within Pakistan, Al-Qaeda and affiliated components within the global jihad movement would be in a far weaker position than they currently hold, their oxygen would be severely curtailed and with that so would their operational capability and their global reach. The EU should focus on these aspects.

Morocco

The type of political future Morocco is heading towards is unclear. The king, Mohammed VI, has spoken frequently of the importance of reforming education and the administration, and of tackling poverty and unemployment. Many in Morocco's political elite hope he will transform the constitutional monarchy from one that rules to one that reigns. Most likely he will continue his father's policy of seeking formal candidacy to join the EU. Many political challenges remain. The monarchy has not given up control over key policies, institutions and appointments. The administrative apparatus is Byzantine. Political parties are internally fragmented. Nevertheless, the country is fast moving away from the coercive, unstable, and ethnically and religiously divided systems of so many Arab and African regimes. Competitive elections, protection of civil rights and an open press seem to be pushing Morocco inexorably towards a more democratic European future.

Like the rest of the Arab world, Morocco suffers from high foreign debt, unemployment and protectionist barriers. Reforms have been slow. Literacy, and particularly female literacy, is amongst the lowest in the Arab world, while regional and social inequalities are exceptionally great. The kingdom would gain little from aligning with the Middle East and Africa, the two most marginalized regions of the global economy. Its economic destiny lies with Europe. Morocco already conducts 65 per cent of its trade with Europe, and the bulk of foreign investment comes from the north. European companies are buying privatized utilities and preparing to build much of the country's new infrastructure. And the number of European tourists (2 million in 1999) flocking south to the Atlas mountains and the beaches of Agadir will rise as new European tourism investments are completed.

Morocco's 1996 Association Agreement with the EU ties the country's future to Europe. It forces Morocco to lower tariffs progressively until, by 2010, there is basically free trade. High rates of unemployment and illiteracy will drag down growth. Poor public education, a lack of private schools and a limited spread of English will hamper adaptation to the global information age. However, there is cause for optimism. Moreover, almost 1 million Moroccans live legally in Europe. Already channelling massive remittances to their families in Morocco, the cultural values and skills they learn in Europe will be even more widely diffused back home, as ease of cross-national communication accelerates. Every summer an astonishingly large "people connection" is formed between Europe and Morocco: hundreds of thousands of Moroccan nationals living in Europe drive across the Strait of Gibraltar by ferry to northern Morocco. Co-opting Morocco on an economic and political scale would be an effective policy strategy.

Indonesia

The Bali terrorist attack not only has exposed the weaknesses of Indonesia's government and security apparatus but also has forced its neighbours and the United States finally to confront a problem they have been avoiding. The country with the world's largest Muslim population, Indonesia, was known as a secular, tolerant society with a majority that practises a moderate form of Islam. But in recent years, Islamist radicals have gained momentum in Indonesia and its Southeast Asian neighbours. Indonesia is a vast archipelago with porous maritime borders, a weak central government, separatist movements, corruption, a floundering economy and a loosely regulated financial system, characteristics that could make Indonesia fertile ground for terrorist groups.

In the aftermath of the Bali bombing in Indonesia, the recent unravelling of involvement of Jemaah Islamiyah (JI) and its local allies points to the growing threat of terrorism in the Southeast Asian Region. This radical outfit seeks to establish a pan-Islamic state covering the regions of Malaysia, Singapore, Indonesia and the southern Philippines.

Over recent years, Indonesia has seen the proliferation of Islamic ideas with external support from Saudi Arabia, Pakistan and others in the Middle East. Like in Pakistan's madrasas, there exists an entire educational system, the Pesantren, independent of the government, giving the Islamists access to the children of the poor. Thus the rapid process of liberalization and globalization has seen the rise of political Islam in Indonesia with strong links to issues in the Arab word.

The Indonesian Government has a narrow path to tread in protecting Indonesia from terrorist activity and ensuring the country is not used by terrorist networks as a sanctuary, and preventing the spillover of radicalism from Islamist organizations to moderate Indonesian Muslims. The JI still has operational capability and the means and will to create mass casualty attacks. The challenges for the government still remain immense. The EU needs to be aware of these factors.

However, Indonesia remains a young democracy "in-the-making". In the past six years the process of democratic reform has been pursued on all sides, but many obstacles remain. Although Indonesia has developed from an authoritarian system to a democracy and gone from military to civilian rule, numerous challenges are yet to be overcome and the Indonesian democracy remains "unpredictable". Addressing the radical elements in the Pesantren as well as the foundation of JI is a necessity and supporting Indonesia to do this an EU policy goal.

The internal dimension: shaping doctrine for counter-radicalization

Although the background contributing factors for radicalization are diverse, the European Union, as a civic power, is well-equipped to deal with them and can pursue a multifaceted and multidimensional strategy calling upon the variety of means and instruments at the disposal of the EU and its member states. This is for instance exemplified by the vast trade links the EU and its member states have with the Middle East. At the same time, an advantage of the European Union is that experiences from various governments can be exchanged, compared and adopted. The European Union requires a wide-scope, multifaceted approach to the problem of radicalization and it is capable to do so. Collecting, combining, focusing and structuring European-wide research efforts in fields related to counter-radicalization is necessary. The security research component of the EU's 7th Framework Programme for Research and Development is suitable for this.

Hearts and minds in the internal realm

The British experience of applying constrained use of force and pursuing "hearts and minds" campaigns is applicable in internal policy as well as in foreign policy. Islamic terrorism has its source in other parts of the world. Religious and ideological contradictions make it practically impossible to reconcile with these terrorists. However, several catalysing factors can be taken into account. First of all, as mentioned above, it must be recognized that three factors lead to foreign policy becoming a source of radicalization for a part of the Muslim population in the European member states. Second, it must be recognized that internal policy can have a radicalizing effect as well. Concerning the latter, a strategy of moderation and dialogue with the moderate segment of the Muslim population is required. Foster a climate of moderation and dialogue with the moderate elements in Muslim communities. Prioritize "hearts and minds" policies, and avoid stigmatization. Respect the group identity and decrease the socio-economic lag. Politicians and public figures have a special responsibility in this. On the other hand, deal decisively with extremists in EU states through a policy of isolation and neutralization. Close radical web sites and "charities", arrest or expel persons conducive to radicalization, close breeding grounds for radicalization and disrupt processes of recruitment. Such attempts may require more covert and secretive actions than usual. They are, however, necessary in order to minimize the negative backlash in the media, which fuels radicalization. This leads to a tense relationship with the rule of law, and a balance between efficacy and legality must be struck. Intelligence services and policy have a special responsibility in this.

A programme for doctrine development

From the analysis above follows that one of the key aspects of an EU approach should focus on the identity formation of young Muslims. Nevertheless, there is a serious lack of expertise and competence in the field of policy-oriented approaches to radicalization and recruitment in the European Union. There are no centres of excellence nor is there accessible information which universities, research institutes, think-tanks or policymakers can use to deal with aspects of this topic. The development of a centre of excellence in the field of European radicalization is a necessity in order to provide conceptual knowledge to policymakers. In terms of topics, research across the EU is diffuse and should take place instead within the confines of a singular effort, an EU research programme on radicalization and recruitment. With sufficient EU funding, expertise in this area could be developed. Key to achieving this is bringing together policymakers, academics, experts and practitioners in order to create a research programme designed to support the EU and its member states in developing policy from a conceptual perspective regarding effective radicalization counter-strategies. Bringing the scattered efforts together of European universities, think-tanks and research institutes is essential. Existing research efforts often take place on the fringe of larger study programmes and do not form core research areas for these centres, but they are nonetheless very important to understanding radicalization and recruitment. Bringing them together under a single centre of excellence, or EU research programme, will greatly enhance the EU's capacity to shape an effective doctrine.

An EU White Book on radicalization and recruitment should be developed, focusing on doctrine; the threat, conceptual approach and the means to deal with it. Recruitment histories should be detailed (both in and outside the EU),[20] and the ideological/semantic foundation of terrorist groups understood. Cross-national doctrines regarding counter-radicalization strategies should be produced, taking the case of Singapore (as a small and effective country in the fight against radicalization) as a starting point. Analyses of "what went wrong" terrorist attacks should be developed, but more importantly should be complemented with "what went right" analyses concerning thwarted terrorist attacks. Over the past years numerous large-scale or NBC-related attacks have been foiled or prevented, the foiled attack on the Strasbourg Christmas market being a very relevant case both in its scope and organizational complexity and its pan-European effect. Understanding how these attacks were planned and how they were foiled can lead to effective European lessons learned. The EU should organize a series of meetings to obtain greater insight in, and compare practices in, all areas relevant and mentioned in this chapter, with the objective to formulate policy. Several more priority areas are identified below that suffer from lack of expertise and understanding and will contribute to shaping policy.

- Prison recruitment counter-strategies need to be analysed and developed.
- Greater understanding needs to be developed regarding how to create, mobilize and aid Muslim civil society for EU policies. A strong and capable Muslim civil society is key to limiting recruitment among Muslim youth within the EU, but also for fostering stability in the Middle East.
- The Western world has encountered instances of radicalization and recruit-

ment before. During the 1950s and 1960s black Americans were marginalized and politically disenfranchised, which led to several becoming radicalized, giving birth to the violent Black Panther movement. Following a few turbulent years, the peaceful Civil Rights Movement, led by Martin Luther King, prevailed. Understanding the dynamics of this timeframe and how these movements developed can be helpful in understanding current difficulties in European states.

- Assess to what extent positive discrimination or affirmative action programmes can be effective in diminishing the socio-economic lag of the Muslim minority.
- Cross-national comparisons and *lessons learned* of legislation practices regarding the fight against terrorism, notably emergency legislation. The absence of well prepared emergency legislation in the face of anti-systemic terrorism leads to improvised and dangerous measures of the sort witnessed after 9/11, such as the legal controversy over Guantanamo Bay or the rendition of suspects to countries practising torture.
- Compare the various types of legislation in terms of their compatibility with human rights (such as the freedom of speech) through an open comparative discussion among EU states.
- Comparing European and international anti-terrorism action plans and drawing conclusions for "best practices".
- The Internet dimension of radicalization and recruitment needs to be examined. EU member states need to make sure that various forms of media, including the Internet, are not used to spread hatred. Existing legislation needs to be assessed for its appropriateness in dealing with radicalization. This concerns, for instance, the EU's directive "Television without Borders" (97/36/EC) or the Council of Europe's initiatives in relation to the media.
- Comparisons of educational reform to limit radicalization. The Jordanian example can be instructive.
- Establish best practices for the integration of population of non-European stock, notably from the Muslim states world. A follow-up to the *Ministerial Conference on Integration* held in Groningen (November 2004) is required. The conference identified four success factors for minimizing radicalization among minority youth. These were the development of a mentorship network, anti-racist and community dialogue efforts, developing a non-violent counterculture and engaging youth with radicalization alternatives. Follow-up conferences should focus on the implementation and assessment of the success factors.
- Recognize that the stigmatization of social groups in the public arena is a strong factor contributing to radicalization and develop effective awareness of this among policymakers and public figures.
- Develop a public–private security initiative. Private companies and entities are well endowed to aid removing the background contributing factors for radicalization. Companies operating in Morocco, for instance, have much to gain with stability in that country. Public–private partnerships in

microeconomic projects with relevance to reversing radicalization in deprived areas are similarly effective.
- Step up efforts to monitor records on Internet and mobile phones.

The doctrine required for European member states is determined by three key elements. First of all, although it is imperative that European states defend their interests and enhance security, the pursuance of (military) interventions in the Muslim world without effective "hearts and minds" campaigns reinforces the paradigm of extremists that Western states are waging a crusade against Islam. Because Western foreign policy is at the core of the extremist's paradigm, it leads to the observation that the roots of terrorism cannot be resolved. Rather the factors leading to radicalization and recruitment need to and can be influenced. Second, this yields significant consequences for internal and external policies. Effective "hearts and minds" campaigns in both policy realms are necessary in order to separate the moderates from the radicals, and third, once this has occurred, policy efforts must be focused on isolating and neutralizing the radical elements. Establishing a coherent programme which is supported by the EU and focuses research on the various elements mentioned above is essential for developing an effective doctrine. For only through the development of a well-balanced doctrine, composed of elements of "soft" and "hard" approaches, and combining internal as well as external policies, will European states be able to manage the threat posed by anti-systemic terrorism.

Notes

1 This was a report originally prepared by the *High-Level Working Group on Terrorism in Europe* advising Dr Gijs de Vries, EU Counterterrorism coordinator.
2 A.P. Schmidt and A.I. Jongman, *Political Terrorism* (SWIDOC, Amsterdam and Transaction Books, 1988), p. 5.
3 Council Framework Decision on Combating Terrorism, 13 June 2002, (2002/475/JHA).
4 The 9/11 attacks were not unique in their operational components, but rather based upon two preceding (attempted) attacks. In 1970 the PFLP (Popular Front for the Liberation of Palestine) performed a multiple hijacking of airplanes and in 1994 members of the GIA (Armed Islamic Group) turned a commercial airplane into a missile by attempting to fly it into the Eiffel Tower. The combination of these two elements, however, was unique.
5 This term was used by A. Carter, J. Deutch and P. Zelikow, "Catastrophic terrorism", *Foreign Affairs*, November–December 1998, pp. 80–94.
6 S. Shay, "Cultural Terrorism and the Clash of Civilizations", ICT Papers on Terrorism (The International Policy Institute for Counter-Terrorism, The Interdisciplinary Center, Herzliya, Israel, 2002), pp. 69–96.
7 For example: *Daily Telegraph*, C. Wilstead, Letters to the Editor, 14 September 2001. In this letter a teacher tells the story of pro-bin Laden expressions being voiced in a British classroom by 15-year-olds following the 9/11 attacks and stresses that these children do not consider themselves to be part of Western society.
8 For example: T. Ali, *The Clash of Fundamentalisms: Crusades, Jihads and Modernity*, Verso, (London, 2002); B.R. Barber, *Jihad vs. McWorld: Terrorism's Challenge to Democracy*, Ballatine Books (New York, 1995 and 2001); B. Lewis, *What Went*

Wrong? The Clash Between Islam and Modernity in the Middle East, Perennial, (New York, 2002); B. Lewis, *The Crisis of Islam: Holy War and Unholy Terror*, Weidenfeld and Nicholson (London, 2003); A. Rashid, *Jihad: The Rise of Militant Islam in Central Asia*, Yale University Press, (New Haven, 2002).
9 Barber, *Jihad vs McWorld*, p. xvi.
10 D.J. Gillet, "US Strike Against Terrorist Forces", *American Forces Press Service*, 20 August 1998.
11 National Commission on Terrorist Attacks, *The Military*, Staff Statement no. 6 (2004).
12 AIVD, *Van Dawa tot Jihad*, p. 15, www.nctb.nl/.../Van%20Dawa%20tot%20Jihad_tcm91-130733.pdf.
13 "Al Qaeda's next target?", *International Herald Tribune*, 4–5 December 2004.
14 This segment draws heavily from a report drafted by Taarnby, M., *Recruitment of Islamist Terrorists in Europe: Trends and Perspectives*, Research Report funded by the Danish Ministry of Justice, 14 January 2005.
15 AIVD, *Nota Rekrutering voor de Jihad*, 2002, p. 19.
16 Leeuwen, van M., "Ronselen in Europa voor de Heilige Oorlog", *Justitiële Verkenningen*, Ministerie van Justitie, no. 2, 2005, pp. 84–95.
17 Smith, C.S., "Islam in Jail: Europe's Neglect Breeds Angry Radicals", in *New York Times*, 8 December 2004. See for more information on prison recruitment also Razavi, E., *Freres Musulmans* (Godefroy, Paris, 2005) and Khosrokhavar, F., *L'Islam dans les Prisons* (Balland, Paris, March 2004).
18 For more information see Napoleoni., L., *Terror Inc: Tracing the Dollars Behind the Terror Networks*, (Seven Stories Press, New York, 2005).
19 United Nations Development Progamme, *Arab Human Development Report: Building a Knowledge Society*, United Nations, New York, 2003.
20 For instance, an excellent study regarding the attack on Theo van Gogh was performed by Petter Nessen, *The Slaying of the Dutch Filmmaker: Religiously Motivated Violence or Islamist Terrorism in the Name of Global Jihad?*, FFI Rapport, available at http://rapporter.ffi.no/rapporter/2005/00376.pdf.

2 Where does the radicalisation process lead?

Radical community, radical networks and radical subcultures

Peter Waldmann, Matenia Sirseloudi and Stefan Malthaner

Introduction

In current research on Islamism the question of individual radicalisation processes is playing a major role. Which Muslims prove to be susceptible for radical messages, how does their swing towards a militant attitude manifest itself? Who exerts an influence on them, and participates in the process of conversion introducing them into the extremist milieu? How is the individual development process towards religious extremism to be described? At what point are crucial decisions made and where can they be interrupted?

Many studies on this subject assume that (of course with certain aberrations) there is an ideal type of radicalisation process: beginning with certain types of personality, which are more responsive to an offensive interpretation of Islamic doctrine than others; specific experiences and stages in their career; their arriving (within the group) within the radical milieu before arriving at a provisional end from which they will be recruited into an Islamic terrorist group as new blood.

In a recently published study, John Horgan pointed out how careful one should be to draw conclusions about specific individual dispositions for terrorist activities. Furthermore, he has shown how diverse and multifaceted the circumstances can be and how winding the ways along which the indivual is inducted into the terrorist group or its preliminary stage of radical milieu.[1] In this contribution we want to elaborate on this point of view through a more precise analysis of what is meant by radical milieu: the aim and final purpose of the individual radicalisation process. We assume that depending on the milieu, the candidate of the possible attack is not only differently inducted, socialised and "orientated", but also different radical milieus because of their unique profiles attract different indivuals.

In the title we expound three different substrata of the radicalisation process or, to be precise, radical mileus.[2] Radical communities emerge primarily on a subnational level (e.g. the Shiites around Hizbollah in the Lebanon or the Chechnian milieu of resistance in Russia). One particular characteristic is the close connection to a certain region and territory over which the fight for liberation and ownership takes place. Radical communities are mainly militant exponents of an ethnic or religious minority who live in the region and insist upon their autonomy.[3]

The opposite to radical communities are transnational radical networks. With them the connection to particular population groups or geographical entities is only vaguely recognisable. Transnational networks establish themselves in a special sphere disconnected from common concepts of space and time, whose parameters are crucially dependent upon the ideology they are sworn to. From this ideology they deduce aims, enemy concepts, convictions and behavioural ideals.[4]

Somewhere between these points of extreme, subnational radical communities on the one hand and transnational radical networks on the other, are the "radical subcultures". Radical subcultures are principally found at a national level and emerge as a side effect of a national protest movement.[5] As a mix between the two ideal types they exhibit a specific instability and fragility. Depending upon the situation and their orientation, they tend towards either one or other of the two poles.

The description begins with an explanation of the radical community and transnational radical networks which will then be contrasted in a kind of provisional appraisal. That will be followed by a section on protest movements and radical subcultures. In the last section we will have to ask where within this the migrant colony radical groups can be found, whether they constitute a particular type or need to be related to one of the types we have already defined.[6]

The radical community

In a recently published paper the conditions of emergence and structural characteristics of that subtype of radical social substratum – the radical community – were thoroughly explained. Here it should suffice to trace some of its characteristics; selecting contrasting character traits to transnational radical networks has been given priority and was uppermost in our mind when selecting them. Successively we will deal with the recruitment base of radical communities, the backgrounds and the attendant circumstances of the radicalisation process. Finally we will talk about the relation of the radical community towards the terrorist groups and their immediate and broader social surrounding.[7]

Radical communities emerge within ethnic and/or religious minorities, sharing features like language, origin and history, religious belonging and as a rule they more or less claim a particular region or bigger territory within a nation state as their region of settlement. This means that their recruitment base is restricted from the beginning. Admittedly one cannot rule out the possibility that third persons may join them (we might think of the Muslims who voluntarily go to Chechnia, to participate in the fight against Russia). But the nucleii of these communities are those who belong to the autochthonous concerned minority as their birthright.

A central characteristic of the ethnic or religious minority is the ascribed belonging of the individual by origin. Structurally viewed we are dealing with a hybrid form: on the one hand, minorities who have held their ground in a confrontation with a particular majority, often exhibit definite modern characteristics, for example they give rise to internationally operating companies or strong infrastructures. We find an ambitious motivation, a willingness to be mobile and not infrequently a cosmopolitan orientation. But on the other hand they often keep the traits of traditional communities where personal, especially face to face, contacts are more important than formal relations. The social ranking of the individual is based less upon individual achievements and qualities than upon its position within a social and familial network, with the collective as a whole exercising considerable control over the members.[8] Even if members of this community have spent several years abroad, for example because of their studies or a professional career, once they have returned home they are considered and see themselves as part of the old relational network and its roll call of duties.

Whether consciously or unconsciously, the autonomic ambitions of ethnic or religious minorities are closely related to the control they exert over a particular region as a precondition to collectively survive and further evolve. If we follow history over a long time, we can see that the ideological vindication for resistance against and delineation from the central state and the majority may change: from a socialistic to a nationalistic and eventually to a religious justification.[9] What remains as their main motivation is to retain autonomy as a religious cultural group, and a type of sovereignty over a certain territory. Minorities react more energetically if their territorial base is threatened for whatever circumstances precisely because they have to make the best of their limited area of influence in which to assert themselves.[10]

Such a threat is normally the main reason for radical tendencies within a minority and the emergence of a radical community. The reasons and motives of such collective mobilising episodes can be diverse, for example an external invasion, civil war or increasing political control resulting in the violent repression of the minority through the central state. In singular cases it is possible that the imminent threat is preceded by a protest movement from the members of the minority revolting against discrimination. It is not the movement itself but the reaction of the majority or the central state in the form of repressive attacks that leads to the syndrome of distress facilitating the appearance of radical communities.[11]

They exhibit certain characteristics. First of all they are based on a defensive impulse. Once started they can develop their own dynamic which perpetuates itself after the emergency situation caused by external attack. But the cohesive forces clearly weaken as soon as the situation begins to ease off and the voices urging to return to a normal open society increase.

With that we have indirectly addressed the second trait of radical communities. The term "community" is chosen with caution: the theory states that under repressive pressure parts of the minority undergo a regressive step in which they leave their modern characteristics behind and transform into a traditional community along the lines of the classic structural analysis of F. Tönnies. This partial mutation can be explained by the new situation with which the minorities are confronted. The quasi-siege, which they have been forced into, leads to institutions closely bound to the central state falling apart and being of no more use for members of the minority as they are controlled by the enemy, for example the security services, especially police, education and training institutions, state-controlled mass media, possibly hospitals and welfare centres.[12]

In other words the minority is forced to mobilise self-helping forces and resources of solidarity to cope with the difficult situation. It moves – metaphorically speaking – closer together, traditional forms of association and channels of communication are revived, as it prepares for resistance. Admittedly this is only one of various forms of reaction, additionally we find opportunism, conformity to the new situation, apathy and indifference. Where a certain willingness not to accept one's fate without resistance and to take up the fight with the new threat exists, radical communities emerge. To a large extent they seal themselves off from the rest of society and subjugate their members to an ever greater social control, which is perfectly normal in traditional communities, but atypical for modern societies.[13] At the same time they create a fertile environment, from which terrorist organisations draw their new recruits.

It should be made clear that the described radicalisation is a matter of collective fate, where the options for individual behaviour only play a subordinate role. Herein we find the third characteristic of radical communities. For the individual young man or woman there is no obligation to get involved or even join a terrorist group, but by doing so, they meet the expectations of their immediate social environment, insofar as their behaviour is considered "normal" and invites respect, if not admiration (the latter if they decide to participate in armed fighting). By no means can we talk about an increasing dissociation of the individual from its family or the community altogether along the course of the radicalisation process. On the contrary they remain embedded within their primordial social relational network which supports them with the necessary moral and material help.

The internal relationship of the terrorist association with the radical community, and its relation to the wider minority-community, describes consecutive phases of representation and delegation and more precisely control.[14] If the radical community represents a large part of the not-immediately integrated broader minority population, then armed units represent the military avant-garde of the radical community.[15] Both, the radical community and its terrorist avant-garde show, in different ways, the striving for autonomy and the will to resist for the minority as a whole. However, representation is not synonymous with congruence; each level of consecutive phases has its boundaries and maintains a certain independence.

The radical community (and this applies even more so to the broader minority population) is by no means willing to condone all the violent actions perpetrated by the armed group and may be unwilling to cover these actions up. In particular cases it may also veto or even threaten to renounce its allegiance to this group.

Likewise, the terrorist units do not accept every candidate from the radical community to be admitted as a member, applying a strict selection criteria. Finally, each "level" reserves certain rights for objection resulting in a subtle balance of mutual support and control between each group. The barriers are repealed when this balance is disturbed by a spectacularly unjust measure or manifest threat from the majority or the central state. In this scenario, a deeply rooted defence syndrome is awakened and solidarity throughout the whole community guarantees a unified resistance against the common enemy.

Transnational radical networks

The internationalisation of terrorism is not a new phenomenon. During the nineteenth century, anarchists had already travelled around Europe, meeting each other in different places scattered throughout the continent. Various social revolutionary terrorist groups during the 1970s and early 1980s in Germany, Italy and other Western countries also aspired towards a globalisation of their armed struggle against capitalism and imperialism, but they were not particularly successful in realising their far-reaching plans.[16]

The first group that suceeded in mobilising broader international public interest in its activities were Arafat's Palestinians. The attack and subsequent hostage-taking of Israeli sportsman during the 1972 Olympic Games in Munich managed to turn the attention of around 800 million people towards the Palestinian problem. Only since the funding of Al-Qaeda by bin Laden and his companions in the early 1990s can we really talk about fully developed and functioning transnational terrorism. From the outset, Al-Qaeda was designed transnationally and pursued a transnational strategy and recruitment policy. Even though the Al-Qaeda organisation only exists now in fragments or as a kind of "state of mind" on the international stage, the various terror groups and groupings which have developed on the margins of and with reference to this first Islamistic Internationale have formed the interconnected transnational radical network in the sense that we now understand it.[17]

As much as the field of recruitment for subnational radical communities is restricted, that for transnational Islamist networks is virtually unlimited – people from every social strata, state, culture and yes, even religion can join. As Olivier Roy has stressed, the number of converts to switch from Christianity to Islam and immediately follow a radical movement has greatly increased.[18]

At best, gender and age impose limits on membership – in transnationally operating cells, women are as rarely found as elderly men. Beside that, the less tied to a locality and unsettled the individual, the less anchored they will be in a social, national or religious community; the more frequently the individual comes into contact with different cultures and societies, the more likely they will be to show a disposition to join a radical transnational Islamist network (ceteris paribus condition taken as read). This connection usually reinforces a dissociation from the social milieu of origin; if the first generation of fighters around bin Laden in Afghanistan overwhelmingly returned to their native countries after the expulsion of the Soviet Union, then the second and third generation of Al-Qaeda members and followers have, on the whole, cut the connections with their families and place of origin.[19]

If radicalisation occurs within ethnic or religious minorities as a response to an encroaching challenge affecting an entire section of the population, the approach and integration into a transnational radical network appears as an individual developmental process carried out over several stages. Its starting points are often feelings of personal dissatisfaction and insecurity, possibly triggered by different experiences and conditions and failure to earn social acknowledgement and integration.

The person concerned is gripped by a deep unease regarding their previous way of life, which leads to an identity crisis, attended by a withdrawal from social interaction and the termination of prior relationships. This crisis is often overcome through the exertion of influence by a close friend or relative who offers themselves as a spiritual leader. The experience of conversion (or a revival of faith) replaces the doubt with a new self-confidence instilling the individual, at the same time, with religious zeal and turning him into a religious fanatic. From this point on, his brothers in the radical faith are his family and everything before this conversion now seems irrelevant.[20]

This may be a simplistic description of an individual's path to integration into a cell of transnational terrorism, but it is sufficient to point out the important differences to the radicalisation of subnational ethnic or religious communities previously described. Here – a personal decision to join a religious brotherhood often taken after a long period of searching; there – a collective fate which offers the individual only limited opportunites to free himself from the pressure of mobilisation. Here – a decision taken in an hour of inner need for which, seen from an external point of view, there is no compelling reason (Muslims joining transnational Islamist networks come from relatively prosperous families and live themselves in a comfortable situation); there – an external crisis with a far-reaching effect on everyday life. Here – the breaking off of social contact based on family belonging and origin after entering the community of fate; there – the holding onto tradition and milieu of origin which support the process of radicalisation.

We have already emphasised that one of the main reasons for the emergence of a radical community is the attachment to a piece of land encompassing place of settlement, basis of livelihood, guarantee of identity and promise of future all in one. It is the defence of this territory against foreign domination with whatever inadequate means available that gives the terrorism of minorities its specific nature and determines its strategy and tactics. A comparable basis for terrorism is lacking in the war waged by transnational terrorist networks against the West and especially the United States. In its place we find a religious or pseudo-religious conviction or ideology providing only very vague objectives and directives. The concept of an enemy who is to be defeated is as woolly as the strategic and tactical means with which the aspired-to end state shall finally be achieved and for which positive reference group of oppressed and deprived people the fight of liberation is being fought for.[21] The clear contrast to the type of defensive war waged by ethnic or religious minorities is that this is an offensive war in which different enemy and religious groups are also included making this a kind of world revolution.

The difference between the two forms of radicalisation and their substrate, the radical milieu, also apply to the relationship between terrorist groups in the stricter sense and their immediate and broader social environment. As we have already stated in the case of the radical community, different levels and groups can be clearly distinguished. As all members of the concerned minority do not automatically belong to the radical community, a clear boundary exists between the radical community and the terrorist units. Both stand in a symbiotic and complementary relationship with one another, but partially diverge in their aims and interests. With radical networks these differentiations lapse. The cells of the network are armed avant-gardists and support group in one; fulfilling each role either successively or simultaneously based on the division of labour. A mother group which accompanies their actions affirmatively, sometimes also critically, does not exist.[22]

This lack of being "earthed", that is, being linked to a broader social group or stratum, has its consequences. What is most important here is that no more scruples exist to intensify the violent actions unlimitedly. Terrorists bonded to ethnic and religious minorities will show consideration for them, and cannot operate completely free. If the symbolic content of an attack, for example, is only low and causes little damage but is followed by a powerful repressive response from the state, under which the whole minority suffers, the terrorists will have to expect criticism from the ranks of their followers. The same is true when they commit an attack whose brutality is grotesquely out of proportion. In other words the mothergroup and the closer supporters assembled in the radical community exert a certain control over the terrorists and their actions.[23]

Such a minimum of control is unknown in transnational terrorist networks. As they do not depend on anybody, they do not have to account to anybody for their actions.[24] Their only principles guiding their actions are the maxims of their ideology and the consensus of their own cell, which constitutes family, homeland and often suicide squad in one. As all the cells are sworn to the same ideas of hate, the same Manichaeic view of the world; their mutual relation and coordination exercises no braking effect, only a further intensification of the destructive commitment of the members.

Looking more precisely at these cells, they are released of any inhibiting control in a double sense: on the one hand, they lack a connection to a territory and a social reference group to which they have to justify their actions; on the other hand, at an international level, the controlling authority comparable to that wielded by the state at a national level, which could effectively oppose their violent canpaigns, is missing. Up till now, the international community hasn't had the strike power and enforcement capibility in order to take on the job.

Provisional appraisal

We can summarise the points already discussed in Table 2.1. As we can see from the table (which is, of course, a simplification of the structures and processes in reality), the pushing and stimulating forces creating and maintaining a radical milieu are very different in the case of subnational minorities and those of transnational Islamist networks. Accordingly, we should take care not to make generalisations about one type of radicalisation process at an individual level as if there were only one, universally valid career path towards becoming a terrorist or towards joining the immediate social environment of terrorists.

Our observations are confirmed, if only by superficial empirical confirmation, when we compare Muslims primarily represented in Al-Qaeda's transnational network with those who fight primarily at a national or subnational level. It becomes clear that the two categories of militant Islamists barely overlap. Transnational terrorism tends to attract Egyptians, Kuwaitis, Yemenis, Saudis, Algerians and Moroccans, whereas Palestinians, Afghans, Shiites from Lebanon or Muslims from Chechnya are rarely represented. The latter groups, however, form the bulk of fighters committing themselves at the national and subnational level in the concerned regions (though these two levels are not always so nicely separated as we shall immediately see).[25]

Radical subcultures

Radical subcultures can neither be equated with transnational radical networks nor do we find them in radical minorities. They are rather related to the level of nation state and emerge as a byproduct or split off of national protest movements.

This simple characterisation needs clarification. It is particularly based on a certain conception of social movements. This term can be defined both narrowly or widely. If we understand it to mean all forms of socio-political mobilisation, through which social evils are denounced and existing power relations are challenged, then social movements are imaginable in every historical and spacial context. In this sense, the transnational Islamist networks we have already described could also be understood as part of a global movement against the hegemony of the capitalistic economic system and the leading world role of the United States.[26] We prefer to remain with the original concept of social movements, as elaborated by Charles Tilly. According to him, social movements are a phenomenon that developed in the nineteenth century in particular. The forms of collective political mobilisation understood by this term challenge national power holders and demand the removal of certain social evils by circumventing elections or regular political channels. The protest movement par excellence of the nineteenth century was the Labour Movement.[27]

The regarding of the state as the protest movement's implied target is important. It was, after all, the nineteenth-century European nation state that succeeded for the first time to impose the monopoly of power, having tried to do this for

Table 2.1 Provisional appraisal

	Radical community	Transnational radical networks
Recruitment base	Very limited; only members of the concerned ethnic or religious minority are considered.	Virtually unlimited; individuals from many different cultures, social strata, nations, even religions can join the radical network.
Conflict-constellation	The conflict is tangible and precisely defined. It is about defensive actions against dangers to a social collectivity, to which the individual is related in various ways. Ultimately the power of disposal over a certain territory disputed by the majority is at stake. The threat comes from the central state, the majority or an external power.	The conflict is extremely abstract and vague. This is as true for the invoked danger as it is for the objects of the network, the strategic guidelines of the fight and the section of population (reference group) who allegedly needs liberating. In place of territorial defence as a uniting bond is a common belief in salvation or an ideology. Not resistance and defence, but an offensive reshaping of existing power structures is the aim.
Relation of individual and collective	Strong connection between the fate of the individual and the fate of the collective. Members of the minority, especially ones who live in the territory, are held responsible for the collectivity by its enemies and at the same time monopolised by the collective when an attack or an occupation occurs. Parts of the minority transform into the radical community which increases the power of disposal and control over the individual. The radicalisation process is linear and continous. They do not isolate themselves from the community but are regarded as its most noble representatives and enjoy great respect.	The radicalisation process is based on highly individual developments and decision-making processes, during crucial phases close friends or relatives play a key function. It seems to be a complicated career in stages, in the course of which the persons concerned free themselves from conventional relationships (family, milieu of origin, nation) and find their way into the religious network. Accordingly, we cannot speak about representation of or admiration by the milieu of origin. In its place we find a close relationship to cells within the network (revolutionary intimacy).[1]
Internal structure and external demarcation of radical milieu	The radical community separates itself from the social environment through mistrust and communication barriers. Internally, we find a division of labour between the community as "mothergroup" and its armed avant-garde – the terrorists. It is a mix of symbiosis and mutual control. The transition from community to terrorist unit takes place through self-selection and selection by the unit.	There is no clearcut outward boundary to the network. The individual gains access relatively easily through friend, friends of friends and the Internet. The project group and support group merge into one single social substrate internally. Apart from recruitment by a friend, self-recruitment is the main criterion for the connection to the network.

Note
1 V. Nahirny, "Some Observations on Ideological Groups", p. 399.

centuries. As a result of this, the repertoire of methods and means of protest movements to draw attention to their causes was significantly reduced. They could demonstrate, organise parades and call strikes but a broader incitement to violence would put them in the wrong and would have provoked a massive repressive response of state power.

It seems necessary to emphasise this restriction within protest movements present from the very beginning because it explains the motivation and mood of the majority of people within them; and keeping this in mind the position of radical splinter groups can also be more easily understood. Usually these splinter groups have further-reaching and possibly extreme goals in view and would not shrink from using tougher means, including violence, in order to achieve them. They can be concentrated within the high command of a movement or established on its margins, but normally they do not represent intentions and involvement of the majority of the movement's members.

Most of those who join a movement do not want to run the risk of a serious confrontation with the state's security forces. Dissatisfied about a certain social evil or generally unhappy with the social or political situation, they are ready to give vent publicly to their grievances. They possibly even would not shrink from non-conventional methods to make their cause heard to the political decision makers. However, the average demonstrator has not only something to win, but also something to lose. If the "price to pay" for challenging the state's power turns out to be too high, they will, at some point, step back from further escalation and would prefer a pragmatic policy of concessions. It is exactly at this point where a small group of persistent, risk-taking individuals detach themselves from the mass movement and those recoiling from final consequences, and a radical subculture, ready to use violence, emerges.[28]

The term "subculture" is chosen because it clearly differs from the forms of radical milieu already described. Subcultures assume the existence of a prevailing norm culture. In this case we mean that wherever the state has established a monopoly of power, the perpetration of violence by private actors is no longer permitted – it is regarded by society as taboo and therefore outlawed. The violent counter-cultures that develop under these circumstances can only exist in illegal niches underground.

Conversely, in societies disintegrating into different ethnic or religious fragments, the state usually does not have a definite monopoly of power. There is a deep, historically justified knowledge within the minorities about only partly being able to rely on the central state in emergency situations when they are thrown back to armed self-help.[29] Radical communities are the militant expression of this consciousness. Its members do not conceal their aggressiveness when distressed even if they do not openly resist the occupiers (they delegate violent resistance to the terrorists). Transnational networks, on the other hand, exist in a legal grey area outside the single nation state's jurisdiction in which their members evade effective control through mobility.

Structurally radical subcultures are a hybrid phenomenon between the extreme poles of the radical community and the radical networks. Depending on the circumstances they may tend towards one or the other pole. For example, one has to expect that in the case of external occupation or an invasion of the nation state, a radical subculture that possibly already exists is expanded and takes on the traits of a generalised milieu of resistance, i.e. a radical community. An example of tendency in the other direction is illustrated by the social-revolutionary terrorist organisations during the 1970s which spread throughout the West. Although they overwhelmingly operated in the national sphere, they showed some clear affinities to current networks of global jihad fighters, as much for their utopian secularised visions of salvation as for their blurred strategic ideas.[30]

If we apply the criteria found in Table 2.1 on radical subcultures, the following picture emerges: concerning the recruitment base, it is broader than that of radical communities, but smaller than the almost unlimited catchment area of transnational networks. The nation state and its population remain the defining sphere of reference. Whoever joins the protest movement, one cannot rule out the possibility that at some point disappointment about unsatisfying development or sheer failure forces them underground.

The conflict constellation is primarily determined by the clash between the movement and the dominant state power. Here we have to consider that protest movements do not emerge in order to defend the existing standards of living, but rather aim to change the distributive status quo of rights and property. Depending on how flexible the state is (particularly its security forces) and how it copes with this challenge, the conflict can either escalate towards violence or be settled peacefully.[31] The involvement of the individual is an accurate reflection of this general dynamic. There is certainly an "objective" cause for joining the movement, for example a general social evil, an overdue political reform which has been repeatedly delayed, but to what extent the single participant in a movement makes the general cause a matter of personal interest, identifies with collective protest action or distances himself from it, strongly depends on the whole course of the movement, especially when brought into conflict with the state's security apparatus.[32]

Roughly speaking, we define two stages through which the indivual goes in their radicalisation process. The first is the individual's decision not to accept a certain social evil or a development viewed as threatening without opposing it and doing something about it. In countries in which political opposition is suppressed and the right to demonstrate is not guaranteed, taking this step can be a risk. In any case, it means the person concerned stands out from the majority of those who are also dissatisfied, but at the same time too lethargic or scared to translate this into practical behaviour.

The participation in the protest movement may also include a readiness to gain attention for the seriousness of the cause through unconventional methods on the margins of legality, for example sit-down strikes or road blockades. As a rule, this does not (or at least not yet) include the intention of getting involved in an open confrontation with the state. This intention manifests itself in the second stage when the conflict escalates or a failure of the movement looms, so that the activists are forced to think about giving up the protest or continuing it underground. Herein lies the crucial threshold over which the transition into a radical milieu takes place. Those who cross this threshold have either already partially acquired a taste for hard fighting in prior clashes and tend to enjoy "all or nothing" decisions or have become devoted to the fight for ideological reasons. It is also possible that somebody is drawn into the underground current by chance, for example, because they have a friend who is already part of the radical milieu.[33]

It is certainly the case that with the partial sudden change of a protest movement into a radical subculture the scope for freedom and options for individual behaviour are drastically diminished. As much as movements are open in principle, radical subcultures present themselves as closed. The terrorist organisations at their centres are, to quote D. della Porta, "greedy institutions". On the one hand, they make sure that for security interests the radical suculture consistently seals itself off from the outside and cuts all contacts with non-members; on the other hand, they subjugate their members to a rigorous control of behaviour and belief and do not tolerate any deviant opinion. They conspicuously resemble transnational radical networks in all these traits including the absence of a mothergroup, external to the radical subculture, which could exert an influence over them. In any case, networks exhibit a unity and ideological conformity that seems to be of a more voluntary and less compulsive nature, whereas at the national level, presumably due to state pressure, internal discipline and strict control of behaviour can become a real obsession for these groups.[34]

Terrorist groups operating at the national level and supported by radical subcultures were, until recently, the most common form of terrorism. Though, that does not mean that they were necessarily the most successful. For a reasonably effective nation state, terrorist groups questioning its sovereignty would not pose any serious threat. It has numerous advantages over these groups, for example a lead in legitimacy and weightier resources at its disposal, especially concerning the potential for sanctions. Needless to say, the state has no intention of letting such groups become real rivals. It is only when the state's basis for legitimacy is strongly weakened, for example, appearing as the henchman or lacky of a foreign state, not being able to defend itself against a foreign invasion or by transforming itself into a crude apparatus for repression, that the radical groups have a chance to win a broader following. Additionally, these groups have the opportunity to withdraw their radical demands and to arrange terms with the state power or move onto the international level, where they can evade the constraints of state control.[35]

Tentative observations on radicalisation in colonies of migrants

About 13.5 million Muslims live in Europe who partially internally reject the Western lifestyle. Minority groups within these colonies of migrants work themselves up into radical hostility against the Western value and economic systems.

The question is how to categorise these emerging radical milieus. On a purely theoretical level three possible alternatives may be considered:

- they can be related to one of the three types already described;
- they represent a radical milieu of their own; or
- they have no independent meaning but function merely as a "reservoir" and recruitment base for the three previously described radical substrata.

With respect to the first alternative – that radical attitudes in migrant colonies correspond to one of the three discussed types of radicalisation – we can surmise that they might share one or other of those characteristics, but we cannot assume a real congruence. Migrant colonies, for example, because of their particular ethnic and religious standing, exhibit certain common features with autochthonous minorities, suggesting we can deal with radicalisation tendencies given birth to within migrant colonies in the same way as we do with "radical communities".

But parallelity does not take us far because migrant colonies are lacking the comparable attachment to a piece of land and its history which classic minorities have. Furthermore the causes for their possible militancy lie in the refusal to recognise them as full citizens and to integrate them into the host society, as opposed to a situation of acute threat. Similar doubts are to be raised against the second classification of radical groups in migrant colonies as subcultures. The question we are immediately confronted with is, to which national context do these subcultures refer to?

Taking Turkey as reference point at the national level, it seems unfitting to talk about a subculture when a group operates far away from this state in Germany or the Netherlands. A reference to the Western host country might be more appropriate, but we have to take into consideration that the real point of reference for the migrants is often their home rather than their guest country. We also encounter difficulties in categorising the radical milieu of migrant colonies as part of transnational radical networks. The networks are intended as supra- rather than subnational, but the individual radically minded Muslim is not able to make this transitional jump. Still, both migrant milieus might form an excellent field of recruitment for transnational radicalisation and terrorism.

Could radicalisation tendencies in migrant milieus be labelled as a separate type of radicalisation? Doubtless first- and also second-generation migrants are in a very special situation. The multiple challenges and frustrations they are confronted with mean that reactions of dissatisfaction, anger and protest are not unexpected. Yet we must consider that migration is primarily an individual initiative, possibly also a family undertaking, therefore it is not a collective fate and a collective reaction is not to be taken as a matter of course. Even if such collective actions take place, for example the emergence of a Europe-wide movement demanding more consideration and explicit recognition of Islam in a European context, the goal would nevertheless be about more integration, more respect for the immigrants and their cultural and religious heritage, rather than the dismantling of European rule of law and a transformation into an Islamic kind of state.

For Muslims, whose parents and grandparents have taken the responsibility for the strains of emigration and temporary or enduring social uprootedness in order to participate in Western prosperity, it would make no sense to launch a frontal attack against state and societal constructions producing this prosperity. Even radical splinter groups, which possibly emerge at the margins of such an extensive protest movement, could hardly free themselves from this logic. For the same reason, so-called parallel societies of which there is currently much discussion are possibly alarming in some respects, although it is unlikely that they will become the nucleus of an independent terrorism from the migrants' milieu.[36]

Still remaining is the third and most plausible alternative from our point of view, describing the radical potential doubtlessly contained in migrant colonies as a type of reservoir and supply base for the three previously mentioned main forms of radical milieu.

It is well known that the ethnic and religious immigrant enclaves in the West maintain tight relations with the minorities from which they possibly derive, supporting them if they get into great difficulties. In general this takes place through financial contributions, but one cannot rule out the possibility that occasionally some young man in the "diaspora" decides to "temporarily" return to his country of origin, in order to participate directly in the fight for liberation. Americans of Northern Irish origin fighting for the IRA in the 1970s, or Muslims setting off from Germany to Chechnya in order to join the resistance against Russian occupiers, are examples for such a voluntary involvement in a "radical community". For the host country left by the person concerned, their involvement does not present a direct danger. Nevertheless we have to consider that the immediate participation in an armed conflict regularly results in an intensification of radical tendencies if the person returns.

Less harmless is the second variant, in which groups try to influence and form policy in their home country from the host country as a type of outsourced radical subculture, as was for a long time the case with the now forbidden Kaplan sect, a Turkish association in Germany, or with the French offshoots of the Algerian GIA.[37]

On the one hand, such groups pursue status quo interests, that is, they are not willing to risk their existence, which is guaranteed by the liberal rule of law in the host country. On the other hand, it is not ruled out that the conflict with the political power holders of the country of origin also spills over to the host country and threatens its inner security. Often the political discourse of groups operating in exile is ambigious with a dishonest effect. They profit from the good conditions of the host country in order to bring forward the opposition in their home country, trying to reform the system without seriously planning to return there ever again.

The most explosive constellation from our point of view is the role radical milieus in migrant colonies can play as a supply base for radical transnational networks. Indeed, social and cultural uprootedness of migrants and their offspring, discrimination and social marginalisation, and identity and orientation problems typical for young Muslims in the West can make them vulnerable to fundamentalist religious messages. The more sensitive and unstable youth may be brought to the point of searching for acceptance in the community of faith of transnational networks.[38] From the perspective of the networks, the migrant colonies could fulfil a special role; they could not only serve as supporters and reserves, but also be protagonists in a global violent campaign. Due to the vagueness and abstractness of the redemption messages and specific strategy, and the missing bond to a concrete section of population, one cannot rule out the possibility that members of these cells could target even those Western countries in which they themselves grew up.

Notes

1 Horgan, John: *The Psychology of Terrorism*, (London: Routledge, 2005), chapter 3 and 4; see also Waldmann, Peter: *Terrorismus. Provokation der Macht*, 2nd edn, (Hamburg: Murmann, 2005), chap. 9.
2 The term "radical milieu" will be used in the following as a general term for the social substrate of the radicalisation process; specific terms shall draw the attention to the variability of partial radical milieus.
3 The reference to a piece of land for the characterisation of radical communities is not unproblematic. The author himself has emphasised that the fight for a piece of land is a characteristic of guerilla warfare, while terrorists primarily intend to impress people with the spectacular nature of their attacks – and not occupy land but their "psyche". The relationship between guerilla warfare and close attachment to land has a long tradition in military history; it has been especially emphasised by Carl Schmitt in his Partisans Theory. It was also C. Schmitt who predicted the end of the classic partisans, because under conditions of modern technical-industrial warfare, especially aerial warfare, partisans have no chance. It remains to be seen to what extent C. Schmitt is right in respect to the future of partisan and guerilla fighters. Even if partisans no longer continue to exist in their traditional form, there is no doubt that they have found a partial successor in the form of the terrorist bound to a certain territory and its population. See P. Waldmann, *Terrorismus: Provokation*, op. cit., p. 19; Schmitt, Carl: *Der Nomos der Erde*, 4th edn, (Berlin: Dunker & Humbolt, 1997); Schmitt, Carl: *Theorie des Partisanen*, (Berlin: Dunker & Humbolt, 1963); Llanque, Marcus: "Ein Träger des Politischen nach dem Ende der Staatlichkeit. Der Partisan in Carl Schmitts politischer Theorie", in: Herfried Münkler (ed.): *Der Partisan. Theorie, Strategie, Gestalt*, (Opladen: Westdeutscher Verlag, 1990), pp. 61–80. More general on territoriality, Münkler, Herfried: *Vom Krieg zum Terror. Das Ende des klassischen Krieges*, Zürich 2006 (Vontobel-Stiftung: Zürich), p. 56.
4 On the concept of ideological groups (developed along the lines of the Russian anarchists of the nineteenth century) see Nahirny, Vladimir: "Some Observations on Ideological Groups", in: *American Journal of Sociology* LXVII (1961/62), pp. 397–405. Generally on ideologisation and deterritorialisation of armed conflicts H. Münkler, *Vom Krieg zum Terror*, op. cit., p. 53ff.
5 Neidhardt, Friedhelm: "Über Zufall, Eigendynamik und Institutionalisierbarkeit absurder Prozesse", in: Ders.: *Gewalt und Terrorismus. Studien zur Soziologie militanter Konflikte*, (Berlin: Wissenschaftszentrum Berlin für Sozialforschung, 1988), p. 178; P. Waldmann: *Terrorismus. Provokation*, op. cit., p. 160ff.
6 In this chapter we intentionally do without the common differentiation between social-revolutionary, ethnic-nationalistic and religious terrorism. In other words we assume that the classification developed here enjoys a higher analytical relevance and

explanatory power than the usual distinction along the lines of the ideology represented by the radical groups.

7 See Waldmann, Peter: "The Radical Community. A Comparative Analysis of the Social Background of ETA, IRA, and Hezbollah", in: *Sociologus*, 55(2) (2005), pp. 239–257. As we mentioned at the beginning of this chapter, the concept of the radical community goes back to Frank Burton, a British anthropologist, who coined it at the end of the 1970s in an analysis of the Northern Irish IRA. See Burton, Frank: *The Politics of Legitimacy. Struggles in a Belfast Community*, (London: Routledge, 1978).

8 P. Waldmann, "The Radical Community", op. cit., p. 245ff.

9 The Palestinian fight for liberation against Israeli supremacy was fought for a long time under a secular socialistic banner. The rise of Hamas, and with that the swing towards a religious justification for the resistance, dates from the first intifada, i.e. 1988. See e.g. Reuter, Christoph: *Mein Leben ist eine Waffe*. Selbstmordattentäter, (München: C. Bertelsmann Verlag, 2002), p. 156f.

10 On the territorial factor see, besides literature cited in footnote 3, P. Waldmann: *Ethnischer Radikalismus. Ursachen und Folgen gewaltsamer Minderheitenkonflikte*, (Opladen: Westdeutscher Verlag, 1989), chap. 4 and Stein Rokkan and Derek W. Urwin: *Economy, Territory, Identity. Politics of West European Peripheries*, (London: Sage, 1983).

11 P. Waldmann, "The Radical Community", op. cit., p. 241ff.

12 Ibid., p. 244.

13 Ibid., p. 247.

14 Ibid., p. 250.

15 Generally on the problem of sympathisers and reference groups of terrorist organisations see Malthaner, Stefan: "Terroristische Bewegungen und ihre Bezugsgruppen: Anvisierte Sympathisanten und tatsächliche Unterstützer", in: P. Waldmann (ed.): *Determinanten des Terrorismus*, (Weilerswist: Velbrück Wissenschaft, 2004), pp. 85–138.

16 P. Waldmann, *Terrorismus: Provokation*, op. cit., p. 51ff.; Della Porta, Donatella: "Gewalt und die Neue Linke", in: W. Heitmeyer, J. Hagan (eds): *Internationales Handbuch der Gewaltforschung*, (Wiesbaden: Westdeutscher Verlag, 2002), pp. 479–500, 491.

17 On Al-Qaeda, Gunaratna, Rohan: *Inside Al Qaida. Global Network of Terror*, 2. Aufl., (London: Hurst, 2003); Sageman, Marc: *Understanding Terror Networks*, (Philadelphia: University of Pennsylvania Press, 2004); P. Waldmann, *Terrorismus. Provokation*, op. cit., Exkurs, p. 149f.

18 Roy, Olivier: *Globalised Islam. The Search for a New Ummah*, (London: Hurst, 2004), p. 47; see also M. Sageman, *Understanding*, op. cit., p. 77.

19 M. Sageman, *Understanding*, ibid., p. 74ff.

20 Puschnerat, Tania: "Zur Bedeutung ideologischer und sozialer Faktoren in islamischen Radikalisierungsprozessen. Eine Skizze", in: U. E. Kemmesies (ed.): *Terrorismus und Extremismus. Der Zukunft auf der Spur*, (München: Luchterhand-Verlag, 2006), pp. 217–235, 222. Puschnerat emphasises that the process of conversion can be recognised in their external behaviour, see also M. Sageman, *Understanding*, op. cit., p. 50, 91.

21 O. Roy, *Globalised Islam*, op. cit., p. 19, 46f., 55f. emphasises the deterritorialisation of global Islamism, for which the "ummah", i.e. the community of believers, becomes a more or less abstract entity, and he puts it in line with Third World movements. Generally on radical communities of discourse. Apter, David (ed.): *The Legitimation of Violence*, (New York University, 1997). On the rise of Islamic ideology and movement see Scheffler, Thomas: "Islamischer Fundamentalismus und Gewalt", in: Urike Kronfeld-Goharani (ed.): *Friedensbedrohung Terrorismus. Ursachen, Folgen und Gegenstrategien*, (Berlin: Lit-Verlag, 2005), pp. 88–111, 100f.

22 The characteristics of networks are particularly stressed by M. Sageman, *Understanding*, op. cit., p. 139ff., p. 147f. He also mentions the lack of social mothergroups for fighters of global jihad.
23 P. Waldmann, "The Radical Community", op. cit., p. 250.
24 Münkler speaks about the new indiscriminate terrorist attacks, which are accompanied with a more and more blurring contour and lacking of consideration of potential sympathisers and party members of terrorists. *Vom Krieg zum Terror*, op. cit., p. 83.
25 M. Sageman, *Understanding*, op cit., p. 70ff.
26 Ibid., p. 137.
27 Tilly, Charles: "Social Movements and National Politics", in: Charles Bright and Susan Hardin (eds): *Statemaking and Social Movements. Essays in History and Theory*, (Ann Arbor: University of Michigan Press, 1984), pp. 297–317, esp. 303ff.; Charles Tilly u.a.: *The Rebellious Century 1830–1930*, (Cambridge, MA: Harvard University Press, 1975). More general on the theory of social movements see Rucht, Dieter: "Gewalt und neue soziale Bewegungen", in: W. Heitmeyer, J. Hagan (eds): *Internationales Handbuch der Gewaltforschung*, (Wiesbaden: Westdeutscher Verlag, 2002), pp. 461–478.
28 On tensions between radical minority groups and the mainly peaceful majority in the protest movement see Donatella della Porta, "Gewalt und die neue Linke", op. cit., p. 492. On a more general classification of the relationship between conflict escalation and terrorist campaigns see Sirseloudi, Matenia: "How to Predict the Unpredictable: On the Early Detection of Terrorist Campaigns". *Defense and Security Analysis* Vol. 21, No. 4, 2005: p. 377f.
29 In Northern Ireland reservations against the British state regarding loyalty and a considerable distrust could be observed as well in the minority of Catholics as in the majority constituted by Protestants. P. Waldmann, *Ethnischer Radikalismus*, op. cit., p. 285ff.
30 This is one of the major theses of Olivier Roy, who sees a clear continuity between the Marxist movements of the 1970s and the current wave of protest of radicalised Muslims. O. Roy, *Globalised Islam*, op. cit., p. 46ff. On social-revolutionary groups see Waldmann, Peter: "Social-Revolutionary Terrorism in Latin America and Europe", in: Tore Bjørgo (ed.): *Root Causes of Terrorism*, (London: Routledge, 1995), pp. 154–163.
31 The behaviour of the security forces as a key factor for the development of protest has repeatedly been emphasised. See D. della Porta, "Gewalt und die neue Linke", p. 487 ff.; P. Waldmann, *Terrorismus: Provokation*, op. cit., p. 172ff.
32 Apart from that, individual characteristics play an important role, for example general preparedness for the use of violence, temperament and risk behaviour.
33 D. della Porta, "Gewalt und die neue Linke", op. cit., p. 492ff.; F. Neidhardt, "Über, op. cit., p. 182f.; P. Waldmann, *Terrorismus. Provokation*, op. cit., p. 174.
34 On the whole thematic complex see Della Porta, Donatella: *Social Movements and Violence. Participation in Underground Organizations*, (Greenwich/London: JAI Press, 1992), especially the contributions in the first volume edited by Martha Crenshaw.
35 From different researchers it has been pointed out that Islamist movements at the national level, confronted with the risk of failure, have found moderate ways and changed the course towards a more political pragmatic one. Vgl. O. Roy, *Globalised Islam*, op. cit., p. 74f.; T. Scheffler, "Islamischer Fundamentalismus", op. cit., p. 105, and the article of Isabelle Werenfels: "Zähmung der Islamistischen durch Einbindung ins politische Leben", in: *NZZ*, 21. März 2006, p. 5. On the migration of unsuccessful Islamists at the national level towards the transnational one see M. Sageman, *Understanding*, op. cit., p. 25 (example Egyptians).
36 See T. Puschnerat, "Zur Bedeutung ideologischer und sozialer Faktoren", op. cit., pp. 217, 228f.

37 On the Kaplan community see Schiffauer, Werner: *Die Gottesmänner. Türkische Islamistischen in Deutschland*, (Frankfurt am Main: Suhrkamp Verlag, 2000). On GIA see Brynjar Lia and Åshild Kjøk, "Islamist Insurgencies, Diasporic Support Networks, and their Host States: The Case of the Algerian GIA in Europe 1993–2000", *Kjeller FFI/Rapport*, 2001/0378, 2001, p. 9f.
38 For a similar argument see Marc Sageman and Olivier Roy. See M. Sageman, *Understanding*, op. cit., p. 93, 149; O. Roy, *Globalised Islam*, op. cit., pp. 2, 23, 30, 69.

3 The physiology of Al-Qaeda
From ideology to participation

Christina Hellmich

Introduction

Al-Qaeda, the first multinational terrorist group of the twenty-first century, embodies the new enigmatic face of terrorism. Few other issues – if any at all – have received more public attention, yet speculations about the strength and extent of Al-Qaeda, bewildering descriptions of a shadowy network, undercover terrorist cells, new arrests and imminent dangers create alarm but not much clarity. "Al-Qaeda not driven by ideology" is the conclusion reached by a Pentagon intelligence team,[1] while according to Stephen Schwartz, amongst others, "Osama bin Ladin and his followers belong to a puritanical variant of Islam known as Wahhabism".[2] Drawing extensively from the writings of Quintan Wiktorowicz, more recent discussions consider Al-Qaeda as a sub-group of the Salafi movement, characterized by "strict adherence to the model of Prophet Muhammad and rejection of a role for human reason and desire".[3] According to this logic, "Salafis are united in their religious belief. Islamic pluralism does not exist."[4]

Yet, the process of applying the doctrines of Islam to socio-political change, the very concept that defines the nature of Islamic fundamentalism, is essential to the logic of Al-Qaeda. Confusion of this kind is likely resulting from the fact that Islamic fundamentalists *see themselves* as the true believers – or Salafi – strictly following the divine guidance of the Prophet and retrieving its fundamental basics (*usul*). The simultaneous denial and demonstration of cognitive adaptation to reality is evident, for example, in Sayyid Qutb's well-known political interpretation of the Quran.[5] In reading his commentary, one is continually struck by the interplay between Qutb's own ideas and the Quranic text, showing that he did not find the truth in the script itself but rather in what he believed to be its meaning. The same process is evinced when bin Laden calls upon fellow Muslims to fight the enemies of Islam, the Zionist–Crusader invasion: he has transferred the words of the holy text into the current political situation and interpreted their meaning within this novel context. Although it is not the aim of this chapter to conceptualize the diversity of the Salafi movement, it suggests that it is not rewarding to throw out the concept of Islamic fragmentation with the Orientalist bathwater. The perception of Islamic unity is challenged by cultural diversity, a variety of strands of thought and multiple interpretations. In the words of James Piscatori, "ideas concerning issues from popular participation to social justice are far from stagnant, and Quranic meanings are nothing if not ambiguous".[6]

A more pertinent line of inquiry into the mechanisms underlying Al-Qaeda's politics of violence would be to focus specifically on questions about the organization's inner logic. What is the connection between religious and political parameters blurred by the rhetoric of bin Laden? Where does his logic spring from? How does it impact the rationales and self-perceptions of Al-Qaeda's followers and supporters? How does it motivate them to carry out terrible acts of violence and forsake the most basic of human instincts – survival? How can we explain the translation of Al-Qaeda's ideology into participation? The answers to these questions will shed a new light on the rationale of Al-Qaeda and its ability to influence a wider audience, which is critical in defining an effective counter-terrorism strategy.

Islamic fundamentalism and the inner logic of Al-Qaeda

An inquiry into the physiology of Al-Qaeda should begin with an analysis of the ideological connection between Islam and politics that defines the nature of religious fundamentalism. The term, which originally applied to an early twentieth-century American Protestant movement, has entered the vocabulary of the social sciences as a designation for conservative, revivalist religious orthodoxy. Yet, it is the more recent rise of fundamentalist movements, specifically in a range of Islamic countries, and the increased magnitude and frequency of terrorist attacks and suicide bombings carried out by Islamic fundamentalists, that has generated a wide-ranging response in both academic and policy circles.[7] The result of this increased attention is an enormous amount of literature that interchanges terms such as "Islam", "Islamic fundamentalism", "Islamism", and more recently "Islamic extremism" or "Islamic terrorism", while referring to the actual participants as "zealots", "Muslim fanatics" or "militants". On the surface, the decision to join an Islamic fundamentalist movement such as Al-Qaeda seems irrational – who would willingly sacrifice their own life?

In this chapter, the understanding of Islamic fundamentalism is based on a combination of two ways of looking at religion, namely as a source of meaning and as incorporated into reality.[8] The underlying hypothesis is that religion consists of socio-cultural symbols that convey a conception of reality and construe a plan for it. These symbols are related to reality, but not a reflection of it, as understood in the cultural anthropology of Clifford Geertz.[9] Important to note here is the distinction between "models of reality" and "models for reality". The former relate to the representation of objects. They are both concrete by displaying structural congruence with the depicted object, and abstract as they are views, religious dogmas or doctrines prescribed to effect conditions with which they are not congruent.[10] On the other hand, whether metaphysically or rationally, models for reality relate to human perceptions of how reality ought to be designed. As such, they are normative and consequently can only be penetrated interpretatively.[11]

In Islam, human conceptions of reality are not based on knowledge, but on the belief in the divine authority of Allah and the revelation of the Quran as the ultimate truth, immutable and universally valid for all people regardless of time and space.[12] Most discussions – and this holds for both Western, and to a significant extent Muslim scholarship – of Islam and politics assume that Islam makes no distinction between the religious and political realms.[13] This view of inseparability finds support in over forty references in the Quran, and the example of the Prophet, at once a spiritual leader and the head of a political community.[14] It further shows in the creation of the "Islamicate" as the creation of the Islamic *umma* and the caliphate, the political order of the Islamicate.[15] Yet, a careful reading of the historical record indicates that politics and religion became separable not long after the death of the Prophet and the establishment of dynastic rule.[16] Notably, this early historical background is strikingly different from the modern fundamentalist claim for an Islamic state and a corresponding *sharia* – (Islamic legal system) bound Islamic government. The call for a *dawla Islamiya* (Islamic state) made by all contemporary Islamic fundamentalists is based on the belief that a *nizam Islami* (Islamic system) forms the centre of Islam. Yet, this assumption is exclusively held by Islamic fundamentalists, not the religion of Islam as revealed in the Quran and the *hadith* (collection of the tradition of the Prophet). These neo-Arabic terms used by contemporary Islamic fundamentalists are non-existent in any classical Islamic source, which leads to the conclusion that the notion of an Islamic system exemplified by an Islamic state is an "invention of tradition".[17] In other words, Islamic fundamentalism is the result of adapting Islamic concepts to socio-political change.

While it is not the aim of this chapter to judge the underlying intentions of the individual, it does suggest that it would be misleading to assume that the role of religion in political conflicts is merely instrumental. It contests the popular view that in the case of Islamic fundamentalism religion serves as a mechanism for obtaining political legitimization and is being abused for cross-political ends. In contrast, fundamentalists throughout the world act and perceive themselves to be the true believers.[18] Although it may contradict an exclusively spiritual understanding of religion, to comprehend the inner logic of Al-Qaeda and the motivation of its recruits it is crucial to acknowledge that Islamic fundamentalists advance a concept of Islam that sees no contradiction between belief and political action. Despite vastly different origins and agendas, Islamic fundamentalists are united in their beliefs of being the "true believers". As a direct consequence, many Muslims see those believers who equate their political interpretation of Islamic sources with Islamic religious belief as particularly keen and devout Muslims, persecuted by unjust bureaucracies. It is for this reason that many Muslims see a hero in bin Laden. In the words of a young Pakistani interviewed on Al-Jazeera, "bin Ladin is not a terrorist. That is American rhetoric. He is a good Muslim fighting for Islam. I named my son Osama – I want him to become a believer just like him."

Al-Qaeda's ideology: sources, influence and appeal

While the process of adapting Islamic concepts to structural changes explains the origins of Al-Qaeda's ideology in theory, questions related to its appeal and impact on individual believers as well as ideological influences and sources necessitate a closer look at the socio-political context and intellectual leadership. In general, the Muslim world has not been isolated from the processes of modernization and the advent of mass education that, among other factors, have influenced the development of modern political societies and produced new identities, opportunities and inequalities. Two results of these social and political changes are particularly important for the advancement of Islamic fundamentalism. The first is the fragmentation of religious authority "whereby the meaning of scripture no longer needs to be interpreted by a religious establishment but, rather, lies in the eyes of the beholder".[19] The second one is a process by which basic questions such as the actual meaning of Islam and how it affects – or rather should affect – the conduct of life come to the fore in the consciousness of believers. In other words, what does it mean to be a Muslim in a world that bears no resemblance to the glorious past of Islam? This development is also referred to as the objectification of Muslim consciousness.[20]

As it is becoming more and more difficult to say with reassuring finality what is Islamic and what is not, the issue of precisely who establishes the guidelines for "proper" Islamic behaviour is of vital importance. In the words of the Sorbonne-educated leader of the Muslim Brothers in Sudan: "Because all knowledge is divine and religious, a chemist, an economist or a jurist are all '*ulama*'".[21] Hence, it is perfectly feasible that someone without religious training in the traditional sense like Osama bin Laden may obtain the status of a religious authority in the eyes of his followers. By addressing timely issues of grave concern in the Muslim world and formalizing the return to the golden age tradition as a straightforward solution, he provides both a powerful indictment of the waywardness of Muslim societies and a blueprint for action. Thus, the turning towards the Islamic tradition and its interpretation becomes a way of legitimately criticizing the existing status quo, providing religious guidance and facilitating revolutionary and incremental changes.[22]

Ideologically, bin Laden started off as a member of the Muslim Brotherhood – which, one might note, is not a Wahhabi-oriented organization – to eventually join forces with Abdullah Azzam, a legendary Arab fighter against the Soviet Union in Afghanistan.[23] Upon setting up Al-Qaeda in the mid-1980s, the Muslim Brotherhood broke off its links with bin Laden, who politically, had gone his own way. As the name of the newly founded organization suggests, the idea behind Al-Qaeda was the establishment of a "base" that would bring together different Islamic fundamentalist groups and coordinate their activities. Yet, the organization failed to attract the mainstream of the radical Islamic fundamentalist movement in Arab countries. With few exceptions, these groups maintained the view that action should be confined to each groups' nation state. However, some of the key Islamist figures, including the leader of the jihad movement

Ayyman al-Zawahri, began to change their outlook to that of a more internationalist revolutionary movement. His decision to join Al-Qaeda was based on the belief that the Islamic fundamentalist groups within their individual states were prevented from achieving any significant change on the domestic fronts because of a common external enemy. Hence, on the leadership level, Al-Qaeda brings together individuals with both strong religious sentiments and previous terrorist records who regard their actions as a much needed act of defiance against the "real enemy" – that enemy being the source of all ills affecting the Muslim world, primarily the US because of its support for Israel and the corrupt dictatorships in the Middle East.

The basis for the ideology of violence that has become the political world view of Al-Qaeda can be found in al-Zawahri's treatise published in 1996, entitled *Shifa' Sudur al-Muminin* (The Cure for Believer's Hearts). The way he adapts Islamic principles to the present political situation and derives the implications for proper Islamic conduct becomes evident in the analysis of three interrelated issues. The first is primarily of political nature: by ranking Palestine as the primary problem, he concludes that all Arab and Muslim regimes have lost their credibility by the mere fact that they have accepted the authority of the UN and the legitimacy of Israel. Thus, invoking the Palestinian issue allows for declaring these governments, especially Saudi Arabia with its close ties to the US, the main supporter of Israel, to be outside the fold of Islam.

The second issue is that of personal consequences that arise in this particular political context for the individual believer, expressed in al-Zawahri's interpretations of personal responsibility in Islamic law. In essence, every Muslim who in any way supports these "un-Islamic" regimes places himself outside the fold of Islam. It is not possible to take refuge in the claim that they merely followed orders as only God's orders are to be followed, which includes the acceptance of taking personal responsibility. For Al-Qaeda's internationalist struggle, this argument is expanded to Western governments. The inherent logic could be expressed as follows: as citizens of these countries, Muslims vote, and even if they don't vote, they pay taxes, and therefore support "un-Islamic" governments. As such, they lose their status of innocent non-combatants in Islamic law, rendering them to be legitimate targets in the case of an attack. A frequently encountered point of criticism to this logic is, for example, the mentioning of children, who are specifically exempted from being combatants in Islamic law. In response to the main corpus of Islamic theology which clearly rejects the concept of collateral damage, al-Zawahri propounds the ideas of the greater good and the need to react to exceptional circumstances. Clearly expressing his personal opinion, an overpowering enemy and limited resources allow for a more lax interpretation of the law. It is precisely this logic that also allows him to handle the clear and absolute prohibition of suicide under Islamic law. Drawing on the idea of martyrdom in the Christian sense, he draws on examples of captured Muslims who were asked to recant on pain of death, and refused. Viewing this refusal as suicide for the glory of God that was not condemned by Islamic theologians, he concludes that committing suicide for the greater good is equally legal. Obviously, the essence of this adaptation of Islamic principles to the political situation is the complete separation between the "true believers", i.e. the Islamic fundamentalists, and the "enemy", now including all Muslims who are in any way connected to non-Islamic regimes, rendering them to be legitimate targets in the fight for the glory of Islam.

Thus, the key to the ideology of Al-Qaeda, as indicated above, lies in the political view of the situation in Muslim societies in general, and the Middle East in particular. It is an intellectual concept that is not based on the main schools of Islamic theology, but a new ideological starting point that results from the application of Islamic principles to socio-political change. With its political goals reinforced by the teachings of the Quran, exemplified by the content and rhetoric of recruitment videos and training manuals, the organization creates powerful imagery embedded in the collective consciousness of the Muslim community.[24] Thus, the message provided by Al-Qaeda inspires its followers to commit violent acts of destruction while being fully convinced that they are fulfilling the ordained will of Allah.

From ideology to participation

Individuals do not typically wake up with a sudden desire to commit themselves to the global jihad. Such a decision is usually preceded by an extensive socialization process that includes exposure to Al-Qaeda's ideas, debate and deliberation. Only when they are convinced that the organization represents the "true" version of Islam is he or she likely to "join". However, many Muslims sympathize with Al-Qaeda's mission and see bin Laden as a particularly devout believer, but only a marginal fraction of that group eventually becomes actively involved. Hence, sympathizing with an organization is not the same as participating in it. Acting according to one's beliefs and principles is not always easy. Indeed, action mobilization is related to the classic social psychological problem of the relationship between attitude and behaviour. Countless laboratory and field studies have studied the predictive powers of attitudes, and repeatedly arrived at the conclusion that attitudes are poor predictors for behaviour.[25] Numerous studies of social movements have reached the same conclusions with regard to the ability to use sympathy for a movement as a predictor of movement participation.[26] Yet, the extent to which positive attitudes predict supportive behaviour – that is participating in the organization's activities – remains an unresolved question.

Research on demographic profiles of Islamic fundamentalists tends to suggest that recruits frequently come from particular socio-economic and educational backgrounds.[27] However, not everyone from that background eventually joins an Islamic fundamentalist movement, while individuals with entirely different profiles do. Even if one were to accept the argument that particular constituencies have a greater propensity to join because of a shared set of grievances and psychological stressors, there must be other mechanisms to explain why this commonality translates into participation in some cases but not in others. This is particularly noteworthy as neither socio-political discontent nor personal crises necessarily translate into some form of active protest or collective activity. From Arab defeat in the 1967 war with Israel, the failure of secular modernization projects, economic malaise, blocked social mobility and political alienation to a more personal sense of cultural weakness, racism, humiliation, victimization, family feuds or simply the lack of life's purpose and subsequent religious seeking, the literature is replete with inexhaustible lists of precipitating factors.

Although scholars debate the relative importance of these factors, there is general agreement that individuals join Islamic fundamentalist movements in response to crisis and in search of new meaning. Yet, while grievances of whatever kind may provide an impetus for participation in Al-Qaeda, many other factors including the level of repression, resource availability or social support networks impact the individual's decision about participation. In the words of Leon Trotsky, "the mere existence of privation is not enough to cause an insurrection; if it were, the masses would always be in revolt".[28] These observations lead to the key question: Why do certain individuals actively participate in Al-Qaeda whereas others do not?

Towards popular support: collective action frames

At the most basic level, every social movement, including Al-Qaeda, has a mobilization potential, which by definition includes every individual that could theoretically be mobilized by that movement.[29] Hence, a mobilization potential consists of people who share certain beliefs and values, in other words, those who are sympathetic to a given collective action frame. As adherence to a particular collective action frame is supposed to be a necessary condition of – and first step towards – participation, we first need to understand how a collective action frame is generated. And because adherence to a collective action frame does not necessarily translate into participation, we then need to identify the additional conditions presumably needed to impel a person to actually participate.

According to Gamson, a collective action frame is "a set of action-oriented beliefs and meanings that inspire and legitimate social movement activities".[30] In other words, collective action frames are a set of collective beliefs that serve to create a state of mind in which participation in collective action, such as participation in the global jihad, appears meaningful. In his analysis, Gamson distinguishes three components of collective action frames that can readily be identified in the case of Al-Qaeda: first, a sense of injustice; second, an element of identity and third, the factor of agency. A sense of injustice arises from moral indignation to grievances, such as the perception of the poor state of the *umma* (community of all Muslims) as being the direct result of US foreign policy. More specifically, bin Laden portrays the presence of US troops in Saudi Arabia, capable of controlling access to the holy sites, as a direct threat to Islam.[31] This concept of threat and injustice is then extended to other parts of the Muslim world by demonstrating the ongoing suffering and blood-letting of co-religionists in Palestine, Iraq, Kashmir and Chechnya to name but a few. Inequality, however, is not the only condition to spark anger and moral outrage. Studies on emotion indicate that anger is the emotion expressed by people who hold an external agent responsible for an unwanted situation.[32] Anger seems to depend on causal attribution, the identification of some agent who is to be blamed for the undesired situation – a mechanism clearly obvious from Al-Qaeda's logic that blames the situation of the Muslim community on the impact of the Zionist–Crusader alliance. But for anger to motivate collective action it must be shared. These observations bring us to the second component of collective action frames, identity. The identification of a "they" who are held responsible for a negative situation implies an ongoing "us". And in defining a "we" the identity component of collective action frames highlights the fact that these frames are sets of collective beliefs. Thus the grievances these frames encompass are also shared, it is a group that feels disadvantaged, ill treated or discriminated against.[33] Thus, the identity component not only emphasizes the commonality of grievances, it also establishes the group's opposition to the actor held responsible for the grievances. And, as mentioned earlier, for Al-Qaeda "the enemy" includes all Muslims who are in any way connected to non-Islamic regimes.

Agency refers to the belief that one can alter conditions or policies through collective action. A sense of injustice and of identity may be necessary conditions for movement participation, but merely sharing grievances and finding an enemy to blame is not enough to impel individuals to engage in battle. Individuals must become convinced that they have the power to change their condition. A rather extensive literature affirms that protest takes place in the belief that collective action can successfully eliminate grievances.[34]

As a brief look at one of bin Laden's lectures suggest, it is his genius at manipulating images and symbols, as well as his ability to tap into a wellspring of legitimate Muslim and Arab resentment of US foreign policies, that explains his popular support. Following a highly emotional presentation of suffering Muslims around the globe, bin Laden summarizes the state of the present situation. In theoretical terms, he creates a strong understanding of injustice and identity – us versus them.

> And the world is on fire. Our Muslim brothers and sisters in Palestine and Iraq are suffering under a Zionist–Crusader invasion. The crusader forces control the holy land, eating its riches and controlling its people. And this is happening while Muslims all over the world are attacked like people fighting over a piece of bread.

> Oh you who believe! What is the matter with you, that when you are asked to march forth in the Cause of Allah/Jihad, you cling heavily to the earth? Are you pleased with the life of this world rather than the Hereafter? But little is in the enjoyment of the life of this world as compared to the hereafter.
>
> (9:38)

Backed by legitimacy derived from an appropriate Quranic citation, bin Laden has created a situation that allows him to present a straightforward case. Invoking the miserable state of the *umma* – or "us", he refers to the enemy "them" in a symbolic phrase as the "Zionist–Crusader invasion". He further provides strong assurance of a powerful agent, namely they themselves as a group of true believers, by making clear that God will be on the side of those who march forth faithfully, despite the risk of physical harm. The citing of the full story of how a small number of believers managed to overcome an overwhelming enemy with the help of Allah – the Quranic equivalent of the biblical account of David and Goliath – exemplifies this intention.

> But those who knew with certainty that they were going to meet Allah, said, "How often a small group overcame a mighty host by Allah's leave!" And Allah is with As-Sabirun. And when they advanced to meet Goliath and his forces, they invoked: "Our Lord! Pour forth on us patience, and set firm our feet and make us victorious over the disbelieving people." So they routed them by Allah's leave and David killed Goliath and Allah gave him the kingdom and taught him of that which He willed.
>
> (2: 249–251)

The victory of David over Goliath provides a powerful confirmation that righteousness, "us", will triumph over evil, and as such can be seen as an incentive for the audience to have faith in Allah even under the most daunting circumstances.

Collective beliefs do not reside in the individual, but are "out there". From this point of view, individual beliefs are appropriated collective beliefs. Accordingly, in explaining the generation of collective action frames, we must account for two separate and distinct processes: the social construction of collective beliefs into a collectivity and the appropriation of a smaller or larger proportion of those beliefs by an individual member of that collectivity. As indicated when introducing the components of collective action frames, injustice is not an objective phenomenon. After all, as scholars have argued time and time again, many situations that could be considered social problems, never become an issue.[35] Before a collective action frame can be generated, evaluations of existing circumstances must be cast as shared grievances, which in turn must be transformed into demands to be presented to the authorities held responsible for the negative situation. Thus, collective action frames are not any kind of shared beliefs, but concern conflicts in a society. Controversial issues are debated and themes and counter-themes structure the debate: social reality is too complex to allow only for one single interpretation. This reality, moreover, is subject to ideological moulding. Proponents of different views will define a situation differently, according to their particular bias and the varying definitions that confront one another. In this context, social actors intentionally or unintentionally influence the generation of collective action frames through either deliberately persuasive campaigns or news discourse. Although news discourse does not necessarily promote one particular definition of situation, it is in the nature of situation analysis to emphasize different issues and events in relation to prior understandings of a given phenomenon, cultural and social background or access to resources to name but a few. In other words, the effect of news discourse on the formation of collective action frame is far from neutral. For example, the haunting image of the Palestinian father holding his dying son made news on CNN on at least five different occasions in 2000, while Al-Jazeera has continually shown the very same image throughout the past six years. Similarly, images of violence against Muslims around the globe are equally common features, creating a lasting awareness of ongoing aggression.

Present studies highlight an individual's willingness to expose him or herself to the movements' message as an essential prerequisite. This theory is based on the assumption that most individuals will reject Al-Qaeda and like-minded organizations as "extreme", "militant" or "irrational", and that the "extreme" messages are not just out there.[36] However, in the light of what is shown in the Arab media discourse and the recent protests in many Muslim countries, this assumption deserves to be treated with caution. The messages of banners and speeches delivered during these protests did not merely reject the bizarre cartoon illustrations of the Prophet, but communicated a much broader, political agenda that could have been taken right from an Al-Qaeda propaganda video: "How can there be a dialogue between Muslims, ('us'), and the West, ('them') when 'they' are killing 'us' and taking 'our' land and holy places by force and attacking Islam?"[37] A careful reading of the messages of those who protested in the Arab streets suggests that the political message and logic of Al-Qaeda resonate with large segments of Muslim societies.

Overcoming barriers to participation: beyond selective incentives

While the generation of collective action frames helps to explain why many are sympathetic towards Al-Qaeda's ideology, it is only a minor fraction of those who sympathize that eventually becomes actively involved. How, then, does Al-Qaeda gain participants? Resource mobilization theory proposes that in order to initiate participation, a movement must influence the perceived costs and benefits of participation. Consequently, the motivation to participate has frequently been defined as a function of these perceived costs and benefits, where participation is facilitated by powerful selective incentives (material, solidary and/or purposive).[38] While this argument has been proven in numerous social psychology experiments, some authors have started to question whether this theory can effectively explain why individuals participate in radical Islamic fundamentalist organizations. According to Wictorowicz,

> such movements demand total adherence and submission to the movement ideology, self-sacrifice in high risk activism, and the abandonment of previous life styles. They rarely offer selective incentives that offset the

enormous costs and risks associated with participation; and while networks, moral shock and frame alignment may expose an individual to a movement, alone they do not explain why the individual, after initial exposure, decides to participate irrespective of costs and risks.[39]

With this assumption, Wiktorowicz falls victim to the limited perception of what might be called an "outside-in" approach. From this "outside" perspective, Al-Qaeda has nothing to offer to offset the high opportunity cost of participation, however, the picture is dramatically different when perceived from "within". For those who embrace the logic of Al-Qaeda, in other words, those "within" the collective action frame, the organization provides something much more meaningful than selective incentives in the traditional sense: the true meaning of life and ultimate salvation. Joining the cause – surrendering one's life to Allah and answering His call to jihad – means overcoming the greatest fear of mankind, the eternity of death. This conviction is clearly evident among the members of Al-Qaeda: whether in a prison in Iraq or a courthouse in Virginia, they seem to have conquered the fear of death. Of the twenty hijackers active on 11 September, no one shrinked back or dropped out. Without exception, they went willingly and seemingly without any hesitation to their own deaths. If counter-terrorism measures are only as accurate as the analysis on which they are based, it is a matter of grave importance that we look at the phenomenon of Al-Qaeda through the only lens that matters: the one from within.

It has already been established that individuals join Al-Qaeda in response to some kind of crisis and in search of new meaning. And whether actively seeking or encountering by chance, the logic of Al-Qaeda and the call to engage in jihad are relentlessly expounded on myriad jihadi web sites, in video- and audio-tapes of bin Laden, al-Zawahiri and other senior Al-Qaeda personalities, or by radical cleric lay-preachers speaking in mosques or addressing informal circles of adherents in more private settings.[40] The struggle is cast in narrow defensive terms: extolling the duty of the faithful to defend Islam by the sword. Imitation by example is encouraged through the depiction of the sacrifices of past martyrs coupled with messages about the importance of continuous battle against the enemies of Islam. Another glance at both the style and rhetoric of Al-Qaeda's messages gives a sense of how powerful and influential they may be to an already sympathetic:

> You are the best community ever brought forth to mankind. The goodness is in you, it comes forth from your hands and from under your feet. You are the best people, bidding to honour and forbidding dishonour, and believing in Allah.
>
> (3: 110)[41]

Thus, forever, let there be one nation, calling for good, enjoining honour and fighting dishonour, those are the prosperers.

The statements above mark the beginning of an "educational" speech by Osama bin Laden. The pairing of the Quranic citation and bin Laden's practical application firmly establish two fundamental principles of Islam as well as their direct consequences for the present, which can be summarized as follow. First, the *umma* – which includes all Muslims regardless of ethnic origin – is the community most favoured by God, which implies – at least according to bin Laden – the need to act as one nation as well as the pursuit of what is honourable, i.e. allowed, or rather expected, under Islamic law, and the prevention of that which is sinful. And second, it reinforces what might be regarded as the cardinal principle of Islam, the duty of every sincere Muslim to "obey God and his Messenger".

> And obey Allah and the Messenger that you may obtain mercy. And march forth in the way (which leads to) forgiveness from your Lord, and for Paradise as wide as the heavens and the earth, prepared for the pious.
>
> (3: 132)

> We testify that there is no God but Allah, He alone, and no associate with Him.

Indoctrinated with divine imperatives and an ideal model for reality, the audience is presented with the fact that the actual reality of the present situation is nothing like it ought to be. Pronounced in a highly dramatic tone which is hardly reflected in the following translation, bin Laden declares that it is the duty of every sincere Muslim – note here the concept of personal responsibility – to correct a situation in which members of the *umma* are subjected to unacceptable levels of pain and corruption by an outside force. Interestingly, bin Laden's observation of reality is now followed by a quotation from the Quran. Structuring his argument in this manner, he not only makes it impossible to question the Islamic integrity of his solution to the problem (who could question the guidance and will of Allah), but also increases the credibility of the invoked threat of eternal hell and the promise of heavenly rewards if this path is followed (selective incentives and disincentives).

But what is happening to us? The world is on fire. Endless suffering, increasing corruption, horrendous abuse. Just look at Iraq. Look at Palestine. Look at Kashmir. Atrocities are committed against our brothers and sisters. Yet, they are part of our community, and they deserve our sympathy and our support.

> Oh you who believe. Obey Allah and obey the Messenger and render not vain your deeds. Verily, those who disbelieve and hinder from the path of Allah, they will die as disbelievers and Allah will not forgive them. So be not weak and ask not for peace from the enemies of Islam while you are having the upper hand. Allah is with you and will never decrease the reward of your good deed.
>
> (47: 33–34)

With this provision of divine guidance and powerful incentives the next part of the video triggers emotional outrage by presenting scenes of Muslims suffering at the hands of the enemy, motivating the audience even further into taking action. Throughout this section, Islamic music of different styles is played, adding to the powerful emotional force of the images presented. But,

> Oh you who believe! What is the matter with you, that when you are asked to march forth in the Cause of Allah/Jihad, you cling heavily to the earth? Are you pleased with the life of this world rather than the Hereafter? But little is in the enjoyment of the life of this world as compared to the hereafter.
>
> (9: 38)

> Oh Muslims, do you (plural) want to walk along the straight path and please God? Do you (singular) submit to the will of Allah?

The way in which this quest if formalized reveals the significance of the moral endeavour that it creates for the individual in the audience. First, in terms of format, the initial part of the question addresses the audience as a homogeneous group, while the second part is directed specifically towards the individual. By changing from speaking to the audience as a whole to addressing the individual, bin Laden engages every listener in a moral dilemma. Second, in terms of content, the question invokes a line from the opening *sura* of the Quran, which is recited several times during the prayer: "do you want to walk along the straight path?" (*sirat al-mustaqim*). The answer of every Muslim to this inquiry can only be in the affirmative. The same holds true for the second part, which is the condition for pleasing God: to submit to His will. The combination of style and content here is manipulative by virtue of the fact that it is simply not possible for the individual Muslim to answer any of these questions negatively. Assuming the intention to communicate his message in the most effective manner, it is hardly surprising that the subsequent lines carry an almost apocalyptic tone:

> Oh Brothers, we all must fulfil the commands that He has placed upon us. We testify that there is no God but Allah, no associate with Him. He is the all-knowing, the most superior, and the ruler of all mankind. To Him we are held responsible on the day of resurrection. There will be no way to hide from God and His judgment.

The example illustrates an atmosphere of risk, opportunity and decision, which furthers the individual moral dilemma. Also note the repeated use of incentives.

> Nobody who dies and finds good from Allah in the Hereafter would wish to come back to this world, even if he were given the whole world and whatever is in it, except the martyr who, on seeing the superiority of martyrdom

would like to come back to the world and get killed again in the cause of Allah.

But "If you (singular) march not forth, He will punish you with a painful torment and will replace you by another people, and you cannot harm Him at all, and Allah is able to do all things.

(9: 39)

In his closing sentence, he summarizes the central message of the address:

When you fight those who disbelieve, smite their necks till you have killed and wounded many of them.

(47: 4)

If you give up jihad, you give up Islam!

With its political goals reinforced by the teachings of the Quran, bin Laden creates powerful imagery embedded in the collective consciousness of his audience. Each word, symbol or concept is loaded with historical meaning and emotion that is hard to measure unless the protagonists' culture and history are thoroughly understood. Carl Gustav Jung, the Swiss psychologist, called the deeply rooted and commonly shared feelings that are evoked as a result of this kind of rhetoric the "collective consciousness". "Utilized towards specific goals, this can serve as a powerful instrument to drive a people to commendable activities or heroism, or move them to destructive behaviour at critical moments of human society or community."[42] Once unleashed, these collective emotions are very difficult to contain and could possibly be directed along a destructive course.

Joining the global jihad – recruiting the toughest

While the process of overcoming barriers to participation through intensification of belief and faith presents a critical step towards participation, it is not yet a sufficient condition for joining Al-Qaeda and the global jihad. Finally, the critical element to joining the cause is the accessibility of a link to the network. Without it, the individual or group of committed worshippers is more likely to undergo a process of progressive isolation. This is not to say that such isolated groups may be conveniently ignored. The opposite is the case as they may involve individuals with very specific knowledge and training, for example, in the field of science that could be utilized towards lethal acts of destruction. Such an "individual response" to the call for jihad would be difficult to predict and virtually impossible to pre-empt.[43]

However, for joining Al-Qaeda the actual encounter with a formal member is crucial. Without someone to facilitate communication, affiliation and organize for a potential recruit to attend training facilities, prospective members remain sympathizers.[44] To become formally accepted into Al-Qaeda, a new recruit needs to attend a training camp (until recently in Afghanistan, Malaysia, the Philippines or the Sudan) and subsequently undergo evaluation for suitability. The extraordinary standards to which new recruits are held are evident from the guidelines for training Al-Qaeda, "the pious group and the pioneering vanguard", which states:

> It must jump into the fire of the toughest tests and into the waves of fierce trials. The training leadership shares with them the testing march, the sweat and the blood. The leadership must be like the motherly warmth of a hen whose chicks grow under its wings, throughout the long period of hatching and training. This vanguard has to abstain from cheap worldly pleasures and must bear its distinct stamp of abstinence and frugality. In like manner it must be endowed with firm belief and trust in the ideology instilled with a lot of hope for its victory. There must be strong determination and insistence to continue the march. The provision consists of meditation, patience and prayer. They must be aware of the existence of anti-Islam machinations all over the world.[45]

According to Sageman, Al-Qaeda offered the opportunity to join its ranks to only 10 to 30 per cent of the trainees. Once found worthy of joining, the commitment was sealed with an oath of loyalty to Al-Qaeda and Osama bin Laden.[46] In this light, it seems reasonable to conclude that the process of joining Al-Qaeda and the global jihad bears more resemblance to a high profile profession that is wanted by many but achieved only by the best. Al-Qaeda, with an abundance of sympathizers and potential recruits, accepts only the toughest into its ranks.

In sum, the final acceptance into Al-Qaeda marks the end of a process that divides into three stages: first, becoming sympathetic towards Al-Qaeda's ideology through what has been described as "adhering to collective action frame"; second, a period of overcoming barriers to participation through intensification of belief and commitment; and third, the act of being formally accepted into the network following a trial period of close observation in the training camp.

Conclusion

In the light of the ongoing war against terrorism, it is all too evident that Al-Qaeda's messages, with their appeal to powerful imagery embedded in the collective consciousness of the Muslim community and their juxtaposition of political goals with the teachings of the Quran, resonate with large segments of the Muslim world and inspire his followers to commit terrible acts of destruction while being fully convinced that they are fulfilling the ordained will of Allah. Contrary to this perception from within, Al-Qaeda advances an intellectual concept that is not based on the main schools of Islamic theology, but a new ideological starting point that results from the application of Islamic principles to socio-political change. Despite the damage and losses of key leaders that Al-Qaeda has suffered since the beginning of the war against terror, it stubbornly adheres to its fundamental raison d'être: continuing to inspire and motivate the broader community. Its exhortations continue to resonate widely when many Muslims harbour a deep sense of resentment and humiliation over the invasions of Afghanistan and Iraq, the continued suffering of their co-religionists in Palestine, Chechnya or Kashmir, the ill-treatments of Abu-Ghraib and Guantanamo, or yet another UN security council resolution condemning Israel's actions vetoed by the United States.

However at the end of 2006, the current Al-Qaeda exists more as an ideology than as an identifiable, unitary terrorist organization. "It has become a vast enterprise – an international franchise with like-minded local representatives, loosely connected to central, ideological or motivational base but advancing the center's goals at once simultaneously and independently from one another."[47] Because of Al-Qaeda's structural changes and continued, if not increased appeal, our concern should no longer be focused on those officially connected to the network, but those who operate independently, motivated by the very same desire to defend Islam and harm the enemy. For this reason, the current "kill or capture" counter-terrorism strategy is unlikely to weaken Al-Qaeda and unable to undermine its popular appeal: there will be dozens of new recruits for every individual that we detain, interrogate and torture. Thus, the success of any counter-terrorism effort will depend on its ability to counter Al-Qaeda's ideological appeal by addressing three interrelated elements of the organization's success: the continued resonance of Al-Qaeda's message, its continued ability to attract recruits from an increasing pool of sympathizers and its capacity for continual regeneration.

Notes

1 "Al-Qaeda not driven by Ideology", *The Washington Times*, 5 June, 2003.
2 S. Schwartz, *The Two Faces of Islam*, (New York: Random House Inc., 2002), p. 1.
3 Q. Wiktorowiscz, "Anatomy of the Salafi Movement", *Studies in Conflict and Terrorism*, Vol. 29, 2006 pp. 207–239.
4 Ibid., p. 208.
5 S. Qutb, *Fi Zilal al-Quran*, (London: MWH London Publishers, 1979). An insightful discussion of Qutb's interpretation is R. Nettler's "Guidelines for the Islamic Community: Sayyid Qutb's political interpretation", *Journal of Political Ideologies*, Vol. 1, No. 2, 1996, pp. 183–196.
6 J. Piscatori, "Islam, Islamists and the Electoral Principle in the Middle East", *ISIM Papers*, (Leiden: ISIM, 2000), p. 46.
7 F. Halliday, "The Politics of Islam – A Second Look", *British Journal of Political Science*, Vol. 25, No. 3, 1995, p. 400.
8 N. Luhmann, *Funktion der Religon*, (Frankfurt: Piper Verlag, 1977), p. 16 and B. Tibi, *Islam between Culture and Politics*, (New York: Palgrave, 2001), p. 28.
9 C. Geertz, *The Interpretation of Cultures*, (New York: Basic Books, 1973), pp. 87–95.
10 Tibi (2001), p. 28.
11 Ibid. p. 29.

12. Ibid. p. 29 and J. Baumann, *Gott und Mensch im Koran: Eine Strukturform religiöser Anthropologie anhand des Beispiels Allah und Muhammed*, (Darmstadt: Piper Verlag, 1977), p. 9.
13. D. Eickelman and J. Piscatori, *Muslim Politics* (Princeton: Princeton University Press, 1996) p. 46.
14. Ibid. p. 46.
15. These are the terms used by Marshall G.S. Hodgson, *The Venture of Islam: Conscience and History in a World Civilization*, 3 vols. (Chicago: University of Chicago Press, 1974).
16. Several authors provide different dates for the separation of functions and institutions from Islam: see for example N. Coulson, *A History of Islamic Law*, (Edinburgh: University Press, 1964) pp. 128–129 or B. Lewis, "Politics and War" in *The Legacy of Islam*, eds. J. Schacht and C. Bosworth (Oxford: Oxford University Press, 1979) pp. 156–209.
17. Tibi (2001), p. 2.
18. Ibid. p. 17.
19. J. Piscatori, "The Turmoil Within", *Foreign Affairs*, May/June 2002, accessed on 14 May 2003 at: www. foreignaffairs.org/2002/the-turmoil-within.html.
20. Eickelmann and Piscatori (1996), p. 38.
21. Turabi quoted in Ibid. p. 43.
22. Eickelman and Piscatori (1996), p. 35.
23. For an excellent discussion of the misunderstood Wahhabi connection, see M. Azzam, "Al-Qaeda: the misunderstood Wahhabi connection and the ideology of violence", The Royal Institute of International Affairs, Briefing Paper No. 1, February 2003.
24. For a detailed discussion of an Al-Qaeda recruitment video, see Hellmich, C, "Al-Qaeda: hypocrites, terrorists, fundamentalists? The view from within", *Third World Quarterly*, Vol. 26, No. 1, 2005, pp. 39–54.
25. For a recent overview see R. Perloff, *The Dynamics of Persuasion*, (London: Lawrence Erloff, 1993).
26. See for example B. Klandermans and D. Omega 1987, "Potentials, Networks, Motivations and Barriers: Steps towards participation in social movements", *American Sociological Review*, Vol. 52, 1987, pp. 519–531.
27. See: Saad Eddin Ibrahim, "Anatomy of Egypt's Militant Islamic Groups: Methodological Note and Preliminary Findings", *International Journal of Middle East Studies*, Vol. 12, No. 4, 1980, pp. 423–453; Saad Eddin Ibrahim, "The Changing Face of Egypt's Islamic Activism", in Ibrahim (ed.) *Egypt, Islam, and Democracy*, (Cairo: The American University of Cairo Press, 1996); Hamied N. Ansari, "The Islamic Militants in Egyptian Politics", *International Journal of Middle East Studies*, Vol. 16, No. 1, 1984, pp. 123–144; Henry Munson, Jr., "The Social Base of Islamic Militancy in Morocco", *Middle East Journal*, Vol. 40, No. 2, 1986, pp. 267–284; Susan Waltz, "Islamic Appeal in Tunisia", *Middle East Journal*, Vol. 40, No. 4, 1986, pp. 651–670.
28. Leon Trotsky quoted in J. Goodwin and T. Skocpol, "Explaining Revolutions in the Contemporary Third World", *Politics and Society*, Vol. 17, 1989, p. 490.
29. Klandermans and Omega (1987).
30. W. Gamson, *Talking Politics*, (Cambridge: Cambridge University Press, 1992) p. 7.
31. Osama bin Laden bases his claim about the illegality of the presence of US troops on a statement of Prophet Mohammad in which the Prophet says: "Expel the polytheists from the Arabian peninsula."
32. B. Major, "From Social Inequality to Personal Entitlement: The Role of Social Comparisons, Legitimacy, Appraisals and Group Membership", *Advances in Experimental Social Psychology*, Vol. 26, 1994, pp. 293–355; B. Parkinson and Manstead, "Making Sense of Emotions in Stories and Social Life", *Cognition and Emotion*, Vol. 7, 1993, pp. 295–323; I.J. Roseman, R.P. Abelson, and M.F. Ewing "Emotion and Political Cognition: Emotion Appeals in Political Communication", *The 19th Annual Carnegie*

Symposium on Cognition. "*Political Cognition*", edited by R. Rau and D. Sears, (London: Lawrence Earlbaum, 1986).

33 The concept of shared grievances is not new in the literature on political protest. The best known exemplar of such a concept is "fraternalistic" deprivation, which appears in the relative deprivation literature. W.G. Runciman, *Relative Deprivation and Social Justice*, (London: Routledge and Kegan Paul, 1966), J. Martin, "The Tolerance of Injustice", pp. 217–242 in *Relative Deprivation and Social Comparison: The Ontario Symposium*, Vol. 4, (New York: Lawrence Earlbaum, 1986). In all cases, comparison yields the feeling that one – or one's group – does not receive the rewards, treatment or recognition it deserves.

34 D. McAdam, *Political Process and the Development of Black Insurgency*, (Chicago, University of Chicago Press, 1982); D. McAdam, *Freedom Summer*, (New York: Oxford University Press, 1988), M. Schwartz and S. Paul, "Resource Mobilization versus the Mobilization of People: Why Consensus Movements cannot be the Instruments for Social Change", pp. 205–224, in *Frontiers of Social Movement Theory*, eds. A.D. Morris and C. McClurg, (New Haven: Yale University Press, 1992).

35 S. Hilgartner and C.L. Bosk, "The Rise and Fall of Social Problems: A Public Arenas Model", *American Journal of Sociology*, Vol. 94, 1988, pp. 53–79.

36 Q. Wictorowicz, "Joining the Cause: Al-Muhajiroun and Radical Islam", Conference Paper accessed under http://yale.edu/polisci/info/conferences/IslamicRadicalims20/papers.htm, p. 7.

37 For example, a group of women in the Sana'a protests repeatedly communicated the following message: "How can there be a dialogue between Muslims and American/European nations while they are killing Muslims and taking hold of their lands and sacred places by force and attacking Islam?"

38 A. Oberschall, "Loosely Structured Collective Conflicts: a theory and an application", *Research in Social Movements, Conflict and Change*, (Greenwich, Conn.: JAI Press, 1980).

36 Wictorowicz, "Joining the Cause", p. 6.

40 See for example C. Hellmich, "The Role of the *Khutba* as a Medium for the Communication of Islamic Fundamentalism: the case of Yemen", unpublished MSc thesis, Oxford University, 2003.

41 The translations of Quranic citations are based on M. Taqi-ud-Din Al-Hilali and M. Mushin Khan, *Translation of the Meanings of The Noble Qur'an in the English Language*, Riyadh: King Fahd Complex for the printing of the Holy Quran, 1419 AH.

42 C.G. Jung, insert, cited in W. Schulz, *Psychologie des Widerstandes*, (Frankfurt: Westman Verlag, 2002), p. 27. See also C.G. Jung, "The archetypes and the collected unconsciousness", in H. Read, M. Fordham and G. Adler (eds), *Collected Works*, Vol. 9. (Princeton: Princeton University Press, 1936). For an insightful discussion of the dynamics and contexts of social movement participation, see Bert Klandermans, *The Social Psychology of Protest*, (Oxford: Blackwell Publishers Ltd, 1997), particularly the chapter on "The Transformation of Discontent into Action", pp. 64–93. On group dynamics and the perception of justice, see for example M. Wenzel, "What is social about justice? Inclusive identity and group values as the basis of the justice motive". *Journal of Experimental Social Psychology*, Vol. 38, 2002, pp. 205–208; and T. Tyler and M. Belliveau, "Tradeoffs in justice principles: definitions of perceived fairness", in B. Bunker and J. Rubin (eds.) *Conflict, Cooperation and Justice*, (San Francisco: Jossey-Bass, 2002), pp. 291–314.

43 See for example C. Hellmich and A. Redig, "The question is When: Al-Qaeda and the reality of bioterrorism", *Studies in Conflict and Terrorism*, Vol. 30, 2007, pp. 375–396.

44 Similarly, see M. Sageman, *Understanding Terror Networks*, (Philadelphia, University of Pennsylvania Press, 2004), p. 121.

45 Abdullah Azzam, "Al-Qa'idah al-Sulbah", *Al-Jihad*, April 1988, p. 4.
46 Sageman (2004), p. 121.
47 B. Hoffman, "Combating al-Qaeda and the Militant Islamic Threat", Testimony to the House Armed Services Committee on 16 February 2006, (Virginia RAND Corporation, 2006).

4 Joining jihadi terrorist cells in Europe

Exploring motivational aspects of recruitment and radicalization

Petter Nesser

Introduction

What are the most typical motivations and drivers for young Muslims who join jihadi terrorist cells in Europe?[1] When he was asked about why he decided to go to team up with an Al-Qaeda-associated militant clique, and attend training in paramilitary camps run by Al-Qaeda[2] in Afghanistan, the French jihadi and terrorism convict David Courtallier said:

> "I couldn't see a way out", referring to his "dead end" life in a small village in the French Alps. Recalling his first mosque visit, he said: "It was impressive, all these people in the process of finding themselves. There was a serenity that showed on their faces". About the Afghan experience he said: "Going there was going to be great.... I had never traveled ... I was taken care of totally".[3]

These kinds of subjective and superficial motivations for seeking out jihadi milieus stand in sharp contrast to Mohammed Siddique Khan's and Shehzad Tanweer's justifications for why they blew themselves up in London's subway network on 7 July 2005. Khan and Tanweer talked politics, and described themselves as warriors, fighting a defensive war against Western aggression towards Muslims in all corners of the world, specifying the conflicts in Palestine, Iraq, Afghanistan, Chechnya and Kashmir.[4]

When looking at the biographies of core members of militant Islamist cells in Europe, one is struck by how different they were as persons, and how their motivations and radicalization paths differed from one individual to the next. Indeed, suspected and convicted terrorists in Europe encompassed multiple nationalities and ethnic backgrounds, ages and professions, social backgrounds and personalities. Some of them were strongly politicized, whereas others cared little about politics.

Faced with this complexity, we must ask ourselves if it is possible to detect some systematic differences between different terrorist cell members and their motivations for joining a terrorist cell. By comparing and contrasting the social backgrounds, personal characteristics and roles played by core operatives in eight different terrorist cells that operated in Europe, I came up with a tentative typology (I will also refer to it as a model) of terrorist cell members.[5] The typology was inspired by categories developed by scholars on right-wing extremism.[6] In this chapter, I try to take the model one step further by specifying common motivational factors that correspond to the different "types" of terrorists.

As pointed out by Peter Waldmann, the current state of the art research on the psychology of terrorism largely dismisses notions that some people have "individual dispositions" for terrorism, meaning that there exists no "terrorist profile".[7] I would like to stress that my approach does not contradict this finding. The typology of terrorist cell members presented here should not be confused with psychological profiling. One cannot, based on how I depict the terrorists, draw the conclusion that people displaying similar traits might be predisposed for terrorism. For such a purpose, the characterizations are too general and the sources upon which they have been made, too limited and biased. However, I do believe that the typology can be helpful for analytical purposes, in terms of understanding the internal dynamics of terrorist cells, identifying typical motivations for joining cells, and thinking about different strategies for countering radicalization. The advantages, disadvantages and limitations of the model will be discussed in more detail as we proceed.

In the following chapter I will first offer a brief overview of Islamist militancy in Europe since 2006 and address some new tendencies that have been observed over the past two years. Second, I will present and discuss the typology of terrorist cell members. Third, I will apply the model in case studies, surveying the backgrounds and recruitment narratives of core members of two well-known terrorist cells that operated in Europe. I argue that the selected cells constitute good examples on jihadi terrorism in the European context.

I draw two main conclusions. First, the most important motivational factor in the formation of the terrorist cells was a desire for activism, be it social, political or religious, or various combinations of the three. The reason for this is that the leading personalities whom I refer to as "entrepreneurs" (because they "build" terrorist cells) embrace violent ideologies and take part in terrorism through activism, and seemingly through more proactive, conscious and intellectual processes than other members of cells (relatively speaking). The entrepreneurs are mainly politically motivated activists and idealists, who, above all, call for social and political justice and fair treatment of fellow Muslims around the world. Data I will present in this chapter suggest the terrorist cells coalesced mainly as a result of interaction between such committed activists and what might be referred to as "the jihadi infrastructure", and mainly in response to politics at local, regional and global levels affecting Muslims.[8]

Second, the followers or "foot soldiers" of terrorist cells (who in fact constitute the majority of operatives) appear to become militants more passively, for a host of other reasons than activism and idealism. These reasons include personal problems, loyalty to friends and relatives, deprivation and lack of options, adventure and youth rebellion, etc. They seem to end up in jihadi milieus in a more coincidental manner because they encounter and befriend charismatic entrepreneurs, or because they are related to such persons in one way or another.

Jihadi terrorism in Europe – background, the general picture and some new tendencies

Jihadi terrorism in Europe is not a post-9/11 phenomenon. In the early to mid-1990s, the Algerian jihadi organization GIA[9] established networks in France and other European countries. These networks provided support for the local GIA fighting the secularist military regime in Algeria. Between 1994 and 1996 the GIA perpetrated a series of terrorist attacks in France, in protest against its political and military support for the Algerian regime. In response, French authorities cracked down hard on the organization. GIA members then relocated to the UK, and contributed to making London the hub for Islamist extremism and militancy in Europe. In 1998, coinciding with Al-Qaeda's bombing of the US embassies in Kenya and Tanzania, Algerian terrorists belonging to the GIA offshoot GSPC conceived of new attacks against French interests in Europe. After the 9/11 attacks, Europe has experienced rising levels of terrorism activities in Europe, intensifying after the invasions of Afghanistan and Iraq, and culminating in the Madrid and London bombings in 2004 and 2005.

Whereas the GIA's operations in France were mainly motivated by developments in Algeria, the new current of jihadi terrorism in Europe involved Muslims who had more complex motivations for becoming militants, and who were either associated with or inspired by Al-Qaeda.[10] Because the threat has evolved with time, I find it useful to talk about the situation before and after the Madrid bombings. The Madrid investigations revealed certain changes in the terrorist profiles, organizational affiliations, as well as motivational and operational patterns, which became more evident in subsequent cases in the UK, the Netherlands and in Scandinavia.[11]

Before the Madrid bombings in 2004, jihadi terrorism in Europe was dominated by North African immigrants.[12] They were recruited and radicalized through interaction with friends, relatives and acquaintances belonging to the European networks of the GSPC, Moroccan Islamic Combatant group, Libyan and Tunisian Islamic fighting groups and Al-Qaeda, centred in the UK (in radical mosques, in immigrant centres, in prisons and so forth). GSPC and Al-Qaeda were the dominant and most organized groups. The operatives were in their mid-20s or mid-30s. Their occupations varied, but most had low levels of education, and survived on odd jobs, temping, social welfare or criminal activities. There were a few examples of educated persons with steady jobs amongst the leading personalities in the terrorist cells, but they constitute a minority. After connecting to the jihadi underworld in Europe, they travelled to Afghanistan, where they received terrorist training in camps controlled mainly by the GSPC and Al-Qaeda. Core operatives met and befriended leading figures of these organizations, who in some instances would give guidelines for attacks in Europe, as well as logistical and financial support. Typically, the North Africans would plan and prepare mass casualty terrorist bomb attacks (sometimes suicide attacks). Their target selection reflected their affiliations with the Algerian jihadis, their European support networks and Al-Qaeda in Afghanistan. Accordingly, they frequently targeted the Algerians' European archenemy, France, and Al-Qaeda's enemy number one, the US.

The Madrid operation occurred after a series of key developments such as the invasion of Afghanistan, the destruction of Al-Qaeda's training camps, the arrests of a large number of Al-Qaeda lieutenants, the weakening of Al-Qaeda's core organization, the invasion of Iraq and the rise of the jihadi resistance against the coalition, tightened security inside the US and inside Europe after 9/11, communiqués by the Al-Qaeda leaders specifying all the European contributors in Iraq as legitimate targets, and last but not least the proliferation of and sophistication of the jihadi Internet. The combined effect of these developments was a totally different operational environment for the jihadis. It caused debates amongst the militants about why the jihad should continue, and in what way. Moreover, it provided militant leaders and ideologues with new arguments, symbols and means of communication that could be used to mobilize potential recruits amongst Muslim youth in Europe and other parts of the world. By 2004, Iraq had become the main strategic focal point for the militants, something which became evident for Europeans when jihadis launched attacks in Madrid in order to put pressure on Spanish authorities to pull their soldiers out of Iraq.[13]

Madrid marked a tendency towards the formation of terrorist cells that were inspired by, rather than associated with, Al-Qaeda.[14] After Madrid, militant milieus in Europe have undergone a twin process of Europeanization and juvenilization. In the wake of Madrid, police in many countries uncovered terrorist cells that were composed of younger people, even teenagers, most of them born and raised in Europe. Many had some level of education and technical skill. They were very Internet savvy, and they looked to the Internet for ideological inspiration, strategic texts and tactical advice, selectively cutting and pasting what legitimized the use of violence in Europe.[15] Along with, and probably as a result of, the juvenilization tendency, jihadi terrorist cells in Europe have become more ethnically diverse, and there have been several examples that women or girls have been involved in terrorist activities. As observed by Lindsay Clutterbuck, there have also been an increasing number of incidents over the last couple of years involving singletons, or "lone actors", who planned acts of terrorism in Europe.[16] This might indicate a tendency towards a more "individualized jihad", which is a strategy advocated by one of the leading Al-Qaeda theoreticians, Abu Musab al-Suri, but it is too early to conclude on this at the moment.[17]

The rapid changes in the sociology of jihadism in Europe make it very difficult to generalize about the terrorists' motivations, personal characteristics and recruitment narratives (the very reason why I attempted to develop a typology). To the extent I dare generalize, the terrorists can be described as quite normal, but somehow troubled young adults. They appear to have been lax about religion before they became involved with extremists and militants. Several have been described (or have described themselves) as not being pious Muslims in the past (who, for example, did not pray or go regularly to the mosque, they smoked, drank alcohol, used and dealt drugs, were involved in crime, etc.) Some claim to have been exposed to racism in Europe. Others allege that they have been persecuted by European police and security services. Some went through personal crises before they were recruited to militancy, such as divorce, death in the family, etc. However, these are all troubles experienced by non-Muslim immigrants and ethnic Europeans alike, without causing similar levels of violent radicalization. Through connecting with Europe's jihadi underworld in radical mosques, immigrant centres, cafes, private apartments, gyms, prisons and so forth, or by surfing extremist web sites, they appear to have experienced "cognitive openings",[18] become "newborn Muslims", and explored jihadi doctrines. They attended sermons of extremist and militant preachers in European cities. Recruiters showed them propaganda movies of injustices against Muslims in Algeria, Bosnia, Chechnya and Palestine. Or, they accessed such propaganda material on the Internet. They were advised to go to Afghanistan, Pakistan or Saudi Arabia to learn more about their religion and their obligation to wage jihad.

The broader picture is that radicalization appears to be caused by various combinations of personal problems, social frustrations and grievances, deprivation and yearning for identity, adventure and youth rebellion, and political grievances related to Europe, the Muslim world, as well as global politics. However, as we will see in the following, the relative importance of different kinds of motivations seems to vary between the terrorists.

A tentative typology of jihadi terrorists in Europe

In order to try and detect systematic differences in the reasons why terrorists embraced violent jihad, I tried to categorize them according to their backgrounds, activities, personalities and roles. As I have highlighted in the introduction, leading experts consider the search for a "terrorist profile" to be futile. Efforts to try and categorize terrorists might therefore be considered somewhat controversial. Moreover, surveying secretive, ultra-violent terrorist networks is by definition methodologically challenging. It is highly difficult, and sometimes impossible to obtain sufficient amounts of reliable sources to conduct meaningful analyses. In addition there are problems connected to identifying units of analysis (for example, who are/are not actual members of the terrorist cell), and finding ways of identifying as well as "measuring" motivations. Another difficulty which relates to terrorism studies in general is that there is no consensus on the meanings of central concepts such as terrorism, radicalization and recruitment.

Considering the methodological pitfalls, I am obliged to stress the limitations of the model as well as the empirical findings. The typology should be seen as an empirical systematic description (based on the available sources) of the different features of core members of eight jihadi terrorist cells that operated in Europe (and that pursued very similar goals through similar means), nothing more, and nothing less. I also have to stress that descriptions of character traits should not be considered professional psychological or psychiatric evaluations.

However, through a sustained and systematic collection of open source material over the past four years, I have been able to empirically document the terrorist cells and the backgrounds of the members in a surprisingly comprehensive manner. Although the picture is not complete, and there are certain imbalances in the level of detail I have managed to obtain in the descriptions of different cells and people, I argue that this material provides a solid empirical basis for analytical generalization about motivational aspects of recruitment processes. The sources and the use of sources will be discussed briefly in connection with the case studies below. As noted in the introduction, my analysis focused on the core group of each terrorist cell, the cell leader and the cadre who were posed to participate in the attacks. Based on observations of what they said and did, and how others depicted them, I singled out four main categories of cell members that recurred across cases: the *entrepreneurs*, the *protégés*, the *misfits* and the *drifters*. As we will see, each category appeared to embrace jihadism somehow differently. Of course, these are "ideal types" discerned by backgrounds, characteristics and roles. The categories are by no means exhaustive. Some cell members defied categorization, while in other cases, it was impossible to find sufficient information about them. In addition, certain cells were dominated by one category of people, for example, some cells feature more misfits (i.e. people with troubled backgrounds, such as drug addicts and criminals) than others.

The entrepreneurs

The heads of the cells, the entrepreneurs, are critical for terrorist cells to coalesce and go operational. They proactively connect with jihadi networks, and they proactively recruit, socialize and train their cadre. Once a cell is consolidated, entrepreneurs are in charge of its operational activities. They also control the cells' external relations with the jihadi infrastructure, operational and ideological mentors. Sometimes, entrepreneurs have been jihadi activists in their original home countries, and sometimes they have received training in Afghanistan, Pakistan, Chechnya, Bosnia or other places (in future cases they might possess fighting experiences from Iraq). They are typically (but not always) senior to and more experienced than their accomplices, and socially well-functioning. Some are educated and employed; others lack higher education, but get by on odd jobs, welfare, legal and illicit business activities, as well as funding by jihadi individuals or groups such as Al-Qaeda. Several have wives and children.

The entrepreneurs are charismatic religious and political activists possessing a strong sense of justice. They are passionate about and committed to social and political causes and demand respect from their surroundings. They are not militants for their own sake, it seems, but out of what they consider a religious duty to defend others. One might say they want to do good for those they consider "their people" or "their communities", based on ethnicity, common background and destiny, faith or other bonds. They seem to be genuinely concerned with the situation for fellow Muslims on the European scene and globally, and typically enraged by the suffering of Muslims in places such as Palestine, Chechnya, Afghanistan, Kashmir, Iraq and so forth (i.e. the conflicts addressed most often by Al-Qaeda). Entrepreneurs are not into party politics, but some dedicate themselves to NGO activism. They have high aspirations, and sometimes they have failed ambitions on their records.

Entrepreneurs embrace jihadism gradually through intellectual processes, activism, idealism and a call for social and political justice. Frustrated with political affairs and poor prospects of having much influence through non-violent means, the entrepreneurs will seek alternative ways to making a difference. They might then become attracted to the action-oriented religious interpretations disseminated by extremists and militants. In the end they take on a "project" for concrete individuals and groups associated with Al-Qaeda, or within the framework of Al-Qaeda's doctrines. Entrepreneurs are typically well read and sometimes they contribute with their own ideas through preaching or writing texts.

The protégés

The protégés are similar to the entrepreneurs, but junior and inferior to them. They are typically second in command of cells. Protégés are also devout idealists and activists with strong personalities and a strong sense of justice, and they are very close to, and seem to be admiring, their mentors. They seem to embrace militancy through a combination of loyalty to the leader and intellectually justified activism (social, religious and political). The dominant motivation, parallel to the entrepreneurs, appears to be political grievances related to the treatment of fellow Muslims locally and internationally.

Protégés tend to be very intelligent, well-educated and well-mannered persons, who excel in what they do, professionally, academically and socially. Through being educated, they might provide the cells with needed expertise (for example, bomb making or IT skills). Skilled, but at times very young, they have limited life experience, and might be impressionable and quite easily manipulated by elders they respect and look up to (such as the entrepreneurs).

The presence of such characters in the cells tells us something about the sophistication of the entrepreneurs and the ideology they convey to their cadre. It indicates that jihadism appeals to highly intelligent, socially skilled and well-off people, social segments that, according to classical rational choice arguments, would have a lot to lose by engaging in terrorist activity.

Indicative of the entrepreneurs' and the protégés' commitment is that I did not manage to find examples of these characters turning informant after they were arrested. On the contrary, in trials and in rare press interviews, captured entrepreneurs and protégés show no signs of remorse for being involved in terrorism, and appear consistent in their belief that terrorism is a legitimate means of armed resistance and an individual duty for Muslims worldwide.[19]

The misfits

The misfits are individuals that perform less well socially, and they often have troubled backgrounds as well as criminal records. They appear to be less ideologically committed than the entrepreneurs and the protégés. They also appear to have somewhat "weaker" and more hesitant personalities, and display more personal vulnerabilities than the former. Misfits typically join the militants to cope with personal problems or out of loyalty to their friends, or some combination of the two. One might characterize motivation for teaming up with militants as some sort of personal salvation or "self-healing".

Misfits might be recruited in prisons, or they might meet militants in the criminal underworld (as criminal activities are used to finance terrorist cells). The misfits are seldom well-educated, but they are typically streetwise and physically fit. Several of the misfits were into sports, and some of them were very talented.

The age of the misfits varies, but typically they too are younger than the entrepreneurs. They might be old friends or acquaintances of the cell leader or one of the other cell members, and the jihadis may propose to "straighten them out" and get them back on the right path by joining the jihad. Misfits do not enjoy a high status within cells, and at times there have been serious controversies between misfits and other elements of a cell, including the leader.

Some misfits have displayed violent tendencies and some have been convicted for acts of violence before they became involved with militants. Because they are physically fit, inclined to show violent tendencies, and familiar with criminal practices, the misfits are well suited for the execution of important practical tasks at the preparatory and operational level, such as being in charge of acquiring weapons and bomb making materials. As opposed to the consistency of the beliefs of entrepreneurs and protégés, we found at least two examples that misfits have turned informant after their arrests, and that they rejected terrorism as an illegitimate means of struggle.[20]

The drifters

The drifters do not constitute a well-defined category. It is indeed difficult to differentiate the drifters from entrepreneurs, protégés and misfits because they might have similar educational backgrounds, professions and general backgrounds. Drifters differ by having less specific reasons for teaming up with the jihadis in the first place. They tend to be people who are "going with the flow" rather unconsciously. The dominant motivations for joining appear to relate to social networks and commitments.

They do not come across as ideologically committed activists before they hook up with people belong to the militant networks. It appears more as if they become members of the cells by being in the wrong places at the wrong times, or having social ties to the wrong people. It seems as if the drifters could have gone in a very different direction if they had connected with other people and other milieus. It is their social networks (friendship, common background, shared experience) which determine where they end up, more than personal grievances associated with the misfits, and more than political grievances associated with the entrepreneurs and the protégés.

Possibly because of their "volatile" characteristics and dubious devotions, drifters are typically not entrusted with the most important tasks in the group, and they might not be privy to details about the terrorist operation. However, they do fulfil important support functions for the group. At times, recruitment of drifters also seems to involve stronger elements of youth rebellion, search for adventure and lack of viable options, than is the case for entrepreneurs, protégés and misfits.

Case studies

In the following case studies, I apply the typology to surveys of the recruitment narratives of core members of two well-known terrorist cells that operated in Europe. The first case is the cell headed by the French-Algerian terrorism convict Djamel Beghal that planned and prepared suicide bomb attacks against American targets in France and in Belgium in 2001. Beghal's cell was associated with Al-Qaeda and several North African jihadi organizations, most prominently the GSPC. I consider this terrorist cell typical of cells that were detected prior to the Madrid operation in 2004 (in terms of the terrorists' backgrounds, organizational affiliations, as well as operational and motivational patterns). The second case is the Al-Qaeda-inspired group headed by the British-Pakistani Mohammed Siddique Khan that executed the London attacks on 7 July 2005. I consider the London cell typical of terrorist cells revealed in Europe after the Madrid bombings.

My analysis of the recruitment narratives revolves around three main questions. First, who were the terrorists, what were their social characteristics? Second, what were the most important reasons they teamed up with militants and became involved in terrorist activities? And third, how did they become involved with militants and terrorist activities?

Note on sources

The analysis is mainly based on press sources, official reports and judicial documents. I have also accessed transcripts of interrogations and interviewed officials with first-hand knowledge about investigations into jihadi terrorist cells that have operated throughout the region. Given the nature of the research object, namely secret and violent terrorist networks, primary sources conveying the terrorists' points of views are quite hard to come by, and sometimes impossible to obtain. The available sources are therefore necessarily somewhat biased towards the perspective of prosecutors and investigators.

Nevertheless, through daily collecting of articles from local and international media outlets, databases and jihadi web sites, dating back to 2000, I have gathered a fair amount of biographical data and characterizations from more independent sources (friends and acquaintances, colleagues and family members), as well as statements and writings attributed to the terrorists, that enables us to balance the narratives to some degree.

The Beghal network

In the autumn of 2001, European security services (with assistance from American counterparts), detected and dismantled a terrorist cell headed by the French-Algerian Djamel Beghal. According to French and Belgian authorities, this cell planned and prepared suicide bomb attacks against American interests in France and Belgium (alleged targets: the American embassy in Paris and the American military airbase Kleine Brogel in Belgium).

The overall picture concerning the formation of the cell is that the charismatic cell-leader Beghal recruited and socialized his accomplices by converting them, feeding them with propaganda and setting them in contact with jihadis in Europe and Afghanistan. The sources I have accessed suggest that radical mosques and secretive meetings in apartments and other meeting places were the main venues of recruitment and radicalization. Moreover, the sources suggest that sermons of militant preachers had profound effects on core operatives. In addition, it seems that propaganda material provided by Al-Qaeda and like-minded groups, such as videotapes of suffering of Muslims in Chechnya and Palestine, were used quite extensively as a tool for the recruitment, indoctrination or socialization of operatives.

Following are the backgrounds and recruitment narratives of convicted members of Beghal's terrorist network according to the typology.

Djamel Beghal

In my interpretation, Djamel Beghal can be characterized as a "prototype" jihadi entrepreneur. He was a social and religious activist who was politicized, and in the end took on a terrorist project for Al-Qaeda and its associates. He appears to have embraced violent ideologies gradually between 1994 and 1997. His radicalization accelerated under the influence of militant clerics in London from 1997 onwards, and, according to the French verdict, by 1998, Beghal was considered "operational".[21]

Beghal was born in Algeria in 1965, but grew up in the French working-class suburb Corbeilles-Essone. He has been described as intelligent and charismatic, and someone who integrated well – at least on the surface. He spoke French fluently, married a French woman and they had three children. I found no accounts about secular educational background (and therefore assume he has no higher education from French universities). Workwise, he appears to have got by on odd jobs and temping. It appears Beghal was a non-violent religious and social activist before he became politicized and radicalized through his interaction with GIA activists in France, and his sympathizing with their struggle against the Algerian regime and its French allies.

According to the French verdict, in 1994 he belonged to the non-violent Jamaat Dawa wa Tabligh, the pietistic missionary movement which alongside its promotion of Islamic faith provides help to the poor and needy. He studied religion and was inspired by several Islamist intellectuals and preachers, including moderate, so-called "progressive reformists" such as Hassan al-Banna's grandson, the Swiss academic Tariq Ramadan. According to the *New York Times's* biography, Beghal was rounded up in the French counter-terrorism campaign against GIA activists as early as 1994. The same source claims that between 1994 and 1997 Beghal started to preach in "storefront mosques" and Islamic centres, and that he raised money for Chechen separatists and Muslims in Bosnia.[22]

According to the French verdict, Beghal first became known to the Direction de la Surveillance du Territore (DST) in 1997, after he was arrested in connection with a crackdown of the so-called "Abbas Benbellil Network" (GIA network). Later the same year he moved with his family to Leicester, UK, and became a student of the militant preachers and ideologues Abu Qatada and Abu Hamza at the UK centre for Islamist militancy, the Finsbury Park mosque in London. Beghal soon was amongst most extreme (Takfiri)[23] worshippers at the mosque. Qatada appears to have been the most important inspiration for Beghal at this point. Omar Mohammed Othman aka Abu Omar aka Omar Abu Omar aka Abu Qatada enjoys a high standing in the militant Islamist underground milieus worldwide. He is considered one of the most important ideological mentors for militant groups such as the GIA/GSPC, Al-Qaeda, al-Tawhid and several other extremist and militant groups operating in the West and in the Muslim world. According to the French verdict, Beghal was also inspired by and in contact with the Paris-based Egyptian preacher al-Hariri (Cheik Abdallah), as well as the Moroccan militant preacher Mohammad al-Fizazi in Morocco (Beghal denied this in court).

By moving to London, Beghal followed the tracks of many GIA leaders and operatives before him, who had relocated to London after French counter-terrorism cracked down on the GIA networks in France. In Leicester Beghal established his own pro-GIA group, and in London he forged contacts with prominent members of the Algerian groups GIA, GSPC and FIS, Tunisian Islamic Fighting Group, Libyan Islamic Fighting Group, Moroccan militants and Al-Qaeda.

Influenced by Qatada, Beghal started to recruit accomplices for militant activities in about 1998. He converted friends and relatives and introduced them to conservative Islam and extreme ideas. In interrogations, several members of Beghal's group characterized each other as Takfiris.[24]

Members and affiliates of the cell portray Beghal as very charismatic, active and enthusiastic, and knowledgeable about Islam. Several said he was the one that converted them to Islam. He was the entrepreneur, the fixer, the organizer of the activities of the militants. He was always on the move, giving orders, making appointments, moving money, people, documents and messages. Indicative of Beghal's wish and ability to influence and control his social networks is that, at one point, he appears to have been involved in the abduction of the children of a Libyan friend (from their British mother) in Norwich, UK, in 2000, in order to send them to Libya.[25] In the UK, Beghal and his followers sometimes approached Muslims on the streets and actively tried to convince them about their duty to participate in jihad. Beghal's cadres were feared even by other extremists because they were viewed as too fanatical.

Djamel Beghal travelled extensively together with fellow Mujahidin in Europe and in the Muslim world (Saudi Arabia, Morocco and Afghanistan). Beghal became a professional recruiter for militant groups. He facilitated trips to camps in Afghanistan for potential Holy Warriors. He was indeed crucial to the conversion, radicalization and recruitment of the members of his terrorist cell, as well as people outside his immediate circle.

In 2000 he moved with his family to Jalalabad, and trained in the Derunta training complex together with the other members of the terrorist cell. In Afghanistan, he met several top Al-Qaeda leaders such as Osama bin Laden himself, Ayman al-Zawahiri, Abu Zubaydah and Abu Hafs "The Mauritanian". In 2001 Beghal received a mission from one of bin Laden's top aides, Abu Zubaydah, to form a terrorist cell and start preparations for an operation in Europe.[26]

From amongst his extensive circle of extremist friends he selected a group of operatives which would plan and prepare terrorist attacks against US interests in Europe to be launched during the spring of 2002. Core members of the cell were friends and relatives, such as the young, intelligent, computer engineer Kamel Daoudi, the former professional soccer player Nizar Trabelsi, and Beghal's brother-in-law, the Frenchman Johan Bonte. According to a testimony Beghal gave to interrogators in Dubai (which was later retracted because he claimed he had been tortured), he received three symbolic gifts (toothpick, prayer beads and a flask of incense) from Osama bin Laden as a sign that Beghal's operation cell had "The Sheikh's" blessing.[27]

Kamel Daoudi

Like Beghal, his protégé Kamel Daoudi was born in Algeria (in 1974) and raised in France from the age of five. Mentored and inspired by Beghal and radical preachers in Paris and the UK, Daoudi appears to have embraced militant Islamism through intellectual processes and through political activism in support of the Algerian militant Islamists' battle against the Algerian regime and France.[28]

In his memoirs written in prison, which were published in part by the *New York Times*, he expresses strong hatred against the Algerian regime for annulling the 1992 elections and sending the country into a bloody civil war, and by extension against France and the West for letting it happen and supporting it. In his own words,

> The West hated us because we were Arabs and Muslims. France did everything possible to ensure that Algeria would not be an Islamic state. It backed an illegitimate and profoundly one-sided regime by sending weapons, helicopters and even the Foreign Legion (not many people know about that). The massacres committed by the Algerian army were the last straw for me. I could no longer study serenely.[29]

According to himself, Daoudi had a happy childhood. His father was an immigrant hospital worker in France who supported his wife and children in Algeria before he brought them to Europe in 1979. Daoudi lived up to his father's ambitions for him to excel in school and he received good grades. He took classes in French, English, Spanish, Arabic, Latin and ancient Greek, flirting with the idea of becoming an anthropologist or a paleontologist, but pragmatism made him choose a technical education instead. At school, French kids made fun of the intelligent youngster because of his Arab name and for his (according to him) "excessive modesty in the eyes of French children". At one point he also dreamt about becoming a fighter pilot, but because of poor eyesight he settled instead for aeronautical engineering at a French University. When the civil war began in Algeria, he "started to worry about religious and political questions". He was antagonized by France for sending weapons, helicopters and legionnaires to Algeria to support the Algerian army, and by extension other Western nations. Moreover, he saw as yet another sign of a conspiracy against Muslims in France the fact that he and his family were evicted from their middle-class apartment and had to move back to the gritty Paris suburbs.[30]

Daoudi portrays his radicalization as an intellectual process, which involved reading "the great contemporary writers of political Islam" (in French and English). He also travelled to Algeria to see for himself the suffering of his native countrymen that was facilitated by the former colonial power. In the typical manner of "Al-Qaedaism", Daoudi links the war in Algeria with injustices against Muslims in Bosnia, Iraq (Gulf War), Kosovo Afghanistan and Palestine, and blames it all on the Christian–Jewish Crusader alliance "influenced by atheism". He ends his memoirs by reassuring that his "ideological commitment is total".[31]

Daoudi appears to have been close to Beghal. It seems Beghal was central in his conversion to Islamist extremism, and he was trusted with important tasks in the group, such as securing communications on the Internet and bomb making. Daoudi lived in Beghal's flat with another accomplice in 1998 after Beghal had relocated to Leicester.[32] A sign of Daoudi's commitment is that he never excused his actions and never became an informant. He also appears to have been highly secretive about his activities and contacts (keeping family and wife in the dark about what he was up to).

Nizar Trabelsi

Nizar Trabelsi was born in Sfax, Tunisia in 1970. Trabelsi could probably be characterized as the social misfit amongst Beghal's closest accomplices, although he also displayed some level of idealism and manipulative behaviour most often associated with entrepreneurs.[33]

It is believed that Trabelsi was the designated suicide bomber for planned bomb attacks against either the American embassy in Paris or the American airbase Kleine Brogel in Belgium.[34] He himself admitted in court to have planned and prepared an attack in Belgium, known as "operation Muntasir (victorious)", acting on orders from Al-Qaeda. According to the French verdict, the plans were masterminded by Al-Qaeda's military leaders, and sponsored by bin Laden.[35] Trabelsi's statements and actions suggest a different recruitment path and a different level of commitment than Beghal and Daoudi. He appears to have embraced militancy mainly as a means to cope with personal problems and out of loyalty to friends and role models, such as Djamel Beghal, and Al-Qaeda's emir bin Laden.

It is also fair to characterize Trabelsi as an atypical Islamist extremist. He was a talented footballer who played on the Tunisian national team in his youth. In 1989 he became a professional player for the German club Fortuna Dusseldorf. He played for several German teams before his career went downhill and ended in 1995. He appears to have made a decent income, and at one point he even owned his own restaurant. According to former team-mates and coaches, Trabelsi came across as a kind, shy and moderately religious person who did not talk about politics. They have explained to the press that, despite this, he had serious problems fitting in amongst his colleagues, and that he was hassled because of his ethnic background and religion.[36]

Faced with racism and other problems such as a failed marriage, Trabelsi started underperforming on the football field, which resulted in cancelled contracts. Trabelsi first found comfort in drugs, and became involved in crime. Between 1994 and 1998 the former athlete and restaurant owner was charged with several crimes (in Germany, Belgium and the Netherlands), including cocaine trafficking.

In 1996, in Dusseldorf, Trabelsi's life took an unexpected turn. According to the French verdict, he met the Al-Qaeda-associated Baghdad Meziane aka "Abu Abdallah from Leicester", a friend of Beghal and a follower of Qatada. Abu Abdallah was the one who formally converted Trabelsi to Islam. In 1997, he met with Djamel Beghal and was fascinated by his eloquence and knowledge about Islam.[37] He became part of Beghal's circle and attended sermons of Qatada in London. As part of his ideological indoctrination and jihadi activism, he travelled extensively between European countries (Germany, Belgium, the Netherlands and UK), and out of the region to Saudi Arabia, Yemen, Pakistan and Afghanistan. He trained at an Al-Qaeda camp in Jalalabad in 2000, bringing along his second wife (who stayed at a special location for the women of the mujahidin).

In Afghanistan he met Daoudi and others who would constitute Beghal's terrorist cell. Also, when in Afghanistan, according to himself, he encountered bin Laden on several occasions. He claimed "The Shaykh" stood up for him when he was criticized by Arab mujahidin for handing out money to Afghans, and helped him get listed for suicide bombings – although "the list of martyrs was full".[38] Trabelsi claimed to have visited bin Laden at a house in Jalalabad two times, staying several days each time, and in court he boasted about having played football in bin Laden's courtyard.[39] During these visits he said he became "deeply impressed" by bin Laden, and that he came to love him "like a father".[40]

Despite his encounters with prominent Al-Qaeda leaders (he also claimed to have met al-Zawahiri, Abu Zubaydah and Abu Hafs al-Masri), Trabelsi appears to have been an outsider in Beghal's group, and according to his second wife, the two of them were viewed by the others as impure Muslims. Moreover, it appears that there were, at times, critical tensions between Beghal and Trabelsi related to the latter's religious credibility and money issues. During the trial, Trabelsi said he no longer supported bin Laden and Al-Qaeda, and, using a soccer metaphor, he said that "there will be no second half" in his involvement in terrorism. He also provided useful information to the authorities about militant networks operating in Europe.[41]

The Courtallier brothers and Johan Bonte

The French butcher's sons and former Catholics, David and Jerome Courtallier, and Beghal's brother-in-law Johan Bonte appear to have been at the fringes of the terrorist cell. It seems they drifted into Beghal's network mainly through their social networks (friendship and kinship), in a more coincidental manner. Their backgrounds resemble that of misfits in the sense that there were some troubles (drugs and youth rebellion), although not of the more serious kind.

There is not much in their statements and actions pointing to sincere ideological commitment and activism. It seems safe to assume, however, that once they had become part of Beghal's group they were socialized and indoctrinated into the jihadi worldview. Still, there is little to suggest that rage over the suffering of Muslims in places such as Chechnya and an altruistic urge to provide help for victims of war was what drew them to extremist circles in the first place.

David and Jerome Courtallier were handsome, athletic young men from the French Alps, who excelled in sports and were popular with the girls. After their father's business collapsed, and their parents divorced, they started to abuse drugs, and soon found themselves in a situation with few good prospects for the future. David was advised by "friends" to go to the UK to change his life. He moved there and started frequenting mosques and encountered extremists.

In 1997 it appears both brothers lived in Leicester, and were under the influence of radicals. Later, David lived for a while in an apartment belonging to Djamel Beghal, and encountered several key suspects in the case. His extremist friends urged him to go to Afghanistan for training and so he did, although his motives for going appear mixed; a combination of boredom, lack of options and urge for adventure. He commented to the press, "Going there was going to be great ... I had never traveled ... I was taken care of totally".[42]

Johan Bonte does not come across as an ardent activist either, but rather someone who got to know the charismatic Beghal through his sister, and became part of Beghal's gang of militants. Bonte's short prison sentence (one year) probably indicates that he played a subordinate role in the activities of the cell. However, he knew the key players well and interacted with them regularly. He travelled with members of the group to Belgium. He stayed with Beghal and his wife for a while in Leicester and interacted with well-known jihadis. Also he did practical favours for Beghal, and in interrogations he referred to Beghal and the milieu surrounding him as "our group".[43]

The London bombings

On the 7 July 2005, a terrorist cell composed of three British nationals of Pakistani origins and one of Jamaican origin launched a terrorist attack against the Underground and a bus in central London. The terrorist cell was headed by the 30-year-old social worker Mohammed Siddique Khan. At the time of writing, we do not know whether Al-Qaeda was implicated in the planning and preparations for the attacks. In a video tape published in July 2006, produced by Al-Qaeda's media production company al-Sahab and featuring the testament of one of the bombers, Shehzad Tanweer, the organization took credit for the attacks and boasted that it had supported and trained core operatives of the cell. However, the tape does not show the London bombers together with known Al-Qaeda members, and although one cannot rule out that Al-Qaeda was involved, it might very well have been a propaganda stunt by the organization trying to convince the world that it maintains an operational capacity.[44]

Massive investigative efforts have yet to disclose direct links to Al-Qaeda operatives or leaders, according to the "Report of the Official Account of the Bombings in London on 7th July 2005 (hereafter Official Account).[45] Although no-one has been able to confirm direct links to the core of Al-Qaeda, the group of Siddique Khan was clearly inspired by Al-Qaeda's ideology and acted within its strategic framework. Moreover, according to the Official Account, it can certainly not be ruled out that Mohammed Siddique Khan and Shehzad Tanweer might have had meetings with Al-Qaeda associates in Pakistan in 2005. According to the Official Account, there are also indications that Khan might have been in Afghanistan for training in the late 1990s, but authorities have not been able to verify this.

A closer look at the backgrounds and recruitment narratives of the London bombers reveals striking similarities with the group of Djamel Beghal. For example, the leading personalities in the cell, Khan and his protégé Tanweer, appear to have been ardent social and political activist who were genuinely concerned with the situation for fellow Muslims internationally. It seems quite certain that they were the ones taking the lead in establishing the cell, organizing the attacks and interacting with the jihadi infrastructure. Recruitment appears to have involved contacts with radical milieus and frequenting radical mosques in the UK, listening to sermons of well-known militant preachers, exposure to propaganda material such as ideological texts and films, and possibly spending time in training facilities in Pakistan.

Mohammed Siddique Khan

Mohammed Siddique Khan (30) aka "Sid" must be considered the entrepreneur of the terrorist cell behind the London bombings. Press reports and the Official Account strongly suggest he was central in recruiting and radicalizing the other members of the cell, and that he was in control of the activities of the cell. There are several parallels between the role played by Khan and the role played by Djamel Beghal.

Khan was born and raised in Leeds, UK. His parents were immigrants from Pakistan. Khan lived close to the Beeston area of Leeds all of his life. He moved to the nearby area of Dewsbury after he got married in 2001, but continued to work in Beeston. Khan enrolled at Leeds Metropolitan University in 1996 to study business. According to the Official Account, it was at the University he first developed "a vocation for helping disadvantaged people". During his studies he worked part-time as a community worker. At University he also met his future wife. She was a British Muslim of Indian origin, who was a committed social activist too, concerned with women's rights, and who allegedly held anti-Taliban views. Other sources bear witness of Khan's activism at this stage. In 1997, Khan participated in a demonstration in Leeds arranged by The Kashmiri Welfare Association. The Association rallied against a decision by Leeds City Council allowing a housing company to build houses on a location which they had hoped could be used for a new community centre. At this event, Siddique Khan gave an interview to the *Yorkshire Evening Post* in which he stated that "a centre is needed more than anything around here. There are a lot of problems for youths and we need somewhere to meet. The existing centre is too small."[46]

When he finished his studies, Khan got a job as an advisor, or a "learning mentor" at a local Hillside Primary School. He worked there between March 2001 and November 2004, when he quit after a period of frequent absences. From the start he appears to have been extraordinarily committed to the job. He was well regarded by his colleagues and the pupils' parents. Youths looked up to him and saw him as a father figure whom they nicknamed "Buddy". His work appears to have been primarily focused on assisting children from immigrant families arriving in the UK. It seems that Khan was successful both professionally and in the private domain. He had a steady job, in which he was given much responsibility. He had one child together with his equally committed social worker wife, and the couple was expecting a second one. Moreover, it seems the couple had a decent income and could afford to buy their own house and a car. However, according to the press, the couple was experiencing some marital problems and split up after having their first child in May 2004.[47]

Khan was vocal and outgoing in his social activism, and he has been quoted in several newspapers. For example, in 2002 he was interviewed by The Times in connection with the work he was doing, expressing pride that some of the children he mentored said that school was "the best school they have been to", but at the same time he expressed frustration that the city council was not providing sufficient funding for regeneration of his home town.

Khan also ran an Islamic bookshop in Leeds, and he established two local gyms with government funding. The first one was established in February 2000, in the name of the Kashmiri Welfare Association, a charity associated with the Hardy Street mosque in Beeston. The second gym was set up in 2004 on Lodge Lane in Beeston, as part of the Hamara Centre charitable foundation's youth programme. The latter had not been officially opened, but all the members of the terrorist cell trained there in the months before the operation. They also met at the bookshop ran by Khan, and in the basement of a local mosque. There are no openly available records about what really went on in these meeting places for young Muslims in Leeds. Rumours and hearsay in the local community point in different directions. Some say they were places in which extremists lectured and in which youngsters could watch propaganda on DVD, videos and on the Internet. One friend of Shehzad Tanweer, who was interviewed by the *Washington Post*, says he once saw Tanweer and Khan watching a DVD of an Israeli soldier killing a Palestinian girl in the bookshop. Others contest such descriptions and deny that the gyms, bookshop and youth clubs were extremist hubs.

Although vocal about social activism, Khan did not express political opinions openly. Colleagues and friends noticed that he gradually became more religious, but he did not voice extreme political views, and publicly opposed the 9/11 operations in the US. The highly politicized video testament which was released after the bombings stands in stark contrast to the way in which he has been portrayed by others, namely as a religious observant, but non-political person, focused on social activism at the local level. Although difficult to pinpoint when, Khan connected to the jihadi infrastructure through extremists in London. According to unconfirmed press reports Khan, Tanweer and Lindsay had been observed attending the sermons of radical sheikhs in London, such as Abu Hamza.[48] According to UK authorities the names of Khan and Tanweer popped up at the fringes of an investigation of an alleged terrorist cell which was dismantled in March 2004 (this case which is referred to as "Operation Crevice" involved a group of young British-Pakistanis suspected of planning and preparing terrorist bomb attacks in London[49]).

Shehzad Tanweer

Shehzad Tanweer (22) appears to have been Siddique Khan's protege, and his narrative parallels that of Kamel Daoudi, an intelligent youngster who embraced the doctrine presented to him by the mentor mainly through intellectual processes and in response to politics. Tanweer, who was nicknamed "Khaka", was also raised in Beeston, Leeds. His parents were Pakistani immigrants to the UK, and he had three siblings. Tanweer's father came to the UK to study textile manufacturing. He built a business including a butcher's shop and a fish and chip shop, in which Tanwer would occasionally work. Tanweer's family is financially well off and well respected in the local community. The Tanweers have in fact been described as the "classic immigrant success story".[50]

According to the press, the Tanweer family was moderately religious and attended Friday sermons at the local mosque, but they rarely prayed five times a day. Tanweer studied Sports Science at Leeds Metropolitan University. He excelled as an athlete and especially as a cricketer. He reportedly dreamt about becoming a professional cricket player. Tanweer has been described as an intelligent and socially adept person, who received good grades at school and university. Friends describe him as a handsome and lively young man with a sense of humour. There is no evidence he experienced social problems of any sort, or that he was exposed to racism. He was known to take care of his appearance. He was fashionably dressed, wore expensive sportswear and owned his own car. Although he was well off and had good prospects for obtaining personal success, Tanweer seems to have cared as much about other people as he did about himself. Like his mentor Siddique Khan, it appears Tanweer was an idealist with a social consciousness and a vocation for community work and activism. For example, he used to volunteer to organize sports activities for children at a local community centre, and it appears he was doing social work for the non-political Jamaat al-Dawa wa-al-Tabligh missionary movement.

The radicalization of Tanweer is a puzzle. A childhood friend interviewed by the *Washington Post* said Tanweer did not express an interest in politics, and during their time together she had never seen him read newspapers or watch television news. To her knowledge, Tanweer had not attended demonstrations against the UK involvement in Iraq and Afghanistan.[51] However, other friends talk about Tanweer's "political and religious transformation" when he was turning 18, when he allegedly distanced himself from British traditions and behaviour and started hanging out with Islamist extremists. Some friends point to 11 September as a radicalizing factor for Tanweer, and one portrayed this event as an eye-opener. At some point Tanweer met Khan at one of the gyms in Beeston. According to the Official Account, Tanweer "had known him a little" when he was a child, but after they met again they seem to have grown very close to each other.[52] It appears that this special relationship with Khan was the factor that pushed Tanweer into a more radical direction. The two spent much time together. Sometimes they were together with the other members of the cell Jermaine Lindsay and Hasib Hussain, and other times they were on their own. They attended various Islamic events in Leeds and the nearby areas. According to press reports they also travelled to London and attended the sermons of Abu Hamza at the Finsbury Park mosque.[53]

Khan, his accomplices and other youths who frequented the gyms, the bookshop and the mosque-basement, organized physical outdoor activities such as white-water rafting and paintball games. Khan and Tanweer went on a camping trip together in April 2003 and on a white-water rafting trip in June 2005. In November 2004 Khan and Tanweer travelled to Pakistan and stayed there until February 2005. In Pakistan, Tanweer stayed with his family in Punjab, whereas Khan was at an unknown location, in which he allegedly met with Kashmiri militants or Al-Qaeda operatives. The fact that only Tanweer accompanied Khan on this trip to Pakistan supports the theory that Tanweer was Khan's protégé and the most trusted member of the cell.

Tanweer's alleged statements to his relatives in Pakistan provided the first glimpses into how Tanweer had been politicized through interacting with Khan and other extremists. The relatives noticed that he had changed his appearance and acted in a more religious way when he was in Pakistan. He grew a beard and prayed five times a day. He initiated discussions about religious issues and politics and he vehemently criticized UK policies in relation to the conflict in Kashmir, the country's involvement in Iraq and Afghanistan, and he expressed admiration for bin Laden and Al-Qaeda. He referred to bin Laden as his personal hero, and said "everything he did was right", that "America had made Muslims suffer all over the world", and "that India was committing great atrocities against the Muslims", according to relatives.[54] It seems the conflict about Kashmir was a very important element in his political motivations. He was an ardent supporter of the separatist movement, and used to send money he received from his father for personal use to buy coats for Muslim fighters in Kashmir.[55] He also displayed strong anti-American sentiments and hatred against the West in general. He was reportedly very upset about the deaths of civilians in Iraq.[56] Accounts about an earlier visit to the family in Punjab together with his father for a period in 2002 suggest he was less devout and politicized at that time than he appeared during the visit in the run-up to the 7/7 operation.

In the video testament published by al-Sahab in July 2006, Tanweer appears as a full-blown jihadi echoing the messages of the Al-Qaeda leaders, specifying the countries in which Muslims suffer at the hands of the UK government (Palestine, Afghanistan, Iraq and Chechnya) and placing the responsibility directly with the victims of the London operation, "the non-Muslim of Britain", "those who have voted in your government", the "government that has openly supported the genocide of 150,000 Muslims in Fallujah".[57]

Hasib Hussain

The trail of the youngest of the London bombers, Hasib Hussain (18), depicts a youngster who in several ways might be characterized as a social misfit. Certain elements of his life story echo the background of Nizar Trabelsi. Hussain, it seems, became vulnerable to indoctrination by extremist friends and role models because he failed to adjust properly to his social environment, was frustrated, and lacked viable options and skills to deal with his own situation.

Hussain lived with his family in the Leeds suburb of Holbeck his entire life. Reportedly, the teenager had a slightly more troubled social background than the other members of the cell. According to *The Times*, Hussain and Tanweer were good friends, but they were quite opposite types of person. Hussain struggled at school and had problems fitting in socially. He is also said to have lived in the shadow of an older brother who was an excellent athlete and did well in school. From September 1998 till July 2003, Hussain attended Matthew Murray High School, completing vocational business studies. Hussain did not succeed academically. He was keen on sports, such as cricket, hockey and football, but he was not a very talented athlete according to friends, relatives and acquaintances interviewed by the press.[58]

According to his father, Hussain "never did anything wrong", and he was "never a bit of a bother" to the family.[59] Other sources contradict this, saying that Hussain at one point was a rebellious youth.[60] He reportedly spent time drinking in pubs, smoked marihuana, and was involved in fights with racists. The Official Account confirms he was involved in racial tensions, and that he was abusive to a teacher at school on one occasion.[61] According to press reports he was also questioned by police over shoplifting once. In July 2003 he dropped out of school after five years of education resulting in mediocre grades and no formal qualifications.

In 2002 Hussain reportedly stayed in Pakistan (outside Islamabad) for four weeks. According to some sources, it was his parents who sent him there in order to "straighten him out". According to the Official Account, the whole family went to Mecca for Hajj early the same year. Around this time, friends and acquaintances in the UK noticed that Hussain had become more religiously observant. He started to wear traditional Islamic robes, grew a beard and prayed regularly. He read religious texts, said he wanted to become a cleric, and openly voiced sympathies for Al-Qaeda and 9/11 in school. In this phase he appears to have met regularly with the other members of the group in homes, gyms, mosques and the Islamic bookshop. We have not come across accounts of Hussain attending sermons of radical preachers, as is the case with his accomplices Khan, Tanweer and Lindsay. However, in all cases we have surveyed, operatives had relations with, or were inspired by, known radical clerics, so it would be highly surprising if Hussain was never exposed to such sermons.

According to Hussain's brother, Khan was a friend of the family and would visit them regularly. Indoctrination, however, appears to have been confined to the other meeting places. Hussain's father had reportedly expressed concern about his son's close relationship with Khan.[62]

Jermaine Lindsay

The Official Account describes Jermaine Lindsay (19) aka "Jamal" as an outsider in Khan's group. For one thing, he had a different background. He was born in Jamaica in 1985 to a British mother and a Jamaican father who would take no part in his son's life. Lindsay might be characterized as a drifter based on the fact that his conversion and radicalization seem to be somehow more coincidental and were related to less specific grievances than those of his accomplices. The way we interpret the available sources, it seems social networks (friendship and kinship) were decisive factors why he ended up amongst extremists and militants.

We found no reports of serious problems in childhood other than the lack of a father figure and accounts of one of his stepfathers having been harsh with him. In press reports and the Official Account he has been described as intelligent, artistic and musical. Friends have portrayed him as someone "fascinated by world affairs, religion and politics". He was also interested in and good at sports. In fact, has been described as a "fitness fanatic" who was into martial arts and body-building. I came across no evidence that Lindsay, before his involvement with the group, translated his interests in politics and religion into activism on behalf of others, such as was the case with Khan and Tanweer.

Lindsay converted to Islam shortly after his mother, who did so when she had a relationship with a Muslim in 2000. This suggests that he may have been quite spontaneous and easy to influence. His sister said to the press that he changed markedly after conversion and that "he was not my brother any more".[63] He took the name Jamal and started to study Urdu. It appears that it was during the time of his conversion that he met and befriended Khan and the other members of the cell in the first gym set up by Khan.

Lindsay married a British convert he met in an Islamic Internet chat room, and the couple was expecting their second child at the time of the attacks. His wife explained to the press how Lindsay acted strangely for some time before the operation, "secretly sending text messages and disappearing three times a week". She suspected that he was having an affair. In reality he was probably hanging out with his accomplices in the gyms and other meeting places such as the bomb factory at 18 Alexandra Grove in Burley, or going to extremist meetings and sermons in London and other cities.

According to *The Times* he was observed together with Khan and Tanweer listening to the extremist preacher Abu Hamza in the streets of London after police closed the Finsbury Park mosque in 2003.[64] The Official Account notes that Lindsay was strongly influenced by the Jamaican extremist preacher Abdallah al-Faisal (currently imprisoned in the UK). Lindsay attended a sermon by this preacher, and listened to his tapes.[65] Friends and acquaintances have told the press that after his conversion, Lindsay travelled around the UK in search of religious guidance.

Concluding remarks

In this chapter I have focused on motivational aspects of radicalization and recruitment of jihadis in Europe. The case studies do seem to support and substantiate my hypothesis that there are some systematic differences in why people decided to join the jihad in Europe. However, they also exemplify some of the difficulties and drawbacks of such attempts at categorization, as well as the limits to obtaining a complete picture of the inner workings of terrorist networks.

I argue that the case studies indicate that there are three main motivational paths to the jihad in Europe, varying between members of cells. Entrepreneurs and protégés (Beghal, Daoudi, Khan and Tanweer) seem to be motivated mainly by ideology and activism. These bright and committed activists despair because they fail to make a political difference through non-violent means. Their statements and actions indicate that they are very rational in the way they embrace jihadism. It appears as if they themselves make the necessary decisions and proactively establish ties to jihadis. They approach radical mosques, preachers and propaganda. They listen to, and let themselves become inspired by militant clerics. They justify their actions with reference to politics, and they appear to share Al-Qaeda's worldview. There is no meaningful way of measuring their religiosity, but they frame their political grievances in religion, appear to be genuinely convinced that they are Holy Warriors, and seem to long for martyrdom.

Misfits (Trabelsi and Hussain), appear to be driven mainly by personal grievances, problems and frustrations, at least in the early phase of the radicalization processes. They appear to find themselves at the passive, or "receiver's" end of the recruitment process. Jihadi recruiters approach them more often than the other way around. Their narratives indicate that they accept the religious and political ideas promoted by the recruiters, mainly as a means of dealing with their personal failures. They seek a new start to their lives.[66] In search of a new meaning and direction in life they encounter "recruiters" such as Beghal and Khan through their social networks. The recruiters introduce the seekers to the jihadi networks and ideology. Those who join in this way appear to be less committed in their adherence to jihadism than the leading personalities.

The drifters (Courtallier brothers, Bonte and Lindsay) appear to have less specific reasons for becoming militants. They are not ideologically committed to social, religious or political activism, and they have no serious social problems. They come across as relatively well-functioning individuals. It appears as if drifters have mixed motivations for joining, but that already established social ties to relatives and friends who are extremists are the decisive factors.

One of the potential advantages of identifying systematic differences in motivations for joining is that it might enable us to establish what kinds of motivations "count more" than others for jihadi cells to form and go operational.

Unfortunately, it is still commonly believed, amongst experts and non-experts alike, that the rise of Al-Qaeda-type terrorism is the result of religious indoctrination or "brainwashing". Furthermore, many still believe that all jihadi terrorists are the same, bearded, irrational, religious fanatics with no earthly ambitions whatsoever.

Religious symbols and religious framing are certainly important aspects of recruitment. However, the way I interpret the available data, systematized and analysed according to the typology, in the European context, politics count more than religion. I argue that without charismatic and politically motivated activists taking the lead, few if any of the cells uncovered in Europe in recent years would have materialized.

According to European security officials, there have been several episodes in which groups have formed, acted very suspiciously, discussed attacks, but without going any further. One possible explanation for this phenomenon, which might be derived from the case studies, is that these groups lacked the crucial charismatic activist entrepreneur types such as Mohammed Siddique Khan who was able to radicalize his cadre to the point they were prepared for martyrdom.[67]

By studying the motivational aspects in a more differentiated manner, we might be able to think in a more differentiated way about counter-radicalization also. For example, entrepreneurs and protégés appear to be socialized and committed to the extent they will not change until they are convinced that the worldview they have adapted does not reflect reality. These militants will consequently pursue the violent path aiming to fulfil their utopian goals.

Misfits and drifters on the others hand appear to be substantially less committed to the jihadi cause, and might thus be more receptive to so-called "de-radicalization" initiatives aimed at steering youngsters away from radicalism and offering them exit opportunities and viable alternatives to violent activism. Because misfits and drifters appear to constitute the majority of operatives, the observation might leave some room for careful optimism concerning development of counter-radicalization strategies.

At the same time as there are advantages, there are of course also considerable limitations to the approach of the current chapter. First, as it focused on motivational aspects, it does not systematically capture the means and methods used by the recruiter to seduce recruits, the discussions, experience sharing and team-building activities that led the recruits to join the group and become jihadis. Moreover, I have not, at this point, been able to sufficiently document and depict the various phases of recruitment, the social interaction and cognitive processes that eventually lead a subject to become a terrorist. For state of the art theorizing and empirical surveys on the role of social networks and socialization processes in recruitment for extremist and militant groups the reader should consult the works of Quintan Wiktorowicz and Marc Sageman.[68]

Although we have not focused on these aspects per se, the individual case studies do indeed illustrate the importance of social networks and group dynamics in recruitment for all of the operatives, and they indicate that recruitment for some individuals is a gradual and lengthy process, whereas for others it is a more spontaneous enterprise.

As discussed above, the typology of terrorists has limited use for the detection of individual terrorists. However, it might help identify particularly suspicious constellations of individuals. When a small social unit within a radical Islamist community contains all the key character types – an entrepreneur, a protégé, misfits and drifters – it may be an operational cell in the making.

As a tool for mapping and understanding the reasons why terrorist groups form, on the other hand, I believe it may be highly relevant. In order to reach a better understanding of radicalization processes, academics should continue to conduct systematic, micro-level, empirical studies of the various roads into militant milieus and terrorist networks. Moreover, there is a need to further develop analytical categories which allow us to capture differences in why and how people become terrorists. This chapter is one of my contributions to that end.

Notes

1 Definitions: In this chapter we use the term *jihadi* about militant Islamist individuals and groups that use this term to describe themselves. Typically, these are individuals and groups associated with Al-Qaeda and the like. However, the way we use the term jihadi does not include mainly nationalist-separatist groups such as Hamas and Chechen separatists, even though they sometimes describe themselves as jihadis. *Terrorism* is here defined as acts (or intended acts) of political communicative violence, mainly targeting civilians or "soft targets", aimed at spreading fear amongst, and paralysing those governments and populations who are perceived as, enemies. For a well known and widely used terrorism definition, consult US State Department's "Pattern's of Global Terrorism", www.state.gov/s/ct/rls/crt/2003/31880.html. Terrorism is thus defined as jihadi if it can be attributed to clearly identifiable militant Islamist or jihadi individuals and groups. *Radicalization* is here defined quite narrowly as the reasons for, and the processes through which, Muslims engage in terrorist activities; the crucial defining factor being the intention and capacity actually to participate in acts of terrorist violence.

2 In this chapter we utilize a very strict definition of Al-Qaeda. The term is used about the core group of people dominated by ethnic Arabs interacting with the top Al-Qaeda leaders for shorter or longer periods of time. My use of the word corresponds, by and large, to Jason Burke's expression "Al-Qaeda hardcore", see Jason Burke, *Al Qaeda, Casting the Shadow of Terror*, (London: I.B. Tauris, 2003).
3 "Bin Laden's invisible network", *Newsweek*, Vol. 119, No. 45, 2001.
4 "London bomber: Text in full", *BBC News* 2 September 2005, http://news.bbc.co.uk/1/hi/uk/4206800.stm; "wasiya fursan ghaswat London [Testaments of the Knights of the London attacks]" *al-Sahab Media Production* July 2006, downloaded from the Jihadi web site *firdaws*, www.alfirdaws.org/vb/showthread.php?t=14619 on 12 July 2006.
5 Consult Petter Nesser, "Profiles of Jihadist Terrorists in Europe", pp. 31–49, in Cheryl Bernard, *A Future For the Young*, IMEY, RAND Corporation, September 2005 www.rand.org/pubs/working_papers/2006/RAND_WR354.pdf; the terrorist cells surveyed for this article were: (1) The Strasbourg Cell (2000), (2) The Beghal Network (2001), (3) The Tawhid Cell (2002), (4) The Chechen Network (2002), (5) The Madrid Cell (2004), (6) The Hofstad Group (2004), (7) The Operation Crevic Group (2004) and (8) The London Cell (2005).
6 Consult, for example, Helmut Willems *et al.*, *Fremdenfeindliche Gewalt: Eine Analyse von Täterstrukturen und Eskalationsprozessen*, Bonn, 1993; Helmut Willems, "Development, Patterns and Causes of Violence against Foreigners in Germany: Social and Biographical Characteristics of Perpetrators and the Process of Escalation", in Tore Bjørgo (ed.), *Terror from the Extreme Right*, (London: Frank Cass, 1995), and a modified version of Willems typology in Tore Bjørgo, *Racist and Right-Wing Violence: Patterns, Perpetrators, and Responses* (Oslo: Tano Aschehoug, 1997).
7 Consult professor Waldmann's contribution in this book and also John Horgan in Andrew Silke *et al.*, *Terrorists, Victims and Society*, (West Sussex: Wiley, 2003); Tore Bjørgo et al., *Root Causes of Terrorism, Myths, Reality and Ways Forward*, (London: Routledge, 2005); Tore Bjørgo, *Racist and Right-Wing Violence: Patterns, Perpetrators, and Responses* (Oslo: Tano Aschehoug, 1997); Marc Sageman, *Understanding Terror Networks*, (Philadelphia: University of Pennsylvania Press, 2004).
8 By "jihadi infrastructure" I refer to: First, support networks for local jihads in the Muslim world, in Europe and elsewhere. Second, sanctuaries and training facilities such as those run by Al-Qaeda and like-minded groups in Afghanistan. Third, the ideological superstructure disseminated by Al-Qaeda ideologists and strategists through the jihadis own media apparatus, through the public media and through the Internet. In recent years, after 9/11, the invasions of Afghanistan and Iraq and crackdowns of militant Islamist networks around the world, the physical infrastructure has been weakened, whereas the virtual networks and the jihadi Internet has become more important for disseminating ideology and propaganda, strategic and tactical advice and training.
9 GIA – Groupe Islamique Armé (Armed Islamic Group), militant group formed in Algeria when the Algerian army cancelled the general elections in the country in early 1992 after the moderate Islamist party FIS (Front Islamique du Salut – Islamic Salvation Front) seemed to have won enough votes to seize power. The group initiated a terrorist campaign in France in the mid-1990s because of France's support for the Algerian regime. GSPC – Groupe Salafiste pour la Prédication et le Combat (Salafist Group for Preaching and Combat), is an offshoot of the GIA that gradually, since the late 1990s, has developed close ties to Al-Qaeda, and now is being perceived as an integrated part of Al-Qaeda's global alliance.
10 Petter Nesser, "Post-millennium Patterns of Jihadist Terrorism in Western Europe – Part 1", JANE's Terrorism and Insurgency Centre, 27 May 2005, www.janes.com/security/international_security/news/jtic/jtic050531_1_n.shtml; Petter Nesser,

"Post-millennium Patterns of Jihadist Terrorism in Western Europe – Part 2", JANE's Terrorism and Insurgency Centre, 8 June 2005, www.janes.com/security/international_security/news/jtic/jtic050608_2_n.shtml; Petter Nesser, "Jihadism in Western Europe After the Invasion of Iraq: Tracing Motivational Influences from the Iraq War on Jihadist Terrorism in Western Europe", *Studies in Conflict and Terrorism*, June 2006, www.ingentaconnect.com/content/routledg/uter/2006/00000029/00000004/art00002.

11 Most of the perpetrators of the Madrid attacks were first-generation Moroccan immigrants who were connected to the Moroccan Islamic Combatant Group, a group formed by Moroccans in Peshawar in 1993 aiming to overthrow the Moroccan regime and establish an Islamic state. The broader network involved other nationalities such as Algerians, Tunisians, Syrians and Egyptians, as well as a few Spaniards at the fringes. Investigations have failed to establish direct links between the so-called Leganes Group (those who actually placed the bombs on the trains) and Al-Qaeda, but associates of this group are believed to have maintained close relations with Al-Qaeda and received training in Afghanistan. Some members of the broader terrorist network were very young. In terms of political motivations, the operatives appear to have found a common cause in resisting the US led invasion of Iraq. Consult Proceedings 20/2004, Indictment of April 10, 2006, Court of First Instance Number 6 of the Audencia National [Spanish National Court], www.elmundo.es/documentos/2006/04/11/auto_11m.html.

12 One notable exception from this was a Jordanian-Palestinian terrorist cell supervised by al-Zarqawi that operated in Germany in 2002, and prepared terrorist attacks against Jewish targets in German cities; consult, for example, Petter Nesser, "Jihad in Europe", Kjeller: Norwegian Defense Research Establishment, 2004, report 2004/01146 www.mil.no/multimedia/archive/00043/Jihad_in_Europe_43302a.pdf.

13 Petter Nesser, "Jihadism in Western Europe after the Iraq War"; Thomas Hegghammer, "Global Jihadism after the Iraq War", *Middle East Journal*, Vol. 60, No. 1 (2006) www.mil.no/multimedia/archive/00076/Global_Jihadism_Afte_76427a.pdf.

14 Consult Proceedings 20/2004, Indictment of April 10 2006, Court of First Instance Number 6 of the Audencia National [Spanish National Court], www.elmundo.es/documentos/2006/04/11/auto_11m.html.

15 Jihadi strategic texts and training manuals have been widely distributed, and can easily be accessed on the Internet, on pro-Al-Qaeda web sites, propaganda outlets for Al-Qaeda and associated groups, and on discussion forums in which Al-Qaeda sympathizers communicate with each other, such as muntadiyat shibkat al-hizba, www.alhesbah.com/v/index.php; shibkat muhajirun al-Islamiyya, www.mohajroon.com/vb/, or libraries such as al-Qaidun, www.qa3edoon.com/. Training manuals contain practical advice on how to recruit fighters and how to form Jihadi cells. They also contain bomb-making instructions, recipes for poisons, advice on how to communicate, how to do reconnaissance, security precautions and so on.

16 Consult Lindsay Clutterbuck's contribution in this book.

17 Consult Brynjar Lia, *Architect of Global Jihad: The Life of Al-Qaeda Strategist Abu Mus'ab Al-Suri*, (London: C. Hurst & Co Publishers, 2007).

18 Quintan Wiktorowicz, *Radical Islam Rising, Muslim Extremism in the West*, (Oxford: Rowman & Littlefield Publishers, 2005).

19 Consult, for example, interviews with Salim Boukhari in the *Guardian*, "A Jihad Warrior in London", 9 February 2004, www.guardian.co.uk/g2/story/0,3604,1143819,00.html, and the memoirs of Kamel Daoudi in Elaine Sciolino, "Portrait of the Arab as a Young Radical", *New York Times*, 22 September 2002 http://topics.nytimes.com/top/reference/timestopics/subjects/i/islam/index.html?offset=50&query=BIOGRAPHICAL%20INFORMATION&field=des&match=exact.

20 Consult, for example, Peter Bergen, *The Osama bin Laden I Know*, (New York: Free Press, 2006), pp. 261–266, Marcella Andreoli, "Under Orders From Usama", *Panorama*, 22 April 2004 via FBIS.

21 French verdicts against Djamel Beghal, Kamel Daoudi and Nabil Bounour, dated 15 March 2005, with author.
22 Steven Erlanger and Chris Hedges, "Missed Signals; Terror Cells Slip Through Europe's Grasp", *New York Times*, 28 December 2001, www.pulitzer.org/year/2002/explanatory-reporting/works/122801.html.
23 Takfir means literally deeming someone as an infidel, and refers to excommunicating Muslims who do not follow the same type of conservative interpretation of the Quran and the ahadith (prophet traditions).
24 Confidential source.
25 Lewis Smith, "Father Accused of Plot to Abduct Children to Libya", *The Times*, 20 April 2005, www.timesonline.co.uk/article/0,,2-1577045,00.html, this incident was also referred to in the French verdicts.
26 French verdicts against Djamel Beghal, Kamel Daoudi and Nabil Bounour, dated 15 March 2005, with author.
27 Steven Erlanger and Chris Hedges, "Missed Signals".
28 Bruce Crumley, "The Boy Next Door. How a mild-mannered science student became the target of an international terrorist hunt", *Time Europe*, 25 August 2003, www.time.com/time/europe/eu/magazine/0,13716,182925,00.html; French verdicts against Djamel Beghal, Kamel Daoudi and Nabil Bounour, dated 15 March 2005, with author.
29 Elaine Sciolino, "Portrait of the Arab as a Young Radical", *New York Times*, 22 September 2002, http://topics.nytimes.com/top/reference/timestopics/subjects/i/islam/index.html?offset=50&query=BIOGRAPHICAL%20INFORMATION&field=des&match=exact.
30 Ibid.
31 Ibid.
32 French verdicts against Djamel Beghal, Kamel Daoudi and Nabil Bounour, dated 15 March 2005, with author.
33 For example, in Afghanistan, Trabelsi handed out money to poor Afghans (something that infuriated other members of the groups and Arabs in Al-Qaeda); consult Marcella Andreoli, "Under Orders From Usama". In the trial in Belgium, a psychiatric report described him as "an incorrigible manipulator"; consult Mark Eeckhaut, "Trabelsi Wanted To Kill Americans", *De Standaard*, 28 May 2003, via FBIS.
34 French investigators believe the target was the American embassy in Paris, whereas a Belgian court that convicted Trabelsi was convinced that he wanted to blow himself up near the canteen on the US airbase Kleine Brogel in Belgium, close to the Dutch border.
35 French verdicts against Djamel Beghal, Kamel Daoudi and Nabil Bounour, dated 15 March 2005, with author.
36 Consult, for example, Sebastian Rotella and David Zucchino, "In Paris, a Frightening Look at Terror's Inconspicuous Face; Probe: Officials say plot against U.S. Embassy offers insight into recruitment and training of ordinary young men", *Los Angeles Times*, 21 October 2001.
37 French verdicts against Djamel Beghal, Kamel Daoudi and Nabil Bounour, dated 15 March 2005, with author.
38 Peter Bergen, *The Osama bin Laden I Know*, pp. 269–272.
39 Mark Eeckhaut, "Trabelsi Wanted To Kill Americans".
40 "Al-Qaida trial opens in Belgium", *The Guardian*, 23 May 2003, www.guardian.co.uk/alqaida/story/0,12469,961838,00.html); Peter Bergen, *The Osama bin Laden I Know*, pp. 269–272.
41 "Defense Pleads for Leniency in Belgian Al-Qa'ida Terrorist Trial", *Agence-France-Presse*, 10 June 2003, via FBIS; Marcella Andreoli, "Under Orders From Usama".
42 "Bin Laden's invisible network", *Newsweek*, Vol. 119, No. 45, 2001.
43 Confidential source.
44 "wasiya fursan ghaswat London [Testaments of the Knights of the London attacks]".

45 UK Government report, "Report of the Official Account of the Bombings in London on 7th July 2005", available at http://news.bbc.co.uk/2/shared/bsp/hi/pdfs/11_05_06_narrative.pdf.
46 *British Muslims Monthly Survey* for September 1997, Vol. V, No. 9, http://artsweb.bham.ac.uk/bmms/1997/09September97.html.
47 Paul Tumelty, "An In-Depth Look at the London Bombers", *Jamestown Foundation, Global Terrorism Analysis*, 28 July 2005, http://jamestown.org/terrorism/news/article.php?articleid=2369753.
48 Sean O'Neill and Daniel McGrory, "Abu Hamza and the 7/7 Bombers", *The Times*, 8 February 2006, www.timesonline.co.uk/article/0,,2-2030129,00.html.
49 Consult, "Momin Khawaja Constitutes the Canadian End of the Conspiracy", *Ottawa Citizen*, 23 March 2006, www.canada.com/ottawacitizen/news/story.html?id=408dc2ed-d950-4ee5-a4b7-392eb5faaf34&k=75162.
50 Sudarsan Raghava, "Friends Describe Bomber's Political, Religious Evolution, 22-Year-Old Grew Up Loving Western Ways and Wanting for Little", *Washington Post*, 29 July 2005, www.washingtonpost.com/wp-dyn/content/article/2005/07/28/AR2005072801991.html.
51 Ibid.
52 UK Government report, "Report of the Official Account of the Bombings in London on 7th July 2005".
53 Sean O'Neill and Daniel McGrory, "Abu Hamza and the 7/7 bombers".
54 Peter Foster and Nasir Malick, "Bomber idolised bin Laden, says Pakistan Family", *The Telegraph*, 21 July 2005, http://telegraph.co.uk/news/main.jhtml?xml=/news/2005/07/21/nimam221.xml.
55 Louise Male, "Bomber whose Hero was Osama bin Laden", *Leeds Today*, 22 July 2005, www.leedstoday.net/ViewArticle2.aspx?SectionID=39&ArticleID=1093857.
56 Peter Foster and Nasir Malick, "Bomber Idolised bin Laden, says Pakistan Family". Louise Male, "Bomber whose Hero was Osama bin Laden"; Sudarsan Raghava, "Friends Describe Bomber's Political, Religious Evolution".
57 "Wasiya fursan ghaswat London [Testaments of the Knights of the London attacks]".
58 Ian Cobain, "The Boy who didn't Stand Out", *The Guardian*, 14 July 2005, www.guardian.co.uk/attackonlondon/story/0,16132,1528199,00.html; Ben Macintyre, "Hitch-hikers to Heaven who created Hell on Earth", *The Times*, 16 July 200, www.timesonline.co.uk/article/0,,22989-1696094,00.html.
59 Jeremy Armstrong, "My Hasib must have been Brainwashed", *Mirror*, 2 August 2005, www.mirror.co.uk/news/tm_objectid=15806384&method=full&siteid=94762&headline=my-hasib-must-have-been-brainwashed-name_page.html.
60 Paul Tumelty, "An In-Depth Look at the London Bombers", *Jamestown Foundation, Global Terrorism Analysis*, 28 July 2005, http://jamestown.org/terrorism/news/article.php?articleid=2369753.
61 UK Government report, "Report of the Official Account of the Bombings in London on 7th July 2005".
62 Jeremy Armstrong, "My Hasib must have been Brainwashed".
63 Paul Tumelty, "An In-Depth Look at the London Bombers".
64 Sean O'Neill and Daniel McGrory, "Abu Hamza and the 7/7 bombers".
65 UK Government report, "Report of the Official Account of the Bombings in London on 7th July 2005".
66 Quintan Wiktorowicz, *Radical Islam Rising, Muslim Extremism in the West*, (Oxford: Rowman & Littlefield Publishers, 2005).
67 Confidential source.
68 Marc Sageman, *Understanding Terror Networks*; Quintan Wiktorowicz, *Radical Islam Rising, Muslim Extremism in the West*.

Part II
Understanding radicalisation in context

5 Radicalisation and recruitment in Europe
The UK case

Mark Huband

As a ball of fire erupted from the World Trade Center, tumultuous cries of "Allah akhbar" echoed around the main hall of the Quaker meeting house in London's Euston Road. Five hundred people sat watching an out-of-focus film of the 11 September 2001 terrorist attacks, as children played among the seats and adults cheered when the Twin Towers crumbled.

The irony of the Quaker meeting house – a citadel of peaceful reflection – having been rented out for the purpose of drawing together so many people filled with hatred and anger made the meeting – some six months to the day before the London bombings of 7 July 2005 – all the more significant. Presiding over the gathering was Omar Bakri Muhammad, former head of the Salafist group *al-Muhajiroun*, which had been disbanded a short while beforehand. Among the other speakers was Abu Izzadeen, a convert to Islam who subsequently became the most extreme public voice of jihadist-Salafism in the UK as head of *al-Ghuraaba*, the group which replaced *al-Muhajiroun*.

Although none of the 7 July bombers – nor the would-be bombers arrested after the attempted suicide bombing of London on 21 July 2005 – were known to have attended the January 2005 meeting, the radicalised environment in which they had moved was vividly on display at the Quaker hall.

Three factors were made clear by the speakers which illustrate the key trends and patterns in the radicalisation process in the UK. These factors, which will be the central themes of this chapter, are as follows.

First, it is evident that among the most vocal of those who are already radicalised, there is a clear intention to explain the apparently unstoppable conflict between Muslims and the *kufr* (non-Muslims) in the West – and specifically in the UK – as resulting from the decision by Western leaders to commit aggression, both against Muslims in the UK and abroad.

This process of explanation has involved seeking both to define the identity of the "British Muslim", and to make clear how this community relates to the plight of Muslims in other parts of the world. The strategy is given a historical veneer by explaining that a *"Covenant of Security"* which allegedly existed between Muslims and the *kufr* – whereby both sides would leave each other in peace – has been broken as a result of Western aggression, and that therefore Muslims have a right to launch a *defensive* jihad.

Accompanying the view that Western aggression is the cause of the current conflict is a second feature of the radicalisation process, specifically a growing sense of the need to strictly and starkly define the distinction between Muslims and non-Muslims *in the West*. A "Muslim identity" that is created in isolation from mainstream society in the UK is now taking shape. This process has two facets: isolation from Muslims seeking to promote integration with the wider society, and isolation from non-Muslims altogether.

Before his forced departure from the UK for Lebanon in 2005, the former leader of *al-Muhajiroun*, Omar Bakri Muhammad, was the most outspoken advocate of isolation. Following his departure, his successor Abu Izzadeen took up this cause even more virulently, until he was silenced following his conviction by a British court in 2008 of terrorist fundraising and inciting terrorism overseas.

Omar Bakri made his views clear:

> The mosque is no longer a mosque in the UK. Many of the Muslim youths don't go, because they are dominated by communities that have sold out to unbelievers. Three things make the mosques not mosques. One is that the mosques are promoting integration; the second is that the mosques allow MPs to make politics in the mosques; a third is that Muslims are spied on in the mosques. The Islamic identity has been deserted. I cannot be a Muslim and live in the UK. We have been forced to make a stand. We are not going to be integrated. Some Muslims believe they are British citizens. It's really very strange. Either you migrate, or you prepare yourselves.[1]

Accompanying these two issues – the justification for conflict and the defining and refining of a distinctive Muslim identity – is a third feature of the radicalisation process, and the one which is most likely to determine the depth of the root it ultimately establishes.

After they had been ousted from their main focal point – the Finsbury Park mosque in North London – in 2003, the radicals sought to build an underground network whose public presence is felt in web sites and at demonstrations.

The radicalised minority sought to create a firm foothold throughout the Muslim population by developing an organisational strategy allowing it to promote its cause, and by providing an ideological framework in which the radicalisation process can take place. By using the Internet, distributing literature at street stalls, keeping its plans secret and cloaking itself in an aura of mystique, it has been able to attract a following among those – mainly young Muslims – among whom there is the greatest disillusionment with moderate Muslim leaders. The radical community – which came to be focused around the *al-Ghuraaba* group – is thus defining itself both as an alternative to those in control of the mosques, as well as using increasingly confrontational language to distinguish itself from non-Muslim Britain. This is the isolated minority from whom the threat to the UK is most likely to come. The tailoring of a counter-terrorism strategy to address the challenge from them will be the concluding element of this chapter.

Looking for *jihad*: the breaking of a "covenant"?

The "Covenant of Security" talked about widely among radical Muslims in the UK has only emerged as a theme since it became evident among the radicals that they could make great play of the fact that – in their view – this arrangement had become null and void. It is notable that among those most vocal in the UK about the disbandment of this "covenant" are two converts to Islam – Abu Suleiman and Abu Izzadeen. However, it is also correct to argue that the historical circumstances in which the West's alleged "breaking of the covenant" in fact took place prevailed long before this "breakage" was identified by the UK's Muslim radicals as having occurred.

It is more accurate, historically, to say that the radicals found it convenient to argue that the "covenant" had been broken only when they became emboldened enough to argue, first, that it had existed in the first place, and, second, that Western behaviour towards Muslims amounted to the breaking of this arrangement. No effort has been made to identify when "the West" agreed to abide by this supposed agreement.

Abu Yahya Abderahman, a vocal proponent of conflict, made this clear in 2005 at the London conference on Euston Road:

> We are no longer living with the kufr with a covenant of security. That means that we are at war. For years we have been living in peace. They have violated the covenant. If they are going to come together to fight us, we now realise we have to have a global coalition to fight them. We are at war. It's time for brothers, sisters and children to prepare. Prepare as much as you can, whether with sticks or stones or bombs. Prepare as much as you can, to defeat them, to terrorise them. That is what the message of Mohammed was. Just by terrorism alone. Is it not the case that when Sheikh Osama bin Laden speaks that kings and queens and prime ministers stop to listen? Why? Because he terrifies them. Thus, you have to want to give up your lives for the sake of Allah. He gave us this life, and he wants you to give it back. The Mujahideen in east and west are calling for you to give up your lives. We want to be part of the hadith of The Messenger. And what is the hadith? That the jihad is going to continue. And if the governments of the west don't want to behave [we will] give them a 9/11 day after day after day after day.[2]

Abu Suleiman, a convert to Islam, added:

> Even when the kufr attacked the Muslim umma we remained at peace in this land because we have this covenant. But it doesn't mean that we remain silent. We are people who motivated the youth to join the struggle, the jihad. But still we remained true to the covenant. While they attacked the Muslims in Iraq we remained true to the covenant. Even when the Muslims were attacked by some people in this country we remained true to the covenant.

> The Muslims will always keep the treaty. It's the infidel who broke the covenant. The covenant is always broken by the kufr. We live by the covenant because it's a treaty. But even though we have this treaty, we didn't neglect our other duties.[3]

The assertion that a "covenant" existed between Muslims and non-Muslims has thus become a key feature of the historical context in which the more publicly vocal proponents of violence have argued their case among Britain's radicalised minority. Even so, the idea that a "covenant" – even unwritten – exists as the basis for peaceable co-existence between Muslims and non-Muslims in the UK is not recognised by anybody but the radicals: moderate Muslims have not heard of such an arrangement, and non-Muslims are not aware that any such understanding ever existed.

Historical inaccuracy and a tremendous lack of clarity as to the intellectual and ideological foundation for the radicalisation of Muslims in the UK is a major element in the search for purpose, language and meaningful action which dominates the perspectives of Britain's jihadist-Salafists. Most vivid in the discourse of these individuals is the sense of a lack of belonging to the wider community. A member of Women's Da'wa UK told the seminal London meeting in January 2005:

> Muslim women should either migrate or prepare themselves. We are in a time of fitna. It is essential that we instil this warrior mentality into our children. It is important that our children have a passion for jihad. Turn your houses into dar-al-islam. Make sure that you nurture your children. A Muslim woman isn't an emotional woman. A Muslim woman will say to them: we don't have friendship with the kufr. We want to put fear into the hearts of the enemy. We want to make sure that our children carry the spirit of jihad in their hearts.[4]

Another woman voiced similar sentiments, saying:

> You can't avoid your children being taught kufr subjects in the national curriculum. You should teach them how to teach Allah exclusively. We should encourage them to teach role models like Abdullah Azzam and Osama bin Laden. There is no benefit to them being in school. In school they are indoctrinated with nothing but love for the unbelievers. Don't wait for people in your community to set up Islamic schools. It will be too late then.[5]

Among Muslim scholars as much as among counter-terrorism strategists there is a wide range of opinion as to whether the circumstances that have encouraged this lurch towards jihadist-Salafism are rooted in the changing sociological conditions of Muslims in the UK, or in the newfound language of defiance and violent rejectionism that has become a global phenomenon. It is certainly the case that attempts following 11 September 2001 to dilute the radicalism that has taken root within Britain's Muslim community have thus far failed. Moreover, the tension between older and younger Muslims is complicating any efforts to do so. As Humayun Ansari, whose studies of Britain's Muslim community are widely respected, said:

> The older generation has emotional bonds with the countries of origin. Among the younger generation there is a problem. They find themselves in a sort of vacuum: they don't have these links, and they don't accept what the older generation says about religion or culture. Their experience tells them that there's not much on offer here. So, how does one become empowered if there is alienation? Then, religion does play a role. They haven't rejected the secular way of thinking. But as a matter of identity, Islam is becoming more important.[6]

The sociological conditions into which the post-9/11 language of extremism has been inserted have provided some already fertile ground for radicalism, as well as having inspired those who would otherwise perhaps have remained inactive had Osama bin Laden not emerged as a global figure. There is no doubt that policy responses – of the United States in particular, and the UK as its key ally – to the 9/11 attacks have yet to produce a clear strategy for incorporating the global perspective of Muslims in the West. Following a range of studies of radicalisation undertaken since 9/11, Humayun Ansari concluded:

> There wasn't a tremendous upsurge in the attraction to jihad post-9/11.
> There's a multiplicity of views within the Muslim communities. This makes it quite complex in terms of coming to any conclusions. You can't arrive at any hard and fast views. There isn't a normative view. For example, regarding jihad, views are individual. It's seen as a spiritual struggle. It's not militaristic. One is talking about a spectrum, from moderate to extreme. And there is a mass of people who operate somewhere in between.[7]

Even so, the failure by moderate Muslims to overtly influence UK government policy on issues that are of particular sensitivity to Muslims, at a time when the radical message is clearly taking root within a minority in the UK, has given the radicals plenty of time to seek to define the relationship between the Muslim and non-Muslim communities. In the immediate aftermath of the 9/11 attacks there was a common view among Muslims as to the impact of policy and the policing of policy. The sentiments remain strong. Sheikh Ibrahim Moqra, imam of the Masjid Umar mosque in Leicester in the English Midlands wherein there is a well-established Muslim population, said: "The anti-terror legislation has caused a lot of problems. No Muslims are happy with it. By and large things were reasonably good before 11 September 2001. Now, Muslims are being treated as if they are a Fifth Column."[8]

Mohammed Naseem, chairman of the council of Birmingham Central Mosque, reflecting on the impact policy has had on the relations between different generations of Muslims in the UK, concluded:

The greatest threat is when the values of the society are being eroded. I don't think the Muslim community can be isolated as one section of the British nation. What is happening is going to affect everybody. There is only one Muslim community, though they come from different lands. But they are being looked at at this time as one community. Muslims are beginning to understand that they are the targets of whatever campaign is reigning. We are moving towards dictatorship in the perception of the threat. The younger generation understand this, and the older generation trusted the values of British society. For the older generation it is obvious to see, that these values have changed, though I think that both generations are realising that changes have occurred. The older generation is not likely to be radicalised. The younger generation don't say "British Muslim". They just call themselves "British". The question of Britishness doesn't arise. What we question is the way society is being run. That's what everybody is questioning.[9]

Sensitivity to the impact of policing – from Muslims who are affected by it, human rights groups who have raised the issue from a legal perspective, and from radicals who have sought to portray it as a part of the "breaking of the covenant of security" – has been acute. For the radicals, tough policing has also become a potent means of mobilising opinion. At the London conference in January 2005, the radical Abu Izzadeen said: "If the police come to my house, I am going to kill them."[10]

Senior counter-terrorism officials regard prevention of attacks – and the use of robust means to make it known to radicals they are under surveillance – as taking priority over the preservation of harmonious relations with the Muslim community. Only as the police and Security Service started to feel – from 2006 onwards – that they had begun to get to grips with the terrorist threat, did they focus more routinely on trying to keep Muslim leaders informed of their actions in order to diminish animosity. As a senior security official said in 2006:

We have to factor in what the community impact is going to be when we plan operations, and we are highly conscious that one could be exacerbating the problem we are trying to resolve. But it hasn't stopped us doing the things we feel we need to do.[11]

A striking feature of the counter-terrorism effort during the eight years since the 9/11 attacks, however, has been the difficulty counter-terrorism strategists have experienced in accepting the motivation for emergent jihadist-Salafist sentiments in the UK. In general terms there has been great difficulty accepting that the condition of the lives of Muslims *within the context of the UK* has been *the* single most significant factor. A senior counter-terrorism strategist said:

The radicalization escalator is something that has been running for quite a long time. The determining factors are foreign policy issues. Bosnia was definitely a field of jihad in the 1990s. There are some continuing underlying issues, like the Palestinian question. But it's difficult to get data. It's not getting a lot better. You have a much bigger pool. The population of North African refugees was relatively small. We have a large pool of people from the Muslim faith community. You have a bigger pond in which you are fishing. The critical difference between the two communities was the community impact. The police arresting people who are recently arrived has a different impact than people who have families and communities here. And there is the potential that security operations are in themselves possibly destabilizing for relations with the community.[12]

He continued:

We have to factor in what the community impact is going to be when we plan operations. We are highly conscious that one could be exacerbating the problem we are trying to resolve. It hasn't stopped us ding the things we fell we need to do. Taking over Finsbury Park mosque was a very delicate thing to do. It was very carefully planned. Explaining is part of it. We need to help people understand what we are doing. A high proportion of our agents are Muslim. They take a lot of risks, and it is extremely valuable intelligence. At the community relations level, the police have got good relations with mosques. But the sort of people who will be in contact with the police, aren't the kind of people [who will be the cause of concern].

The complexity of identifying who is on the "radicalisation escalator" – and what their motives are – was made clear by Abu Hamza al-Masri, the radical imam of the Finsbury Park mosque in North London who began a seven-year prison sentence on 7 February 2006 after being found guilty of soliciting murder and inciting racial hatred. Abu Hamza said:

I think Osama bin Laden is a phenomenon rather than a person. He is speaking the minds of many many Muslims. But in the future the best approach won't be the one he has taken. The biggest mistake of Osama bin Laden is that he has avoided the scholars of the [Saudi] regime, whom he views as corrupt. He should be addressing them and taking them on. The emotional people will keep killing and they may do some operations. But they won't make any difference, because the West is too big. Al-Qaeda has always been a provider, but not a structure. They can't prove anything solid. The feeling in the hearts will be there. But it's not according to God's agenda: He first said that we should get our own house in order. Osama bin Laden will be a phenomenon – an emotional one. He will go down as a struggle. But it will be known that he was mistaken. Al-Qaeda will continue in Yemen, Somalia, Saudi Arabia and the Gulf. Because it's going to be difficult for them to communicate, it might be some sub al-Qaeda [groups] like in Pakistan, where people will be operating and trying to reform themselves from the inside. But regarding al-Qaeda worldwide, it won't strengthen itself. People are wanting to distance themselves from al-Qaeda. Al-Qaeda has narrowed itself, and everybody has suffered.[13]

Crucial to Abu Hamza's observations is the recognition of this "distance" between the catalyst for the radicalisation – the activities of al-Qaeda – and the motivation for new radicalisation, planning and activity way beyond the physical area in which the core of al-Qaeda can be and is active.

In its official report of the London bombings of 7 July 2005, the UK government sought to crystallise its thinking with regard to its understanding of the trends with which the Security Service (MI5), the police and other agencies had been grappling since September 2001. The "distance" as defined by Abu Hamza between the epicentre of global extremism – focused on the Middle East and to varying degrees structurally centred on al-Qaeda and the re-emergent Taliban now active in Afghanistan and Pakistan – and the motivations of the four London suicide bombers, was made clear in the UK report, the central thesis of which is summed up in an annex to the main report and which is worth citing in full. The report stated:

ANNEX B
RADICALISATION IN CONTEXT

1   What we know of previous extremists in the UK shows that there is not a consistent profile to help identify who may be vulnerable to radicalisation. Of the 4 individuals here, 3 were second generation British citizens whose parents were of Pakistani origin and one whose parents were of Jamaican origin; Kamel Bourgass, convicted of the Ricin plot, was an Algerian failed asylum seeker; Richard Reid, the failed shoe bomber, had an English mother and Jamaican father. Others of interest have been white converts. Some have been well-educated, some less so. Some genuinely poor, some less so. Some apparently well integrated in the UK, others not. Most single, but some family men with children. Some previously law-abiding, others with a history of petty crime. In a few cases there is evidence of abuse or other trauma in early life, but in others their upbringing has been stable and loving.

2   As for the process of radicalisation, there are a number of factors which have, in the past, contributed. Attendance at a mosque linked to extremists may be a factor. This will normally have nothing to do with the official mosque hierarchy, but rather extremists identifying potential candidates for radicalisation on the margins. However, evidence suggests that extremists are increasingly moving away from mosques to conduct their activities in private homes or other premises to avoid detection.

3   The influence of an extreme spiritual leader may also be important, either through direct meetings and sermons or via video, DVD and written material. But evidence suggests, again, that radicalisers will

increasingly keep potential recruits away from too strong an association with a public figure. As such, extremists are more and more making extensive use of the internet. Websites are difficult to monitor and trace; they can be established anywhere and have global reach; they are anonymous, cheap and instantaneous; and it requires no special expertise to set up a website. The internet is widely used for propaganda; training (including in weapons and explosives); to claim responsibility for attacks; and for grooming through chatrooms and elsewhere.

4   The role of personal mentors and then bonding with a group of fellow extremists appears to have been critical in many cases. Mentors may first identify individuals from within larger groups who may be susceptible to radicalisation; then "groom" them privately in small groups until individuals in the group begin feeding off each other's radicalisation.

5   There appear to be a number of common features to this grooming. In the early stages, group conversation may be around being a good Muslim and staying away from drugs and crime, with no hint of an extremist agenda. Gradually individuals may be exposed to propaganda about perceived injustices to Muslims across the world with international conflict involving Muslims interpreted as examples of widespread war against Islam; leaders of the Muslim world perceived as corrupt and non-Islamic; with some domestic policies added as "evidence" of a persecuted Islam; and conspiracy theories abounding. They will then move on to what the extremists claim is religious justification for violent jihad in the Quran and the Hadith (the Hadith are the accounts recording the words and deeds of the Prophet Muhammed by people who knew him); and – if suicide attacks are the intention – the importance of martyrdom in demonstrating commitment to Islam and the rewards in Paradise for martyrs; before directly inviting an individual to engage in terrorism. There is little evidence of overt compulsion. The extremists appear rather to rely on the development of individual commitment and group bonding and solidarity.[14]

The most prominent feature of this "official" version of the radicalisation process is that there is no single "profile": neither among those seeking to radicalise others, nor among those vulnerable to radicalisation, nor among those who are ultimately driven to kill. The absence of a single profile has a range of implications. But primarily one lesson should be drawn from the multifarious character of the radicalisation process in the UK: there are many people from many different backgrounds with the potential for becoming radicalised.

However, it is not enough to say that the single factor unifying them is their experience of Islam. Another common feature exists as a bond between them: this is their experience of the UK, its way of life, its political realities, its strengths and its weaknesses. In many cases it is the experience of life in the UK which has been a much more common feature over a longer period of the "radical's" experience; religious observance, the lure of the radical agenda, the promise of action as a means of breaking out of a humdrum existence – these things come later.

A senior UK security official said:

> There's not from our perspective any kind of demographic profile of an Islamic extremist. There is a whole range of motivations that could play a part. The way that people are radicalized in each group is different. There are push factors: government policies, ideologies within Islam, extremist rhetoric. How it is justified is different for each individual, and may be determined by the media. One specific path is that in most individuals the first stop has been with the mosques that are linked to Islamic extremism. Also, links to Islamic leaders, peer pressure. There is always the need for ideological justification.[15]

It would be wrong to conclude that the common experience of life in the UK – either for those born into Muslim households, or those drawn to Islam who then convert – is blameworthy for the terrorist acts which have now resulted. Most people in the UK do not, for example, live in the brutalised environment that Northern Ireland has been over much of the past 30 years. The attraction of the various armed groups in Northern Ireland to the young who signed up over the years is rooted in the extreme polarisation of the society that has prevailed in that part of the UK – a polarisation that has evidently been heightened as violence has spiralled and revenge become routine.

But "historical" conflict of the kind to which – in various phases – Northern Ireland has been subject, has no comparison in the experience of Muslims *within the UK* mainland, whatever claims the young firebrands may make about a "covenant" having been breached. Even so, it is evident that the radicalism *has* taken root among some Muslims, the hatred *is* real and strong, and the motivation is not lacking, as the events in London in July 2005 and the car bomb attack on Glasgow airport in July 2007 proved. But if life for the Muslim community is not brutalised – in the way that it has been for many in Northern Ireland, or for other communities who revert to terrorism – and thus lacks a common cause rooted in seeking to respond directly to real and immediate aggression, what is fuelling the anger and inspiring the violent response?

The section quoted above from the UK government's report into the London bombings of 7 July 2005 makes clear that "ideas" are a fundamental part of the radicalisation process. In generating, diffusing and engaging in debates – even at a distance – about ideas, those lured by extremism seem at least to share a keenness to feel engaged in issues beyond the immediate experience of their lives.

The experience of Jermaine Lindsay, a convert to Islam of Jamaican origin who was one of the four suicide bombers on 7 July 2005, is instructive. The UK report provides a snapshot of his life in the UK, which again is worth quoting in full:

31 Lindsay was the outsider of the group. He was born in Jamaica on 23 September 1985. His mother was 19 at the time. His natural father remained in Jamaica and appears to have played little role in Lindsay's subsequent life. His mother moved to Huddersfield the following year with another man. This first stepfather is described as having been harsh to Lindsay. The relationship broke up in 1990. Lindsay was closer to his second stepfather who stayed with the family until 2000. He had 2 younger stepsisters.

32 Lindsay was a bright child, successful academically at school and good at sport. He is described as artistic and musical. As a teenager, he became interested in martial arts and kickboxing. Like the other 3 he was physically fit and regularly worked out.

33 Lindsay's mother converted to Islam in 2000. He converted almost immediately thereafter and took the name "Jamal". His behaviour around this time was mixed. At school, he is said to have begun associating with troublemakers and was disciplined for handing out leaflets in support of Al Qaida. At his local mosque and in Islamic groups around Huddersfield and Dewsbury, he was admired for the speed with which he achieved fluency in Arabic and memorised long passages of the Quran, showing unusual maturity and seriousness. He began wearing the traditional white robes.

34 It is believed that he was strongly influenced by the extremist preacher Abdallah al Faisal (also of Jamaican origin) now serving a prison sentence for soliciting murder, incitement to murder and incitement to racial hatred and distributing material of a racial hatred nature. Lindsay is believed to have attended at least one lecture and to have listened to tapes of other lectures by him.

In 2002, his mother moved to the US to live with another man, leaving Lindsay alone at the family home in Huddersfield. This has been described as a traumatic experience for Lindsay, for which he was ill equipped. He left school, and lived on benefit, doing occasional odd jobs selling mobile phones and Islamic books.

36 He married a white British convert to Islam, whom he had met over the internet and subsequently at a "Stop the War" march in London, on 30 October 2002. They lived initially in Huddersfield but moved to Aylesbury in September 2003, where his wife's family lived, although they continued to spend time in and around Huddersfield thereafter. Their first child was born on 11 April 2004. While in Aylesbury, Lindsay worked as a carpet fitter, a job he had obtained with the help of his brother-in-law, until early 2005. He was unemployed at the time of the bombings.[16]

A leading academic, who has advised UK security officials on extremist tendencies and the *potential* for terrorist networks to operate *within* the fabric of British society, told a recent London meeting of counter-terrorism officials and experts:

The UK jihadist community is much more heterogeneous than we give it credit for. We are seeing terrorism isn't something we can separate from society. It's embedded in it. There's movement from legal to illegal functions. People become involved in terrorism for a set of reasons. But once they are involved, a lot of other reasons take over. Are personality traits part of the profile of the terrorist? I doubt it.[17]

The absence of a clear profile suggests that a key element in the radicalisation process is the personal choice of the radical. Some individuals *choose* to look for jihad while others don't. Within the context of the UK the issue of personal choice is key. This is in part due to the geographic distance between the UK and the most dynamic areas of jihadi activity, and the relatively benign environment within the UK, which strongly supports freedom of worship. Despite issues related to schooling and the national educational curriculum, it is difficult for the Muslim in Britain to identify *religious* grounds within the context of the UK which could be used convincingly to argue that Muslims in the UK are under attack in a concerted way that would justify launching a *defensive* jihad in response.

However, the radicals who have emerged have argued this very point. The question is: how and why have they done so?

Muslim and British – the radicals, the mainstream and the *kufr*

At the heart of the evolving jihadist-Salafist effort to entrench the radical element within the Muslim community in Britain is an extensive effort to give substance to the Muslim identity within the context of the West in general and the UK in particular. The speakers at the London conference of January 2005, whose views are quoted earlier in this chapter, provide a taste of how deeply felt is the wish among the most outspoken radicals to separate Muslims from non-Muslims. But among those who are not intending to travel to the areas where jihad is currently being fought – until recently Iraq, though now likely to be Pakistan and Afghanistan – the need to establish a body of ideas which will define the role, relationships and purpose of Muslims in the UK who are intent on remaining there is becoming more pronounced.

The most prominent means by which this is being done is through a small number of Internet-based publications overseen by the groups spawned by *al-Muhajiroun*, chief among them being *al-Ghuraaba*. The group – whose name translated means "the strangers" – used its web site (which has been through numerous changes of name) both as a forum for propagating ideas, and as the centre of an organisational nexus for its supporters. Deprived of a particular mosque within which to focus its activities, supporters learned of planned demonstrations, book sales and other activities, by reading the site or emailing its administrators.

While it is highly likely that the organisational aspect of the web site was its primary purpose, the more thought-provoking content it carried before its disappearance provides some pointers as to how far the UK's Salafists have reached in defining their perspective and aims. On 30 May 2006 a lengthy piece of analysis[18] appeared which sought to guide Muslims in the UK – and elsewhere in the West – as to how they should define their identity while living among the non-Muslims – the *kufr* – with whom they are at odds. At the heart of the *al-Ghuraaba* analysis is the intention of justifying – as well as promoting, and even celebrating – the intense feeling of alienation from non-Muslim Britain (it is no coincidence that the group chose to call itself "the strangers", thus stressing their separateness from society, but doing so using the term "ghuraaba" which is a Koranic reference to those who were early adopters of Islam). This is done by stressing the primacy of the individual identity, and then explaining that identity purely as a product of belief – belief that is the result of the "perfection" Islam has offered its adherents. The following excerpts from the analysis give a clear sense of how such groups relate to wider UK society:

> The identity is the reality of every person and every individual that distinguishes him from anybody else, therefore the identity is related to his personality, which in turn composes the mentality of the person, composes of the emotions and the feelings of the person and it is related to his physical and character and behaviour...
>
> Furthermore, the identity of the individual is different from the identity of the society, because it could be that you have an Islamic identity and yet you are living between the man-made identities of the Kufr society. So the identity is what forms and shapes the behaviour, character and thoughts etc and could be completely different from what is prevalent where you live. In our case, the identity we carry is completely different from the identity of the society and this is an almighty tradition...
>
> Hence, whenever somebody's identity starts to match and reconcile with the society where he lives, then he will start to integrate and lose his identity, he will no longer feel any clash; but when there is a clash of identities, he will feel strange and will be strange and that is how The Prophet said...

What is clear from the group's analysis is that the writer is seeking a clash with the wider, non-Muslim society, and is stressing the "strange" or "stranger" (that is, the "*ghuraaba*") identity which the entire analysis argues is an "almighty tradition" rooted in the experience of the first Muslims, who were also "strangers" in the time of the Prophet. This "strangeness" makes the "clash" with the wider society of non-believers not only inevitable but divinely sanctioned, as the "clash" is fundamental to the assertion of the identity. The article continues:

> So when someone is conscious about the identity clash, he feels from his own soul and Nafs that he belongs to that identity, that he is part and is proud of that identity and will lead to him fighting for that identity, he will love and hate according to whether or not the people share that identity; he will have friendship according to that identity and will have animosity

against those who do not carry that identity. That is because the identity has a fundamental effect on his beliefs and ideas, on his behaviour and personality. The identity is a controller of the will have an impact on his personality...

That is why, when he has a clear understanding of his identity, he will never be a hypocrite nor double faced nor have double standards. Verily, Islam has its own identity and will it never reconcile with the identity of the Kufr societies that are based on Kufr law and on man-made systems...

But rather the Muslim has his own identity that is based on Islam and though he may be living in a society that carries a Kufr identity. That is also why it is inevitable that they will clash with each other...

It is noticeable that the expectation of a "clash" with the *kufr* is rooted in the apparent impossibility of Muslims and non-Muslims coexisting. This is a markedly different explanation from that expressed at the London conference in January 2005 – whose key speakers became part of *al-Ghuraaba* – which made clear that Western aggression had broken a "covenant", and therefore Muslims must respond. Indeed, one view expressed at the London conference was that "for years we have been living in peace" but that Western action now justified a different approach. A year or more later, the same people appear to have sought new justification for "a clash" – founded not on "the other's" behaviour but on a creed that is far more intrinsic to Islamic belief. Thus, the analysis continues:

So the fundamental pillar of the identity is the Aqeedah, the belief, the Tawheed. Also the identity is based on the culture, civilisation and history and even the language of the Qur'an. The Arabic language is part of our identity, so when we are speaking about the identity, we are speaking about all the detailed components that are independent of all other identities. There is no way to be Muslim and Kafir at the same time, or to be "Muslim and western" or "Muslim and Arab" or "Muslim and Asian" at the same time...

That is not because it is bad to be born in Arabia, but your identity has nothing to do with where you are born, it is about to have the correct belief and culture and you combine that with all your personality and behaviour and carry it with you...

Seeking to divorce the "Western Muslim" from the West or any other regional or national identity is a potentially powerful means by which the writer (or writers) can seek to build the foundation for a "global" Muslim identity established within the West as a direct challenge to non-Muslims. Achieving this will allow Muslims in the UK and elsewhere whose identity has a racial aspect – Pakistani, Arab, South Asian, etc. – to build a challenge based purely on their religious identity, by which they clearly hope to attract "white" converts. As the writer states:

In addition, know that when we speak about the identity in relation to his belief, we find that the Muslim is always loyal to his belief; the true

Muslim always implements Islam and always has alliance and animosity based on that belief. The most noble and highest element of his identity and the most noble thing to be attributed to him is to be attributed to the most perfect Deen with the most honourable book revealed to the most honourable messenger in the most honourable language, in the most honourable month of the year on the most honourable night, with the most perfect Shari'ah and guidance for all of mankind that Allah praised it in the Qur'an.

We are a nation that has its own Islamic belief, its own Islamic concepts, culture, behaviour, history; its own identity. So the fact that they are living in Europe, in UK, France or Italy etc that does not mean that they have a British identity or French identity; their identity is unique and they must interact and call the people away from their Kufr identity and to the Islamic identity...

And so we cannot follow the Arab traditions or the Asian culture or the western culture. The only Shari'ah we are obliged and indeed allowed to follow is the Shari'ah of Islam; and the only culture and identity that we follow is the culture of Islam. So make sure that your identity is pure and free from any other culture; not to be poisoned by the Jewish identity, or western or Asian or Arab identity and that is why the prophet (saw) asked the Jews to give up everything that they had and they replied...

So we do not want to be like them, or even look like them. We cannot wear western clothes that are known to be part of the western fashion; the Muslims will always address the disbelievers and say, "you are free from what I am doing and we are free from what you are doing"...

So May Allah make us stick to our Islamic identity and save us from all British values, customs, culture and identities. Ameen.[19]

Among converts to Islam, the non-racial, non-regional approach to building – or receiving – an identity is both complex and dynamic. In a recent study of the role of converts within the radicalisation process in the UK, a common characteristic of those whose views were canvassed was that they were drawn to Salafism because they were looking for an "ideology rather than a faith".[20] The study also found that a large proportion of those who had converted were raised in religious families, many of them in Roman Catholic homes. Several had also come from families with members serving in the armed forces, and some were assessed as being "uncomfortable with their ethnicity", while others had travelled abroad and had a

> romantic idea of travel. But despite all these characteristics, it is difficult to identify a neat pattern. Many converts drawn to salafism seem to be seeking an ideology rather than a faith. But conversion is a very isolating experience, as the converts often don't feel they fit into their local mosque. Because of this, salafist groups like *Hizb-ut-Tahrir* become appealing.

The study went on to say:

> The converts find the all-encompassing appeal of Islam attractive. But, equally, politics is a motivating factor, with Islam being used to reflect their political aspirations. Among those who had been a part of al-Muhajiroun there were people who were low achievers but who still wanted to express their anger. The more fundamentalist the group, the more the group helped the individual convert, and groups like Hizb-ut-Tahrir are actively trying to bring converts, while many converts don't have the ability to distinguish between radicals and moderates.

Just as is clearly identified in the analysis by *al-Ghuraaba*, the UK study of converts focused on the question of *identity*. The discovery of personal identity by establishing a firm belief in Islam is clearly the path advocated by *al-Ghuraaba* and other of the Salafists that have spearheaded the radicalisation process in the UK for much of the past decade. The UK study of converts stated: "For some, Islam is a fashionable way of forging a new identity. Islam offers a new discipline, with the mosque becoming the centre of their universe, though the reasons given for conversion do appear to have been *learned*."

It is this process of *learning* which appears fundamental to the perspective and actions of Britain's Muslims. The sentencing of Abu Hamza al-Masri, as well as the ongoing detention of Abu Qatada – a highly influential imam whose video-taped sermons appear to have been as inflammatory as anything said by Abu Hamza – reflects the view in the UK that the influence of "mentors" is profound. Muslims growing up in an atmosphere of extremism are undoubtedly vulnerable.

But this truism is made more so by a further study which examined the views of British Muslims of mostly south Asian descent.[21] The study, published in March 2006, canvassed the attitudes of Muslims between the ages of 16 and 44 from a wide range of socio-economic backgrounds, all of whom were asked their opinions of jihad, martyrdom and terrorism. The key findings of this study were:

> ...*regarding attitudes towards jihad:*

- A large proportion understood jihad to mean either a "Holy war" or a "Muslim war", fought for Allah against "those who threaten the existence of Islam".
- A common understanding was of jihad as a struggle against oppression, which could be "the oppression of the Muslim people", or, equally, the oppression of their beliefs.
- In one way or another, jihad was interpreted as a fight for Islam primarily against "non-Muslims", a "fight for justice", a "fight against those who deny Muslims their rights" and "treat [them] unfairly".
- In the absence of the community taking responsibility to counter this unfair treatment, some respondents felt that individuals could "take matters into their own hands".

- A small minority, however, did not see this "fight" in physical terms, but described it instead as a mental or emotional one, which helped to "purify" someone for Allah. Many respondents also referred to jihad as "a struggle", not necessarily implying physical violence or death but rather a constant striving for faith.
- Some viewed jihad in terms of an inner struggle for the sake of peace and truth within oneself. For them, there was more to jihad than a "war" in the crudest sense. Instead, this "war" or "struggle" could be a personal "inner struggle". One respondent introduced the concepts of "lesser" and "higher" jihad, and argued that the concept is often manipulated for political ends by Muslims and non-Muslims alike.
- Another more general definition of jihad involved "keeping Islam alive" or "spreading Islam".

...regarding attitudes towards martyrdom:

- Eleven respondents specifically stated that martyrdom (*shahid*) meant death or dying in the name or cause of Allah. They saw it as defending the cause of Allah, thus "protecting the faith and those who practise it".
- One respondent suggested that by doing this "we will have paradise".
- Another stated that dying for Allah's cause meant dying "in battle against non Muslims". Thus, martyrdom meant giving one's life in the name of Islam, including dying while fighting for the right to be a practising Muslim and to be recognised as one.
- One respondent, however, stressed the difference between dying for your beliefs in war and suicide killings which were considered to be "very wrong". Another said that this action was very important but added "only in extreme circumstances". A third respondent understood this act as giving one's life a sense of justice.
- Some respondents understood and described martyrdom in terms of it being the "highest sacrifice". This sacrifice could be in the physical form, such as sacrificing one's life for one's beliefs, for "the Islamic cause".
- Some also raised questions as to the theological or conceptual aspects of the term "martyrdom", and implied that, though it was a significant concept, it was not necessarily important to them in their everyday life. They were more critical not only of the term but of how it was being misrepresented.
- One respondent blamed "shrewd politicians disguised as clerics" for misguiding people. Another argued that martyrdom "represents a theological justification for extreme actions that ultimately prolong the injustice that provokes those actions in the first place".

...regarding circumstances when acts of violence can be justified within Islam:

- 58 per cent of the sample argued that acts of violence against Muslims could not be justified within Islam.
- 47 per cent said that violence could not be justified against non-Muslims either.
- 19 per cent agreed that the use of violence could be justified against Muslims, whereas 26 per cent justified the use of violence against non-Muslims.
- Overall, the sample justified the use of violence against non-Muslims rather than Muslims.
- In general, those respondents who identified strongly with being Muslim (as opposed to being British) were more ready to feel that, in some circumstances, Islam could justify acts of violence.
- 29 per cent of those for whom being Muslim was very important indicated that there were circumstances when they felt that acts of violence against non-Muslims could be justified within Islam (23 per cent also justified actions of violence against Muslims).
- 20 per cent of those for whom being British was very important felt that acts of violence in the form of suicide bombings against military targets could be justified in Islam, again contrasting with a higher percentage (36 per cent) of those for whom being Muslim was very important.
- Those respondents, who indicated that they thought of themselves as British, were much less ready to say that violence could ever be justified within Islam. Regarding violence against non-Muslims, this was 10 per cent, as against 52 per cent of those who said they did not think of themselves as British; likewise, regarding suicide bombings against military targets, this was 13 per cent as against 66 per cent of those who did not think of themselves as British.

...regarding suicide and suicide-bombings:

- Suicide, defined as taking one's life for personal as opposed to political or ideological reasons, was viewed as *haram* (prohibited) by most of our respondents.
- [But] the sample's order of priority regarding when violence is not justifiable was, firstly, suicide (76 per cent) secondly, suicide bombing civilian targets (68 per cent), and, thirdly, suicide bombing military targets (42 per cent).
- While the majority of the sample agreed that suicide was not justifiable in Islam, a substantial minority of respondents thought that suicide bombing could be justified by Islam. 32 per cent said it was justifiable for suicide bombers to target military targets. 15 per cent justified the targeting of civilians.

- The order of priority regarding when violence is justifiable in Islam was, firstly, military targets (32 per cent), secondly, civilian targets (15 per cent), and, thirdly, self harm (8 per cent).
- The most common view of the sample was that violence could be justified only in self defence or out of desperation. But, while some respondents stated they "abhorred" the "killing of civilians", or "the idea of a suicide attack", and that this could "never be justified", they then seemingly contradicted themselves by saying that violence was justifiable in self-defence or desperation.

Humayun Ansari, the academic who conducted this study, concluded from his findings:

> At the popular level, most religious belief is not very theological. As expected, the majority of our respondents were not profound analysts of the Quran. For a vast proportion of these "believing" Muslim men and women, "Islam" tended to stand in a rather jumbled half-examined way, with the result that many possessed conflicting understandings. For example, on the one hand, many believed that they understood why some people might be driven to commit acts that were viewed by others as acts of "terror". At the same time, they denied that such acts could be the work of Muslims, that indeed Muslims were even capable of committing such horrific acts ... Hence, as the findings of this research suggest, Muslim suffering and grievances elsewhere are deeply felt by Muslims in Britain, and influence their attitudes towards the issues that have been under discussion here.

But Ansari added:

> Their understanding of the role of violence, together with their interpretations of Islamic texts in resolving conflicts, would seem to be shaped in complex and fluid ways. In essence, they would seem to be influenced more by individual and collective experiences and perceptions of the political contexts, both domestic and international, than by acceptance of some reified and homogeneous prescriptions from the past. At the same time, interaction between past and present practices, ideas and realities forms part of the attitude-framing process. As the responses of our sample highlight, interpretations and understanding of issues such as jihad and martyrdom must be located in the context that exists at any given time for their impact to be properly and fully understood.

Confronting the radicals: strategies for counter-terrorism

For converts to Islam as much as for those born into the faith, the process of *learning* has created a great range of attitudes towards belief and religious practice. As Humayun Ansari says of the Muslims whose views he canvassed:

Their understanding of the role of violence, together with their interpretations of Islamic texts in resolving conflicts, would seem to be shaped in complex and fluid ways. In essence, they would seem to be influenced more by individual and collective experiences and perceptions of the political contexts, both domestic and international, than by acceptance of some reified and homogeneous prescriptions from the past.

It is this process which has been taken up very assertively by Salafist groups in the UK. The purpose of this "educational" role is twofold: first, to assert an identity vis-à-vis the *kufr* with whom the global jihad is being fought, and – second – to seek to distinguish the Salafist cause from mainstream attitudes within the Muslim community. Although issues such as the invasion of Iraq clearly played into the hands of the Salafists – as an example of aggression by the *kufr* – there is still a need for groups in the UK to mobilise Muslims *within* the UK context who have no *personal* experience of such aggression and whose *real* ability to identify *genuinely* with all Muslims everywhere in the world – the global *umma* – is weak or non-existent.

Central to developing counter-terrorist strategies appropriate to the evolving reality of Muslim life in Britain is an understanding of the range of attitudes within the Muslim community, in particular the reasons why most Muslims are *not* likely to be drawn into terrorist activity. Equally, it is a major challenge to establish how the different tendencies within the totality of the UK's Muslim population regard the issues that have enflamed Muslim opinion in general. The use to which these issues are put by the radicals – as vehicles for mobilisation, and proof of *kufr* aggression – is clearly not the same as the response of the moderate mainstream, even though the anger within the mainstream over these same issues is just as great as it is within radical circles. What is different is the response: the radicals take these issues as proof that they can never live with the *kufr*, while – generally speaking – the mainstream take these issues as proof that there should be far greater *integration* of Muslim attitudes into the policymaking arena: Muslim sensibilities should matter in *real* ways, and "British" policy on emotive issues such as Palestine should reflect *real* sensitivity to the perspectives of British Muslims. In short, the mainstream view is that to prove Britain really is multicultural, British foreign policy should reflect the *interests* of British Muslims as an integral part of *British* interests.

The ineffectiveness of the Muslim mainstream at influencing British foreign policy has been one factor contributing to the ability of the radicals to widen their pool of recruits. The fundamental battle in the West – just as within the Middle East – is not really between Muslims and the *kufr* but between Salafists and secular Muslims. However, an important issue facing those involved in developing counter-radicalisation strategies is that there is a great deal of crossover between individuals, groups and ideas. As Anthony McRoy, a leading British writer on religion has written in *From Rushdie to 7/7: The Radicalization of Islam in Britain*:

We have seen that Islamic radicalism in the UK is not a monolith, and we must be careful when referring to "Muslim radicals" because they are a very diverse body. Most are participationist, but some are rejectionist, and even among the latter there are very different nuances. In fact, some expressions of Muslim radicalism are now the dominant and guiding forces in British Islam. At the start of the twenty-first century many British Muslims remain quite alienated from government policies in many ways, notably on foreign policy matters. As was demonstrated by 7/7, some are violently inclined, but most are much more confident and able than they were when [Salman] Rushdie's book [The Satanic Verses] first led to public awareness of their distinctive identity. Like everyone, they learned from their mistakes. But something else has occurred, too: the traditional, subcontinental Islam, with its cultural accretions, has lost out to challenges from the contextualised radicalism of Mawdudism, Qutbism and Khomeinism, and even from home-grown strategies, as with the [Muslim Public Affairs Committee]. In particular, Muslims are more confident in their British identity, partly as a result of their own social engineering policies, partly through natural integration, but also because of more positive public attitudes – such as the mass turnout at anti-war rallies over Iraq. Again, as a consequence of this war, Muslims have managed to implement strategies for tactical voting, and have seen the fruit of it. This holds out the prospect for a more peaceful and cohesive future – Insh'allah.[22]

McRoy's expectation that the increasing confidence of Britain's Muslim population will dilute the tendency towards rejectionism raises the question of whether the [possibly] increasingly isolated pool of extremists ready to commit acts of terrorism will be influenced by these broader social currents within the UK, or whether it will continue to be most strongly influenced by the ideological pull of a creed influenced more by *global* trends than by the realities of the UK alone. It should always be assumed that the extremists can be influenced by social currents – if things improve for British Muslims, then some who could have been lured by extremism may instead be pulled by a "moderating tide". This leaves the hard core – the individuals who, for personal or other reasons, have embarked on a course from which no wider social currents are going to deter them.

It is these people who are the major cause of concern, and the London bombings of 7 July 2005 were the point at which the intelligence gathering which had led UK officials to regard a terrorist attack as inevitable gave the British security establishment the insight into something which they knew was there but could not have seen until it actually happened.

The conclusions of the official report into the 7/7 bombings are an instructive guideline as to how far – even "after the event" – the UK authorities have reached in establishing a substantial understanding of the threat Britain faces. Briefly, these conclusions[23] are:

- The case demonstrates the real difficulty for law enforcement agencies and local communities in identifying potential terrorists. All four [terrorists]

were open about their strict religious observance but there was little outward sign that this had spilled over into potentially violent extremism.
- There is little in their backgrounds which mark them out as particularly vulnerable to radicalisation, with the possible exception of Jermaine Lindsay. Khan, Tanweer and Hussain were apparently well integrated into British society.
- In the absence of evidence of other methods, the process of indoctrinating these men appears principally to have been through personal contact and group bonding ... Their indoctrination appears to have taken place away from places with known links to extremism.
- Their motivation appears to be typical of similar cases. Fierce antagonism to perceived injustices by the West against Muslims and a desire for martyrdom.
- The extent of Al Qaida involvement is unclear. There was contact with someone in Pakistan in the run up to the bombings.
- It remains unclear whether others in the UK were involved in radicalising or inciting the group, or in helping them to plan and execute it.

As the terrorist attacks of 11 September 2001 become the *past*, and are replaced in the public mind by subsequent atrocities and their consequences, discussion within the UK about the challenge from extremist Islam has become more frank as knowledge has improved and understanding deepened. Sir David Omand, until recently the British government's Intelligence and Security Co-ordinator wrote recently:

The most effective weapon of the terrorist at present is their ideology. And that is driven by underlying strategic thinking on the part of their leaders. If we are to prevail – as we can and will – then the struggle of ideas, as much as the tactical battle on the streets, has to be won. Like other terrorist groups in the past, members of al-Qaeda will adjust their message to take advantage of weaknesses they see in our policies, and to exploit our differences. We see this in their use of the Internet and video technology. The international terrorist ideology now has a life of its own beyond the lives of the men in the cave that spawned it. Like a biological parasite, it can only live off the energy of its hosts, mutating as it spreads, into forms that can infect previously untouched groups, particularly if their natural immunity is low. Even if the original source is destroyed we are left with the spread of this ideological virus as a continuing danger.

That is what we have been seeing with the radicalisation of small groups within the UK itself. We thus badly need a counter-narrative that will help groups exposed to the terrorist message make sense of what they are seeing around them. We should not be diverted in this task by bogus fears that to search for the understanding needed to underpin our strategy is a step towards excusing or even condoning such beliefs. And we need international understanding of such a narrative. If the United States and Europe deploy very different rhetoric and send signals that can be interpreted as contradictory, then we will lose ground. The UK has had to learn hard lessons in that respect in responding to terrorism in Northern Ireland. Attempts to brand the terrorists evil, mindless or mad – however apt as a description of highly violent individuals – was read by all sides in the community as confirming the view of the extremists that successive governments of the day did not understand, or were not prepared to acknowledge, the historical roots of the terrorist campaign. The circumstances were very different, but the parallel may suggest that we are still at a relatively unsophisticated stage in our thinking of how to present internationally and domestically what will be a long campaign. We even lack language with which to describe the essential features of the threat and its ideology without risking giving offence to Muslims around the world – hence my use of the British government's preferred euphemism, "international terrorism".[24]

Omand was the architect of the UK's counter-terrorism strategy in the post-9/11 period – abbreviated to the "4 Ps": Prevent, Pursue, Protect and Prepare. He was thus as affected by – and perhaps as responsible for – the shortcomings which he identifies and which became evident within the UK security establishment. The most striking point raised by Omand is this assertion that "The most effective weapon of the terrorist at present is their ideology", a point which he follows up with the challenge: "If we are to prevail – as we can and will – then the struggle of ideas, as much as the tactical battle on the streets, has to be won."

That this analysis of the threat to the UK was written several months after the 7 July 2005 bombings makes this assertion all the more significant, as it recognises that one root of the problem lies within the society wherein the terror was spawned – that is, *within the UK itself* – owing at least in part to the refusal of "successive governments ... to acknowledge the historical roots of the terrorist campaign". Omand had his supporters and detractors within UK security circles while occupying the position of Intelligence and Security Co-ordinator, his detractors criticising him for identifying where the intelligence community should focus its efforts even though he himself was not an intelligence professional despite having been director of the Government Communications Headquarters (GCHQ).

His prescription for the future made clear the struggle within the security establishment. While on the one hand it has sought – and continues to seek – to implement an effective counter-terrorism strategy that is primarily aimed at saving lives, it has only relatively recently been able to consider detailed ways of tailoring the counter-terrorism strategy to a profound understanding of the issues – personal, social, political, religious, geo-political – that underlie the threat.

A senior counter-terrorism officer reflected on this:

> It's not our role to consider all the additional consequences of what we do. Our primary aim is to prevent atrocities, save lives, and make the public feel secure. We know that there are vast issues and that we are – in a sense –

dealing with the tip of the iceberg when we spy on people, bug telephones, intercept Internet traffic, knock down doors and arrest people. But the counter-terrorism strategy has in essence to be informed primarily by knowledge of specific threats – of which we are currently dealing with around 100 simultaneously in the UK – while we have to leave to others the task of social engineering and developing foreign policies which can dilute the anger. Bridging the gap between understanding the underlying issues and designing a counter-terrorism strategy in response to that deeper understanding just isn't possible in the current climate, when the threat is real, urgent and highly dangerous. There are too many lives at stake for us to become overly academic.[25]

However, the problem with this approach was made clear prior to the bombings of 7 July 2005. Three months before the bombings – and thus several months *after* the London conference of *al-Muhajiroun* whose proceedings were described at the beginning of this chapter – a senior UK counter-terrorism strategist had said:

We feel that we are seeing the finer grain of the picture. But the overall picture has not changed ... For the UK Muslim it is still very much the external jihadist story. Most of it is about the traditional issues of contention: the Middle East. Much of this activity revolves around the idea: what can we do to help?[26]

He continued:

We have not detected signs that there is a wish among British Muslims that they are wishing to act within the UK, against the authorities within the UK. We haven't detected that. We are more focused on the risk of attempts that are potentially externally inspired. This isn't going to self-generate from within the UK, from people with a sense of injustice. We must expect quite determined attempts to get people in here to try and create chaos. [In general] you can plan together for an operation that might take a year to plan. What they [within the UK] don't have is the self-starting professional knowledge. So they will get caught. They are not professional at it. They lack that knowledge of how to run a terrorist cell.

He added:

But it's only a matter of time. The knowledge is very replicable. What we need to watch out for is somebody arriving from outside. But there isn't much command and control left in al-Qaeda central that we can detect. We have slowed the process down a lot by the arrests that we have made. But we haven't stopped it, and we must expect it to pick up again. What would accelerate it would be more influence from outside.

The views of this official – whose personal influence lay right at the heart of the UK government's counter-terrorism policymaking process – could evidently not have been more mistaken, as the events of 7 July 2005 showed. None of the terrorism investigations that have taken place in the UK has taken place without part of the inquiry taking place abroad – often in Pakistan, but also in Saudi Arabia, Jordan, other parts of Europe, or the United States. However, this focus distracted those very same security officers from seeing the reality of their own country, despite MI5 having established a regional presence in major UK cities in 2004 and opening fully-fledged regional offices in 2005. The "finer grain" of the terrorist threat – as the senior counter-terrorism strategist cited above calls it – was perhaps too fine for those fighting it to see. Perhaps this is because it is within their own country, and the biggest challenge they have is in trying to work out how an outwardly socialised man in his bedroom in the north of England or an educated Iraqi doctor living in Scotland could be a more immediate threat than a well-armed man sitting in a cave in Afghanistan.

The absence of "intelligence" prior to the 7 July 2005 bombings was – it has to be said – in part due to the absence of resources available to track every lead and place even "unlikely" targets under surveillance for long periods of time. A senior UK counter-terrorist police officer said:

> The day of the 7 July bombing made one thing clear: the intelligence gathering had been a failure. MI5 simply had nothing to offer. Nor did the police Special Branch (which also has an intelligence gathering role, but which was folded into the newly-created Counter-Terrorism Units created in 2006). The entire effort on 21 July 2005, when the second lot of bombers nearly got away with it, was due to classic policing. It was a manhunt of the kind we would do for any criminal, and intelligence about terrorism and terrorists played absolutely no part in our success in finding the would-be bombers.[27]

Despite this scepticism, however, other senior police officers have made clear that intelligence – by which a body of convincing knowledge can lead to an understanding of the phenomenon during its developmental stage – is becoming a useful tool for wholly new reasons. Peter Clarke, head of the Metropolitan Police anti-terrorist branch (SO-13) and later the head of the newly created Counter-Terrorism Command until his retirement in 2007, said:

> We need to give ourselves the choice of whether to intervene with arrest and prosecution, or whether some other form of disruption better serves the overall public interest – and the way we have achieved this represents one of the most fundamental changes in the way in which counterterrorism is delivered in this country. There is no longer a sequence where intelligence material becomes mysteriously translated into a product that is admissible in court as evidence. There is obviously some material that has to be protected, but for the most part we are now running the intelligence and evidential

tracks in parallel – in fact, I prefer to think of it all as information, and we just need to gather and handle it in a way that gives us choices as to how to use it. This obviously requires high levels of trust and co-operation between the intelligence world and law enforcement – but I would like to think that the generation of this trust and the level of co-operative working has been one of the great success stories of the past few years.

Clarke's conclusion reveals clearly that the UK's efforts to counter both radicalisation and the terrorist threat it has spawned have been troubled, with the institutions at the forefront of the strategy clearly learning as much through error as through trial. He makes clear that what was believed only a few months earlier – that the terrorists were amateurs who relied on external assistance – was totally wrong and verged on the arrogant, saying:

> We know that the terrorists we are facing in the UK are well-trained, highly motivated and confident of achieving their goals. There has been, without doubt, a shift in our understanding of the scale and intensity of the problem ... The recalibration since 9/11 has not only been in the scale of our response, but also in our understanding of the terrorist networks in the UK. In early 2002 we regarded ourselves as net importers of terrorism ... We then came to know that the UK was an exporter as well as an importer of terrorism ... There are hugely important and sensitive issues at stake here. We are still at the stage of trying to understand the evolving nature of the current threat. In just the past few years our perceptions, and indeed the reality of the threat, have changed completely. There is no reason to suppose this will change – we must all be prepared to learn.[28]

Notes

1 Omar Bakri Muhammad, interview with the author, 5 January 2005.
2 Abu Yahya Abderahman, London, 8 January 2005.
3 Abu Suleiman, London, 8 January 2005.
4 Member of Women's Da'wa UK, London, 8 January 2005.
5 Member of Women's Da'wa UK, ibid.
6 Humayun Ansari, interview with the author, 14 December 2004.
7 Ibid.
8 Sheikh Ibrahim Moqra, Imam of the Masjid Umar Mosque, Leicester, interview with the author, 17 December 2004.
9 Mohamed Naseem, chairman of the council, Birmingham City Mosque, interview with the author, 4 January 2005.
10 Abu Izzadeen, London, 8 January 2005.
11 Senior security official, interview with the author, 7 May 2006.
12 Senior security official, interview with the author, 12 May 2006.
13 Abu Hamza al-Masri, interview with the author, 7 February 2005.
14 www.homeoffice.gov.uk/documents/7-july-report.pdf?view=Binary. pp. 31–32.
15 Senior security official, interview with the author, 3 June 2006.
16 UK report on 7 July 2005 bombings, op. cit., pp. 18–19.
17 Leading expert on terrorist profiles, London, 28 April 2006.

18 www.alghurabaa.co.uk/Deen/walaa_baraa/identity.htm.
19 Ibid.
20 Private, interview-based study of 34 converts in the UK who have been associated with Salafist groups.
21 Humayun Ansari, "Attitudes to Jihad, Martyrdom and Terrorism" article in: *Muslim Britain: Communities Under Pressure*, edited by Tahir Abbas, (London, Zed Books, 2006).
22 Anthony McRoy, *From Rushdie to 7/7: The Radicalization of Islam in Britain*, (London, The Social Affairs Unit, 2006), p. 235.
23 UK report, op. cit., p. 27.
24 Sir David Omand, "Countering International Terrorism: The Use of Strategy", article in *Survival*, vol. 47, no. 4, Winter 2005–2006, pp. 107–116.
25 Senior UK security official, interview with the author, 3 June 2006.
26 Senior UK counter-terrorism strategist, interview with the author, 5 April 2005.
27 Senior UK counter-terrorism police officer, interview with the author, 16 July 2005.
28 Peter Clarke, Deputy Assistant Commissioner and Head, SO13 Anti-Terrorist Branch, Metropolitan Police. Speech to the Royal United Services Institute, London, 15 February 2006.

6 An overview of violent jihad in the UK

Radicalisation and the state response

Lindsay Clutterbuck

Introduction

The objective of this chapter is threefold: to examine the ways in which violent jihad has manifested itself in the UK, predominantly since the events of 11 September 2001 in the USA; to explore the processes of radicalisation and recruitment to terrorism in a wider context and finally, to analyse the UK response to the current threat posed by radicalisation and recruitment.

There are numerous difficulties in carrying out research in this area in the UK and these must be constantly borne in mind. Foremost among them is the current lack of authorative and reliable open source material. Only a very small number of cases have come to trial, yet alone completed one. In advance of any trial, the judicial system in the UK imposes strict controls on the release into the public domain of any material that may prejudice the defendant's right to a fair trial, hence much information remains unknown until that point.

A further complicating factor must also be considered. The time delay between defendants being charged with offences and their eventual trial is now of such a length that the events at issue may have occurred two or even three years before.[1] This situation means that the information that enters the public domain as the consequence of its revelation at a trial is always subjected to a "time-lag" between its occurrence and its revelation. For example, due to the legal necessity for both the so-called "Ricin trial" and the trial of Abu Hamza to be completed, the full details surrounding the police search of Finsbury Park Mosque in January 2003 and the materials that were found there could not be put into the public domain until three years later.[2] The final caveat is that the number of trials that have yet to be held is not insignificant. As of February 2006, sixty defendants had been charged with various offences relating to violent jihad and were remanded in custody awaiting trial.[3] By June 2006, the figure had increased to nearly seventy and by October it had reached ninety.[4] Only when the legal process has run its course over the next few years will it be possible to obtain a clearer and more comprehensive picture of terrorist activity related to violent jihad in the five years since 9/11.

The challenge faced by the UK is a difficult one due both to the scale of the threat and its complexity. These difficulties are further compounded by the multidimensional way in which the threat can manifest itself, the range of individuals who become involved in it and the differing motivations that underlie their involvement. As well as countering those who are determined to carry out attacks, there is a pressing need to apply effective measures to mitigate the process of radicalisation and prevent the recruitment of people into terrorist activity. To add to the difficulties of the counter-terrorism practitioner, this must be done whilst simultaneously trying to identify and understand its causal factors and underlying dynamics in order to devise effective counter-measures. Dealing with this paradox is one of the most critical tasks currently facing the UK government, the intelligence agencies and the police.

The rise of violent jihad in the UK

For obvious reasons, the events that occurred in London during July 2005 tend to be at the forefront of any consideration today of how violent jihad has impacted on the UK. On 7 July 2005, four suicide bombers, three of them UK-born and one UK raised, detonated homemade explosive devices on three Underground trains and a double-decker bus in London. Fifty-two people were killed and many hundreds were seriously injured.[5] Simultaneously with the rescue and recovery operations, a massive investigation immediately began to determine what exactly had occurred and who else may have been involved in perpetrating it. Fourteen days later, on 21 July 2005, four alleged suicide bombers launched further coordinated attacks on the London Underground and a bus. None of the devices detonated and they fled. A further rucksack containing homemade explosive was later found in some bushes, indicating that a fifth bomber may have set out on the same task but had abandoned the attempt.[6] Six men are now awaiting trial on charges of possessing explosives and conspiracy to murder and a further six people will face a separate trial accused of assisting an offender and failing to disclose information on terrorism.[7]

Speaking in 2006 on the first anniversary of the 7 July bombings, the Commissioner of the Metropolitan Police, Sir Ian Blair, revealed that since then three more terrorist operations had been discovered and disrupted. He went on to state "We are now in a position where the threat is both internal and external ... it is very grim ... There are, as we speak, people in the United Kingdom planning further atrocities."[8] Just over a month later on 10 August 2006, police arrested twenty-four people in the London area as a result of "Operation Overt".[9] In an echo of the "Oplan Bojinka" plot of Ramzi Yousef that had been disrupted in January 1995, they were held on suspicion of conspiring to detonate explosives on a series of passenger aircraft leaving Heathrow en route to cities across the USA.[10]

On 10 November 2006 the Director General of the Security Service in the UK (MI5) stated in a rare public speech that since 7 July 2005 "five major conspiracies in the UK" had been thwarted and that the Service had already seen this year an "eighty per cent increase in case work since January".[11] In practical terms, they were aware of "some 200 groupings or networks, totalling over 1,600 identified individuals ... actively engaged in plotting, or facilitating, terrorist acts here and overseas".[12]

Taking into account these pronouncements and the events since 7 July, it therefore appears that the threat to the UK from terrorists motivated by violent jihad is real, substantial and continuing. However, in order to put the current situation into context, a longer-term historical view is also required. The UK, and in particular the British mainland, has seen numerous acts of "international terrorism" in both the nineteenth and twentieth centuries. Indeed, many of the operational and tactical elements seen in terrorist attacks today were first deployed from 1881 onwards by the Irish-American members of Clan na Gael and the Skirmishers who travelled from the USA to the British mainland to carry them out. Their objective was to carry on a campaign of terrorism that was designed to cause such a public outrage that it would force the government to withdraw from Ireland.[13]

Their innovations were many; from devising the very concept of a "campaign of terrorism" itself to their invention and use of novel mechanical and chemical timing mechanisms to detonate their explosive devices, the manufacture of explosives in "kitchen workshops" and obtaining their financial support by fund-raising amongst sympathisers abroad.[14] As a consequence of this, measures were devised and implemented to counter them. Many still remain as important elements of the UK counter-terrorism response, for example: the gathering and operational use of intelligence; developing a systematic approach to the surveillance of suspect individuals and groups; the scrutinising of passengers as they arrive at and leave UK ports to identify those involved in terrorism and the use of UK detectives to carry out investigations abroad into potential terrorists who might wish to target the UK.[15]

Moving forward into the twentieth century, incidents of international terrorism began to occur regularly but intermittently in the UK. Unlike the consistently recurring episodes of Irish republican terrorism throughout that period, the attacks were motivated by a variety of differing causes and were carried out by disparate individuals and groups. Initially, they were associated with opposition to the British presence in India.[16] The cause of Indian nationalism was later superceded by a number of attacks in Britain arising out of the administration of the British Mandate in Palestine, particularly during the period from 1947 to 1948.[17]

Perhaps surprisingly, the series of British counter-insurgency campaigns carried out in Malaya, Kenya, Cyprus, Brunei, Borneo and the Gulf States between 1948 and 1967 generated no terrorist attacks within the UK.[18] However, these campaigns did have a great impact on the British armed forces, leading to the development of a distinct sub-set of military doctrine and capability known as counter-insurgency (COIN). Subsequently, the concept and doctrines of COIN were first used in the development of the counter-terrorist strategies employed by the police and military in Northern Ireland and then in turn, on the mainland of the UK itself.[19]

Foremost amongst the key principles derived from these campaigns was the realisation that driving a wedge between the insurgents and the communities upon which they depended for food, shelter, recruits and information was the cornerstone of successful counter-insurgency. Without the active cooperation of the population, particularly in providing accurate and timely information and intelligence on the activities of the insurgents, the insurgents stood a far better chance of achieving their own military and political objectives. Consequently, in addition to day-to-day COIN and counter-terrorism operations, significant efforts needed to be made by the government, military and police if they were to win the battle for the "hearts and minds" of the population.[20] As will be seen, this concept now lies at the centre of current efforts in the UK to ensure that the flow of "community intelligence" is developed and utilised against the current threat from violent jihad and in stopping the radicalisation of individuals.

From the late 1960s onwards, international terrorism once more began to occur in the UK itself, predominantly on the streets of London. Its return coincided with a series of terrorist attacks throughout the British mainland carried out from 1974 onwards by a reinvigorated IRA, thus compounding the difficulties of those responsible for dealing with it.[21] A plethora of groups, mainly but not exclusively linked to the wider conflict in the Middle East, carried out shootings, bomb attacks and aircraft hijackings in the UK or against UK citizens and UK assets overseas. Their causes encompassed Palestinian, Armenian and Sikh nationalism whilst their targets ranged from diplomats to their own nationals, from the aircrew of national airlines to businessmen. Some attacks were not only encouraged by foreign governments but were also carried out by their agents. Foremost amongst these state-sponsors of terrorism were Libya, Iran and Iraq, but the murders of dissident nationals from the Seychelles, Yugoslavia and Bulgaria also took place.

From amongst this apparently inchoate mass of international terrorist attacks that have taken place in the UK over the last thirty years of the twentieth century, a strategic theme can be identified. From a counter-terrorism perspective, there are two key elements. First, whilst all of these attacks took place in the UK, the UK itself was only the venue and *not* the target. Second, as the perpetrators were foreign nationals, at some stage, they had to travel to the UK from overseas. Indeed, even the IRA had to send its operatives on the British mainland from "overseas" in Northern Ireland or Ireland.[22] As far as the British mainland was concerned, as well as international terrorism, Irish terrorism also arrived from "outside" even though it was perceived of as an internal, domestic terrorist threat. Until about 2003, these two fundamental certainties underpinned the operational level of the counter-terrorism response on the British mainland, both against Irish republican and international terrorism.

The 1990s saw the rise of a different form of international terrorism, this time based on the ideology of Islamist extremism. It differed from the existing pattern of international terrorism in that its exponents committed no terrorist attacks in the UK and where they did espouse or support political violence, the targets involved were located in other countries. Under the anti-terrorist legislation that existed at the time, police jurisdiction was geographically limited to offences committed in the UK and this constrained the possibilities of executive action in cases where the offence would ultimately be committed abroad.[23] However, where attacks did occur, police investigations generally led to arrests, charges and convictions in court.[24]

There were several events in this period that assumed an even greater significance in the light of subsequent events. Foremost amongst these was the war in Bosnia between 1992 and 1995. It played a critical role in the development of violent jihad both in the UK and in Europe. Bosnia provided a theatre of war at the heart of Europe where exponents of violent jihad could participate in "military operations", but perhaps its greatest impact came in the opportunities it presented to those who wished to encourage and spread their message of violent Islamist extremism.[25] They found London, with its wide variety of diaspora communities, its central role in the Middle Eastern press and media networks and its high level of tolerance to publicly aired extremist views, to be particularly suited to their activities.

In 1994, Osama bin Laden took advantage of these opportunities to open an office in London, operating under the name of the "Advice and Reformation Committee". Over the next few years, it was instrumental in ensuring the distribution of *fatwas* issued by bin Laden and statements from Al-Qaeda.[26] The Advice and Reformation Committee was closed down in the aftermath of the Al-Qaeda bomb attacks on the US Embassies in Nairobi and Dar es Salaam on 7 August 1998. Its three organisers, Khalid Fawwaz, Ibrahim Eidarous and Adel Abdel Bary were arrested pending extradition to the USA to stand trial in connection with the attacks.[27]

A further, ultimately more alarming indicator of things to come occurred in November 2000 when two men of Bangladeshi origin were arrested in Birmingham in possession of a substantial quantity of a homemade explosive called HMTD, plus numerous documents and computer files relating to the manufacture and use of explosive devices. At their trial, one man was acquitted but Moinul Abedin was found guilty of planning to cause an explosion and sentenced to twenty years imprisonment. No indication of a motive or target emerged at the trial.[28] However, since then, a little more information concerning these events has emerged into the public domain. In 2003, the Director of the UK Security Service stated "It is not known for what purpose they intended this explosive but it is certain that it was for use in the UK".[29] The Home Secretary, John Reid, recently went further, commenting in the aftermath of the operation against the alleged Heathrow plotters in August 2006 that the government believed that this was the first "Al-Qaeda plot" that was planned in and targeted against the UK.[30]

By 2001, if anyone was still under the misapprehension that terrorism driven by the ideology of violent jihad would have little or no impact in the UK itself, a series of events in the four months from September to December must surely have dispelled it. They included: the deaths of sixty-four UK citizens at the hands of Al-Qaeda in their attack on the World Trade Center; a clear link between the suicide bombers who killed the leader of the Northern Alliance in Afghanistan, Ahmad Shah Massoud, and the preparations made in the UK for that attack; the discovery of a predominantly North African money-raising and facilitation network in Leicester which led back to Al-Qaeda and finally, in December, the attempt to destroy in mid-air a flight from Paris to Miami. It was carried out by Richard Reid, a petty criminal from south London and a convert to Islam, who attempted to detonate explosives concealed in his shoes. The involvement in violent jihad of UK citizens and foreign citizens resident in the UK had both become an unmistakeable reality.

Characterising the threat from violent jihad today

Nearly five years after the attacks in the USA on 9/11, the threat to the UK has increased dramatically. A recent government report to Parliament states "that the scale of the threat is potentially still increasing and is not likely to diminish significantly for some years" and the events of August 2006 seem to bear this out.[31] The activities of violent jihadists in the UK are far more complex and cover a much greater scope than might be suggested if the focus is maintained solely on the attacks on the London transport system in July 2005 and the alleged conspiracy against aircraft uncovered in August 2006.

An analysis of the publicly available information on the cells, networks and indeed individuals linked to violent jihad in the UK indicates that they are not homogeneous. A large degree of diversity can be seen in the ways that they are established, controlled and organised and in the activities that they engage in. These range from supporting, financing and facilitating terrorism in the UK and abroad, to the radicalising and recruitment of individuals and finally, the preparation and carrying out of terrorist attacks in the UK itself. In the latter case, the objective of achieving mass casualties through the use of suicide terrorism has been achieved once, failed once and appears to have been planned or prepared on other occasions as well.

In order to encapsulate as many of their multifarious activities as possible into a holistic representation of violent jihad in the UK, it is helpful to aggregate the information into four categories. Three of the categories are centred on the participants in violent jihad and one is centred on their activities. The categories of the typology thus produced cover the motivation of those involved in it, those who are known to have participated in it, the way that the participants are organised and structured and finally, how their activities manifest themselves. Each of these four categories is now examined in turn.

Motivation for involvement in activity related to violent jihad

How and where an individual becomes involved in violent jihad is inextricably bound up in their own personal philosophical justification of why they wish to do so. There are two forms of jihad that advocate the use of physical force, the first of which is "offensive jihad".[32] The use of offensive jihad is only justified in very specific and well-defined circumstances, but where these are met, the enemy may be attacked wherever they are found, including in the enemy's own country. However, it is not the motivating factor behind the violent jihad that we see today and to all intents and purposes, offensive jihad can be set to one side as a causal factor in the context of current terrorist attacks driven by violent jihad.[33]

Second, there is "defensive jihad", where the prospective jihadist takes a decision that they are prepared to fight and die in defence of fellow Muslims and Muslim lands. It is a long-standing and well-understood concept in Islamic legal sources.[34] The duty to undertake it is placed on an individual and therefore it is their personal decision whether or not to engage in it. It is defensive jihad that encompasses all of the terrorist activities that are now seen in the UK. In practical terms, once an individual has taken the decision to engage in violent jihad, the justification that they have used to make that decision therefore dictates whether it is undertaken in the UK or overseas.

This situation arises because this individual justification can fall within a number of points that cover a spectrum of violent defensive jihad. At the one end, it is based on the traditional belief that defensive jihad only applies to the defence of Muslims in Muslim lands and consequently, as the UK is not a Muslim country, any individual wishing to engage in it must do so in another country. Since the invasion of Afghanistan by the Soviet Union in December 1979 opened the first substantial modern "front" where defensive jihad could be "legitimately" fought, the opportunities to participate in defensive jihad have progressively widened. Initially, the destinations were Afghanistan, then Bosnia and Chechnya, followed by Kashmir and increasingly today, Iraq.

Accurate numbers of those participating cannot be ascertained but, as previously stated, six Muslims from the UK had been killed in Bosnia by 1995, including a UK citizen who died in the premature detonation of a car bomb that may have been destined for a "suicide" attack.[35] It was not until April 2003 that an event occurred that would bring to prominence the involvement of UK citizens in this type of activity. On 30 April, Asif Hanif from Hounslow, West London and Omar Sharif from Derby launched a suicide bomb attack in Mike's Place, a seafront bar in Tel Aviv, Israel. Hanif detonated his device and died instantly whilst Sharif fled the scene after his device failed to detonate. Three people were killed and many more injured. The body of Sharif was found in the sea several days later.[36]

Since then, a number of arrests have been made in the UK as the police and intelligence services target individuals and networks dedicated to recruiting volunteers to participate in violent jihad overseas and facilitating them to do so. Increasingly, their destination of choice appears to be Iraq.[37]

At the farther end of the spectrum of violent defensive jihad lie those individuals who have shown that not only are they prepared to carry out terrorism in the UK but they are prepared to use suicide terrorist attacks to do so. In these cases, they have pushed beyond the confines and strictures of the traditional understanding of what constitutes the defence of Muslims and Muslim lands. They believe that, as they perceive it, Muslims and the Muslim ummah are under attack throughout the world, and in these circumstances they are justified in attacking the enemy wherever it is possible to do so.

An overview of violent jihad in the UK   151

Marc Sageman introduced in 2004 the concept of the "Global Salafist Jihad" to describe the actions of those who are prepared to carry out violent jihad in circumstances over and above those traditionally encompassed by defensive jihad.[38] The suitability of the name he assigned it can be debated, but undoubtedly the priority of its adherents is "to car[ry] the fight to the 'far enemy' (the United States and the West in general) on its own territory or in third country territory".[39] The first and foremost group exponent of this strategy was Al-Qaeda, but increasingly it has been adopted by other groups, networks and individuals. Some of the initial participants from the UK who undertook this type of activity were Richard Reid (the so-called "shoe bomber"), Sajid Badaat (who trained to carry out an identical and possibly simultaneous suicide mission to Reid) and Andrew Rowe (originally a veteran of jihad in Bosnia and Chechnya).

The third category of individuals in the UK who are involved with violent jihadism are those who have recently arrived in the country from overseas and now reside here. They may be participants in or supporters of violent jihad in other countries and they are generally present in the UK on a temporary, non-active basis. They may be here for "rest and recuperation" or they may be using the UK as a destination to avoid arrest in their own country or a previous country of residence. Individuals have been traced and arrested at the request of the Dutch, Spanish and French governments. On 6 June 2006, a US citizen resident in the UK, Syed Hashmi, was arrested pending extradition to the US where he had been recently indicted on charges of receiving "military gear" intended for use in terrorism.[40]

The final category is a small one, consisting of the criminal opportunists who seek to exploit the situation created by violent jihad for their own financial ends. They are not part of the terrorist networks or groups but appear to view them as a resource to capitalise on. Their activities are driven mainly by the prospect of illegal financial gain for themselves. At best they are unconcerned with the potential end destination and usage of the items they offer for sale and at worst they fully understand the consequences. Generally, their activities encompass the procuring and selling of arms and other equipment. As an example, Hemant Lakhani was convicted in the USA in April 2005 of trying to sell shoulder-launched missiles to an FBI agent posing as a Somali terrorist. He was born in India but had lived in the UK for forty-five years. He received a sentence of forty-seven years.[41]

In July 2005 in the UK, three men were acquitted of trying to acquire "red mercury" with the intention of selling it on to a customer in the Middle East "for use in terrorism".[42] After the trial, the head of the counter-terrorism prosecution unit of the Crown Prosecution Service stated that in their opinion, "we regarded the evidence as credible and the trial ran its full course".[43] It remains to be seen whether and how this type of terrorist support service develops.

One final note of grave concern must be raised over the known potential for criminals to acquire and supply (at a price) radioactive material. Al-Qaeda, at least, is known to be interested in acquiring this type of material to produce a radiological or possibly even a nuclear weapon.[44]

Participants in violent jihad

Until very recently, the UK experience of international terrorism was that it predominantly involved individuals who originated from various countries in the Middle East, from Libya, Iran and Iraq or the Indian sub-continent and who entered the UK as visitors from abroad. Often, the sole purpose of their visit was to carry out one or more terrorist acts before they made their escape out of the country. From the early 1990s onwards, foreign nationals who were resident in the UK also began to become involved in terrorism. Usually, this was related to nationalist struggles in their country of origin and not targeted specifically against the UK. An early example of this arose from the demands of Sikhs for an independent Sikh nation (Khalistan) to be established in the Punjab. A terrorist campaign in India generated support, procurement and fund-raising activity in the UK. It also led to several incidents in the UK itself where Indian diplomats and supporters of rival internal factions were attacked and in some cases killed.

Just as this source of political violence was gradually fading away, the withdrawal of the Soviet Union from Afghanistan in 1989 led to the arrival in the UK of a number of "Afghan veterans", many of whom originated from North Africa. It can be argued that if it was events in Afghanistan in the 1980s that sowed the seeds of violent jihad in the UK, it was the developing war and violence in Algeria and then Bosnia that encouraged its growth throughout the 1990s.

The increasing radicalisation of loose networks of exiles from Algeria throughout that period eventually fed directly into terrorist activity. In September 2001, independently from the aftermath of 9/11, a substantial terrorist support network consisting mainly of North African UK residents was uncovered in Leicester. Its participants were a mixture of those legally and illegally in the UK. Two Algerian individuals who played key roles, Baghdad Meziane (an asylum seeker) and Brahim Benmerzouga, were convicted of an international credit card fraud aimed at raising money for terrorism. The court was satisfied that they were linked to Al-Qaeda, although at that stage the incompletely implemented Terrorism Act 2000 could not be used to charge them with that particular offence.[45]

Despite the fact that UK citizens were travelling abroad to engage in violent jihad, there had been no further substantive indications since November 2000 that UK citizens were either involved in the planning and preparation of large-scale violent jihadist terrorist attacks in the UK or that their targets were to be UK citizens. This perception began to change with the arrest on 30 March 2004 of eight UK citizens, six of whom are of Pakistani descent, and the seizure of over half a ton of ammonium nitrate fertiliser from a self-storage unit in West London. The men are currently on trial accused of possessing the fertiliser with the intention of using it as an explosive to commit a terrorist attack.[46]

Since then, the number of British citizens arrested and charged with involvement in terrorist activities targeted against the UK has increased substantially. Inevitably, not every plan could be detected or disrupted, as became clear after the suicide attacks of 7 July 2005. Three trends now seem to be developing in terrorist activity in the UK. First, the suicide attack is becoming the weapon of first choice; second, the majority of those carrying out the attacks seem to be male, young, UK-born citizens of Pakistani descent (although there is diversity) and third, the recurring involvement in terrorist activity of converts to Islam who originate from other ethnic or religious backgrounds.

Organisation and structure

Traditionally, a terrorist group was just that, a group of people who, to a greater or lesser extent, operated in a hierarchical structure. In the cases of the Irish Republican Army (IRA) and the Palestinian Liberation Organisation (PLO), they were large enough also to function as bureaucracies. In this sense, the most recent "group" to threaten the UK directly has been Al-Qaeda. Since "Operation Enduring Freedom" destroyed its training camps and brought down the Taliban regime in Afghanistan that supported it, and after five years of numerous other operations across the globe targeted against it, the threat presented directly by Al-Qaeda acting as an organised group has lessened.

However, it has not been removed and there are indications that it may have been involved in some way with the recent alleged Heathrow airport plot.[47] In addition, whilst the Al-Qaeda "core" has been degraded, various other terrorist groups affiliated to it and its cause have begun to carry out their own violent jihadist attacks. They range from those with close personal and operational links, such as Jemmah Islamiyyah (JI), to those who have no links at all but who have become inspired enough to declare themselves as followers, for example, the recently arrested "Miami 7" in the USA who allegedly "had taken an oath to Al-Qaeda".[48] In this latter category, each group acts on its own interpretation of the "commander's intent", planning and preparing actions that they believe will meet with the approval of Osama bin Laden and Ayman al-Zawahiri when they become aware of them after the event.

Over the last decade, in parallel to the central core of Al-Qaeda functioning almost as a traditional terrorist group, there has been an enormous increase in the use of network types of organisation by both Al-Qaeda and other terrorists. In the UK, the existence of these network forms first began to be noticed from the early 1990s as individuals, particularly those from North Africa, began to arrive. Many were bound together by the shared experience of taking part in combat operations against the Soviet Union in Afghanistan. These extended networks of "Afghan veterans" and others of like mind took no part in any attacks in the UK itself but concentrated on recruiting, supporting, facilitating and financing terrorism and violence in other parts of the world, for example, Algeria, Kashmir and Bosnia.

Today, a common network form of organisation involved in violent jihad in the UK appears to consist of a small, tightly knit node or cell of individuals prepared to carry out terrorist activity with links into a wider network of individuals who are willing to assist them. These nodes seem to be of two main types. First, where the node is linked internationally both physically (where individuals in it travel) and through its communications system (predominantly using the Internet). An example of this type of organisation was the 7/7 cell in Beeston, West Yorkshire led by Mohammad Siddique Khan.[49]

A second type also exists, where there is no personal contact with other conspirators and the node may be linked internationally only through its communication links. In 2005, such a virtual network was discovered in the UK and in the words of Deputy Assistant Commissioner Peter Clarke, the police National Coordinator of Terrorist Investigations "The people concerned in it have been charged with conspiring to cause an explosion but we don't actually have any evidence they have ever met".[50] Indeed, it is theoretically possible that this type of network may not be linked to anyone else at all outside of the immediate conspirators.[51] However, there is no publicly available evidence of a UK terrorist cell that is both self-radicalised and self-operational.

The final active element involved in violent jihad in the UK is the Lone Actor. A number of individuals have coalesced around both the ideology and methodology espoused by Al-Qaeda, a situation made increasingly possible by modern communications technology and the rapidly spreading access to it. To date, only one individual has travelled to the UK with both the intention and means to carry out a violent act.

In February 2003, Hazil Rahaman-Alan travelled from Venezuela to the UK with a live but defective hand-grenade in his luggage. His motives and target are still unclear, although he stated at his trial that his intention was to use the grenade "as his microphone to the world" in order to draw attention to "the suffering of children and the plight of humanity".[52] Since then, a series of arrests of other apparently unaffiliated or linked individuals have taken place in the UK. They include UK citizens and those of other nationalities who are resident here. There are those who are self-radicalised and act alone and at least one who appears to have acted alone but who is known to have been closely associated in the past with Al-Qaeda.[53]

The potential physical and psychological harm that an individual acting alone can cause to a community should not be underestimated. During a period of three weeks in April 1999, David Copeland carried out a one-man bombing campaign in London. His devices were targeted on successive weeks in areas of London that were focal points for the Afro-Caribbean, Bangladeshi and homosexual communities. Using the knowledge that he had acquired from Internet web sites, his explosive devices utilised a mechanical timer, gunpowder from fireworks and nails to act as shrapnel. They caused the deaths of three people and injured many more. The population of London was accustomed to IRA bombs detonating in their city, but this new type attack, with no prior warning and no post-attack claim of responsibility, caused an unprecedented level of fear and uncertainty.

Manifestation

The way in which a violent jihadist group, network or individual can manifest themselves can be categorised according to where they operate (i.e. geographically) and how they operate (i.e. methodologically). In terms of geography, UK violent jihadists participating in "traditional" defensive jihad cannot do so in the UK and must travel abroad. If their motivation is to participate in "Global Salafist Jihad" then they can do so internationally or within their own country.

As has already been described, UK citizens and residents are known to have become involved in violent jihad in Bosnia from 1992 onwards. Another significant early case was that of Ahmed Omar Saeed Sheikh, a former schoolboy from East London and student at the London School of Economics (LSE). He first became engaged in violent jihad prior to 1994 with a separatist group in Kashmir before he was arrested and imprisoned in India. On Christmas Eve 1999 an Indian Airlines plane from Kashmir was hijacked and Sheikh was one of the three individuals released by the Indian government in exchange for the passengers. His transition to the cause of Global Salafist Jihad was completed by January 2002 when allegedly he led the group who kidnapped and executed the US journalist Daniel Pearl. Pearl had been investigating the links between Richard Reid and Pakistan. Sheikh was arrested, tried and is currently under sentence of death in Pakistan.[54]

A second UK citizen who made the transition to Global Salafist Jihad was Andrew Rowe. Like Richard Reid, Rowe was a convert to Islam. His involvement in violent jihad had also originally begun in Bosnia, where he was wounded, but he later moved on to embrace terrorist activity in other countries, including the UK. After his conviction and sentence to fifteen years imprisonment in September 2005, the police National Coordinator of Terrorist Investigations described him as "a global terrorist [who] has been trained and knows how to use extreme violence".[55]

In terms of terrorist methodology, participants can either act in an "attack" capacity or a "support" capacity, although they are not mutually exclusive. As a consequence of the events in London in July 2005, most attention has been paid to violent jihadist suicide attacks, but evidence also exists of their intent and capability to carry out "conventional" attacks and even attacks involving the use of chemical and radiological-based weapons. One case, involving the potentially fatal poison ricin, has been dealt with at court. An Algerian, Kamal Bourgass, was convicted of conspiring to use it and eight others were acquitted.[56]

In another major case still awaiting a full trial, seven defendants who were arrested in August 2004 have been charged with conspiracy to murder and conspiracy to commit a public nuisance "by the use of radioactive materials, toxic gases, chemicals and/or explosives".[57] A further defendant, Dhiren Barot, a UK citizen of Hindu descent who converted to Islam, pleaded guilty in November 2006 to conspiracy to murder. The prosecution outlined to the court Barot's "plans for the detonation of a radiation dispersal device, more commonly known as a 'dirty bomb', the use of a petrol tanker to cause an explosion and attacks on the London rail or underground network".[58] He was sentenced to forty years in prison.

The activities of those involved in the support and facilitation of violent jihad cover a wide spectrum. They raise and courier money, procure weapons and military equipment and make arrangements for others to travel, often facilitating this by acquiring forged or stolen travel documents. In addition, they undertake the radicalisation of alienated individuals to the point where the most committed of them are ready to be recruited to undertake violent jihad. It can be argued that these figures, as influential as they are in the active radicalisation of others, are at least as dangerous as those who prepared to carry out the attacks. Without their activities, the numbers of potential recruits ready to become engaged in violent jihad and terrorism could be much reduced.

Lord Carlile, the government-appointed independent reviewer of the Terrorism Act, gave evidence in February 2006 to the Home Affairs Select Committee of the House of Commons. Speaking about radicalisation, he highlighted three areas he was particularly concerned about: the potential for foreign imams with extremist sympathies to take up posts in UK mosques, the radicalisation of male students in universities and the occurrence of radicalisation "in a custodial setting".[59]

In the UK, since about the mid-1990s, among the most active and effective people in the radicalisation of individuals appear to have been the "radical clerics". Prominent among them were Abu Hamza al-Masri, Sheikh al-Feisal, Omar Bakri Mohammed and Abu Qatada. Of these, two are now serving sentences in prison after conviction for incitement to murder and soliciting murder (Abu Hamza, seven years and Sheikh al-Feisal, nine years), one is imprisoned under the restrictions of a Control Order, pending deportation from the UK (Abu Qatada) and one voluntarily left the country in 2005 and will not be allowed to re-enter (Omar Bakri Mohammed). Between them, they regularly preached to and spoke with people such as Richard Reid, Sajid Badaat, Andrew Rowe and Jermaine Lindsay. All of these went on to commit, or in the case of Badaat, to train for, terrorist actions in the cause of Global Salafist Jihad.

Concerns have been raised that a number of individuals involved in terrorist activity are known to have attended UK universities or institutes of higher education. There also appears to be a strong indication that they may act as venues where individuals may be "talent-spotted" as suitable for radicalisation and recruitment off-campus.[60] In the immediate aftermath of the July 2005 attacks in London, the UK government established seven short-term, informal Working Groups under the generic title of "Preventing Extremism Together".[61] Their remit was to "develop workable proposals for Government and Muslim civic organisations to take forward". One of the issues that they looked at was "Tackling radicalisation on campuses" and flowing from it came a recommendation that the government and the community needed to work together to "equip Islamic student bodies to take on extremism in universities, whether through smarter use of literature, shared intelligence or closer partnerships with Vice Chancellors".[62]

In the context of violent jihad, prisons can provide opportunities for prisoners who are not radicalised to become so and for those who are radicalised to have their radicalisation confirmed, reinforced and increased.[63] On their release, recruitment into terrorist activity then becomes an easier step to take. There is a need to gather timely and accurate intelligence on potentially problematic prisoners, but on its own this will not be sufficient. It needs to be supported by a wide-ranging series of measures that impact on the problem of radicalisation in prisons, designed around anti-radicalisation (to prevent it happening), counter-radicalisation (to stop it developing when it happens) and de-radicalisation (to reverse its effects if it has happened). A variety of work to counter this is now underway within the UK prison system.[64]

The Home Office employs twenty-three full-time and twelve part-time imams to accommodate the spiritual needs of seven thousand Muslim prisoners in the UK prison system.[65] Specialist training for prison imams has now been identified as a priority and closer links have been forged with the police Prison Advisors Section. Police officers from the Section have been instrumental in developing "a unique mentoring programme, which seeks to identify those Muslim prisoners potentially susceptible to radicalisation or extremist views and which supports them upon their release from prison to integrate back into their local community".[66] Only time will tell whether these prisoners are able to do so on their release.

Emerging key factors in the processes of radicalisation and recruitment

In a public document, originally presented to Parliament, the UK government set out for the first time the most important factors that it believes potentially lead to radicalisation.[67] It sees the process as a two-stage one, beginning with the radicalisation of an alienated individual and then, in a "tiny minority" of cases, that individual may go on to become involved in terrorist activity.[68] It can therefore be characterised not as a conveyor belt, moving all who step onto it inexorably from radicalisation to terrorism, but as acting more like a funnel, where a larger number of individuals are selectively reduced to a much smaller number that may eventually cross over the threshold from extremism into terrorism.

A similar funnel-and-filter phenomenon has been noted in relation to recruitment to the militia movement in the USA, as a variety of legitimate social and political issues are used to draw people within their orbit:

> Once you enter into the large side, having been sucked in by gun control, you are exposed to the other ideas of your new friends. What with speakers at meetings, literature on tables, computer forums and shortwave programs, your universe now includes people who promote racism and anti-Semitism. Such ideas become safer, less remarkable, no longer subject to taboo, believable, part of "the explanation".[69]

The parallels are striking with what is known today of radicalisation in the context of violent jihad.

The UK government report also recognises that there are a range of radicalising factors, with no single factor predominating. The first of these is "the development of a sense of grievance and injustice" that can, in turn, result in a specific anti-Western world-view and a belief in its overt hostility to Islam. A second factor is "a sense of personal alienation or community disadvantage arising from socio-economic factors such as discrimination, social exclusion and lack of opportunity". Whilst no single factor is considered as conclusive, the report goes on to identify the "exposure to radical ideas" as being "important".

Within the context of this exposure, radical literature and material found through use of the Internet have an impact, but "more often, radicalisation seems to arise from local contacts and peers" and may also include "exposure to a forceful and inspiring figure". Figures such as these may be part of an individual's local network of personal contacts or they may have a national or international prominence. In the latter case, "inspiration from a distance is important" and the report acknowledges the key role of the Internet in allowing access to the "flow of radical ideas".[70]

The power of the Internet to assist in the radicalisation of individuals has been acknowledged by Muslim representatives themselves. A range of recommendations relevant to this issue were proposed by the "Preventing Extremism Together" working party. These included the development of a UK web site and information portal, aimed at facilitating access to "a wide range of views and opinions from all the major Muslim schools of thought, presenting young Muslims with a wide range of choice in terms of views within a mainstream spectrum".[71]

Radicalisation: a defining characteristic of violent jihad?

If radicalisation is the response by individuals to a set of conditions resulting in them first becoming sensitised to a "cause" and then undergoing a period of transition that may subsequently lead to them undertaking terrorist activity, then an argument can be made that it is not unique to the current circumstances of violent jihad. History can give us an insight from the past, in particular if we look to the example of Irish Republicanism over the last century.

At the highest level, the reaction of the British government to the defeated Irish Republican insurgents following the Easter Rising in Dublin during April 1916 illustrates how it is possible for a state "to turn the actions of fanatics into the will of a nation".[72] Here, it was the actions of the British government that served to accelerate the process of radicalisation by alienating many of the population. In the weeks that followed the Easter Rising, the court martial and execution of fourteen of the most prominent of the insurgents changed the national mood in Ireland from one of widespread condemnation of their actions to one of outrage against the British government. Throughout Ireland and particularly the Irish diaspora in the USA, the actions of the British government were vilified.[73]

The consequences were dramatic. From 1919, Ireland was in the grip of a full-scale insurgency involving the IRA and its secretive inner core, the Irish Republican Brotherhood (IRB). By 1922, the British had withdrawn from Southern Ireland and the Irish Free State was established.

A review of the memoirs of some of the individuals who joined the IRA at the beginning of the latest phase of terrorist violence, from the late 1960s and early 1970s until the late 1990s, gives some personal insights into why they joined the IRA.[74] This period in time covers the earliest days of the descent from political agitation to street violence and thence to organised terrorism and the emergence from the "old" IRA of the hard-line terrorist group that called itself the Provisional IRA (PIRA). Whilst the parallels are not exact and should not be extended too far, it can be argued that there are some similarities to the situation today as far as violent jihad in the UK is concerned.

The process whereby an individual arrived at a point where they actively began to consider joining the IRA seemed to operate on two levels. At the first level they developed a growing political awareness of global events: the Vietnam War, the student riots in Paris in 1968, revolutionary actions and personalities and state counter-actions. In addition to this, they also began to acquire a growing political awareness of events closer to home and of more immediate personal relevance: the Civil Rights movement in Northern Ireland, the violent attacks on Catholic marches and demonstrations by Protestant mobs, and the partisan way that the Royal Ulster Constabulary (RUC) and its police reserve, the "B Specials" appeared to operate. Often, this awareness was mixed with an increased interest in the historical events, folk memory and romanticised myths that together form a potent element of Irish Republicanism. In the words of J. Bowyer Bell, "This history is rich in events, adventures, disasters and spectaculars and filled with martyrs. The Irish republicans mine the past for whatever the present needs."[75] Indeed, the Easter Rising in 1916, its immediate aftermath and subsequent events remain as a central feature of this milieu.

The end result was that at some point, each individual took two decisions. The first was to do something active "to help" and the second, subsequent decision was to fulfil this decision by joining the IRA. The latter decision may have been triggered by their reaction to a large-scale, highly publicised event such as the introduction of internment on 9 August 1971 or "Bloody Sunday" when, on 30 January 1972, the British Army shot dead thirteen Republican demonstrators in Londonderry. Alternatively, it could also have been a much less prominent traumatic or unpleasant incident that happened to them personally, to a member of their family or to a long-standing friend. From that point onwards, as increasingly committed observers of events, the amorphous "pull" of empathy and anger that they felt was replaced by a very specific internal "push" towards the decision that they must "do something" by joining the IRA. In the context of violent jihad today, they moved from alienation into radicalisation and then took a final step into recruitment by a group or network that was prepared to use terrorism to advance its cause.

The UK state response

Strategic principles

By early 2002, the UK government had put into place its first holistic counter-terrorism strategy based on the prevailing assessment of the current and probable future threat to the UK. The focus is almost entirely on violent jihadism. The strategy known as CONTEST was revised in its current format in 2004 and is designed to cover a three- to five-year time span.[76]

The strategic aim of CONTEST is "to reduce the risk from international terrorism over the next few years so that our people can go about their business freely and with confidence".[77] Two key components that contribute to the creation of a risk are a combination of the threat posed and the vulnerability of the target. The four main "Mission Areas" of CONTEST were designed to impact upon both of these factors. Two of the Mission Areas were aimed at reducing the threat and are based around the themes of "Prevention" and "Pursuit". A further two Mission Areas were intended to reduce vulnerability and therefore focused on "Preparation" and "Protection". Underpinning them all were "two vital capabilities, good assessed intelligence and effective public communications".[78]

Countering radicalisation and recruitment falls within the "Prevent" Mission Area and the measures that it encompasses are designed "in particular to stop the next generation of terrorists emerging". The Missions themselves are categorised into "Domestic" and "Overseas". Domestically, they aim to "tackle radicalisation and its roots" whilst Overseas, they are designed to "help create stability, resolve conflicts, support moderate Islam and reform, diminish support for terrorism, help states to build up their own CT capabilities".

The latest iteration of CONTEST continues to build a cross-government programme of action to counter radicalisation.[79] However, the division of work into "Domestic" and "Overseas" categories within the "Prevent" pillar has been modified to form three areas where it is believed effective action can be taken, irrespective of geographic location. These actions are "addressing structural problems in the UK and elsewhere that may contribute to radicalisation ... changing the environment in which the extremists and those radicalising others can operate; deterring those who facilitate terrorism and those who encourage others to become terrorists" and finally "...challenging the ideological motivations that extremists believe justify the use of violence".[80]

It is this latter category that is now being referred to as the "battle of ideas", a theme strongly linked into a long-standing key conceptual element of British counter-insurgency (COIN) doctrine: the need to win the "hearts and minds" of the communities in which the insurgents operate. In turn, the success or otherwise of the "hearts and minds" element is a critical influence on the effective gathering and utilisation of intelligence; without accurate and timely intelligence, an effective operational counter-terrorism response cannot be planned and implemented.

Operational response to radicalisation and recruitment

At the operational level, intelligence on violent jihadism is obtained from across the globe by national intelligence agencies that utilise complex and sophisticated technological and human resources. The intelligence may lead directly to the discovery of terrorist activity and in these cases, executive action or disruption can follow. However, this "top down" process needs to be complemented by a "bottom up" approach where information and intelligence from within the communities where terrorist activities are most likely to occur is also acquired and then fused with the intelligence from all other sources. It is this local "community intelligence" that is particularly vital to help counter the radicalisation of individuals and their recruitment for the purpose of terrorism in the UK and other countries.

Three types of community information and intelligence must be acquired, fused with "national" intelligence and then assessed before a comprehensive intelligence picture can be obtained of the situation "on the ground". At the first level lies information that is freely available within the community and hence can be acquired openly. In the UK, the responsibility for the acquisition of this type of material lies predominantly with the police of the local area. Not only are they best placed to find and gather it, they are able to channel it into their own Special Branch where it can be assessed and where necessary passed on to the Security Service.

The second type is information given in confidence by members of the local community who wish their assistance to remain covert. Once more, it is the local police that are best placed to perform this function. Finally, there is secret intelligence that is obtained clandestinely by a range of methods from within the community. These intelligence-gathering operations are led by the Security Service, often in close cooperation with the local Special Branch. In all three levels of community information and intelligence gathering activity, it is the police Special Branch that provides "the 'golden thread' of local contact and coverage" that links local communities into the national counter-terrorism strategy.[81]

All three types of community intelligence gathering are dependent, to a greater or lesser degree, on a successful, local-level "hearts and minds" operation to build confidence and trust within each community. At the overt and "in confidence" levels, in order that timely and accurate information can flow, it is vital that local communities trust the police sufficiently to engage with them and pass it on. However, any drive at the local level to engage the "hearts and minds" of the community can be severely curtailed or even stopped unless a simultaneous "hearts and minds" campaign is undertaken at government level.

The value of a high-level counter-terrorism strategy such as CONTEST is that it should provide both a conceptual and practical mechanism for this to occur. Whether it does so and indeed whether it does so effectively is extremely difficult to assess. In October 2005, a confidential report produced in 2004 by the Prime Minister's Delivery Unit was critical of the impact of CONTEST, concluding that much more had to be done to ensure that the activities generated under CONTEST were coordinated, integrated and delivered "real world impact".[82]

Measuring "success" in any meaningful way is difficult to achieve in the context of counter-terrorism as success can be assigned many different meanings. These can range from the absence or otherwise of terrorist attacks to the number of successful prosecutions of terrorists. In any debate over the usefulness of any of these metrics to indicate the achievement or otherwise of "success" or indeed in defining what success actually looks like, one factor always must be borne in mind. The words of the IRA, uttered in the immediate aftermath of their failed attempt in 1984 to kill the incumbent Prime Minister, Margaret Thatcher, summarise it well "Today you were lucky. We have to be lucky once. You have to be lucky all the time."[83]

Conclusion

Terrorism, as a trans-national and international phenomenon, has long afflicted the UK. Its origins, its participants and the causes that they espoused have varied over the last century and a half. During that period, terrorist attacks on the British mainland have been carried out to force a UK withdrawal from Ireland, India and Palestine; as part of the long-running conflicts and wars in the Middle East and elsewhere and the violent activities of the terrorist organisations involved in them; as a consequence of States wishing to suppress dissent amongst their nationals living abroad and in order to advance their own political aims and, finally, as a consequence of the extreme ideological beliefs of others and their willingness to use violence in pursuit of them.

It is this latter category that currently poses the highest level of threat from terrorism to the UK. An illustration of both the scale of that threat and its potential consequences can be seen in the alleged recent conspiracy to board a number of US airliners flying from Heathrow and then destroy them in mid-air.[84] At least twelve individuals are alleged to be closely involved, with others carrying out support roles. All of them are believed to be UK citizens. Reliable information on the alleged participants and their activities is currently minimal, but it appears that once more, a network of individuals seems to have made the journey from alienation to radicalisation and then recruitment into terrorism and having done so, they were prepared to carry out suicide terrorism attacks designed to cause mass casualties.

The current UK approach to counter-terrorism is to be as holistic and integrated as possible. After long historical experience and with many mistakes and miscalculations along the way, it is firmly based on the rule of law and recognises the primacy of the criminal justice system. It relies on close cooperation and coordination between all the security organs of the state: police, intelligence agencies and the military. However, this multi-agency approach also extends into a wide range of other government roles and responsibilities and, in turn, into communities and the public at large. There is a clear recognition that without the full engagement of all of them, the primary aim of CONTEST, "to reduce the risk from international terrorism" will not be achieved as effectively as it could be.[85]

Perhaps the most vital task to contribute to the overall aim will be to slow, contain and reverse the process of radicalisation amongst impressionable young Muslim men living in the UK. The difficulties and challenges that this presents are enormous. Globalisation now means that the flow of information, images, news and propaganda is constant in its output and increasingly accessible to all. Consequently, reducing in any meaningful way its impact on radicalisation will be almost impossible to achieve.

At the other end of the scale, on a more directly personal level, there is much greater scope for local communities, friends and family to make an impact by being aware of the potential for an individual to become radicalised. The police, as a front-line emergency service constantly operating within their local community, must be better prepared and trained to deal with all levels of intervention, particularly if they receive requests for assistance before the individual concerned has become criminally involved. This need for pre-emptive intervention can be at its most acute in cases of juveniles and youths, an age range where involvement in terrorism appears to be becoming more prevalent.[86]

The practitioners of counter-terrorism do not have the option of waiting to see what knowledge can be gained from studying radicalisation and its causes before they move to take preventive or disruptive action. They must act in response to the situation that presents itself. In the meantime, the more information and insights that can be gleaned, based on research and analysis, the better the policy, strategies and operations to counter it will become. The UK government recognises the need for a comprehensive approach and that, "in the longer term it is clear that the answer lies not just with the [intelligence] Agencies but in successfully countering the spread of the terrorist message in the UK and overseas".[87]

Notes

1 For example, the trial of seven defendants arrested in March 2003 accused of conspiring to carry out bomb attacks in the UK commenced in March 2006 and is not expected to conclude until early 2007.
2 Deputy Assistant Commissioner Peter Clarke, National Coordinator for Terrorist Investigations. Speech at the Royal United Services Institute (RUSI), 15 February 2006. www.rusi.org/events/ref:E437B44EF8DA91/info:E43F9D7471E52C/.
3 Ibid.
4 "Countering International Terrorism: The United Kingdom's Strategy", published by TSO (The Stationery Office) at www.tsoshop.co.uk, Crown Copyright 2006 and "Crisis as Terrorist Trials Hit Log Jam", *The Times*, 7 October 2006, pp. 1–2.
5 "Report of the Official Account of the Bombings in London on 7th July 2005", London: Stationery Office, 11 May 2006.
6 "Man Charged over 21 July Attacks", BBC News http://news.bbc.co.uk/go/pr/fr/-/1/hi/uk/4545374.stm.
7 *The Guardian*, 29 April 2006, p. 4.
8 "*Today*" Programme, BBC Radio 4, 7 July 2006 as quoted in the *Evening Standard*, 7 July 2006, p. 8).

9 For details of Ramzi Yousef and his activities, see Rohan Gunaratna, *Inside Al-Qaeda: Global Network of Terror* (London: Hurst and Company, 2002) p. 6 and others and Jason Burke, *Al-Qaeda: The True Story of Radical Islam* (New York: I.B. Tauris, 2003) pp. 101–115.
10 "Five Planes and the Plot to Commit Britain's 9/11", *The Times*, 11 August 2006.
11 "Terrorist threat to the UK-MI5 chief's full speech", *Times Online*, 10 November 2006. Full text of speech by Eliza Manningham-Buller, Director General of MI5 at www.timesonline.co.uk/article/0,,2-2447690,00.html.
12 Ibid.
13 See Lindsay Clutterbuck "The Progenitors of Terrorism: Russian Revolutionaries or Extreme Irish Republicans?", *Terrorism and Political Violence*, Vol. 16, No. 1, Spring 2004, pp. 154–181.
14 See Lindsay Clutterbuck "Countering Irish Republican Terrorism in Britain: Its Origin as a Police Function", *Terrorism and Political Violence*, Vol. 18, No. 1, Spring 2006, pp. 95–118.
15 Ibid.
16 For example, the assassination of Sir Curzon Wylie in London in 1909 by an Indian nationalist extremist, Madan Lal Dhingra. See Richard J. Popplewell, *Intelligence and Imperial Defence* (London: Frank Cass, 1995) p. 125.
17 For a contemporary account of these events, see George Wilkinson, "*Special Branch Officer*" (London: Odhams Press Ltd, 1956) pp. 204–227.
18 A good résumé of the campaigns of this period can be found in *Modern Warfare: British and Commonwealth Forces at War 1945–2000*, edited by Major General Julian Thompson (London: Sidgewick and Jackson in association with the Imperial War Museum, 2002).
19 For the impact of COIN on British military thinking in the period coinciding with their first operational deployment to Northern Ireland, see Frank Kitson, *Low Intensity Operations: Subversion, Insurgency and Peacekeeping* (London: Faber and Faber, 1971).
20 The concept of a campaign for the "hearts and minds" of the population arose out of British COIN operations in Malaya from 1948 to 1960. See John Newsinger, *British Counter Insurgency: From Palestine to Northern Ireland* (London: Palgrave, 2002) pp. 45–55.
21 First significant IRA attacks on the British mainland took place on 8 March 1974 when four car bombs in London detonated or were defused.
22 For an insider's description of the role of the IRA "England Department", see Sean O'Callaghan, *The Informer* (London: Bantam Press, 1998) pp. 112–115.
23 "The Prevention of Terrorism Act 1986" (as amended), HMSO 1986.
24 The most significant of these was on 26 and 27 July 1994 when two car bombs exploded in quick succession outside the Israeli Embassy and the Israeli Joint Appeal offices in London. No one was killed. A number of Palestinians were eventually convicted.
25 By the end of 1995 six British nationals had been killed (according to Al-Qaeda). See Evan Kohlman, *Al-Qaeda in Europe* (London: Berg, 2002).
26 *United States of America v. Usama bin Laden*, United States District Court, Southern District of New York, Indictment. Available at www.terrorismcentral.com/Library/Incidents/USEmbassyKenyaBombing/Indictment/Count1.html.
27 To date, Fawwaz and Abdel Bary remain in custody in the UK. Eidarous was released under Royal Perogative upon a diagnosis that he was suffering from terminal cancer.
28 "Bomb maker jailed for twenty years", BBC News, http://news.bbc.co.uk/1/hi/england/1845218.stm.
29 Eliza Manningham-Buller, Director General of the Security Service, delivering the James Smart Memorial Lecture, 2003, www.homeoffice.gov.uk/docs2/james_smart_lecture2003.html.

30 "Reid tells of 'four terror plots'", 13 August 2006, BBC News, http://news.bbc.co.uk/go/pr/fr/-/1/hi/uk/4788101.stm.
31 "Countering International Terrorism: The United Kingdom's Strategy", published by TSO (The Stationery Office) at www.tsoshop.co.uk, Crown Copyright 2006, p. 1.
32 A good explanation of the concept is provided by Shmuel Bar in "Jihad Ideology in the Light of Contemporary Fatwas", *Research Monographs on the Muslim World*, Series no. 1, Paper no. 1, Hudson Institute. Found online at www.hudsoninstitute.org/files/publications/Jihad.pdf.
33 In November 2001, Osama bin Laden proclaimed "We ourselves are the target of killings, destruction and atrocities. We are only defending ourselves. This is defensive jihad." See interview, "Osama Claims he has Nukes: If the US uses N-Arms it will get the Same Response", *Dawn – The Internet Edition*, www.dawn.com/2001/11/10/top1.htm cited in *What Does Al-Qaeda Want? Unedited Communiques*, Commentary by Robert O. Marlin (California: North Atlantic Books, 2004), p. 41.
34 See John Esposito, *Unholy War: Terror in the Name of Islam* (London: Oxford University Press, 2002) pp. 32–36.
35 Evan Kohlman, *Al Qaeda's Jihad in Europe*, (Oxford: Berg, 2004), pp. 163–168.
36 "Islamists in Britain Plot Israeli Attacks" David Leppard and Uzi Mahnaimi, *The Sunday Times*, 8 February 2004.
37 "UK Arrest in Iraq Attacks Probe" 21 July 2005, BBC News, http://news.bbc.co.uk/go/pr/fr/-/1/hi/uk/4113846.stm.
38 Marc Sageman, *Understanding Terror Networks*, (University of Pennsylvania Press, 2004), pp. 17–24.
39 Ibid. p. 19.
40 "Terror Suspect Fights Extradition", BBC News, http://news.bbc.co.uk/go/pr/fr/-/1/hi/england/london/5054590.
41 *The Guardian*, 13 September 2005, p. 5.
42 "Terror accused in 'Mercury Sting'", BBC News, http://news.bbc.co.uk/go/pr/fr/-/1/hi/uk/4943122.
43 *The Guardian*, 26 July 2006, p. 10.
44 "Al-Qaeda Plotting Nuclear Attack on UK, Officials Warn", *The Guardian*, 14 November 2006, p. 10.
45 "Terror Link Pair Jailed", BBC News, http://news.bbc.co.uk/go/pr/fr/-/1/hi/england/2907853.
46 "Terror Suspects Held in Raids", BBC News, http://news.bbc.co.uk/go/pr/fr/-/1/hi/england/3581687.
47 For example, in January 2006 Abu Baker Mansha was sentenced to six years imprisonment for targeting a British soldier who had won a Military Cross in Iraq "Man Jailed for Iraq Revenge Plot", BBC News, http://news.bbc.co.uk/1/hi/england/London/4650000.stm.

In December 2005 Abbas Boutrab (not believed to be his real name) was sentenced to six years imprisonment for possessing plans and information on how to carry out an attack on an aircraft. He is believed to have "strong allegiance to a terrorist group that is linked to the Al-Qaeda network".

"Al-Qaeda Terror Suspect is Jailed" BBC News, http://news.bbc.co.uk/go/pr/fr/-/1/hi/northern_ireland/4544692.stm.
48 "'Homegrown terrorists' arraigned in court", www.msnbc.msn.com/id/13497335.
49 *The Guardian*, 24 July 2006, pp. 1–2, 6–7.
50 "Court Indicts 29 over Madrid Train Blasts", *The Guardian*, 12 April 2006, p. 22.
51 As in the case of the Oklahoma City bombers, Timothy McVeigh and Terry Nicholls.
52 "Man Jailed over Airport Grenade", BBC News, http://news.bbc.co.uk/go/pr/fr/-/1/hi/england/3581687.
53 "UK Trio Face US Terrorism Charges", BBC News, http://news.bbc.co.uk/go/pr/fr/-/1/hi/world/americas/4438593.stm.

54 *The Guardian*, G2 Section, 23 February 2005, pp. 2–3.
55 *The Guardian*, 24 September 2005, p. 7.
56 *The Guardian*, 14 April 2005, pp. 1–2.
57 "UK Trio Face US Terrorism Charges", BBC News, 12 April 2005, http://news.bbc.co.uk/go/pr/fr/-/1/hi/world/americas/4438593.stm.
58 "British Muslim 'Wanted to Blow up Tube Train under Thames'", *Times Online* at www.timesonline.co.uk/printFriendly/0,,1-2-2440025,00.htm.
59 Select Committee on Home Affairs, Fourth Report, Minutes of Evidence, 14 February 2006, Questions 77 & 82 www.publications.parliament.uk/pa/cm200506/cmselect/cmhaff/910/6021402.htm.
60 "Extremist Groups Active Inside UK Universities, Report Claims", *The Guardian*, 16 September 2005, pp. 1&4 and "They don't Sit with a Sign Recruiting for Terrorists", *The Guardian Education Supplement*, 19 July 2005, pp. 18 & 19.
61 "Preventing Extremism Together Working Groups: August–October 2005", Home Office, www.communities.homeoffice.gov.uk/raceandfaith/faith/faith-communities/.
62 Ibid. p. 18.
63 "Watchdog Warns of Rival Muslim Factions and Pressure from Militants at Jail", *The Guardian*, 21 November 2006, p. 4.
64 For the earliest public iteration of CONTEST and its implications, see Wyn Bowen and Andrew Stewart (eds.), *Terrorism in the UK: Broadening the Government's Counter Terrorist Response – CONTEST*, Defence Academy of the UK, Strategic and Combat Studies Institute, Airey Neave Papers, Occasional Paper no. 50, p. 13.
65 "Do prisons radicalise inmates?", BBC News, http://news.bbc.co.uk/go/pr/fr/-/1/hi/uk/4727723.stm.
66 Op. cit., CONTEST strategy, p. 13.
67 "Countering International Terrorism: The United Kingdom's Strategy", published by TSO (The Stationery Office) at www.tsoshop.co.uk, Crown Copyright 2006.
68 Ibid. p. 10.
69 Kenneth Stern, *A Force Upon the Plain: The American Militia Movement and the Politics of Hate* (New York: Simon and Schuster, 1996), pp. 245–248.
70 Op. cit., CONTEST strategy, p. 10.
71 Op. cit., "Preventing Extremism Together", p. 90.
72 Tim Collins, *Rules of Engagement: A Life in Conflict* (London: Headline, 2005) p. 431.
73 Robert Kee, *The Green Flag: A History of Irish Nationalism* (London: Weidenfeld and Nicolson, 1972, pp. 573–587.
74 For example, see op. cit., Sean O'Callaghan, *The Informer*; Shane O'Doherty, *The Volunteer* (London: Harper Collins, 1993); Maria Maguire, *To Take Arms: A Year in the Provisional IRA* (London: Macmillan, 1973); and Eamon Collins with Mick McGovern, *Killing Rage* (London: Granta Books, 1998).
75 J. Bowyer Bell, "Career Moves: Reflections of the Irish Gunman", *Studies in Conflict and Terrorism*, Vol. 15, no. 1, January 1992, p. 71.
76 Op. cit., CONTEST strategy.
77 Sir David Omand, "Emergency Planning, Security and Business Security", *Royal United Services Institute Journal*, August 2004.
78 Ibid.
79 Op. cit., CONTEST strategy, pp. 11–16.
80 Ibid.
81 "A Need to Know: HMIC Thematic Inspection of Special Branch and Ports Policing", Report by David Blakey, Her Majesty's Inspector of Constabulary (HMSO, 2001) p. 30.
82 "Labour's war on Terror is Failing, says Leaked Report", *The Sunday Times*, 23 October 2005, p. 2.
83 *An Phoblacht/Republican News*, October 1984. Quoting a press statement released by the IRA.

84 Op. cit., Heathrow plot (see Endnote 10).
85 Op. cit., CONTEST strategy, p. 1.
86 Hasib Hussain, one of the 7/7 bombers was eighteen years old. Charges have been laid against others of a similar age or younger e.g. a sixteen-year-old, "Pair in Court on Terror Charges", BBC News, http://news.bbc.co.uk/go/pr/fr/-/1/hi/uk/5083414.stm.
87 "Government Response to the Intelligence and Security Committee's Report into the London Terrorist Attacks on 7 July 2005", p. 7, www.cabinet office.gov.uk/publications/reports/intelligence/govres_7july.pdf.

7 Islamism, radicalisation and jihadism in the Netherlands
Main developments and counter-measures

Edwin Bakker[1]

Introduction

Radical political Islam and radicalisation of Muslims in the Netherlands have been high on the agenda of national and local authorities ever since the devastating attacks on the United States on 11 September 2001. The rise of radical political Islam or Islamism and the radicalisation of young Muslims produced several of them to join the jihad in places like Chechnya and Kashmir, and the murder of the filmmaker Theo van Gogh in November 2004.

This chapter focuses on the growth of radical political Islam in the Netherlands and the radicalisation processes among young Muslims leading to jihadism. In the second part, it will look at the way in which the authorities have responded to these social and security challenges. The chapter concludes with an overview of recent developments, which includes growing resilience to radical political Islam and radicalisation among Muslim communities, the decline of the homegrown threat, and the growth of the threat of jihadism from abroad.

Growth of radical political Islam and radicalisation in the Netherlands

Early development

Radical political Islam and Islamism are defined as political-religious movements that aim to impose a strict version of Islam as the dominant or major factor in the regulation of societies.[2] The first signs of radical political Islam in the Netherlands date back to the 1980s, when individuals and groups started to organise themselves around issues such as the first Palestinian intifada in 1987 and the row over Salman Rushdie's novel *Satanic Verses* in 1988. Following the Rushdie affair, influence of radical political Islam within Muslim communities seemed to increase. Concern about this development led to a number of public reports on radical political Islamist groups' activities, produced by the Dutch Security Service (BVD/AIVD). In 1991, the Service revealed the existence of small groups of "militant fundamentalists" and expressed concern regarding its consequences for the integration of Muslims into mainstream society.[3] A classified study by the Erasmus University of Rotterdam concluded in 1994 that radical political Islamists had indeed attempted to impede the integration process but had not been very successful in their endeavour. Furthermore, it concluded that there were very few Muslims who wanted to challenge existing social structures in the Netherlands.[4]

The idea that the impact and threat of radical political Islam was rather limited was reaffirmed in the 1995 annual report of the Dutch Security Service.[5] From 1997 onwards however, the tone of the reports changed. The 1996 annual report spoke for the first time of information on possible attacks in the Netherlands by a foreign Islamist group, Hizballah, which had been investigated by the Service.[6]

In response to the increase in Islamist terrorist activities worldwide as well as growing concern over domestic developments, the Service published a report on political Islam in the Netherlands. In this report, it described the various political organisations based on Islam. Most of them, in one way or another, rejected Western society and the integration of Muslims into Dutch society, but only small groups of Muslims had radical opinions and were prepared to pursue their ideal through violent means. Some of the groups were supported or influenced by foreign powers such as Iran, Libya and Saudi Arabia. The report also showed that most were established on a national basis. Their focus of interest was on their countries of origin and not the situation of Muslims in the West. Nonetheless, they did try to gain support from this Diaspora by way of taking a strong anti-Western, anti-integration and isolationist position. In the report, the Dutch Security Service did not anticipate that the more radical variants of Islamism in the Netherlands would gain in power and size. However, it did warn that marginalisation of Muslim immigrants could pose a long-term threat with regard to the potential of these groups to grow.[7]

By the end of the century, the threat of Islamism to the Netherlands was still more or less an external one. Threat perceptions were dominated by events taking place outside the Netherlands and beyond Europe. Moreover, in the Netherlands itself, the main players were foreign nationals who predominantly focused on their countries of origin without receiving active support from local Muslim communities. Nonetheless, the number and impact of these groups was growing. One of the reasons for the growth in numbers was the increase in immigrants with an Islamist background, including asylum seekers from Algeria, Bosnia, Chechnya, Egypt, Iraq and Syria. In the Netherlands, these individuals established political-religious organisations that were strongly oriented toward the countries they came from. However, some of these groups also strongly rejected the Western society in which they lived.[8]

Gaining momentum

Until 2000 the growth of Islamism in the Netherlands was gradual and remained rather insignificant. As the aforementioned reports of the Dutch Security Service in the 1990s indicated, radical political Islamic groups did not appear to receive much support among Muslims in the Netherlands. Furthermore, there were no indications of growing radicalisation within Muslim communities. After the turn of the century, however, this situation began to change. Radical political Islam began to gain momentum. This development was greatly propelled as a consequence of the anti-Muslim atmosphere following 11 September, the Madrid bombings in March 2004, and other terrorism-related incidents in Europe and elsewhere.

In the Netherlands, anti-Muslim sentiments increased following "incidents" that could be interpreted as a sign that many Muslims were openly or secretly condoning or even supporting terrorism. For instance, on the evening of 11 September 2001, a group of youngsters of mainly Moroccan descent allegedly was loudly celebrating the attacks on the United States. Journalists were shooting pictures of some of them who had quickly printed a picture of Osama bin Laden. It remains unclear to what extent members of the media incited this small group of teenagers to produce this picture. Nonetheless, the incident provoked a lot of criticism and could be considered one of the starting points for journalists to hunt "scoops" like this by searching for all kinds of worrisome developments within Muslims communities. At one official state-sponsored Islamic school, for instance, journalists found Hamas propaganda and posters glorifying attacks against the West. In addition, a series of arrests of suspected Islamist terrorists led some to question the loyalty of Muslim communities in regard to the Dutch state, norms and values. Despite the fact that many of these reports later turned out to be based on hearsay or misinterpretations of texts and events, and despite the fact that most of the suspected terrorists were released within days or weeks, a lot of damage was done to the image of Muslim communities in the Netherlands.[9]

A Pandora's box had been opened, resulting in the departure of long preserved political correctness to a sterner tone of debate. While in the past, few dared to speak out against (radical) Islam, the Netherlands suddenly became unbridled in its, mostly negative, expressions regarding Islam and Muslims.

These sentiments did not go by unnoticed by the Muslim communities, especially among the younger generation of Muslims. They felt pushed into a corner, insulted and discriminated. In April 2004, in an unprecedented move, the Dutch security service warned about *"a growing number of Muslims who feel treated disrespectfully by opinion-makers and opinion-leaders [...]. In addition, from their perspective, the government's attitude is not impartial enough or not impartial at all."*[10] These feelings were not only shared by a small group of radical political Islamists, but they also existed among many other Muslim individuals who felt loyal to the democratic principles of the Dutch state. In particular, young second- and third-generation Dutch Muslims appeared to feel strongly about the alleged alienation between society and Muslim citizens. In particular, it was found that this group of Muslim youths felt that they were treated disrespectfully, which made them a vulnerable potential target for radicalisation and possibly recruitment processes.

Radicalisation turning into jihadism

The attempts made by representatives of the radical political Islam to radicalise young Muslims and to recruit them for the violent jihad resulted in a number of "successes". In December 2001, it was discovered that young Dutch citizens of Moroccan descent had been killed in Kashmir at the hands of Indian security forces. The two youngsters were believed to be jihadis.

The growth of radical political Islam and the case of the two Dutch jihadis worried many politicians and led to a request for more information about the extent and nature of Islamist terrorism in the Netherlands. A report issued by the Dutch General Intelligence and Security Service, published in March 2004, estimated the number of radical political Islamists to be between 100 and 200 activists.[11] According to the Service, this group included so-called veterans from Afghanistan and Chechnya who played an important role in the development of young Muslims into potential jihadis, as well as several dozen youngsters being prepared for jihad. This jihad includes both conflict areas in the Muslim world and potential targets in the Netherlands and Europe.[12] The conflict areas in the Muslim world that had the interest of young Dutch Muslims included not only Kashmir, but also Iraq and the Caucasus region. In 2005, six of them were ostensibly on a journey to Chechnya or Dagestan. Religious leaders and family members successfully persuaded them to return from Azerbaidzjan and not to continue their assumed journey. It is not clear whether this "trip" was organised by an internationally operating network, an individual recruiter or a more autonomously decided "adventure".[13] In an interview with a Dutch daily, they themselves claimed they had been "on holiday".[14]

With regard to the role of veterans and foreign recruiters, it should be stressed that they were not the only important factor in the development of jihadism. Internal dynamics within groups of radical young Islamists play an important role as well. This was observed from intensive Internet discussions by young Muslims about conflicts such as the ones in Chechnya, Afghanistan and Iraq. These discussions resulted in the development of increasingly radical opinions. The strong anti-Muslim feelings in the Netherlands also contributed to their radicalisation. Consequently, a number of these Muslim youngsters developed an extremely hostile attitude towards the Dutch state and society to the extent that they developed views so extreme that they embraced the use of violence.[15]

As mentioned earlier, their hostile feelings were partly linked to opinion-makers that allegedly treated Muslims and their religion disrespectfully. One of them was the filmmaker Theo van Gogh, who had earned himself a reputation as an outspoken provocateur. In his short film *Submission*, shown on Dutch television, van Gogh demonstrated his adversarial stance towards radical political Islam. It challenged the abuse of women in the Islamic world based on verses from the Koran, which were projected onto the bodies of naked women wearing only veils. The script was written by another known critic of Islamism, the Dutch Member of Parliament of Somali origin, Ayaan Hirsi Ali. Following the broadcasting of the film, both received death threats via the Internet.

Hofstadgroep and Muhammad Bouyeri

One individual who felt Islam was treated disrespectfully by Van Gogh and Hirsi Ali was a young man of Moroccan descent by the name of Muhammad Bouyeri (born 1978). On 2 November 2004, Bouyeri assassinated Theo van Gogh. He was apprehended by police while attempting to die a martyr's death. Other arrests followed, revealing to the general public a homegrown network of young Muslims known as the "Hofstadgroep".[16]

This "group" emerged in 2002 from a diffuse and self-generated autonomous network of approximately two-dozen young Muslims with no proven links with other terrorist "organisations" or "groups". Initially it constituted a group of people that met to discuss political and religious issues. It did not have fixed boundaries and its composition changed over time. Some persons participated in only a few meetings, but then dropped out because of disputes or lack of interest. About a dozen persons can be considered the core of the Hofstadgroep, which even at the time of the arrest of its "members" can best be described as a relatively loose network with only a few key players.

This core group gradually developed very radical ideas on Islam and how to be a good Muslim. Their discussions also started to focus on the idea of the jihad and attitudes towards non-believers, which included the great majority of all Muslims. The most radical ideas of the group have been associated with those of the movement of Takfir wal Hijra – a Sunni-based group, but fundamentalist in nature, borrowing on the Salafist ideology that resembles the Saudi version of Wahhabism. The set of ideas developed by the Hofstadgroep, however, can better be described as neo-Takfir or Takfir-Light.[17] Basically, it places less strict demands on its followers. Nonetheless, it still contains the element of legitimising the use of violence.[18]

The meetings of the participants of the network took place in a few mosques (in particular the As Soennah mosque in The Hague), as well as in individual homes (in particular that of Mohammed Bouyeri in Amsterdam). Most of the (key) participants were young Dutch Moroccans, including Mohammed Bouyeri, Samir Azzouz and illegal aliens such as the Moroccan Nouredine Al Fathni and the only older person of the network, the Syrian Redouan al Issar who is believed to have been the spiritual leader of the Hofstadgroep.[19] Initially, Mohammed Bouyeri was not the most noticeable person within this group of people. He was the one who translated many radical political Islamist texts from English to Dutch and took on the role of "scholar" within this group, which was considered a more passive one.[20]

By 2004, some of the participants in the network had developed plans to use violent means to "defend" Islam. This holds true particularly in the case of Mohammed Bouyeri. In September 2004 he had reached a stage at which he developed the idea not only to threaten but also kill persons who, in his eyes, where insulting Islam or the prophet Mohammed. One of these people was the Dutch filmmaker Theo van Gogh.

Bouyeri's radicalisation process and the killing of Theo van Gogh

To many who knew Mohammed Bouyeri during his childhood it came as a surprise that he would develop such extreme ideas and practices. Bouyeri was born in Amsterdam in 1978 as a child of immigrant parents of Moroccan Berber heritage. He grew up in a low-income immigrant neighbourhood in the west of Amsterdam. In elementary school Bouyeri was an exemplary student and was able to advance on in 1990 to higher general secondary education. In 1995 Bouyeri received his diploma, one of his teachers even praised him as one of the "bright boys" who would "probably succeed".[21] Bouyeri wanted to help his peers to achieve more in Dutch society. He did not have many friends and was shy around girls. At college he did not succeed and switched studies a number of times.[22] After five years, he dropped out all together.[23]

Bouyeri's first encounter with the police occurred in 1997. Bouyeri was involved in a fight with a police officer. Later in the spring of 2000 Bouyeri did not allow his sister to leave the house because of her affair with a Moroccan boy and the police were once again involved. A year later he got into a fight with the, by then, ex-lover of his sister and drew a knife during the fight. For this he was convicted and spent twelve weeks in prison. In prison, religion started to become important to Bouyeri. In his cell he began to study the Koran.[24] After his release from prison, Bouyeri worked as a volunteer at a community centre in Amsterdam. He also began to write columns for a neighbourhood newsletter, voicing the needs of the Moroccan youth in the area. In this period, he tried to organise and receive funding for a new youth centre, but saw his idea rejected by the authorities. Progressively, his writings were becoming of a more radical nature. Under the pseudonym Abu Zubair, he wrote at least a dozen extremist texts on the Internet, in which he made calls upon young Muslims to "wake up" from their paralysing sleep and to actively take part in the "defensive jihad" against the West. It was from these publications that the Security Service began to take notice of Bouyeri and started to tap his phone.[25] In the last phase of his radicalisation process before killing Theo van Gogh, around summer 2004, he is believed to have encountered some misfortune in relation to girls. His status as the "scholar" of the network, sitting behind his personal computer most of the time, was not regarded as high as that of a "true" jihadi with plans to travel to places such as Chechnya or Iraq or to take concrete action in the Netherlands itself. One girl is said to have turned him down as her husband in the spring of 2004, which may have provoked Bouyeri to trade his computer for a gun.[26]

On the morning of 2 November 2004, Bouyeri assassinated filmmaker Theo van Gogh who was biking his way to work. Bouyeri shot him eight times. Van Gogh died on the spot. Bouyeri then tried to cut his throat, nearly decapitating him, and pinned a five-page letter to his chest with a knife. In this letter Bouyeri referred to ideologies of the Takfir wal Hijra organisation and threatened Western governments, Jews and a number of Dutch politicians, including Ayaan Hirsi Ali. After a shootout with the police, Bouyeri was arrested near the spot where he had killed Van Gogh. He had run out of bullets and had been shot in the leg. On the same day and the days that followed, more than a dozen other participants of the network were arrested at several locations. Two of these suspected members of the Hofstadgroep were arrested after a fourteen-hour siege of their apartment in The Hague. One of them threw a hand grenade at the police when they tried to enter the place. Five members of the arrest team were seriously wounded. Later the police shot the same suspect in the arm to force his arrest.[27]

Trials and convictions

In two separate trials, the suspects were tried. The first took place in Amsterdam were Bouyeri was sentenced for the killing of Theo van Gogh. He was, among others, convicted and received the maximum sentence possible: life sentence without parole.[28] He and thirteen other suspects were (also) brought to the court of Rotterdam, which convicted nine of them for membership of a terrorist organisation (i.e. what is known as the Hofstadgroep).[29]

Other arrests and trials would follow. As mentioned earlier, the core of the Hofstadgroep was part of a larger fluid network that included a number of individuals who have been charged and/or convicted of terrorist activities or crimes such as the illegal possession of arms. The most noticeable individual was Samir Azzouz (born 1986). This Dutch national of Moroccan descent had close links to individual members of the Hofstadgroep, though he was never prosecuted for membership of this particular group. In January 2003 he was arrested in Ukraine, together with a friend, while allegedly on his way to join the jihad in Chechnya. In October 2003, Azzouz and three others were arrested in the Netherlands on suspicion of constituting a terrorist cell, but were released for lack of evidence. In June 2004, he was arrested again; this time in relation to an armed robbery of a supermarket. During a search of his house, police found what they believed to be evidence that Azzouz had been involved in planning several attacks in the Netherlands. However, at trial the judge concluded that there was insufficient evidence to convict Azzouz on the charge of planning terrorist attacks. He was only convicted on the charge of illegal possession of firearms and sentenced to three months in jail. In October 2005 he was arrested again with six others on terrorism charges and finally sentenced for planning terrorist attacks and membership of a criminal organisation with terrorist intensions. This group has been labelled by the media as the Piranha group, but is generally believed to be part of the Hofstadgroep.[30]

Different variations of radical political Islam: from dawa to jihad

Following van Gogh's murder and the subsequent arrests of more than a dozen predominantly homegrown jihadis, Islamist terrorism became regarded as the most important security issue in the Netherlands. The authorities exhibited a growing awareness that radical political Islamist individuals and groups appeared to be increasingly successful at targeting and recruiting erstwhile "moderate"

Dutch Muslims. Noting this, a report by the Dutch security service titled *From Dawa to Jihad. The various threats from radical political Islam to the democratic legal order* issued clear warnings about the rapid radicalisation of young Muslims. At the same time, it also sought to contribute to the debate on countering the threats that may emanate from radical political Islam. The report, probably the best overview of the complex and multiform phenomenon of radical political Islam in the Netherlands, investigates three variations of radical political Islam that have manifested themselves in the Netherlands. It lists the different threats posed by these types of Islamism and the effect that radical political Islam has on both mainstream Muslim and non-Muslim communities.[31]

According to the report, in the Netherlands there are three variations of radical political Islam that can be described as "Puritanical", "Muslim National", and "Anti-Democratic". Radical-Islamic Puritanism emphasises resistance against Western oppression, and holds contempt for the way in which human relations are given shape in Western society. Western views on equal rights for women, freedom of speech, respect for ideological multiform, autonomy in privacy and the secular nature of the state are despised. As an alternative, a social order is proposed based on the Islamic morals set out in Sharia. In present day radical political Islam, this radical Puritanism is manifested within such movements as "Salafism" and "Wahhabism", which put primary emphasis on "purifying" Islam from "heretical" influences. Thus, in contrast to other forms of radical political Islam, the goal of radical political Islamic Puritanism is not primarily that of establishing an Islamic state, but of the return of all Muslims to the "purity" of early stages of Islam before it was "tarnished" by the influences of Shi'ism, Hinduism and Western thinking.

According to the *From Dawa to Jihad* report, those following the path of Muslim Nationalism consider themselves to be reacting against both the political and cultural dominance of the West – though their actions are less religiously motivated in this proposed alternative. Thus, Muslim Nationalists focus less on Islam as a religion, and more on what it means to be Muslim in terms of the "imagined community" of the "Muslim nation", and the solidarity between Muslims all over the world.

The prime objective of Anti-Democratic radicals is the realisation of a form of government that is different from a Western, liberal democracy. Supporters of this type of radicalism are often motivated by a general non-acceptance of the democratic forms of government, or by a partial rejection of essential elements of a democracy. Consequently, Anti-Democratic radicals can opt for various strategies to achieve their objective, including both armed combat with the intention of rapidly overthrowing the democratic form of government and insidiously undermining it by gradually winning over the public by means of propaganda or covert financing and influencing.

While all three strands may pursue different objectives, the authors of the report see a particular commonality. Puritanical, Muslim National and Anti-Democratic radical political Islamists all share a strong mobilising force provided by the idea of the umma – the Islamic global community. The umma is seen as a source of inspiration for identification and organisation, and is a fundamental concept that is used by all three variants for the implementation of radical political Islam.

Dawa and jihad

The threats posed by radical political Islam are both violent and non-violent in nature. In its violent form, the threat from radical political Islam is referred to as jihad, and in its non-violent incarnation, it is referred to as *dawa*. Both forms currently present a threat to Dutch society.

While violent jihad against Dutch society poses the most obvious threat to security and democracy in the Netherlands, non-violent dawa as the propagation of radical political Islamist ideology strives for the "re-Islamisation" of Muslim minorities in the West – a long-term strategy of continually influencing them towards extreme puritanical, intolerant and anti-Western ideals. Their goal is for Muslims in the West to reject Western values and standards, propagating extreme isolation from Western society and often intolerance towards other groups such as Jews and homosexuals.

Dawa-oriented radicals encourage Muslims to develop parallel structures in society and often to take the law into their own hands so that they "turn their backs" on the non-Islamic government while setting up their own autonomous power structure based on a specific interpretation of the Sharia. Generally, Islamist radicals of this persuasion pose a threat in that they reject the open nature of Western society, Western respect for diversity, and personal autonomy in the area of ethics and ideology.

In particular, dawa-oriented radicals pose three specific threats. The first is that of radical "isolationism", which involves the isolation of Muslim groups from social and political life. The second is radical "exclusivism", which entails the withdrawal of the Muslim community from society, involving expressions of a strong discriminatory nature towards the rest of society or certain groups within society. The third is that of radical "parallelism", which involves not only a withdrawal from society but also the pursuit of an entirely parallel society within the surrounding population, whereby parallel power structures are developed and the law is taken into one's own hands.[32]

Such a movement might eventually heighten ethnic and religious tensions in the Netherlands, with increasing polarisation as a result of its intolerant message concerning those who do not share its views.[33] This new development is described as Islamic Neo-radicalism which is arguing for the establishment of "Islamised" enclaves within society; physical areas in which Sharia law prevails over Dutch and European legislation.[34] No firm conclusion is possible at this stage, but the existence of such enclaves may serve as sanctuaries for extremist ideology and may become hotbeds for radicalisation.

Different categories of dawa and jihad-oriented groups

According to the General Intelligence and Security Service, four different categories exist in regard to the groups that pursue dawa and jihad. These categories can be divided as Overt Dawa, Covert Dawa, Covert Jihad and Overt Jihad. Each group, comprised of unique characteristics, has a distinguishable composition of radical political Islamic actors. Some groups pursue multiple strategies, so there is not always a clear distinction between networks or individuals that concentrate on dawa and those that concentrate on jihad. Thus, the choice of dawa-oriented groups to pursue non-violent activities does not always imply that they are non-violent in principle. Often such groups simply have not *yet* considered armed jihad appropriately expedient for practical or religious reasons. The same is true among groups pursuing either overt or covert variations of dawa or jihad.[35]

Overt Dawa

The first type of Overt Dawa group is engaged in efforts to create anti-democratic views on the state by non-violent means. This involves non-violent activities by Anti-Democratic political Islam and/or non-violent radical Muslim Nationals, and is currently best demonstrated in the Netherlands by the Arab European League, which hopes to "introduce the Sharia via elections".[36] The second type of group, meanwhile, seeks to overtly propagate exclusivism and parallelism. This group is comprised of non-violent radical political Islamic Puritanism in the Netherlands from Salafist groups such as the ultra-orthodox Jama-at-al-Tabligh Wal-Dawa (Society for Propagation and Preaching) movement.[37]

Covert Dawa

Within the category of Covert Dawa, one group type focuses primarily on the covert propagation of exclusivism and parallelism through the application of hidden agendas under false pretences. This group comprises non-violent radical political Islamic puritans, which is evidenced by radical political Islamic non-governmental organisations (NGOs) from Islamic model countries, such as the radical Puritan Islamic missionary, socio-cultural and finance organisation from Saudi Arabia and the Gulf. Moreover, itinerant imams, radical web sites and recruiters/converters in prisons, mosques and schools can also present this type of threat. The other group pursuing this form of Covert Dawa, meanwhile is preoccupied with covert attempts to undermine the structure of the democratic legal order. This threat involves non-violent Anti-Democratic political Islam, and can be witnessed on the international level by the various branches of the Muslim Brotherhood.[38]

Covert Jihad

The first Covert Jihad group type pursues the subversion of the democratic legal order. This type of threat comes from violent Anti-Democratic political Islam, though at present no examples of this form of threat currently exist in the Western world. The second focuses on the secret encouragement of serious tension among groups in society that may lead to violence. Radical political Islamic Puritanism and violent Muslim Nationalism pose such a threat. The former of which has been demonstrated by the activities of the Hizb ut Tahrir, an international radical political Islamic organisation that is active in the Netherlands.[39]

Overt Jihad

Of these Jihadis, there are some ten to twenty loose-knit structures that can be qualified as Jihadi or terrorist networks.[40] Most of these Jihadi networks are autonomous, acting independently of foreign influence, such as the aforementioned Hofstadgroep. Additionally, there are also a considerable number of locally embedded international networks that are controlled through various means from abroad, or in a manner whereby foreign recruiters residing in the Netherlands play a key role.[41]

In this most extreme category of radical political Islam, the first group comprises individuals and networks in pursuit of exclusivism and parallelism via overtly violent activities. This threat is posed by violent radical-Islamic Puritanism such as the Salafiyya Jihadiyya, which advocates violent radical Puritan Islam, as well as the Takfir wal Hidjra movement in the Netherlands, which contends that all non-Muslims and all moderate Muslims are heretic and should thus be combated by whatever means necessary. In the case of the latter example, this contention was most starkly depicted by the Hofstadgroep, which was connected with the murder of Theo van Gogh.[42]

The second group is characterised by individuals and networks bent on creating anti-democratic views against the state by violent means. This threat is put forth by violent Anti-Democratic political Islamists and/or violent radical Muslim Nationalists, and can be witnessed internationally by the Al-Qaeda network, as well as nationally in the Netherlands by the dozens of second-generation Dutch immigrants "wrestling with their identity", who have struck out for Iraq's Sunni Triangle.[43]

Impact of radical political Islam and radicalisation on mainstream Muslim communities

Within mainstream Muslim communities, the ability to resist the influence of radical political Islam, at least until recently, had been rather low. Moderating individuals and organisations either had insufficient insight into the effects of these radicalising forces or were unable to assess and neutralise these effects. As a consequence, they were unable to counterbalance the forces of Islamic radicalisation.[44] This has especially been the case concerning recent arrivals – and especially those of North African origin – because of a lack of education, frustration and anger at the inability to "make ends meet" in their adopted country.[45] As a consequence, international jihadi networks were impacting mainstream Muslim communities by "stealthily taking root in Dutch society" through the co-opting of estranged Dutch-born Muslim youths.[46]

Moreover, after the murder of van Gogh, radical political Islamic individuals and groups appeared to be increasingly successful at targeting and recruiting erstwhile "moderate" Dutch Muslims.[47] According to the Ministry of the Interior, the murder of van Gogh, along with the terrorist attacks in New York, Madrid and London, served as "trigger events" that directly influenced the radicalisation and jihadisation of many young Muslims in the mainstream, because they channelled latent feelings of political and social discontent in a specific direction. As a result, the attraction of radical political Islam for mainstream Muslim youths seems to have grown, which was displayed through provocative behaviour and the way Muslim youths have applauded terrorist outrages and praised attackers as activists for Islam.[48] Consequently, radical political Islam was able to take hold as a homegrown phenomenon within the Netherlands.[49]

Today, however, counter-forces have gained ground and continue to do so. This development, as well as an explanation of growing resistance of Muslim communities to radical political Islam and radicalisation will be described in the conclusion of this chapter. Next follows an overview of the counter-terrorism and counter-radicalisation policies that might have contributed to this recent (and still fragile) development.

Counter-terrorism and counter-radicalisation policies

High on the political agenda

For non-Muslim Dutch society, the combination of wide-ranging individual freedoms and the rapid stream of immigrants within a short period of time have drastically altered traditional societal relations and placed existing traditions and authorities under pressure. The combination of this pressure, along with the Dutch reaction to the assassination of van Gogh, has resulted in a collision between multiculturalism and liberalism, privacy rights and national security.[50] This became increasingly apparent in the violent reactions amongst the Dutch population following van Gogh's murder, which was shocked not only by the crime, but the manner by which the basic principles of the Netherlands' democratic constitutional state were challenged.[51] Anger, frustrations and fears resulted in numerous arson attacks on mosques and Islamic schools, and many smaller incidents aimed against Muslims. Some individual politicians played a negative role by contributing to the idea that the Netherlands was now at war and that Dutch Muslims in general were a serious threat to society.[52] According to data of the public opinion poll of the Eurobarometer, terrorism became one of the biggest issues of concern in the Netherlands. Asked "what do you think are the two most important issues facing your country at the moment", terrorism jumped from 12 per cent in Autumn 2004 to 40 per cent one year later.[53]

The government and local authorities were given the difficult task of channelling these feelings and maintaining social peace. From 2005 onwards, politicians and executives tried to formulate ways to deal with terrorism and radicalisation of Muslim youngsters. In the years following the van Gogh murder, radicalisation ranked high on the political agenda. Many programmes were launched to increase the awareness of the phenomenon, to investigate the socio-economic situation of young Dutch Muslims, and to try to understand the threat through research and training programmes.

General counter-terrorism and counter-radicalisation policies

In order to combat terrorism, the government is tackling radicalisation to reduce the risk of terrorist attacks. Both local and central government are taking measures to identify, prevent, isolate, intervene and curb radicalisation as well as recruitment before it is too late. Some of the general counter-terrorism measures taken by the government include appointing a National Counter-Terrorism Coordinator, charged with developing policy on national and international terrorism and making threat assessments. Furthermore it expanded the capacity of the general and military intelligence and security services (AIVD and MIVD). These services are responsible for identifying threats and security risks associated with specific individuals, objects and services. The government also gave police, public prosecutors and judicial authorities greater powers and more scope to investigate potential threats. Making it possible to use methods such as wiretapping and surveillance at an earlier stage. Furthermore, it enacted the Crimes of Terrorism Act, which outlaws recruitment and conspiracy for the purpose of committing a terrorist offence. Finally, the Immigration and Naturalisation Service (IND) tries to prevent undesirable guest speakers from appearing in Dutch mosques, in part by monitoring the visa process, and the Ministry of Finance notifies credit institutions if foundations are involved in terrorism or terrorism-related crimes.

In the field of counter-radicalisation, the Netherlands advocates a broad-based approach.[54] Efforts to deal with radicalisation are focused primarily on young Muslims and consist of strategies for handling persons or groups already extremely radicalised and strategies for handling persons or groups potentially susceptible to extreme radical ideas. Such a broad and difficult effort requires joining forces at all political levels as well as involving all parts of society. Their combined efforts should make it as difficult as possible for extremists to radicalise and recruit Dutch Muslims. According to the "Polarisation and Radicalisation Action Plan 2007–2011" of the Ministry of the Interior it should result in the following:

1   The prevention of (further) processes of isolation, polarisation and radicalisation by the (re-) inclusion of people who are at risk of slipping away or

turning away from Dutch society and the democratic legal order. This includes such things as, in particular, inclusion through education, traineeships and work.
2   The early signalling of these processes by administrators and professionals and the development of an adequate approach.
3   The exclusion of people who have crossed clear boundaries and seeing to it that their influence on others is limited as much as possible.[55]

To achieve these goals, the authorities have developed a wide range of strategies and policies. The following elements can be considered key elements of the Dutch approach. First, the authorities promote the integration of Muslims. The priorities include considering specific identity problems of Muslim youths in Western surroundings, introducing anti-discrimination measures and encouraging social and political participation.[56] For example, they have undertaken several policies to address discrimination, including in the labour market, as well as to equip youth with the skills they require to find work. They have also provided financial resources for language training and to encourage young people to complete their schooling, and have increased support for parents to help them equip their children to participate in Dutch society.[57] In addition, the government is actively fighting polarisation and Islam phobia. For instance, anti-discrimination laws have been used in the Netherlands not just to support victims of discrimination, but to allow monitoring and to provide information to citizens and local authorities to enable them to combat those who would exacerbate divisions in society by inciting racism and xenophobia, specifically fear of Islam.[58] Integration is also promoted by policies to end the dependence of Dutch Muslims on imams from abroad, who may lack sufficient knowledge of Dutch society and convey distorted impressions. Imams trained in the Netherlands identify more closely with this country and are better able to reinforce social cohesion.[59]

The second general strategy concerns heightening resistance of the Muslim population to radicalisation. The national authorities are aware of the fact that resolving the problem of possible radicalisation among Muslim youths requires support from the Dutch Muslims. Therefore, the authorities actively support Islamic initiatives against radicalism. Organisations serving social causes are, for instance, encouraged to disseminate more diverse information about moderate versions of Islam via intermediary institutions and the Internet.[60]

The third and final main strategy against radicalisation involves acknowledging, isolating and curtailing these processes. To this end, local authorities in particular need to be properly attuned to persons who drift away from or turn against society. Several major cities in the Netherlands, including Amsterdam, Rotterdam and Utrecht, have drafted their own specific policy.[61]

In addition, the Netherlands has a specific policy for dealing with a number of high-risk sites or hotbeds of radicalisation.[62] Some are Salafist centres and mosques that engage in dawa. Imams and governors of so-called "hotbeds of radicalisation" are closely monitored by the authorities and are held directly accountable for their social responsibility. They are also requested by the authorities to keep recruiters at a distance and to discourage youths from resorting to violence.[63] Intervening in these hotbeds of radicalisation can involve administrative, financial or communication tools, or the options provided for by immigration law. In a few cases preaching intolerance was severely reprimanded and resulted in (attempts at) extraditions of imams to their country of origin.

Finally, it should be noted that the Dutch are keenly aware that the radicalisation and recruitment problem is closely related to situations and developments in other countries. Therefore international cooperation, including exchanging information, learning from each other's experiences, and capacity building in third countries is part of the general strategy. With its foreign policy, the government aims to promote peace, safety, stability, good governance, democratisation and respect for human rights.[64] Whether this can have an impact on radicalisation processes in the Netherlands is difficult to determine, but it can help to create a better context in which more concrete and direct counter-radicalisation policies have a better chance of success. The most tangible and direct of these policies are developed and executed at the local level. The case of Amsterdam is generally regarded as one of the most interesting among the counter-radicalisation policies at the local level.

The case of Amsterdam

The city of Amsterdam is home to up to 180,000 Muslims, which is 24 per cent of the population of Amsterdam. Most of them originate from Morocco (63,000), Turkey (38,000), Surinam (up to 70,000), Egypt and Pakistan.[65] Amsterdam was also home to a number of persons that were part of the Hofstadgroep. In addition it hosts a number of radical mosques, including the most prototypical orthodox Al Tawheed mosque and Salafist centres. Especially after the murder of Theo van Gogh, radical political Islam and radicalisation processes were considered to be an important social issue and a considerable risk posing a threat to the social peace. While there are no statistics on the extent and scope of radicalisation in Amsterdam, reports by the General Intelligence and Security Service have indicated a rise in Islamist radicalism in the years following the van Gogh murder. A study by the Institute for Migration and Ethnic Studies (IMES) of the University of Amsterdam also concluded that radicalisation among youngsters with a migration background was on the increase.[66] Furthermore, as part of a study conducted in September 2006, a survey showed that 2 per cent of all Muslims are susceptible to Islamist radicalisation because they follow certain orthodox beliefs in combination with the perception that Islam is under threat and something must be done about it.[67]

The IMES study entitled Processes of radicalisation: "why young Muslims in Amsterdam radicalise", was part of the "Wij Amsterdammers" (We, the People of Amsterdam) programme and constituted the basis for "Amsterdam Against Radicalisation" plan.[68] The study also included a number of key recommendations. In order to counter radicalisation, the local authorities were urged to do the following:

- to increase societal trust;
- to increase political confidence;
- to increase religious resilience; and
- to find ways of contacting radical youngsters.[69]

In addition, the report points explicitly to the necessity of providing assistance to mosques in countering radicalisation and to the importance of increased insight into the diversity within Islam. The recommendations or the IMES study were translated into concrete actions by local authorities, among others by the coordinating office of the "Wij Amsterdammers" programme. This has resulted in a broad approach, aimed at not only countering radicalisation, but also removing the reasons for radicalisation by way of enhancing social cohesion, bridging ethnic gaps, and strengthening the common identity of all people of Amsterdam.[70]

In order to counter radicalisation, Amsterdam has taken a two-pronged approach. A hard and repressive tactic is employed against "doers": extremists who are suspected to have a willingness to use violence in trying to achieve their ideological goals. Recognising the importance of working together, the city's mayor has teamed up with the police, prosecution and security services. With an emphasis on actively preventing radicalisation, greater privileges have been extended to the police and security forces to disrupt individual actions.[71] The hard approach also includes measures to deal with the breeding grounds for radicalisation that express repression towards radicalism, but mildness towards orthodoxy.

The soft power approach towards radicalisation is aimed at the "thinkers": individuals who do not want to employ violent tactics (yet), but do radicalise in the sense that they are adhering to radical ideologies. With the aim of investing in the intellectual social capital, each individual case is analyzed to ascertain what is needed to turn around the radicalisation process and is followed by suitable interventions. For this specific task, a small unit was created within the department of Public Order, Safety and Security to gather early warning signals of radicalisation in the city and find ways to prevent and counter the process. This unit is called the "informatiehuishouding" (the information house) and constitutes the heart of Amsterdam's counter-radicalisation strategy. Together with the coordinating office of the "Wij Amsterdammers" programme, it develops and advises policy on more specific prevention strategies and activities. The main goals of the specific prevention strategy are increasing resilience and stimulating alternative supply. The focus of this strategy is on the broader Muslim community, first-line professionals and susceptible youth in particular.[72]

Of course trying to deal with a relatively new, complex and constantly changing phenomenon like radicalisation requires regular evaluations and improvement of policies based on lessons learned. In the case of Amsterdam, these lessons are the following:

1 Policies have to be formulated not top–down, but bottom–up.
2 Investing in trust is more important than investing in control.

3 Give room to good ideas and suggestions from society, as society cannot be managed from one's desktop alone.
4 Make sure to have enough budget and a diverse and specialised team to make your promises come true.
5 Be sure the programme has always enough political support.
6 Be aware of the huge political and media sensitivity.[73]

These lessons learned are reflected in new measures and the reshaping of existing ones. Among others, it has resulted in a more intensive cooperation with key partners such as leading figures from the Muslim community and religious organisations in Amsterdam.[74]

Recent developments and concluding remarks

Positive developments

Whether or not the above-described counter-terrorism and counter-radicalisation have an impact on the radicalisation processes in the Netherlands is difficult to determine. Perhaps in a decade or so, one can evaluate the various policies, although this will remain questionable given the many factors that play a role with regard to radicalisation (including difficult to measure psychological characteristics and personal experiences). Perhaps one can only determine to what extent the number of radical Muslims has gone up or gone down – despite of, or thanks to the various policies.

At the moment the speed in which these numbers increase seems to have slowed down. The reason for this may not be the counter-radicalisation policies, but the steadily growing willingness within Muslim communities to recognise and tackle the problems of radicalisation and recruitment. The latest anti-terrorism progress reports of the National Coordinator for Counterterrorism (NCTB) specifically mention this, while also pointing out various initiatives that are currently being taken to foster diversity in the political and religious debate. In addition, a growing number of moderate Muslim groups are starting to copy the influential approaches of radical groups by both producing their own religious products in the Dutch language and by focusing more intensively on issues important to today's Muslim youths.

Since March 2006, the Terrorist Threat Assessments Netherlands issued by the National Coordinator for Counterterrorism have reported that resistance among Dutch Muslims to radicalisation and extremism is on the rise. The leading Islamic organisations realise that violence and polarisation along ethnic and religious lines will fuel existing anti-Islamic sentiments in the Netherlands. According to the 12th Terrorist Threat Assessment Netherlands the many efforts undertaken to boost social resistance and defuse tensions probably tend to appeal to the more moderate wings of the various groups. Nonetheless, an increasingly vigilant community can reduce the likelihood that an individual undergoing radicalisation would turn to violence, and greater social resistance can also restrict the size of the "comfort zone" in which jihadis can operate. However, individuals who are already confirmed radicals and willing to use violence to further their goals may only isolate themselves even further from mainstream society and from their less radical co-religionists, whom they may see as "weak" and overly inclined to compromise, according to the Assessment.[75]

Not so positive news

Since the late 1980s radical political Islam has managed to take root in the Netherlands. Despite some positive developments, in particular the growing resilience among Muslim communities, there are a number of factors that continue to play a role with regard to the future of radical political Islam in the Netherlands. For instance, Islamists are still dominant on the "religious market of ideas". The large majority of European citizens from Muslim descent share core European values, but they are not spreading their views on the religious market of ideas as such. This leaves the field rather open to people with a more radical vision. These radicals, increasingly, use the Dutch language in sermons, training sessions and conferences, and in disseminating relevant literature and audio-visual material. This has enabled them to reach a growing number of young Muslims – most of whom do not speak Arabic. This strong position on the religious market is also reflected in the influence on mosques and (charity) organisations, as well as on the Internet.[76] The latter also plays a role in Jihadi groups becoming much more dynamic, fluid and diffuse. They rely heavily on virtual networks and training, through the Internet, and then shift into actual, operational networks. In a way, the Internet is "the cement" of these networks.[77] Moreover, these networks and radical groups constitute an ongoing threat as their activities may ultimately lead to mounting distrust between Islamic and non-Islamic population groups. As such, radical political Islam also presents a long-term threat to the Netherlands, as polarisation between Holland's ethnic-religious populations may undermine social cohesion, and consequently the democratic order as well. The Netherlands Ministry of the Interior warned of such a development in the first half of 2005.[78] Given the rise in the last few years of the populist political movement with a clear anti-Muslim agenda and the release of the anti-Muslim movie "Fitna" by the leader of this movement, Geert Wilders, these fears seem quite justified. There is the risk that the gap between Muslims and non-Muslims may further increase, in particular as a result of new Islam-related incidents, such as rows over publications (think of the cartoon crisis), foreign policy issues (for instance the conflict in Afghanistan and Pakistan) and new terrorist incidents (such as the attacks in Mumbai or a new terrorist attack in Europe). Such developments and incidents will make it very difficult to bridge the gap between Muslims and non-Muslims. In particular a new terrorist attack might have a devastating effect on intergroup relations. The chance of such an incident is "substantial" according to the latest reports of the National Coordinator for Counterterrorism.

Current terrorism threat level

In the Terrorist Threat Assessment Netherlands of March 2009 it states,

> that there is a realistic possibility that an attack will occur against Dutch interests at home and/or abroad. International jihadist groups still constitute a major threat for West European countries and West European interests. These groups have the capacity and the desire to hit European and Western interests abroad, such as in the Pakistan–Afghanistan border region. They also still intend to carry out attacks against Dutch interests in the Netherlands and abroad. For these groups, the Netherlands is regarded a "legitimate" target because of the presence of Dutch troops in Afghanistan and the alleged insult to Islam in the Netherlands. These international jihadist threats currently constitute the most important component of the threat against Dutch interests in the Netherlands and abroad.[79]

On the basis of this analysis, one could argue that terrorist threat has become more "foreign and less homegrown". The situation in the Pakistan–Afghanistan border region seems to have become of greater concern than the situation in Salafist mosques or the home gatherings of young Muslims in Amsterdam or The Hague. Of course, the continued existence of the terrorist infrastructure in Pakistan is related to the worrisome security situation in the Netherlands and a possible connection between Pakistan and homegrown groups can have devastating effects as we have witnessed in the case of the United Kingdom. Also neighbouring Germany is facing such connections.

According to the same Terrorist Threat Assessment, the threat emanating from the Dutch jihadist networks has generally remained unchanged, which means that the situation around local autonomous jihadist networks in the Netherlands continues to be "relatively calm". There is, however, a quite worrisome new development. As in the case of the UK and Germany it seems that individual members of local autonomous networks have increased their contact with international jihadist groups. According to the National Coordinator for Counterterrorism, this development may lead to these local networks becoming increasingly associated with international jihadist networks.

With regard to radicalisation, the Terrorism Threat Assessment points at the fact that the war in Gaza between Israel and Hamas stirred many emotions in the Dutch Muslim communities. Therefore, it cannot be excluded that the shocking images from the media of Gaza are an additional stimulus for young Muslims, in particular, to turn to radicalism. This risk is increased because political Salafis and the international Islamic movement of Hizb-ut-Tahrir used the events in Gaza to propagate their message, in order to increase their group of adherents. The Assessment continues to point at another relevant development: the increase in the last few years in the number of anti-Islam statements on the Internet.

The Terrorist Threat Assessment is quite positive on the issues of resistance of Dutch Muslim communities against polarisation, radicalisation and terrorism.

According to the report, this continues to be high. It points at the various Muslim organisations that opposed anti-Semitic slogans that were shouted by some, mainly Moroccan-Dutch, young people during protest demonstrations following the war in Gaza. It also mentions the fact that it is furthermore increasingly noticeable that it is becoming possible in Muslim communities to discuss sensitive subjects, such as the position of homosexuals and women in Islam. The National Coordinator for Counterterrorism even observed a growing resistance against (violent) radicalisation in the last few years within the Salafist movement in the Netherlands.

Concluding remarks

Considering the above-described report and the positive and not so positive developments regarding radical political Islam, radicalisation and jihadism in the Netherlands, it remains difficult to give a general assessment of the situation. It is clear that in the last two decades radical political Islam has managed to take root in the Netherlands and has caused serious problems; within Muslim communities, and between Muslims and non-Muslims. So far, with the exception of the murder of Theo van Gogh, it has not (yet) produced serious security risks. Nonetheless, the threat and the social and political problems have been serious enough to spend much money and energy in counter-terrorism and counter-radicalisation policies. The effect of these efforts is impossible to measure. The fact that the level of resistance and resilience among Muslim communities has increased and has remained high is perhaps the most positive development in recent years. The increasing willingness of mainstream Muslim groups to recognise and tackle the problems of radicalisation and recruitment within their own communities may have a mitigating effect on the growth of radical political Islam. This has, however, not led to an apparent cessation or decline of Islamism in the Netherlands. Moreover, it is questionable if the resistance among mainstream Muslim communities will reduce the chance that the Netherlands will fall victim to another jihadi terrorist attack. The fact that some radical Muslim individuals have increased their contact with international jihadist groups and are more internationally orientated than ever before is extremely worrisome. Growing resilience among moderates or non-violent Salafis is not likely to prevent local networks becoming associated with international jihadist networks. In addition, this "foreign" threat is more difficult for the intelligence communities to monitor than that of the (erstwhile) homegrown Hofstadgroep-like networks. Therefore, in the coming years, the Netherlands is still more likely to be confronted with jihadist violence than to see the decline of radical political Islam.

Notes

1 The research of this article is partly based on the research conducted within the framework of the 6th Framework Research Programme of the European Commission "Transnational Terrorism, Security and the Rule of the Law". The author would like

to thank Michael Andrew Berger, Natalie Kraak and Tinka Veldhuis for their input and critical remarks.
2. In this chapter, radical political Islam and Islamism are used as synonyms.
3. Interior Security Service, *Annual Report 1991*, The Hague: BVD, 1992.
4. Buro Jansen & Janssen, *The Nosy State: The Netherlands and the Interior Security Service*, Amsterdam: Fagel, 2002, pp. 108–109.
5. Interior Security Service, *Annual Report 1995*, The Hague: BVD, 1996.
6. Interior Security Service, *Annual Report 1996*, The Hague: BVD, 1997.
7. Interior Security Service, *The Political Islam in the Netherlands*, The Hague: BVD, 1998.
8. Tinka Veldhuis and Edwin Bakker, "Muslims in the Netherlands: Tensions and Violent Conflict", in: Michael Emerson (ed.), *Ethno-Religious Conflict in Europe: Typologies of Radicalisation in Europe's Muslim Communities*, Brussels: CEPS, 2009, pp. 81–108.
9. Ibid.
10. General Intelligence and Security Service, *Background of Jihad Recruits in the Netherlands*, The Hague: AIVD, 2004.
11. Ibid.
12. General Intelligence and Security Service, *Recruitment for the Jihad in the Netherlands*, The Hague: AIVD, 2002.
13. Tinka Veldhuis and Edwin Bakker, "Muslims in the Netherlands".
14. *NRC-Handelsblad*, 27 December 2005.
15. Tinka Veldhuis and Edwin Bakker, "Muslims in the Netherlands".
16. The name "Hofstad" was originally the codename the Dutch General Intelligence and Security Service used for the group, which leaked to the media. The name refers to a popular name for the city of The Hague, which was home to some participants of the network.
17. *De Volkskrant*, 26 November 2005.
18. General Intelligence and Security Service, *The Violent Jihad in the Netherlands: Current Trends in the Islamist Terrorist Threat*, The Hague: AIVD, 2006.
19. Ibid.
20. Transnational Terrorism, Security & the Rule of Law (TTSRL), *The "Hofstadgroep"*, Deliverable 5, Workpackage 6, April, 2008.
21. Albert Benschop, *Chronicle of a Political Murder Foretold, "Jihad in the Netherlands"*, Amsterdam: University of Amsterdam, 2007.
22. Emmerson Vermaat, *De Hofstadgroep, Portret van een radicaal-islamitisch netwerk*, Soesterberg: Aspekt, 2005.
23. Transnational Terrorism, Security & the Rule of Law (TTSRL), *The "Hofstadgroep"*.
24. Albert Benschop, *Chronicle of a Political Murder*.
25. Ibid.
26. Ibid.
27. District Court of Amsterdam, 26 July 2005, 13/129227–04, LJN:AU0025.
28. Ibid.
29. In January 2008, an appeals court overturned the convictions for belonging to a terrorist group because, in the eyes of the judges, no structured cooperation had been established.
30. Transnational Terrorism, Security & the Rule of Law (TTSRL), *The "Hofstadgroep"*.
31. General Intelligence and Security Service, *From Dawa to Jihad. The Various Threats from Radical Islam to the Democratic Legal Order*, The Hague: AIVD, 2004.
32. Edwin Bakker and Michael Andrew Berger, "The Case of The Netherlands", in: Barry Rubin (ed.), *Global Survey of Islamism*, Armonk NY: M.E. Sharpe Publishers, 2009, forthcoming.
33. General Intelligence and Security Service, *The Radical Dawa in Transition – The Rise of Islamic Neoradicalism in the Netherlands*, The Hague: AIVD, 2007.

34 Ibid.
35 Edwin Bakker and Michael Andrew Berger, *The Case of the Netherlands*.
36 General Intelligence and Security Service, *From Dawa to Jihad*.
37 Edwin Bakker, "Radical Islam in the Netherlands", in: Christopher Heffelfinger (ed.), *Unmasking Terrorism. A global review of terrorist activities*, Washington DC: Jamestown Foundation, 2005.
38 General Intelligence and Security Service, *From Dawa to Jihad*.
39 Ibid.
40 General Intelligence and Security Service, *Violent Jihad in the Netherlands*.
41 Ibid.
42 Alison Pargeter, "The Evolution of Radical Islamist Groups in Europe", *Jane's Intelligence Review*, February 2005.
43 Robert Leiken, "Europe's Angry Muslims", in: *Foreign Affairs*, July/August 2005, pp. 128–129.
44 General Intelligence and Security Service, *From Dawa to Jihad*.
45 Alison Pargeter, "The Evolution of Radical Islamist Groups in Europe".
46 Robert Leiken, "Europe's Angry Muslims".
47 Edwin Bakker, "Radical Islam in the Netherlands".
48 General Intelligence and Security Service, *Violent Jihad in the Netherlands*.
49 Edwin Bakker and Michael Andrew Berger, *The Case of The Netherlands*.
50 Robert Leiken, "Europe's Angry Muslims".
51 Albert Benschop, *Chronicle of a Political Murder: Foretold Jihad in the Netherlands*, Utrecht: Forum, 2005.
52 Edwin Bakker, "Wat te doen na de klap", in: S. Harchaoui (ed.), *Hedenddaags radicalisme. Verklaringen en Aanpak*, Apeldoorn: Het Spinhuis, 2006, pp. 195–216.
53 Edwin Bakker, "Differences in terrorist threat perceptions in Europe", in: D. Mahncke and J. Monar (eds), *International Terrorism. A European Response to a Global Threat?*, College of Europe Studies No. 3, Brussels: Pieter Lang, 2006, pp. 47–62.
54 The policy of the Dutch government is reflected in the following reports and parliamentary papers: Parliamentary paper 2004–2005 29754 nr. 4 Memorandum "Van Dawa tot Jihad"; Parliamentary paper 2004–2005 29754 nr. 26 Memorandum "Radicalisme en radicalisering"; Parliamentary paper 2004–2005 29754 nr. 27 Memorandum "Weerbaarheid en Integratiebeleid"; Parliamentary paper 2005–2006 29754 nr. 30 Memorandum "Lokale en justitiele aanpak van radicalisme en Radicalisering"; Parliamentary papers 2004–2006 29754 nrs. 5, 24, 60, 73, 94 Updates on the fight against terrorism; Wetenschappelijke Raad voor het Regeringsbeleid, report nr. 73: "Rapportage Dynamiek in islamitisch activisme"; the "Polarisation and Radicalisation Action Plan 2007–2011" of the Ministry of the Interior, 2006, and "Operationeel Actiepan Polarisatie en Radicalisering 2008", 2008.
55 Ministry of the Interior, "Polarisation and Radicalisation Action Plan 2007–2011", 2006, p. 7.
56 Marije Meines, "Radicalisation and its Prevention from the Dutch Perspective", in: *NCTb, Radicalisation in Broader Perspective*, The Hague: NCTB, 2007, pp. 34–39.
57 CounterTerrorism Implementation Task Force, "First Report of the Working Group on Radicalisation and Extremism that Lead to Terrorism: Inventory of State Programmes". See, www.un.org/terrorism/pdfs/radicalization.pdf.
58 Ibid.
59 Marije Meines, "Radicalisation and its Prevention from the Dutch perspective".
60 Ibid.
61 *Marije Meines*, "Radicalisation and its prevention from the Dutch perspective", p. 38.
62 Parliamentary paper 2005–2006, 29754, nr. 61, 22 December 2005, Letter detailing a framework policy for dealing with hearths of radicalisation.
63 Marije Meines, "Radicalisation and its prevention from the Dutch perspective", p. 38.
64 Ibid.

65 For additional facts and statistics, see www.eumap.org/topics/minority/reports/eumuslims. Last accessed 29 April 2008.
66 Transnational Terrorism, Security & the Rule of Law (TTSRL), *Radicalisation, Recruitment and the EU Counter-radicalization Strategy*, Deliverable 7, Workpackage 4, November 2009, p. 76.
67 Ibid.
68 Gemeente Amsterdam, Redactie team: PAS, IHH, en COT, *Amsterdam tegen radicalisering*, Amsterdam: Gemeente Amsterdam, 2007.
69 IMES, *Radicaliseringsprocessen: waarom moslimjongeren in Amsterdam radicaliseren*, Amsterdam: University of Amsterdam/IMES, 2007.
70 Transnational Terrorism, Security & the Rule of Law (TTSRL), *Radicalisation, Recruitment and the EU Counter-radicalization Strategy*.
71 Gemeente Amsterdam, Redactie team: PAS, IHH, en COT, *Amsterdam tegen radicalisering*, Amsterdam: Gemeente Amsterdam, 2007.
72 Colin Mellis, "Amsterdam and Radicalization. The Municipal Approach", in: *NCTb, Radicalisation in Broader Perspective*, The Hague: NCTB, 2007.
73 Joris Rijbroe, "We the people of Amsterdam", presentation for the Symposium Städte-Kulturen-Sprachen, Mannheim, 19 September 2008.
74 Gemeente Amsterdam, Redactie team: PAS, IHH, en COT, *Amsterdam tegen radicalisering*, Amsterdam: Gemeente Amsterdam, 2007.
75 National Coordinator for Counterterrorism, *Terrorist Threat Assessment Netherlands No. 12*, The Hague: NCTB, 2 March 2006.
76 National Coordinator for Counterterrorism, *Terrorist Threat Assessment Netherlands No. 4*, The Hague: NCTB, 7 June 2006.
77 General Intelligence and Security Service, *The Violent Jihad in the Netherlands: Current Trends in the Islamist Terrorist Threat*, The Hague: AIVD, 2006.
78 Ibid.
79 National Coordinator for Counterterrorism, *Terrorist Threat Assessment Netherlands No. 16*, The Hague: NCTB, 6 April 2009.

8 The Jihadists and anti-terrorist challenges in France
An overview

Jean-Luc Marret

Since the Madrid and London bombings, European countries have become increasingly worried that they may also become the victims of a terrorist attack. Countries such as Denmark, with its pro-NATO line and recent controversy over the Muhammad cartoons, Italy, which has been involved in Iraq, and the United Kingdom where radical Islamism is still very present, are all "potential terrorism targets". Conversely, whilst the threat is ever-present, France has, since 1996, successfully avoided any attack on its soil by operational jihadist cells, although there have been terrorist acts carried out against French interests or citizens around the world.

Yet France is currently facing the challenge of its (sometimes) discontented communities. This discontent is fuelled partly by a quest for identity among third-generation immigrants, but also by radical elements that are operating in the streets, the mosques, the *halal* business. As such, France could be regarded as the "avant-garde" of Europe and sooner or later other European countries could be faced with similar challenges. In this difficult environment, the publication of the Ministry of Interior's White Paper on Terrorism in March 2006 was arguably a political means by which to mobilise citizens. Lately, the reform of the internal security apparatus may be perceived as a real challenge. The creation of a new intelligence agency – the Direction Centrale du Renseignement Interieur (DCRI) – is the most recent initiative in order to enhance and adapt the French anti-terrorism strategy to changing threats.

The purpose of this chapter is to provide an overview of French jihadist networks, other old or emerging threats and to demonstrate how France's situation could foreshadow a similar evolution in countries like Spain, Italy, Germany or the UK.

Statistics, history and realities

Since 1980 (to 2006), 139 people have been killed by terrorist acts in France – one-third of them (46) were killed in five distinct terrorist waves. These were:

- Action Direct, a far-leftist group,
- The State-sponsored FATAH-RC (Abu Nidal Organization),

- The Armenian ASALA,
- The "Lebanese connection" (FARL, CSPPA, PDL, i.e. the Hezbollah),
- And finally, the most deadly, the Islamist Armed Group (or GIA) (Khaled Kelkal and others); 41 French citizens were assassinated in Algeria from September 1993 to August 1996.

Geographically speaking, 37 per cent of all terrorist acts that have occurred in France since 1965 have been carried out in Paris. Since the 1995, Groupe Islamique Armée (GIA) bombings on the Paris metro system, French human casualties have been tourists or citizens working in Arab-Muslim countries (see Figure 8.1).

Threat and sociology of "made in France" jihadism: still a "lumpen-Islam"

France has the largest Muslim (between five and six million) and Jewish communities in the European Union. The majority of this very heterogeneous population has the same relationship to Islam as the "cultural French" have to Christianity, i.e. somewhere between indifference and moderation. However, there is clearly a micro-community of more radical Muslims. It should be noted that in areas where unemployment rates are high the population is particularly sensitive to radical proselytising (*Salafism* or *tabligh*). The October–November 2005 riots in the predominantly immigrant suburbs (*banlieues*) demonstrated how sensitive the situation is currently in these areas. Intelligence assessments have not established, however, a formal and direct causality between "territorial" and multi-ethnic riots (more than simply "ethnic") and radical Islamism or jihadism. Theses riots were probably fuelled mainly by a sort of "local nationalism" or "jingoism" among the various gangs operating in each area.

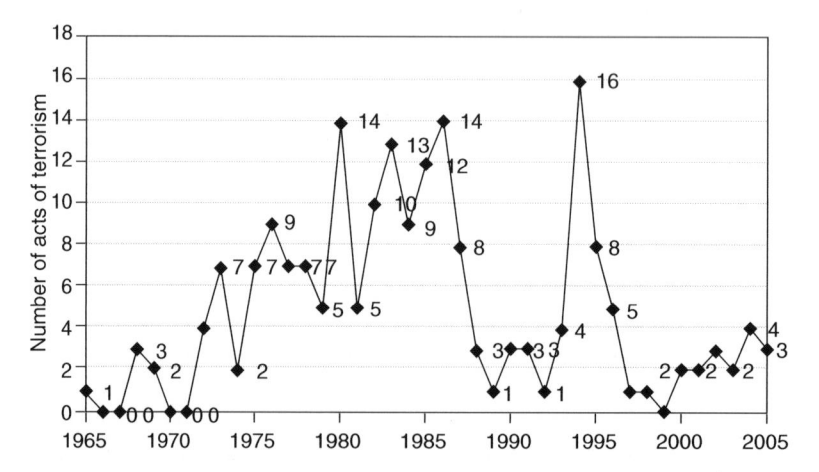

Figure 8.1 Number of acts of terrorism

According to the *Direction Centrale des Renseignements Dénéraux* (DCRG) (now part of the Direction Centrale du Renseignement Intérieur – DCRI), it is estimated that 5,000 Salafists currently live in France and that in 2004, 75 out of the country's 1,700 mosques were Salafist. One of the most tangible indicators of radicalisation is the taking control of mosques. Salafist circles seem bent on infiltrating mosques by subterfuge in order to practise entryism after which they move to take control. This occurs especially in mosques run by the *Tabligh*.[1]

A Salafi (referring to *first Muslim*), from the Arabic word *Salaf* (literally *predecessors* or *early generations*), is an adherent of a contemporary movement in Sunni Islam that is sometimes called Salafism and sometimes identified with Wahhabism. Salafis themselves insist that their beliefs are simply pure Islam as practised by the first three generations of Muslims and that they should not be regarded as a sect. Saudi Arabian Salafis do not like to be called Wahhabis, although this name was acceptable in the past. The word *Salaf* means predecessors (or ancestors) and refers to the Companions of the Prophet Muhammad (the Sahaba), the early Muslims who followed them, and the scholars of the first three generations of Muslims. They are also called *Al-Salaf Al-Salih* or "the Righteous Predecessors". The argument put forward by the Salafists is frequently the same. They claim to embody the *firqat an najra* – the saved sect – that follows the way of the Prophet and will be saved, in contrast to the other 72 "deviant sects" of Islam. A common factor in this proselytising seems to be the speed with which a conversion to Islam occurs. This is also true for new members who are adopted by the group. Compared with Catholic or Jewish proselytising, this speed is striking. Salafist proselytising in France is concentrated in certain locations. For example, according to a report by the *Renseignements Generaux*,[2] radical proselytising through the use of printed matter or cassettes, as well as through direct contact with the faithful, has been taking place in a particular mosque in Stains in Seine Saint Denis.

From the mid-1990s until today, French Muslims who have been involved in terrorist attacks in France have been mainly from immigrant communities, predominantly Algerian. They have generally had a low level of education and have often been Islamicised in jail. At least 70 per cent of those involved in Islamist terrorist acts in France since the mid-1990s have been unemployed. The remainder had manual jobs such as gardeners, security personnel, delivery men or temporary workers. Fewer than five individuals involved had reached graduate level in their education.

Some examples are:

P., born in September 1972, 69 months of unemployment between 1991 and 2002, vocational training certificate in metallurgy, delivery man.

K., born in July 1967, 12 months unemployment between February 2000 and February 2001, self-taught electrician in the meantime. Attempted a conversion course in IT maintenance under a public re-training programme.

K., born in October 1975, watchman, certificate in metallurgy, worked in retailing, a few months' experience in telesurveillance.

C., born in August 1975, qualified in electrical engineering, completed training for job seekers in electronic maintenance.

B., born in March 1967, construction electrician, four months unemployment since May 1999.

The profiles summarised above show obvious similarities to that of Jose Padilla – aka Abdullah al-Mujahir, who was arrested during the summer of 2002 in the United States, on suspicion of intending to build a radiological bomb. Despite these allegations, his reported attempts reveal a weak, indeed ridiculous, level of technical ability. This is not surprising given his background. Padilla, aged 31, had always found it difficult to earn a living. He spent a number of years in a Chicago gang (the Latin Disciples), then in a prison for young offenders, as well as in a fast-food establishment, before trying to begin a new life as a Muslim in the Middle East. His journey was financed by "friends" who took an interest in his education and in his being instructed in the Arabic language. It appears, therefore, that the authorities, and in particular the Director of the FBI, greatly exaggerated the threat Padilla posed, for reasons of internal politics.

Padilla's experiences strikingly resemble the profiles of the young jihadists arrested in France. Like Padilla, the "French" jihadists had no higher qualifications, suffered from long periods of unemployment and displayed various forms of delinquency. They also experienced a sudden conversion to a very conservative form of Islam – some of them during a short prison term – and they then fell rapidly into the hands of an activist or violent network. Moreover, like Padilla they were willing to consider the land they were living in as "Dar ul Harb" (land of war).

As for those who convert to Islam, the basic religious instruction given to new converts does not necessarily allow them to distinguish between the sectarian divisions of Islam. Even worse, as a result of long periods of social alienation and existential confusion, these individuals are in some cases motivated exclusively by a ready-made Islam that is reduced to some basic practices related to clothing, food or prayers, rather than a calm and thorough study of the faith, which is in any case hardly practicable in a prison environment. "Islam plays a dual role", says Robert Dannin, author of *Black Pilgrimage to Islam*. "It gives prisoners a total and complete way to restructure their lives down to the way they eat, the way they dress, the way they break up the day, the way they study and think." Mr Dannin, who teaches at New York University, also says that Islam's self-imposed discipline gives prison authorities a "convenient force" to help them control the prisoners.[3] Over the last 30 years Islam has become a powerful force in the American penal system. In the State of New York alone it is estimated that between 17 and 20 per cent of prisoners are Muslims. According to the experts this figure is reflected across the entire American prison system.[4]

As a consequence, the sociological recruiting base of jihadists around the world does not consist only of the middle classes of Saudi Arabia, Egypt or Yemen, as was the case in the attacks of 11 September. The danger in France and the United States – and indeed more widely in Europe and North America – is also posed by individuals who are to a greater or lesser extent unsocialised. These unsocialised or socially frustrated people of the developed world are not the same as those attracted to jihad in the Arab-Muslim world. The prevalence of well-qualified and socially well-integrated individuals among the terrorists who struck the World Trade Center is a clear indication of this. It is also proof of the sociological divisions that exist within the Islamic world. These educated contemporary Islamists often find themselves caught between two contradictory worlds: between the world of modern knowledge (learned in Western universities, or in overcrowded Arab ones that give few perspectives of social mobility) and that of Islamic culture. As the French orientalist Bruno Etienne has observed, "Ph.D. plus beards equals dynamic and qualified young men".[5] For the time being, those individuals in France that are attracted to jihad do not, for the most part, have the necessary cultural level to be able to conceive and carry out complex terrorist operations. In other words, if Atta was an "officer" by reason of his abilities, France is only producing "soldiers". This does not mean, however, that high-level French Islamic militants are not planning any attacks. They simply have not been detected up to now.

Khaled Kelkal – a profile of a homegrown French jihadist

An example of a profile of a young, homegrown jihadist in France is the case of Khaled Kelkal. Born in 1971 in Mostaganem, Algeria, Khaled Kelhal came with his family to live in Vaulx-en-Velin, a suburb of Lyon. He had four sisters and three brothers. He gradually slipped into delinquency and, in 1990, he was sentenced to four months with probation for trafficking in stolen cars. A few months later he was arrested for thefts using cars as battering rams to enter private properties. He was sentenced to four years of prison.

Serving his time, he met another prisoner called "Khelif", an Islamist who had flown from France to evade prison. Returning to France in 1989 he had been sentenced to seven years in prison. While in jail, Khelif tried to recruit Algerians for radical organisations in Algeria. After his release, Kelkal regularly attended a Salafist or radical Mosque in Vaulx-en-Velin; which was headed by the radical imam Mohamed Minta, a sympathiser of the *Foi et Pratique* ("Faith and practice") fundamentalist/Tabligh organisation. In 1993, Kelkal went to Mostaganem, in Algeria, to visit his family. There, he was probably recruited by one of the radical branches of the GIA, headed by Djamel Zitouni, whose aim was to "punish France".

On 11 July 1995, he was involved in the murder of Imam Sahraoui, in his mosque in Paris. Sahraoui was considered too moderate by the GIA. Four days later, in Bron, a suburb of Lyon, Kelkal opened fire on gendarmes at a checkpoint and evaded arrest. On 26 August 1995, during the jihadist bombing campaign in France, a gas bottle equipped with a detonation system was found near the Paris–Lyon TGV railway, near Cailloux-Sur-Fontaines (Rhône). The device had not exploded, and was found to be similar to the one which had been set off on 25 July in the Saint-Michel RER station. Fingerprints of Khaled Kelkal were found on the bomb, and an intensive search immediately started, with 170,000 photographs displayed in all public places in France.

On 29 September 1995, after several days of a manhunt in the forest of Malval, in hills near Lyon, Khaled Kelkal was found in a place called "*La Maison Blanche*" (literally translated as "White House", but probably a reference to the 6 October bomb that exploded in the Paris Métro). He attempted to resist arrest and was shot dead by the gendarmes of EPIGN (a special counter-terrorist force).

Radicalisation in jail

Jails in France are a place for proselytising. This phenomenon is well known, at least since the beginning of the 1970s with the Tabligh. On 1 June 2005, there were 59,786 prisoners in the French prisons, occupying 51,312 places; prison overpopulation reached alarming levels (4–5 people living in 9 m^2). Some of these establishments posted a density higher than 200 per cent (200 prisoners for 100 places). Condemned terrorists are now more and more isolated in jail to prevent them from recruiting.

A procedure of invitation to tender is in hand to equip 15 penal establishments with a system of integral jamming of portable telephones. The prison authorities recalled that "*30 prisons, among the most sensitive, were using equipment for jamming in certain sectors of detention*" from May 2003, the date of the advertisement of this measurement by the Chancellery following two escapes in Fresnes (the Valley-of-Marne) and Borgo (High-Corsican).

The office of the French Council of Muslim worship (CFCM) chose Monday 2 May 2005 to propose, with the ministry justice, Moulay El-Hassan El-Alaoui Talibi for the post of Muslim general chaplain of the prisons. He would be the first to occupy this function.

On suicide bombings and attempts

The question of suicide attack attempts in France poses a priori a certain number of difficulties which will be analysed with care in the preamble before going further. There are various doctrinal and operational origins. Initially, the minimal definition of a suicide bombing appears simple – an attack perpetrated by an individual whose death results from this same attack. This begs several questions: was the death of the individual planned a priori or was it an unforeseen consequence of the attack itself, for example at the time of detonation was there an unexpected explosion of the improvised explosive device? The know-how deployed to perpetrate a suicide attack can also be variable: for instance a certain amateurism in the operational preparation, the housing of the explosive device or the modus operandi. Another question, was the preparation of the attack the occasion of a formal training procedure or of a psychological control exerted upon the operational militant?

It appears that many attack attempts in Europe, and in particular those in France towards their citizens, proceeded from a very pragmatic process, having little cultural formalisation and which did not show in any of the cases any of the real pressures, gratifications and symbolic systems exerted by Hamas or Hezbollah on their militants. The reasons which can be cited and which will be the subject of an examination starting with examples open to analysis are: the size of terrorist cells which would not enable the exertion of pressure comparable with political organisations like Hezbollah or Hamas, nor the process towards glorification on a scale that exists in the Shiite quarters of Beirut or in Palestine; and the diasporas and cultural origins of the militants concerned, such as Maghrebi Islam, which is different on many points from Shiism or other denominations of Sunnism.

The majority of the detected and dismantled groups expressed at least an intention to make a suicide attack. French counter-terrorist services have been able to detect them and dismantle them successfully before they act. In reality it appears that the chances of success of a suicide attack led by one or more French citizens are far greater outside the country than on their own soil. From the moment terrorists or candidates for martyrdom manage to enter Iraq without being detected, they are highly likely to be able to "die", either by being killed in combat (for example, in Fallujah in 2004), or, the ultimate goal, in a suicide attack. The suicide attack is thus a very uncertain process: there are few candidates and even fewer who are successful.

The French anti-terrorist organisation

The French government's nationwide security plan (Vigipirate), which uses military forces to reinforce police security in Paris and other major cities, remains in effect. This plan increases security at metro and train stations, enhances border controls and expands identity checks countrywide. And very recently, our government has decided to recruit 200 new policemen devoted solely to the monitoring of jihadists in France.

The structures of the French anti-terrorism system are complex and are more the result of historical, legal and constitutional processes, than of an immediate consideration of the present threat. The cornerstone is the 9 September Act of 1986, providing for the prosecution of all terrorist acts. Under this Act, terrorism is defined as an infraction committed by an individual, or a group of individuals, aimed at seriously disrupting public order through intimidation or terror.

The political level

Under the Prime Minister's direction, a political office called the "interior security Council" analyses terrorist threats and the means of addressing them. At a lower level, an interministerial liaison committee against terrorism (CILAT) under the direction of the Ministry of the Interior is charged with coordinating the different administrations (Interior, Defence, Justice, Foreign affairs) for adopting proactive, short-term, anti-terrorist measures. It was created in 1982 after an anti-Semitic terrorist act in Paris.

The administrative level

The operational coordination of the anti-terrorism fight is not new. During the Algerian war in the 1950s, a North African liaison office was created. Later, a bureau of liaison composed of members of the judiciary police, the general intelligence service and the counter-intelligence service organised daily meetings for combating French nationals acting violently in Algeria and in France. A standing coordinating committee was created in June 1976, which became the anti-terrorist liaison bureau in 1982 and the current Anti-terrorist Coordination Unit (UCLAT) in October 1984. Under the direction of the national police chief, the UCLAT facilitates intelligence data diffusions among those concerned in France and in friendly allied countries: it welcomes to France delegations or correspondents of foreign intelligence services devoted to anti-terrorism and has, by bilateral agreements, numerous officers deployed around the world (Germany, Italy, United Kingdom, Spain, etc.). The UCLAT is responsible for implementing the "Vigipirate" plan.

Locally, anti-terrorist coordination can be given to a specialised high official, as in Corsica since the beginning of the 1980s. An office for the fight against organised criminality, terrorism and money laundering exists in the Justice ministry. It can generate preparatory documents in these areas before a law is formulated by the government and the legislative powers. In October 2001, the Ministry of Economy and Finance created a small cell specialised against terrorism financing (FINTER) under the control of the treasury director. Solely concerning the analysis of terrorist threats, let's take a look at two interministerial departments under the Prime Minister: the SGDN (National Defence General Secretariat) and the CIR (Inter-ministerial committee for intelligence).

The operational level

Intelligence

The Direction centrale du renseignement intérieur (Central Directorate of Interior Intelligence, DCRI) is a brand new French Intelligence agency which reports directly to the Ministry of the Interior. It became officially operational on 1 July 2008, through the merging of the Direction centrale des renseignements généraux and the Direction de la surveillance du territoire of the French National Police.[6]

The DCRI is headed by Bernard Squarcini. It is organised into a headquarters and eight departments:

- Economic protection
- Terrorism
- Intelligence technologies
- Violent subversion
- General administration
- Support
- Counter-espionage
- International affairs.

The functions of the DCRI are:

- counter-espionage
- counter-terrorism
- countering cybercrime
- surveillance of potentially threatening groups, organisations and social phenomena, like far-leftist groups.

In that sense, this new organisation is doing what the former services were doing.

The Territorial Surveillance Directorate (DST) and the Central Directorate of General Information (DCRG) were in charge of anti-terrorist intelligence for the Ministry of the Interior. The DST monitored international terrorism occurring in France or against French interests. Its activities were highly classified (1,500 individuals). DST had a counter-terrorist role. Acting as a surgery, this service led the way in dismantling operational or logistical cells.

The DCRG handled national terrorism or internal terrorism. Around 300 members of operational and search sections were acting within the entire territory. This division of labour was not very old (the mid-1980's?) and there was sometimes a redundancy between these two services. Religious or politically violent organisations were sometimes monitored by both of them, particularly the radical Islamist networks. In reality, the division of labour was made geographically (internal–external) and thematically. The DCRG dealt with external terrorist threats linked to separatism (Basque ETA) or far-rightists or leftists. This service was mainly devoted to threat assessment, but could often contribute to the active counter-terrorism phase. The DCRI is an attempt to solve these redundancies and loopholes. The General Directorate for External Security (DGSE) is in charge of intelligence data collection and special operations outside of France; including for counter-terrorism.

Repression

The repression of terrorist acts is the responsibility of the judiciary police (with central direction) and has a national anti-terrorist department (DNAT) created in 1998, mainly focusing on regional forms of terrorism. As France is a very centralised country, the DNAT can rely on regional (SRPJ) and local police structures – for example, the Paris criminal brigade, or the search and intervention brigades – for monitoring terrorist cells. The judiciary police Directorate and the counter-terrorism intelligence service closely cooperate with a special Ministry of Justice Branch with special anti-terrorist judges.

Active counter-terrorism

To arrest an alleged terrorist requires special and well-trained forces. The arrests are usually conducted by the normal anti-terrorism services. When a tough intervention is required, special Ops and Counter-terrorist units are deployed: the GIGN (groupe d'intervention de la gendarmerie nationale), which liberated a French Airbus hijacked in 1994, or the RAID, which not only handles intervention but has monitoring and tailing capacities as well.

The ad hoc *legal framework*

The French specific penal law against terrorism is probably our best weapon. Between 1986 and 1994, step by step, we have created a special legal branch which defines terrorism, oversees the financial welfare of the victims, authorises detention pending trial and carries out a night search. By Western democratic standards, this is probably very tough.

These measures may be linked with other legal means:

- The centralisation of legal pursuits by special anti-terrorist judges. They are formed, motivated and very protected. There is a very useful and fast connection between the judiciary and the police. Specialised courts can prevent juries from being threatened and intimidated by terrorist groups to influence their decision-making abilities.
- Special and legally motivated identity checks.
- The postponement of the intervention of a lawyer until after 72 hours of police custody.
- The night search between 9 pm to 6 am under restrictive conditions defined by the constitutional court.
- Special police custody (four days for terrorist acts versus two days for normal criminality).
- Special sentence reductions for repentant terrorists.

The French National Assembly voted in November 2005 to back the Minister of the Interior Nicolas Sarkozy's new anti-terror bill. The law increases the state's powers of electronic surveillance of its citizens through the use of closed-circuit cameras in public places (like in the UK), the recording and monitoring of Internet activity, and the retention of data that must be made available to the state. The law was passed by 373 votes in favour (by the ruling Union for a Popular Movement and the centre-right Union for French Democracy). The Socialist Party abstained. The 27 votes cast against the bill were those of the Communist Party, three Greens and just three Socialist Party representatives.

The reluctance of the official left to mount any opposition to the government's declaration of a state of emergency during the nationwide youth riots that sparked off on 27 October 2005 has perhaps emboldened the conservative government to toughen its security approach. Riot police were permanently stationed in targeted neighbourhoods, curfews were in operation and the state of emergency, lifting all judicial control over police actions, decreed for 12 days, with the approval of the Socialist Party, was extended for three months with only token opposition from the SP. In one particularly significant incident in relation to Sarkozy's bill, the right of assembly was suspended for 22 hours in Paris on 9 November. The police justified this measure by citing that Internet monitoring had revealed plans for a riot.

On 19 January 2006, the French constitutional Court[7] assessed that the new national anti-terrorism law, submitted by the French Senators, was not anti-constitutional. The Senators were particularly worried about some provisions. The first one was allowing the police to obtain communication data without any judicial order, for preventing and punishing acts of terrorism (article 6). The constitutional council only found it necessary to remove the word "punish" from the article, otherwise considering it in compliance with the Constitution and its human right's preamble, stating that prevention is the role of police forces, and finding that enough safeguards were already provided by the brand new law.

The second one was allowing the police to monitor cars on French roads and highways, taking pictures of licence plates and people in the cars, with various purposes ranging from the fight against terrorism to the identification of stolen cars (article 8). The same article also provides for the monitoring of people in street gatherings during "big events". Again, the constitutional council has not found any constitutional problem with this provision.

This new French anti-terrorism law also provides, in article 7, that the Ministry of the Interior may process passenger name record data collected on any travel by air, sea or rail to or from non-EU countries. The constitutionality of this provision has not been challenged. This article has the claimed objective "to improve border controls and to fight against illegal immigration". With this anti-terror law, and under the guise of the fight against terrorism, France is then directly targeting immigrants and even foreigner residents, especially those from North Africa, since they regularly travel by sea to spend holidays at home. France is now the first EU country to follow the example of the US unilateral decision imposing the transfer of PNR data to US customs and border control authorities.[8]

The main articles of the bill are:

- Internet and telephone providers must give to "specially empowered officers from the national police and gendarmery, information" they kept and processed. The providers will be required to conserve technical data such as phone numbers contacted by the user and localisation of "terminal

equipment". The state information gatherers can largely avoid judicial control: "The present obligation to act in accordance within a determined judicial procedure is too restrictive." Officials designated by the UCLAT will guarantee the purpose to which this surveillance is put. The document assures the public that the content of messages will not be monitored.
- Cars and their passengers can be electronically monitored and filmed, and restrictions on identity checking on transnational trains are to be reduced. Air and transportation companies and travel agents will be required to give the details of travellers.
- The crime of "association with miscreants", or conspiracy, whose terms are very vague in order to be very "flexible", will carry increased penalties: someone found guilty of being an associate will have his or her prison sentence potentially doubled to 20 years in jail, while "leaders and organisers of the association" (i.e. the facilitator) will have their sentences extended to 30 years from 20 years.
- Prisoners can be held without trial for six, rather than four, days. The bill establishes that all cases be assigned to "specialised judges with national powers", meaning the Section Fourteen in Paris.
- The *préfets* (acting under the orders of the Minister of the Interior) will be enabled "to make obligatory the installation of cameras in suitable places so as to improve the detection of operations preparing terrorist acts". A refusal to install the required camera is punishable by a €150,000 fine. A vast programme of provision of the most advanced equipment is envisaged.
- Another significant measure of the bill is the lengthening from 10 to 15 years of the period for which a naturalised French person can be stripped of his or her nationality (with the concept of acts incompatible with the quality of being a French person – *actes incompatibles avec la qualité de Français* – and prejudicial to the interests of France).

A successful cooperation: French–Spanish work against ETA

Almost every week, militants – often operational, sometimes high-ranking – are arrested, either by the Spanish or by the French police. Serious plots are also regularly prevented: some recent sources have indicated that ETA may have plotted to blow up (presumably with a MANPAD – man-portable air-defence system) a helicopter or airplane carrying the Spanish King. Details of the plot were outlined in several CDs which allegedly belonged to ETA and were discovered in 2004 by French anti-terrorism services. The main reason for this success story can be found in the very intense bilateral cooperation between these two countries. This cooperation is not new – Basque terrorism has been a "French–Spanish" issue for many years – but in recent years it has improved. It mixes legal and judiciary means, information sharing and shared field activities (HUMINT, SIGINT and police activities). These cross-border police actions and judicial initiatives against terrorism and financing have paved the way for a broader pan-European response to a phenomenon that has no respect for boundaries. This is true for ETA. It is also true for "global jihad", violence which Spain no longer considers "secondary" after the Madrid attacks in March 2004.

It is striking to observe that many arrests in the two countries occur almost simultaneously. That is certainly indicative of a joint dismantling operation. By operating together to arrest suspects, the two countries' police systems can prevent potential escape. Time matters. This wave of arrests is common in the French–Spanish counter-terrorism history. This can be explained, first, by common understandings of the problem and, second, by a concrete European solidarity. This solidarity was not substantial under the Franco regime, when French authorities were not eager to cooperate with an authoritarian regime.

The two countries have the same Maghrebian diasporas and consequently, very often, the same sort of radical networks to monitor. Threats are similar: Droukdel, the General Emir of the Al-Qaeda organisation in the Islamic Maghreb (AQIM), threatened the two countries in an audio message broadcast on jihadist Internet forums, in September 2008. In October 2007, French and Spanish police (with Belgian help) dismantled a network on suspicion of recruiting Muslims for jihad in Iraq.

"Presumed ETA members" (according to the French official terminology) are often arrested, sometimes very far away from Basque territory, in the French "mainland" territory. One of the most recent eon 25 February 2009, while he was trying to escape police control by carjacking. He had been freed after five years in jail in Spain for being involved in ETA activities. This arrest occurred the same week that another shut down took place in Spain: two suspected members of ETA were arrested. They may have been involved in a December fatal shooting in the town of Azpeitia, near the coastal city of San Sebastian. The victim was the head of a company involved in the construction of a high-speed rail network in the region – a project opposed by ETA. One of the two people arrested seems linked to a suspected ETA member, Manex Castro, who was arrested earlier in the Basque Country just hours before polls opened in regional elections. Castro may have prepared an "imminent" bomb attack.

In April 2009, the French and Spanish services also arrested Ekaitz Sirvent Auzmendi, the "head of the forgery unit of ETA", as he got off a train in Paris. The arrest, as its frequently the case, followed a joint effort by authorities in Spain and France to find Auzmendi. Although French officers of the Sous-Direction Anti-Terroriste (SDAT) (specialised in Basque issues) made the arrest, it came about as a result of cooperation and Spanish officers were present at the arrest.

It has sometimes been claimed, and rightly, that this multi-level daily cooperation is the avant-garde example of a successful and well-integrated intra-European division of labour against homegrown terrorism. It has been gradually shaped on political and field levels, beginning long before 11 September. Some real value-added tools in the bilateral arsenal are:

- The enhancing of special counter-terrorism legislation (in Spain, for instance, detainees suspected of membership in a terrorist group may be

held in incommunicado detention for up to 13 days and may be held in pre-trial detention for up to four years. During incommunicado detention, detainees are held in isolation and do not have the right to a lawyer of their own choosing).
- The possibility of temporary handover of individuals arrested in France to Madrid authorities for interrogation, before being tried in France. Historically, the extradition process was the first resort. Now, the European arrest warrant is the general framework.
- Special police attachés (for instance, nine French liaison officers are currently at the French Embassy in Madrid).
- Liaison magistrates and prosecution teams (the process was formalised and broadened by a Joint Action of the European Union of 22 April 1996). The activities undertaken by liaison magistrates fall into four broad categories:
  1. mutual assistance in the sphere of international criminal law;
  2. mutual assistance in the sphere of civil law;
  3. comparative law;
  4. the forging of links between judicial authorities.
- Mixed patrols on both sides of the Pyrénées. The two countries have both police and gendarmerie nationale/guardia civil – these two types of organisation can easily cooperate in the field.
- Joint inquiry and interview teams (ten groups in 2007 were working on Basque terrorism, organised crime and jihadism) for conducting cross-border stings. Spain and France aim to promote the work of the Frontex agency to reinforce the monitoring of border security of European Union members.
- Immediate release to the state-partner of every intercepted document (since 2003) during a counter-terrorism operation (laptops, propaganda, agendas), etc.
- At the judiciary level, since 2005, the most sensitive information is shared by means of an "early warning system" that involves the French special antiterrorism court (*pôle anti-terroriste du tribunal de grande instance de Paris*) and the *audienca nacional de Espana*.

Conclusion: threat assessment

A terrorist act in France or against French interests around the world could be perpetrated by many actors:

- As usual, but on a low scale, by Basque or Corsican separatist movements.
- Much more seriously, Al-Qaeda in Islamic Maghreb (ex-GSPC). GSPC/Al-Qaeda in Islamic Maghreb now claims to be an umbrella organisation on both sides of the Mediterranean Sea, providing resources and, possibly, an identity to smaller groups, a better pool of expertise, shared know-how, "economies of scale", and an increased sense of support. The label "Al-Qaeda" itself can also potentially induce an increased "public" awareness.

The GSPC has progressively and openly adopted broader goals, from "regionalisation" to solidarity and cooperation with trans-national jihadi networks.[9]
- A Moroccan operational cell (either a non-aligned cell, or one connected to the GICM or to *Salafiya jihadya*). The United States Department of State "Patterns of Global Terror" report states that GICM[10] emerged in the late 1990s, but its founding is believed to date back to the early 1990s, when it was formed by veteran mujahiddin returning from Afghanistan. Morocco first experienced Islamic radicalism in 1969 with the birth of the *Shabiba Islamiya*. This organisation split into two organisations, and one of the groups that emerged came to be known as the Moroccan Combatant Group (GICM). They are believed to operate in the UK, Denmark, Belgium, Egypt, Turkey, Morocco, Spain and France, and, like Algerian groups, to deal in the trafficking of falsified documents and arms smuggling – the cultural practice of *Trabendo*.
- A multicultural operational cell (French-Moroccan-Algerian-African-Converts).
- A non-aligned cell, for instance with non-cultural Muslims, global jihad potentially attracting a broader opposition to Western values and societies.
- The French Army in Afghanistan, a Muslim land, is seen as provocative by local jihadists or by members of the Taliban. Some French radicals are allegedly reputed to be in Pakistan and in Afghanistan.
- Chemical-Biological-Radiological-Nuclear (CBRN): Several attempted CBRN attacks involving substances were foiled recently, in particular in France, but also in the UK, Italy and Spain. The homemade manufacture of ricin learned in Afghanistan, for example, consists of extracting ricin from crushed ricin grains.[11] The method employed requires the use of ricin as a contact agent with the addition of another common agent for percutaneous absorption. The effectiveness does not seem to be guaranteed. In France, the investigation into the "Chechen connection"[12] led to the dismantling of the La Courneuve and Romainville[13] groups. On 16 December 2002, a number of individuals were questioned at La Courneuve. Various electronic components, two 13-kg gas bottles and an NBC protection suit (technical details unknown) were discovered. Some of the suspects questioned claimed to have undergone military training in Georgia between June and September 2001, including with the suspects involved in the ricin affair in Great Britain. On 24 December 2002, the urgent questioning of individuals took place in Romainville. The police found a physics and chemical catalogue, freely available on sale, small items of laboratory equipment, and a list of chemical products for making explosives, including one which generates cyanhydric acid when heated. The preparation of an attack against the Russian Embassy in France was apparently planned. French targets are also believed to have been designated by the group. The questioning of a young radical in Lyon, in January 2004, revealed that he had undergone training in Afghanistan in 2000 where he had learned to use explosives and the making of lethal chemical products by simple steps.

He had engaged in attempts at making chemical compounds in his room and wanted to produce ricin, and maybe botulinum toxin.[14]
- Massive hostage takings are a particular and emerging concern in France among SWAT teams and authorities.
- The far-leftist networks could be, more or less, for the moment in pre-operational phases, or radicalisation phases. Is this the harbinger of things to come? An alleged French activist is presently accused, with others, of sabotaging TGV's overhead lines in November 2008. He is being charged with "directing a terrorist group" by the Paris Prosecutor's office. He is also a founder of the radical, philosophical French journal *Tiqqun*.

Notes

1 See for instance: www.dartabligh.org/.
2 *Le Monde*, 25 January 2001.
3 "Gangs, Prison: Al Qaida Breeding Grounds?", *Christian Science Monitor*, 14 June 2002.
4 Ibid.
5 B. Etienne, *L'Islamisme Radical*, (Paris, Hachette, 1987): p. 202.
6 www.interieur.gouv.fr/sections/a_la_une/toute_l_actualite/securite-interieure/creation-dcri.
7 www.conseil-constitutionnel.fr/decision/2006/2005532/index.htm.
8 www.edri.org/book/print/800.
9 J.L. Marret, "AQMI: A 'glocal' organization", *Studies in Conflict and Terrorism*, Vol. 31, No. 6, 2008, 541–552.
10 www.cdi.org/program/document.cfm?DocumentID=2227&from_page=../index.cfm.
11 www.humanite.presse.fr/journal/2004–01–12/2004–01–12-385985.
12 http://tf1.lci.fr/infos/france/0,,3291198,00.html.
13 http://fr.news.yahoo.com/photos/060320075715.j50zmkjr-photo-vue-prise-en-decembre-2002-romainville-de-l-imme.html.
14 *Le Monde*, 10 January 2004.

9 Radicalisation and recruitment among jihadist terrorists in Spain
Main patterns and subsequent counter-terrorist measures

Rogelio Alonso

Introduction

On 11 March 2004 Spain suffered its worst terrorist attack ever. On that day Islamist fundamentalists killed 192 people and injured hundreds more after ten bombs went off in four different trains full of commuters during the morning rush hour. These terrorist attacks and the collective suicide of seven of those responsible for them weeks later, on 3 April 2004, when Spanish police surrounded the flat where some of the men involved in the 11 March attack (11 M) were hiding, exposed the prominence that the jihadist movement had reached in the country. Spain, which as far back as 2001 had been described by judicial authorities as the "main base of Al-Qaeda in Europe"[1] as a result of the activities of Islamist radicals during the previous decade, had also become a target of violence. The evolution of jihadism demonstrated the extent to which the country had turned into a hub for the recruitment and radicalisation of individuals prepared to commit terrorist attacks in Spain and further away. Over the last ten years almost 200 people have been accused by the Spanish judiciary of being involved in terrorist activities related to Islamic fundamentalism. This chapter will analyse the main patterns in the process of radicalisation and recruitment evident in the networks of jihadist terrorists that have emerged in the country so far. Relying on research based on interviews with significant informants, including members of the security forces and intelligence services, as well as open secondary sources and judicial reports, the author will examine the process of radicalisation and recruitment of the main cells dismantled in Spain. After exploring dominant factors and currents in the process of mobilisation of individuals who over the last decade have joined groups involved in spreading and defending the jihad, an assessment of counter-measures against this particular dimension of the terrorist phenomenon will also be provided.

Indoctrinating and proselytising: neosalafism and the subculture of death

As in the case of other terrorist expressions, those who are sympathetic to religious extremism and terrorism in the name of Islam represent a small but a significant minority disaffected with the country in which they live. The analysis of the information available so far allows for some general conclusions about the socio-demographic profile of these individuals and their processes of radicalisation. To this extent, data relating to 188 persons who were imprisoned in Spain between 2001 and 2005, under suspicion of involvement in jihadist terrorism, showed that most of those engaged in these activities were men born between 1966 and 1975, aged from 26 to 40 at the time of their arrest, and mostly in possession of legal immigration documentation. This particular sample revealed that seven out of ten prison inmates originated from the Maghreb, 69 of them being born in Morocco and 67 in Algeria. Individuals of Syrian and Pakistani origin constituted a minority within a sample in which only eight individuals were Spanish nationals.[2] As can be inferred from this analysis, the limited access to certain sources prevents a more systematic appraisal of a wider sample of individuals, a shortfall which is also evident when attempting to examine the factors leading to the radicalisation of jihadist terrorists in the country. Nonetheless, the assessment of a wide range of sources provides quite a clear picture of the evolution of jihadism in Spain indicating that the process of radicalisation and recruitment generally follows some discernible patterns that will be explained below.

First of all it should be pointed out that irrespective of the origin of the radicals a common denominator emerges. A neosalafist ideology advocated by Islamist extremists constitutes an ever-present pattern that homogenises the diversity of profiles that can be appreciated when analysing their process of radicalisation. Neosalifism is understood in this chapter as a radical interpretation of Salafism which advocates a global jihad as well as the unification of the Muslim world and the setting up of a new caliphate. This radical ideology appears as a key variable that has allowed different individuals to become submerged into the subculture of violence required to pursue terrorist actions. The consolidation of this subculture of death has very often occurred under great influence from individual manipulation carried out by Islamist extremists. Spiritual leaders or other relevant figures have exerted decisive influence on individuals who at certain points have decided to participate in extremist activities espousing a violent ideology like the one referred to.

Charismatic leaders, mosques and private locations

Those leaders usually identified places and clusters for the socialisation of potential recruits which enabled the radical doctrine to spread. Some of the mostly young and male recruits were targeted by extremists but others were recruited through personal contact, often by chance. Ideological indoctrination preceded active involvement in terrorist activities, the influence of peers constituting a very relevant factor in their process of radicalisation as it seems to be in other terrorist cases too. Very often potential recruits were exposed to videos, books, songs, speeches and other sources available through the Internet that justified the use of violence and the jihad; places such as mosques, prisons, Islamic institutions as well as other social and sports meetings becoming propitious for these type of activities which provided an environment for some to gravitate to terrorism. It was through the engagement in this gradual and regular process that the commitment to the cause deepened also leading to involvement in training and fundraising, both inside and abroad, strengthening solidarity bonds among those being radicalised.

These patterns can be clearly appreciated when analysing numerous episodes of radicalised individuals and also in relation to those responsible for perpetrating the terrorist attacks on 11 March 2004 in Madrid. The availability of more information on this particular episode, in which a high number of individuals participated, allows for a more elaborated discussion of an example that reveals representative patterns that are also evident in other cases. The terrorist cell responsible for the 11 M attacks did engage in similar processes of radicalisation and recruitment as other extremists. Certain individuals were in charge of planning the recruitment of newcomers who were attracted into their clusters following a structured and organised procedure, as can be inferred from the explanation provided by one of those who was acquainted with some of the terrorists involved in the 11 M atrocity.[3] In his statement to Judge Juan del Olmo, the magistrate responsible for the investigation, this informant admitted to meeting different members of the group involved in perpetrating the terrorist attacks in Madrid. He recalled encountering on various occasions key radical Islamists such as Sarhane Ben Adbelmajid Fakhet, nicknamed "the Tunisian", Moutaz Almallah Dabas, Hicham Tensamani – imam of the town of Portillo in Toledo – and Mustapha Maymouni. These figures considered themselves to be members of a group which they would refer to as "the brothers of the martyrs". Membership of this group would entail regular meetings in order to discuss issues related to Islam as well as the reasons behind the death of "Muslim brothers" in areas such as Afghanistan, Palestine, Chechnya and Iraq. The religious advice of imam Hicham Tensamani was often sought by members of the group, particularly by Sarhane "the Tunisian", in order to strengthen the link between the grievances of Muslims that featured so prominently in the indoctrination process and the response with which they should be met. The staged process of recruitment and radicalisation meant that terrorist actions were not discussed at every single meeting. In fact, attendants of these meetings understood that those issues would be later discussed in smaller groups once the leaders of the group had identified, through various conversations, those individuals who would be open to more radical stances and once a certain degree of trust had developed among themselves. Videos were also watched at the meetings arranged by the group with the intention of reinforcing the view of a victimised Muslim community, as it was the case with the film recorded at a training camp in Afghanistan which showed youngsters of different nationalities who had travelled to that country to find their death. By resorting to these means, the group developed ideological solidarity bonds with other Muslims who were losing their lives in areas such as Afghanistan and Chechnya, to the extend that they would insist on calling themselves the "brothers of the martyrs".[4] Such an association with "martyrs" who were regarded as "the vanguard of the Muslim nation" enhanced the attractiveness of the offer to approach and join the group.

An example provided by the wife of Mouhannad Almallah Dabbas, one of the individuals charged with taking part in perpetrating the terrorist attacks in Madrid, illustrates how the recruitment and radicalisation process developed. In her testimony to the judge she recalls how different men were brought home by her husband in what seems to be an attempt to lure them into the group. These visitors would watch videos and would listen to religious songs extolling the jihad. One of these songs was used as background music in a video that portrayed military training at a training camp in Afghanistan. This type of music would constantly be played by Mouhannad at home and while driving around, being also used for recruitment and indoctrination purposes, and it would suggest the fact that numerous copies of tapes containing that kind of songs were frequently made. Mouhannad's brother-in-law was one of the individuals brought to the house with the intention of being attracted into the group. He was shown a video in which "infidels" forced a Muslim family to commit obscene acts. The video also contained pictures of a "Chechen martyr" who was led to burial, as well as photographs of Osama bin Laden and Ayman Al-Zawahiri.[5]

Books about bin Laden were also used in the process of radicalisation and indoctrination, the Al-Qaeda leader, commonly referred by them as "the emir",[6] not being the only figure that was seen as iconic for the group of radicals. Abu Qatada, the London-based religious leader of Palestinian origin who was later arrested under suspicion of being involved in terrorism, was a close friend of the Almallah brothers. Abu Qatada was regarded by the two brothers as the Al-Qaeda ambassador in Europe. Amer Azizi was also seen as a "hero" by members of the group because of his courageous escape from Spain when the police were about to arrest him and his decision to "combat" in Afghanistan.[7] Another religious leader, imam Hicham Tensamani, was also seen as an influential figure to whom several individuals were taken in order to listen to his views in the belief that this would encourage them to join the group.

Therefore, relevant figures like the ones alluded to provided role models for the newcomers, exerting very useful influence on them. These leaders organised the proselytising and indoctrination of potential candidates, some of whom would join the theme in their efforts to expand and defend Islam, around different locations. The assembly places that have been mentioned so far were not the only ones where the activists gathered together. The terrace located at the M 30 mosque, the main mosque in Madrid, was also frequented by key figures such as Sarhane "the Tunisian" and Mouhannad Almallah Dabbas and other individuals who would regularly get together in the afternoons, particularly since October 2003 when their daily meetings would last from 17.00 to 21.30.[8] Previous to these meetings, as far back as 2001, other encounters took place among radicals who would get together at various flats with the intention of recruiting and radicalising other individuals, mostly youngsters, some of whom would be contacted at different mosques. These centres provided the opportunity for exchanges of opinions about Islam, enabling the recruiters to approach individuals whose open views seemed to be amenable to more radical inputs. It should be remembered that radical speeches would also be pronounced at some mosques, as the judiciary report on the terrorist attacks perpetrated in Madrid demonstrates when referring to a talk held in 2002 that focused on the "jihad against the enemy in order to liberate not only the Palestinian territories but all Arab territories".[9] Thus some of the youngsters would be approached after prayers, being subsequently invited to watch videos containing speeches of religious leaders such as, for example, the Palestinian Abu Qatada or the Saudi Taham. Invitations to meetings would also follow these approaches.

According to a police informant who also took part in several of the meetings held by one of the groups involved in these activities, at some point of the recruitment and indoctrination process leaders identified numerous geographical contexts in which the jihad could be practised. Although Afghanistan or Chechnya remained countries of great significance and symbolism for those willing to practice jihad, violence was also acceptable and possible at other locations without requiring volunteers to travel away from their country of residence.[10] In fact, one of the radicals involved in the group explained as far back as 2002 that it was not necessary to travel to Afghanistan in order to engage in jihad since this could be done in Morocco and Spain.[11] Moreover, some of the radicals would constantly refer to Spaniards as Jews, depiction they would use in order to justify robberies and other crimes against Spanish citizens. In addition to this, violence against "incredulous governments" in places such as Algeria, Tunisia and Morocco, countries that were not led by "good Muslims", was also justified. The justification of such a violent course of action was also found in different fatwas recited by heart by the attendants to these meetings.[12] As a result of these mechanisms jihad was regarded as a duty of every Muslim as long as "infidels" remained in control of lands "invaded" and "taken from Muslims".

The experience in Spain so far suggests that the process of radicalisation is very often led by charismatic leaders. As regards the cells that took part in the 11 March attacks, Mustapha Maymouni and Sarhane Ben Addelmajid were seen with considerable respect, being regarded as authority figures. The statement provided by one of the police informers who regularly engaged with them is particularly revealing of the variables used in these radicalisation processes led by them. The former would frequently recite verses and songs extolling the jihad while the latter would follow him with very emotional and enthusiastic statements encouraging the practice of jihad. Such a violent course of action was justified by appealing to the example of women who in the time of the prophet had followed the jihad themselves, leading him to question the courage of the men who were listening to him should they not do the same as the women had done.

The information provided to the police and the judiciary by some of those involved with the group suggests that the process of radicalisation and recruitment was structured around two types of leadership, spiritual and organisational, which was exerted by Maymouni and "the Tunisian" respectively.[13] This dual leadership was also careful to guide the process of radicalisation and recruitment, as demonstrated by the warnings of Maymouni to one of the attendants at the group's reunions. Following one of these meetings, Mustapha Maymouni privately congratulated one of the men present at the gathering for his bright personal views expressed on issues related to the practice of jihad. He nonetheless warned him of the danger of "scaring" some of the members present at the gathering since the majority of them lacked a good religious preparation, therefore requiring a slow indoctrination process, particularly in relation to the duty of jihad. Having said that, Maymouni went on to offer him the personal contacts that could assist him in his preparation, religious and otherwise, in order properly to follow the jihad.[14]

The rationale behind the radicalisation process

Findings at the site of the suicide killings in Leganés, on April 2004, proved very revealing of the ideology espoused by the terrorists and the means used to strengthen their ideological and personal commitment to their violent cause.[15] After the explosion Spanish police managed to reconstruct files contained in a computer found at the bomb site which included texts criticising the Saudi Arabian government for not being part of "the community of believers", as well as all non-Islamic governments, which were described as "infidels". Other files contained several references to significant shuras from Qur'an which were interpreted as legitimisation of violence against "Allah's enemies", as well as a video which described the 19 terrorists who killed themselves on 11 September as "examples of mujahideen that should be followed" and "valuable young men who have changed History". The legitimisation framework required by all kinds of terrorists, irrespective of their ideology, was also evident in the rhetoric used by Islamic fundamentalists in Spain, as other police findings corroborated, among them a file found in a computer at the house in Leganés containing a text entitled: "Terrorism: its meaning and its situation from the Islamic point of view". The author of the text distinguished between "good" and "bad" terrorism. Whereas the former was to be directed against people that could cause "harm to humanity", the latter was seen as the violence inflicted by Israel towards Palestine, the United Nations embargo on Iraq, and the USA intervention in Afghanistan.

The computer material discovered by investigators exposed how a combination of factors commonly present in the motivational framework of others terrorist groups constituted very relevant variables of use for the radicalisation and recruitment process in this particular context. In fact the sources exposed a variety of considerations – ideological, utilitarian and emotional, as well as the reinforcement of social and group identities – that could explain the rationale behind the terrorists involvement in the group, also representing key elements in their radicalisation and recruitment process. By way of example, the analysis of the propaganda material used by Islamist radicals reveals a portrayal of terrorism as a useful and necessary means of achieving the objectives pursued by jihadists, not unlike other terrorist groups, also representing an honourable and prestigious response that would provide personal and collective gains for those who practised it, as the following sample illustrates.

Numerous imams' speeches were found, some of them praising the violence that had made possible the "moral defeat of the USSR in Afghanistan". Others complained about "the fall of the Islamic world as a result of Israel's occupation of Palestine", also denouncing Saudi Arabia for welcoming US troops, or the US attempts to "erode the Arab culture and identity", thus stating that "the only way out for a society that has lost everything is jihad". The moral justification of terrorism was strengthened by rhetorical questions such as: "Is it alright to kill a Palestinian but not an American?"; or Osama bin Laden's response advocating jihad: "Would it be fair to tell the lamb to stay still while the wolf is about to eat it?". The reinforcement of such a course of action was provided by pieces produced by Abu Qatada in which he fiercely extolled the jihad and criticised those who didn't follow it. Therefore, not only was terrorism rationalised as necessary and useful in tactical and strategical terms, but also as a reward, since "those who fall in the name of God and their nation, do not die, because they remain alive with God". The legitimacy of jihad was also reasserted through the advantageous comparison with a conflict spot such as Iraq, pictures of terrorist attacks against the US army in the country being a very common feature, as well as photographs and references to Aiman Al Zawhari, some of them taken from Al Jazzera. One of the computer files consisted of a summary of an Al Jazzera programme on the Al-Qaeda leader broadcast in January 2004 in which he provided ample justification for jihadism and attacks on "tyrant governments", "the crusaders against the Muslim world" and those who "have invaded the Muslim territory".[16] This material was complemented by frequent access to Internet chats associated to radicalism that contributed to encourage the use of violence in a way which was perfectly and carefully justified through the narratives summarised above. Documents containing instructions for the use of explosives to perpetrate terrorist attacks at public locations such as restaurants, markets, stations or buses, as well as information about how to behave under police arrest were also logged through these chats by this group of Islamist radicals.

The analysis of life patterns of Islamist activists in Spain expose characteristics shared by members of other terrorist groups throughout the world. Common factors can be appreciated when comparing the recruitment processes of religious and secular organisations.[17] These variables are also evident in the individuals who participated in the terrorist attacks perpetrated on 11 March in Madrid as well as in those jihadists arrested before and after the massacre. Structural, motivational and facilitation factors merged in their process of radicalisation and recruitment. Most of them were part of a closed community of activists poorly integrated in Spanish society who were kept together by a radical ideology. It is clear that terrorism is a group phenomenon in which individuals are greatly influenced by group dynamics.[18] The dynamics that influenced these terrorists approaching and joining the jihadist movement do not differ extensively from the experiences of other participants in the jihad.[19] As with previous experiences of recruitment into social movements, the network channel is the richest source of movement recruits,[20] constituting a key issue in the Spanish case, one in which a social and family set of connections facilitated such a process. As a result, it can be argued that the genealogy of Islamic terrorism in Spain is one of interpersonal links strengthened by kinship and friendship through which social and group cohesion has been fostered. These networks enabled contacts and relationships to the extent that police and judicial investigations in Spain have been able to establish strong connections between some key Islamist figures who were arrested at the end of 2001 and subsequently sentenced in 2005 and those individuals who participated in perpetrating 11 March, as well as others involved in the preparation of various terrorist attacks. In fact the major setback suffered by the network of Islamist terrorists when at the end of 2001 relevant leaders and operatives were arrested by Spanish police could have seriously influenced the process of radicalisation and recruitment of other activists. Such a strike against the infrastructure of the network could have triggered a strong feeling of revenge that would have materialised in the terrorist campaign initiated in March 2004, which was fortunately interrupted by police successes, since other targets and attacks had been planned by the perpetrators of 11 M.

In September 2005 a total of 18 men were sentenced by the Spanish National Court after magistrates found them guilty of membership and collaboration with Al-Qaeda. Imad Eddin Barakat Yarkas, nicknamed "Abu Dahdah", the leader of what has been termed as the Spanish cell of Al-Qaeda, was sentenced to 27 years in prison accused of leading a terrorist organisation and conspiring to perpetrating the 11 September attacks in the United States in 2001.[21] The judicial verdict stated that the men found guilty had engaged over a prolonged period of time, which in some cases went back as far as 1995, in activities of indoctrination and proselytising, financing terrorist cells in different countries all over the world, as well as recruiting mujahideen in order to send them to conflict spots in Bosnia, Chechnya, Indonesia and Afghanistan. Different methods were used for those purposes, among them the distribution of propaganda contained in magazines produced by Islamist terrorist organisations such as the Palestinian Hamas or the Algerian Groupe Islamique Armeé (GIA) and Front Islamique du Salut (FIS). This type of literature, together with Osama bin Laden's speeches and other sources which justified and encouraged the jihad, was on some occasions handed out to regulars outside the main mosques in Madrid.

At that stage of the process of radicalisation, the Internet also constituted a rich source for those willing to spread a radical Islamic ideology, visits to sites dedicated to advocating violence being a constant pattern in the behaviour of those who were convicted in Spain over the years as a result of their association with Islamic terrorism. Video tapes of the so-called mujahideen would also circulate among members of the cells, some of them former combatants in conflict spots such as Bosnia and Chechnya who, on their return to Spain, would continue their commitment to the neosalafist cause by searching for financial support for other "brothers" in those areas, as well as by engaging in the indoctrination and recruitment of newcomers. During that period, the Internet was also used by Islamist radicals in Spain with the intention of recruiting sympathisers, as demonstrated by the sentencing of Ahmed Brahim, whom the attorney accused of Al-Qaeda membership. In April 2002 Brahim, of Algerian origin, was arrested and subsequently sentenced to ten years imprisonment by the Spanish National Court after being accused of setting up a web page aimed at spreading the jihad and attracting newcomers to the cause of Islamic fundamentalism including those who would be willing to become "martyrs".[22]

The current international political scenario has undoubtedly provided a very fertile ground for newcomers into the global jihad, the war in Iraq offering strong motivational arguments for many individuals who may want to join in such a movement. As can be deduced from the propaganda material used by jihadist terrorists in Spain, Iraq has had an impact in their radicalisation. Nonetheless, police and judicial investigations indicate that the commitment to jihadism which is now so evident in Western Europe does precede the conflict in Iraq and even the intervention in Afghanistan, which is also often identified as another explanation for the growing importance of Islamist terrorism in today's European context. It should be remembered that Islamist terrorists had already targeted Europe long before the intervention in Iraq. Previous terrorist attacks had been foiled as a result of good intelligence and effective police work, as demonstrated by plots aborted in London, Strasburg or Rome, where the United States embassy had also been targeted.

Moreover, as it has already been pointed out, some of the men responsible for carrying out 11 M had been committed to jihadism even before the war in Iraq broke out, leading judicial authorities as far back as 2001 to define Spain as "the main base of Al-Qaeda in Europe". The *Situation and Trends Report* produced by Europol in 2003 warned of the risk faced by Spain in the following terms:

> Various terrorist groups comprising the so-called Islamic World Front, under the leadership of Al-Qaeda, as well as the advocates of internationalisation of Jihad on a global scale, continue to pose the greatest threat to our interests as well as to the interests of the other EU Member States. The Spanish Government's support of the military intervention in Iraq by the United States and its Allies constitutes without doubt a further risk factor for Spain, even though it might not be the most decisive or dangerous one.[23]

It should be emphasised that the report did not regard Spain's support for the intervention in Iraq as "the most decisive or dangerous" risk factor, exposing the existence of a terrorist threat in advance of the Iraqi conflict. The explanation lies in the fact that, as investigators learnt from various informers, some radicals had a mind for jihad since at least 2001. A point corroborated by several members of the Spanish intelligence service interviewed by the author who emphasised how since 2002 one of the suicide terrorists, Sarhane Ben Abdelmajid, frequently referred to the need to apply "Islamic justice".

Group dynamics and interpersonal links

Friendships and family bonds have been of great relevance in linking different subgroups in the network of sympathisers and activists, thus facilitating common patterns of radicalisation and recruitment to develop. To this extent police investigations have confirmed the close relationship between various networks of activists illustrating how significant interpersonal links became in order to bring newcomers and strengthen the group cohesion, as one event may illustrate. Three years before the terrorist attacks in Madrid took place, some of the main Al-Qaeda figures in the country attended a Muslim wedding held in the capital between a Spanish woman and a Syrian man. Three of the leaders of the organisation, including Abu Dahdah, shared a table with Sarhane Ben Abdelmajid Fakhet, alias "the Tunisian", one of the seven suicide terrorists who killed themselves in the outskirts of Madrid in April 2004, who acted as a translator during the wedding. Sarhane "the Tunisian" was married to the sister of Mustapha Maymouni, a close associate of Abu Dahdah and a very influential individual in the Al-Qaeda network. It is around these authority figures that ideological and social bonds were knit in the years before the terrorist attacks were finally perpetrated in Madrid. Different mosques in the city enabled contact between individuals, but did not represent the main meeting points where they gathered and conspired, other places such as restaurants, hairdressers and flats being preferred for those purposes. The quarter of Lavapiés, with a great affluence of immigrants, provided some of these meeting points. A restaurant called *Alhambra*, the public phone booth *Nuevo Siglo* – owned by Jamal Zougam, another individual closely linked to the main Al-Qaeda cell in Spain and the group who perpetrated 11 M – and *Abdou*'s hairdressers were all situated in the same street and only metres away from each other. It was at these places that members of the cell regularly met. The back of *Abdou*'s hairdressers was where the radicals purified themselves with water from Mecca and a place where they used to meet for prayers since they did not wish to attend the local mosque which was controlled by a Pakistani who upheld an interpretation of Islam they did not agree with.

In the privacy of these locations the exaltation of the jihad took place, collectively endorsing the activists' radical views of Islam with literature and video footage which portrayed a victimised Muslim community as well as the violent and bloody response to their grievances that mujahideen inflicted on their enemies. This ritual contributed to strengthening the "culture of death", also evident in other suicide terrorists, which makes martyrdom appear as the right thing to do.[24] It is revealing that a copy of one of those video tapes used as a means of indoctrination and of reassuring their beliefs was found in different locations when house searches of Al-Qaeda suspects took place even before the terrorist attacks in Madrid were perpetrated.[25] The tape, titled *Islamic Jihad in Dagestan*, showed the brutality of mujahideen against Russians. The video featured prominently Abdelaziz Benyaich and his brother Salaheddin, alias "Abu Mughen", both dressed in combat fatigues leading a group of mujahideen in Chechnya.[26] The Benyaich brothers had befriended Jamal Zougam in Tanger where all of them came from. Abu Mughen, who lost an eye fighting in Bosnia, became an iconic and venerated figure for the members of the Spanish cell and was welcomed in their homes when he needed refuge, as he did when his eye was operated on at a Madrid clinic in March 1999.

Both brothers were later arrested and sentenced for their participation in the attacks in Casablanca in May 2003 when Islamist terrorists killed 45 people. Another of the Benyaich brothers, Abdalla, was also involved in the jihad and died in Afghanistan while American troops chased bin Laden. Mohamed Fizazi, a religious figure imprisoned after the Casablanca killings who is serving a 30-year prison sentence for his alleged involvement in that terrorist attack, is regarded by police as somebody who greatly influenced youngsters like Zougam and the Benyaich brothers who shared the same background.[27] The relevance of kinship in the jihadist structure is highlighted by the involvement of several groups of brothers such as Rachid and Mohammed Oulad, both killed in the collective suicide of April 2004, Moutaz Almallah Dabbas and Mohannad Almallah Dabbas, as well as Abdelgani Chedadi and Said Chedadi, the latter arrested before 11 M and the former in the aftermath of the terrorist attacks, both of whom run a shop just a few metres away from some of the main regular meeting points of Islamist radicals such as *Restaurante Alhambra* and Zougam's public phone booth, both located in a popular neighbourhood of Madrid. Abdelkhalak Chergi and his brother Abdelhak were also arrested and interrogated under the suspicion of being involved in the preparation and financing of the terrorist attack. In addition to these family ties, cousins were also involved in the cells behind the terrorist attacks. By way of example, Hamid Ahmidan, charged with "membership of terrorist organisation" in April 2006, is the cousin of Jamal Ahmidan, nicknamed "the Chinese", one of the seven suicide bombers who killed themselves in Leganés, a town in the outskirts of Madrid.

A rundown house outside Madrid also offered a meeting point where the radicals behind the 11 M terrorist attacks socialised and reinforced their ideological commitments through the hatred and dehumanisation of Westerners encouraged by the means already outlined. It was owned by Mohammed Needl, imprisoned in Spain while awaiting trial since 2001 for his alleged involvement with the Spanish Al-Qaeda cell and its leader Abu Dahdah. The house had been rented by Mustapha Maymouni before he was sentenced for his involvement in the Casablanca attacks and later on by Jamal Ahmidan, "the Chinese", through the intermediary Sarhane, "the Tunisian". Owing to its secrecy, the shack outside Madrid was used to prepare the bombs used on 11 March. It was also the place where some kind of celebration took place on 21 March shortly after the terrorist attacks had shocked Spain. On that Sunday some members of the terrorist cell and their families gathered together for a barbeque. In fact, as the judicial investigation revealed, it was quite common for the group to get together at a country location in the Madrid province where for the last couple of years some of those involved in the terrorist attacks perpetrated in Madrid used to play football, swim in the river, cook and pray.[28]

Radicalisation in prisons

The type of personal connections described above have also been present in other groups of radicals, as revealed by the dismantling of a cell in Ceuta in late

2006. According to security sources, the radicalisation of some of the leaders of this cell took place inside the jail and through personal contact with radicals involved in another network engaged in the preparation of the infrastructure required to send jihadists to Iraq.[29] In fact, prisons have also constituted an important place for the radicalisation of some of the individuals involved in terrorism in Spain as evidenced by the dismantling of a cell in a jail located in Salamanca in the autumn of 2004. Prison experiences seemed quite influential in the radicalisation process of some of those who took part in the 11 M attacks, particularly that of Jamal Ahmidan, nicknamed "the Chinese". Born in Tetuan, Morocco, on 28 October 1970, he arrived illegally in Spain in 1990 and got involved in petty crime and drugs' smuggling. He was married to a Spanish woman and was the father of an 11-year-old boy when he died. Police sources believe his marriage to a drug addict was primarily aimed at legalising his situation in the country. He spent time in prison between 1992 and 1995 and after his release was detained at least nine times for forging documents and trafficking in drugs. In 1999, while he was held at a detention centre in Madrid where illegal foreigners were kept before being sent back to their country, *the Chinese* started a fire aided by an Algerian internee in an attempt to break out. When he went back to Morocco in 2000 he was sent to prison for three years for drink driving and running over a man while driving under the influence. His time in prison is regarded as a key period in his life where he became radicalised and turned into a religious fanatic. His brother Mustafa says that Jamal gave up smoking, heroin, cocaine and alcohol, although he did not change the way in which he had earned his livelihood. Shortly after being released in 2003 he acquired the explosives used on 11 M, exchanging them for drugs and a considerable amount of money. He also managed to acquire weapons and ammunition through his contacts in the Spanish criminal world. At the same time he became a regular at the mosque in the Villaverde quarter of Madrid, where he would listen to the preaching of a radical imam, Samir Ben Abdellah, who shared with Sarhane "the Tunisian" strict views about Islam.

Imprisonment was also a key period for Allekema Lamari, born on 10 July 1965 in Alger, and another of the suicide terrorists. According to the Spanish intelligence service, while in prison after being sentenced for membership of a terrorist organisation his radicalisation deepened even further and he became fully committed to take revenge for his imprisonment which came to an end in 2002. Before that he came into contact with Rachid Oulad Ackcha, born in Tetuan, Morocco, on 27 January 1971 and another of the seven suicide terrorists. In 1998 Rachid was sentenced to four years in prison after being found guilty of drug trafficking. According to prison officers who met Rachid, during the initial stages of his imprisonment he was not regarded as religiously radicalised but rather as a "normalised inmate with quite a low profile".[30] Nonetheless, there was a three-month period in which he was in the same prison, Madrid III, as one of the relevant figures involved in 11 M, Allekema Lamari. Some intelligence sources argue that this period could have proved decisive in Rachid's process of radicalisation.

Confronting the radicalisation and recruitment of Jihadist terrorists

Preventing and containing radicalisation: a multifaceted approach

Spain's protracted history of confronting violence perpetrated by the Basque nationalist terrorist group ETA has enabled the country to reach a high level of efficiency against this type of terrorism. Different measures implemented over the years provided ample experience which would be used in order to improve Spain's capacities against a new brand of terrorism for which the country was not so well prepared by 11 March. As has already been mentioned, the origins of jihadism can be traced back to the previous decade when the first networks mainly composed of Algerian and Syrian individuals started to settle down in Spain. Although police surveillance led to important successes at the turn of the century, efforts directed to counter Islamic terrorism at the time were considerably restricted given the limited amount of human and material resources available. The emergence and development of the threat since the 1990s raised concerns among the main security agencies, that is, the National Police (*Policía Nacional*), Civil Guard (*Guardia Civil*) and the Intelligence Service (*Centro Nacional de Inteligencia, CNI*). Nonetheless, the commitment to confront Islamic terrorism became stronger as a result of the terrorist attacks in the United States in September 2001 and most definitely after the atrocity perpetrated in Madrid in 2004. In fact the attacks in the United States led to a slight increase in police personnel followed by another small boost after the 2003 Casablanca terrorist attacks in neighbouring Morocco. In this few years the Spanish National Police increased its capacity by 25 per cent, employing up to 70 specialists on Islamic terrorism and doubling those who concentrated on the Maghreb region, which was regarded as the main area of threat.[31]

At the same time the Civil Guard also increased its specialists on the subject, although the 60 experts available were still regarded as insufficient. Despite these efforts police and intelligence personnel, including translators, could benefit from a more generous increase, with initiatives aimed at preventing the radicalisation and recruitment of radicals with the potential to perpetrate terrorist attacks still remaining scarce. It was only after Spain had suffered the major setback on 11 March and the loss of almost 200 people as a result of such an attack that a broader counter-terrorist framework was put into place.[32] In the aftermath of the terrorist attacks different measures were announced by the newly elected Spanish government. The scope of these initiatives coincides with the objectives set out by the European Union's strategy for combating terrorism and the radicalisation and recruitment of individuals: disrupt the activities of the networks and individuals who draw people into terrorism, ensure that voices of mainstream opinion prevail over those of extremism and promote yet more vigorously security, justice, democracy and opportunity for all.[33] The measures implemented by the Spanish authorities in order to fulfil these objectives have included a significant increase in capabilities, the improvement and enhancement of coordination and cooperation between security agencies and governments, a few legislative reforms, the implementation of a programme designed to enhance the protection of targets and the response to terrorist attacks, and, finally, some specific measures aimed at the prevention of radicalisation and recruitment.

Increase in intelligence capabilities

The fact that prior to the massacre perpetrated in Madrid many of the terrorist suspects involved in the 11 March attacks had already been under investigation in the course of investigations vis-à-vis Islamist terrorism and other criminal acts exposed serious intelligence shortcomings that had to be faced. The limited human and material resources available seriously constrained the work that the security agencies could do, thus making it necessary to significantly increase resources, something that was announced immediately after the attacks. The increase in translators and interpreters was particularly important in the aftermath of the atrocity given the surprisingly small number of professionals devoted to such an important part of the investigation process. The vast amount of dialects and unfamiliar cultural and social codes constitute important barriers for a better understanding of the current terrorist phenomenon and the activities of individuals under investigation, hence the absolute necessity of incorporating not only translators but also police and agents capable of working within the communities in question. The complex access to what are very closed clusters remains a daunting task that will require a coherent policy for the recruitment of translators, specialists on the subject, and security personnel qualified to work in such an environment as well as members of minority groups, preferably second generation.

Between 2004 and 2005, 600 new policemen were recruited to fight Islamist terrorism. Three hundred more are currently being trained, the intention being to have over 1,000 specialists in this particular area which requires important expertise and specific knowledge of the subject matter that was not hitherto available. Such an increase aimed at improving the quantity and the quality of intelligence thus requiring more informers, under cover and infiltrated agents, as well as better technical means necessary to intercept communications, and carry out surveillance and scientific investigations. Therefore it was not enough for the two main police bodies in the country to experience such an increase or for the Spanish intelligence service to recruit 300 new members with a view to having 1,000 new agents in the next few years. First of all the new agents would have to be filtered and properly selected before recruitment. Later on they would have to be formed and trained in a slow process which would require existing members to devote some of their time and energy to the newcomers, thus stretching already limited resources until the new agents were fully operational. The limited presence of police and intelligence personnel abroad has also been a problem that the authorities have started to address. As a result, police representatives have been sent to key areas such as Pakistan, Syria, Libya, Algeria, Jordan, Indonesia, the Philippines and Saudi Arabia. However, this should not obscure the fact that in terms of resources, only 10 per cent of Spanish intelligence is deployed abroad.

Strengthening contact networks with the Muslim community

The awareness of the relevance that the processes of radicalisation and recruitment have in the fight against terrorism has increased in the last few years, as demonstrated by the European Union's growing concern for these issues revealed in different statements on the matter since December 2004 when the European Council agreed to elaborate a strategy and action plan to address this problem.[34] The decision by the European Commission to appoint a group of experts to provide policy advice on fighting violent radicalisation is in line with this concern.[35]

Spain's specific initiatives in relation to radicalisation and recruitment can be defined as multifaceted, thus requiring the participation of different ministries in its design and implementation. First of all measures coordinated by the Ministry of Justice will be outlined, followed by other initiatives led by the Ministry of the Interior. Both sets of responses share a common objective, which is the improvement of the relationship between the authorities and the Muslim community in Spain and its main representatives. Although the Spanish state and the Islamic Commission of Spain signed a cooperation agreement in 1992 in which important aspects of the relationship between Muslims and the authorities were set out,[36] many of the issues covered by such a text were not fully developed.

The Office of Religious Affairs of the Ministry of Justice, as the body in charge of the preparation, coordination and implementation of the government's policy on religious matters, including relations with Islamic communities, has been responsible for the assessment and development of the referred agreement. Thus, the Office is in charge of the register of religious entities, the communication with federations and bodies regarded as representatives of Islamic communities, as well as the judicial aspects derived from the relationship between Muslims and the state. By way of example, in the last few years the Office has managed to stabilise the situation of imams who lacked social security benefits offering them the possibility of regularising their situation in the country. It should be remembered that preaching is one of the factors that may influence individuals in order to embrace opinions, views and ideas which could lead to acts of terrorism. Therefore, it is important to monitor those responsible for it, also enabling moderate preachers to fulfil their jobs by lessening the difficulties that may arise for them from a legal point of view. As part of such a process it has been decided to issue permits of residence for imams as a result of their religious activity, which is thus considered a professional one. Such a development is seen as much more effective than the control of speeches by imams made in mosques that was contemplated at some point by the authorities, a measure that was never implemented following the wide criticism it received when announced shortly after the terrorist attacks in Madrid on 11 March. The rejection of such a measure stems not only from the technical difficulties of its implementation, but mainly from the restrictions to freedom of speech that would have entailed, as corroborated by the fact that amendments to the current legislation would have been required if finally introduced.

Education has been a key area in the agenda of the Office of Religious Affairs, a concern that has led to addressing the training of imams but also of teachers responsible for the teaching of Islamic religion to children. Therefore, a commission set up by members of the Office of Religious Affairs and the Islamic Commission of Spain has been involved in setting up courses in primary education in sensitive areas such as Ceuta and Melilla, geographically located in the African continent and home to big Muslim communities, as well as throughout those Spanish autonomous communities where education remains the responsibility of the central government. It is acknowledged that more teachers are needed and that the hour and a half of religious classes per week that the legislation currently allows for may not be regarded as sufficient by some parents who may still deem it necessary to send their children to Islamic schools away from the public system. Another difficulty that this initiative has encountered is related to the lack of didactic material available to teachers. Consequently new materials have been devised after careful consideration by a group of experts who have analysed what content would be the most appropriate for such a purpose. This has been the result of a successful cooperation between a respected publishing company with long experience in the publication of school material, albeit for Catholic schools, and a new foundation created at the end of 2004 by the Ministry of Justice falling under the supervision of the Office of Religious Affairs, named Foundation for Plurality and Life Together (*Fundación Pluralismo y Convivencia*).

The work developed by this Foundation is regarded as particularly relevant in the fight against radicalisation. It aims to encourage freedom of religion by supporting representatives of minority confessional communities as well as educational and cultural activities that may be designed together with similar actions in the area of social integration. It should be stressed that this body is not exclusively oriented towards Islamic communities. Consequently the Foundation also aims at improving mutual knowledge of different communities in society with the intention of overcoming stereotypes, also being concerned about the need to support those federations that represent minority religious groups so they can strengthen their leadership and their role as liaison between society and the administration. Other goals include the development of communities which belong to minority groups and the improvement of their social and economic conditions as well as the encouragement of intercultural and interreligious dialogue through participation in joint initiatives.

The Foundation has financially supported different projects submitted by communities and entities belonging to minority groups with the objective of meeting those objectives. Social and cultural initiatives have been funded enabling local communities to engage in the formation and education of its members. Given that youngsters are particularly vulnerable and susceptible to radicalisation, these projects are seen as an interesting and practical alternative allowing them to get involved in activities that may keep them away from radicals. It is believed that the influence exerted over youngsters by radicals at that particular stage of their lives may be neutralised by their involvement in cultural, educational and sports activities like the ones currently funded by this Foundation. New members of the community who arrive from abroad, very often knowing little about the country of arrival, sometimes lacking an important support network of relatives and friends, can also benefit from such an initiative given their propensity to being lured into a group. In some cases their solitude and boredom can make the group particularly attractive by providing personal reinforcement and support that could also deepen processes of de-individuation, particularly damaging for the individual should the group espouse a radical ideology that justifies the use of violence. Therefore, as part of its strategy the Foundation also hopes to favour the strengthening of social cohesion and the building of responsible leadership at the local level.

The prevention and detection of radicalisation requires ample cooperation from representatives and members of the communities where radicals are more likely to act in their attempt to attract youngsters into their influence. It is at that level that early indicators can be more easily identified providing the opportunity to disrupt the radicalisation process from going further. Such an acknowledgement has led Spanish authorities to increase contacts with Islamic communities through the means previously outlined, also involving the police in this process of improving relations with those who are seen as key players in the detection process. To this extent measures like the ones already described have been complemented by efforts aimed at deepening contacts between the police and the communities; one of the most successful initiatives so far consisting of the devising of an alert system online that allows police to highlight those issues that may be of concern for Islamic communities which have the potential of turning into controversial grievances if they are not properly addressed.

In order to detect sensitive issues with the potential to becoming conflict matters that could be conveniently manipulated by radicals, Spanish police have increased their contact with local communities by promoting liaison officers who can facilitate such communication. Officers who fulfil this role are not assigned investigative tasks in order to enhance their position as some kind of social mediator between the authorities and the community. This figure has been of considerable practical use in managing to defuse situations which otherwise could have been used against the authorities in order to reinforce narratives aimed at delegitimising the State institutions. This has been the case when, for example, intense security presence in certain areas ran the risk of becoming an alienation factor or when some concerns were raised by Muslim women who did not want to uncover their heads when being photographed as was required in order to issue new identity cards. This system has also been used to warn about xenophobic attitudes towards certain Muslim communities at an early stage, preventing that type of situation from deteriorating. Various concerns about security force activities have also been aired through these means, for example when police raids have taken place coinciding with major Muslim festivities or when detentions have not been followed by prosecutions, conveying negative images of the police work without acknowledging the difficulty of such a job and the need to disrupt certain movements of suspects following intelligence but in the absence of sufficient evidence to guarantee prosecutions.

The delicate balance that needs to be struck by police requires a strict adherence to protocols and patterns of behaviour. Despite the efforts already made in this area, some mistakes have been made in the last few years, for example when police detentions have been immediately broadcast on national television in news programmes at prime time showing pictures of terrorist suspects handcuffed and lying on the ground. On one occasion the detention of a Muslim woman dressed according to strict Islamic code was also shown on television only hours after it had taken place, the lady being just a suspect who could well be released shortly after.

The liaison provided by the contacts available, mainly police and representatives of the Office of Religious Affairs who have striven to engage in close dialogue with local communities very often on a bilateral and informal basis, is understood as a key element of the government's strategy in setting up a context where early indicators of radicalisation and recruitment can be detected, communicated and acted upon. As has been described, the nature of this relationship allows for very diverse types of action which also include mediation when imams from abroad are invited by local communities in order to ease procedures to acquire legal documents required to enter the country. Assistance at school level when Muslim children encounter problems, as is quite often the case in the process of integrating young immigrants into the education system of a distinct society, is also included in this type of intervention.

Public diplomacy and the role of the media

As with other previous terrorist expressions of nationalist ideology, the role of the communities of concern is particularly relevant too when confronting violence perpetrated by individuals who espouse a radical and fundamentalist interpretation of Islam. Experience demonstrates that the required delegitimisation and condemnation of violence by the majority will prevent terrorists from increasing their social support.[37] This is a necessary but not sufficient precondition for terrorism to remain a phenomenon confined to a minority. Therefore, counter-terrorism also needs to include measures that encourage such condemnation and delegitimisation, which is particularly efficient when coming from political or religious leaders who are respected in the community, thus being able to exert a positive influence on other members of that particular section of the population.[38] Thus the "battle for hearts and minds" is also part of the counter-terrorist framework against Islamic terrorism, implying initiatives like the ones already described or the fatwa issued against Osama bin Laden by the main Spanish Islamic religious authorities after 11 March, measures which have also been complemented by some other actions on the communication front. As a result of it, contacts with the Arab media and governments in the Arab world have also been intensified. The Spanish government have engaged in a type of public diplomacy aimed at better explaining to a wide Arab audience its foreign policy, the country's factual circumstances and its policies against issues such as immigration, as well as other areas with the potential of becoming mobilisation factors for certain individuals. To this extent, of particular significance remains the role played by certain Arab media, among them *Al Jazzera*, whose particular coverage and interpretation of current affairs contributes to the strengthening of solidarity bonds between Muslims throughout the world by the portrayal of a global victimised and humiliated Muslim community. As a way of example, the detention in September 2003 of Taysir Alouny, *Al Jazeera's* correspondent in Spain and the man who interviewed bin Laden shortly after 11 September, was portrayed by the television station as an attack which would have consequences for a country whose image was going to deteriorate in certain parts of the Arab world.[39] Violence polarises and forces audiences to take part by choosing either the side of the victims or that of the terrorist. Therefore, the media provide "identification machines" since "the terrorist's invitation to identification is brought home to us by the public and the private media".[40] It has proved extremely difficult so far to confront that dimension as well as the great and increasing great influence that the Internet exerts on individuals who can easily access sites where violence in the name of Islam is not only justified but actively and strongly encouraged.

Confronting radicalisation in prisons

Finally, the Spanish government has also introduced some measures with the intention of preventing the radicalisation and recruitment of individuals incarcerated. The dismantling of a terrorist cell inside one of the prisons and the evidence of other cases where radicalisation of prisoners has occurred led the authorities to opt in November 2004 for the dispersal of those inmates who were linked to jihadist terrorism, allocating them to 30 different centres over the country. Dispersal of prisoners constitutes an important policy adopted in the mid-1980s to confront ETA's terrorism and has been maintained since then given its efficiency in preventing the association of members of the same ideology that would strengthen the group's pressure over the individual, raising obstacles in the process of disengagement from the terrorist organisation, also increasing the chances of posing various challenges to the prison authorities. With such a background the dispersal of prisoners associated with jihadist terrorism was also seen as a very positive initiative, although the outcome could vary as a result of the key differences between these types of terrorism. The dispersal of individuals linked to jihadist terrorism may actually enable them to contact other inmates with the potential of being radicalised and recruited, an obstacle that has led the prison authorities to apply a very strict control of communications by this type of inmates. Whereas the nationalist ideology espoused by ETA's activists was unlikely to be an effective tool for the indoctrination of other prison inmates with no connection with the terrorist organisation given the sheer rejection of ETA's objectives by the majority of the Spanish prison population, the same could not be said of Islamism when conveniently manipulated as a means of justifying extremism. The search for new recruits by jihadist terrorists has often extended to marginal groups and crime circles where individuals are prone to accept ideological doctrines convenient for their criminal acts to be seen in a different light. In other words, a radical interpretation of Islam may become a useful instrument to justify previous and further transgressions shielding the individual from his own self-questioning and criticism, which usually ensues decisions that generate negative consequences. The prison environment could provide a facilitational context for such a course of action which requires proper management if further processes of radicalisation are to be prevented.

To this extent the above-mentioned Office of Religious Affairs has started to offer religious assistance to prison inmates through a representative of the Islamic community who is seen by the authorities as a useful link between the prison system and the prisoner. Such a figure should combine a good psychological and religious background since both dimensions are key elements in the strategy required to build a positive rapport with inmates. By presenting this mediator as the main liaison between the prison authorities and the prisoners, it is hoped that this figure will be able to build trust with the inmate to the point of being regarded as a reference figure thus neutralising other possible influences originating from radical quarters. The aide's remit of action goes beyond his role as mediator, including religious assistance but also a didactic dialogue with the intention of facilitating the understanding of concepts such as guilt, offence, crime, remission and responsibility, among others, which are of great relevance for a successful process of resocialisation away from violence and radicalism.

Conclusion

This chapter has outlined the main patterns discernible in the process of radicalisation and recruitment of individuals who have been associated with jihadist terrorism in Spain. Although the majority of the Muslim community in Spain considers itself well integrated in Spanish society, widely rejecting the use of violence,[41] a small minority of members of this community does espouse a radical ideology which condones the use of terrorism. A Pew Research Survey published in June 2006 pointed out that 16 per cent of Spanish Muslims "sometimes" justified violence against civilian targets in order to defend Islam, whereas according to 9 per cent of those polled the use of violence was "rarely" justified, while 69 per cent considered that such a course of action was "never" justified. At the same time, 16 per cent expressed "a lot or some confidence in bin Laden", with just 12 per cent of Spanish Muslims saying that "many or most of the country's Muslims support Al-Qaeda and similar groups".[42] In November 2006 a survey funded by the Spanish Ministry of the Interior indicated that 4 per cent of the Muslim population in Spain regarded violence as an acceptable method in support of religious beliefs. In 2007 another survey carried out by several government departments showed that 90 per cent of Spanish Muslims considered that violence should never be used or justified in support of religious beliefs.[43]

The support for the extremist views expressed by some members of the Muslim community is a result of a process of radicalisation undertaken by individuals who on some occasions will end up resorting to violence. The analysis of the background and profiles of jihadist terrorists in Spain reveals that their radicalisation and recruitment process was influenced by religious, cultural, social, economic and political factors. The importance of these factors varies according to the individual, but a common thread can be appreciated since all of them espouse a radical neosalafist ideology based on a fundamentalist interpretation of Islam. Such an ideology enabled the strengthening of a subculture of violence that has provided the framework for violent actions which are also justified on rational and emotional grounds.

Imams and other charismatic leaders have played a pivotal role in the process of radicalisation of jihadist terrorists in Spain. The specific grievances and personal experiences of victimisation which seemed to be absent from the lives of many jihadist terrorists in Spain were brought directly to them by prominent figures, thus enabling the process of radicalisation through the intense socialisation and indoctrination that followed. Charismatic leaders such as Mustapha Setmariam, Amer Azizi or the Benyaich brothers, who had fought in Afghanistan, Bosnia and Chechnya, were of key relevance in the process of socialisation providing role models of "brothers" who had sacrificed their lives for others. The Internet provided an essential tool in the process of indoctrination and consolidation of the "subculture of death" that would predispose them to violence.

The relevance of charismatic leaders who attract newcomers into the jihadist cause is still evident in the Spanish context. In December 2006 in the Spanish town of Ceuta, located in North Africa, Spanish police arrested several men under suspicion of being about to plot terrorist attacks after having followed a deep process of radicalisation. Two of the suspects were the brothers of Hamed Abderrahaman Ahmed, the Spanish citizen who spent two years in Guantanamo, where he confessed to Spanish police that he had received arms training at a Taliban camp in Afghanistan, later on withdrawing this confession. On his release from Guantanamo he has become a charismatic figure who is seen with considerable respect by youngsters susceptible of being radicalised, as police sources indicate. Furthermore, the return of individuals who have travelled to Iraq, where they have received arms training, some of them taking part in terrorist actions in the name of Islam, is also creating role models for new radicals in Spain.[44] Despite the lack of widespread legitimisation for suicide terrorism within Spanish society, intelligence sources have corroborated that a minority of individuals regard with great respect and admiration those who embraced "martyrdom", the seven suicide terrorists being considered as courageous men and even as role models. There is concern about the fact that certain individuals are being inspired by what they regard as the moral superiority of the suicide terrorists who killed themselves in Madrid and that of other "brothers" engaged in jihadism.

The strategy for dealing with terrorism has evolved over many years in the light of experience, but current responses to international terrorism still maintain some of the key pillars on which previous counter-terrorist campaigns in Spain were sustained despite their distinct features. To this extent the Spanish government still aims at improving and increasing intelligence capabilities as well as enhancing the coordination and cooperation between security agencies and governments in order to disrupt the activities of the networks and individuals who draw people into terrorism. At the same time, the Spanish authorities are committed to ensure that mainstream opinion prevails over extremism within Muslim communities in the same way they tried in the past to strengthen moderate nationalists while isolating radical extremists who supported a terrorist group like ETA and their political front.

Now, as has been the case for previous decades, anti-terrorism still aims at winning the battle for hearts and minds to ultimately ensure that terrorism remains a minority phenomenon, a choice of certain individuals who take the deliberate decision to use violence without achieving widespread legitimisation. To this extent, more attention is being paid to how best to confront the radicalisation that will enable the recruitment of newcomers with the intention in many cases of perpetrating terrorist attacks. A deeper assessment of the effectiveness of certain measures implemented in order to prevent radicalisation and recruitment, as described in this chapter, is not possible yet and it will only be possible with the passing of time, as is usually the case with anti-terrorist policies.

Notes

1 "Al Qaeda convirtió España en la base principal de su red en Europa", José María Irujo, *El País*, 3 March 2002.
2 "Hacia una caracterización social del terrorismo yihadista en España: implicaciones en seguridad interior y acción exterior", Fernando Reinares, *Análisis del Real Instituto Elcano*, No 34/2006, available at www.realinstitutoelcano.org/analisis/929.asp. Nonetheless, subsequent detentions by Spanish police have involved Spanish citizens, as in the case of seven youngsters arrested in Ceuta in December 2006.
3 See, for example, Juzgado Central de Instrucción Número 6, Audiencia Nacional, Madrid, Sumario N° 20/2004, Madrid, Auto, 10 April 2006, pp. 1212–1213.
4 Ibid., pp. 1212–1213.
5 Ibid., pp. 1216–1217.
6 Ibid., p. 1222.
7 Ibid., pp. 1218–1219.
8 Ibid., p. 1219.
9 Ibid., p. 1236.
10 Ibid., p. 1225.
11 Ibid., p. 1235.
12 Ibid., p. 1226.
13 Ibid., p. 1231.
14 Ibid., p. 1234.
15 Ibid., pp. 436–450.
16 Ibid., p. 498.
17 See, for example, two of the most protracted cases of ethnonationalist terrorism in Europe in Rogelio Alonso, *The IRA and Armed Struggle*. London: Routledge, 2007;

and Rogelio Alonso, "Individual motivations for joining terrorist organisations: a comparative qualitative study on members of ETA and the IRA" in Jeff Victoroff (ed.), *Social and Psychological Factors in the Genesis of Terrorism*, pp. 187–202. Amsterdam: IOS Press, 2006.

18 J.M. Post, K.G. Ruby and E.D. Shaw, "The Radical Group in Context: 1. An Integrated Framework for the Analysis of Group Risk for Terrorism", *Studies in Conflict & Terrorism*, 25, 2002, pp. 73–100.

19 See Marc Sageman, *Understanding Terror Networks*. Philadelphia: University of Pennsylvania Press, 2004. The profiles of the four terrorists who died in the terrorist attacks perpetrated in London on 7 July 2005 do corroborate this point.

20 David A. Snow, Louis A. Zurcher Jr. and Sheldon Ekland-Olson, "Social networks and social movements: a microstructural approach to differential recruitment", *American Sociological Review*, 45, 1980, pp. 787–801.

21 In June 2006 the Spanish Supreme Court reduced this sentence to 12 years stating that although Abu Dahdah was definitely a member of a terrorist organisation, he did not take part in the preparation of the terrorist attacks perpetrated in the United States in 2001.

22 *El Correo*, 4 April 2006 and *Siglo XXI*, 6 December 2005, at www.diariosigloxxi.com/noticia.php?ts=20051206112122.

23 *Terrorist Activity in the European Union: Situation and Trends Report (TE-SAT) October 2002–15 October 2003*, Europol, 3 December 2003, p. 37.

24 See for example Ami Pedhazur, "Toward an analytical model of suicide terrorism – a comment", *Terrorism and Political Violence*, 16, 2004, pp. 841–844, and Ami Pedhazur, *Suicide Terrorism*. London: Polity, 2005.

25 Juzgado Central de Instrucción Número 5, Madrid, Sumario (Proc. Ordinario) 0000035/2001 E, 17 September 2003.

26 Ibid., pp. 86 and 289.

27 *El País*, 15 May 2005.

28 *El País*, 3 August 2005.

29 M. Sáiz-Pardo and J.C. García, "La célula terrorista de Ceuta controlaba una de las principales mezquitas", *El Correo*, 19 December, p. 206.

30 Author's interview.

31 Testimony by Jesús de la Morena, senior police officer responsible for counter-terrorism, given before the Commission of Enquiry set up by the Spanish Parliament to investigate the 11 March attacks. Cortes Generales. Diario de Sesiones del Congreso de los Diputados. Comisiones de Investigación, Año 2004, VIII Legislatura Núm. 3, Sesión núm. 7, 7 July 2004.

32 In fact, the inertia associated with a protracted campaign against ETA's terrorism led the Spanish authorities initially to blame the Basque terrorist group for the 11 March atrocity in spite of the fact that jihadist terrorism had clearly emerged as a very serious threat. On the Spanish government's response at the time see Rogelio Alonso, "El nuevo terrorismo: factores de cambio y permanencia", in Amalio Blanco, Rafael del Águila and José Manuel Sabucedo (eds.), *Un análisis del mal y sus consecuencias*. Madrid: Editorial Trotta, 2005.

33 "The European Union Strategy for Combating Radicalisation and Recruitment to Terrorism", Council of the European Union, Brussels 24 November 2005, 14781/1/05 REV 1, JAI 452 ENFOPOL 164, COTER 81.

34 Council of the European Union, 14894/04 (Presse 332), Press Release, 2626th Council Meeting, Justice and Home Affairs, Brussels, 2 December 2004. See also on this issue "Communication from the Commission to the European Parliament and the Council concerning Terrorist recruitment: addressing the factors contributing to violent radicalisation", Commission of the European Communities, Brussels, 21 September 2005, COM (2005) 313 final.

35 "Commission Decision of 19 April 2006 setting up a group of experts to provide

policy advice to the Commission on fighting violent radicalisation" (2006/299/EC), *Official Journal of the European Union*, 25 April 2006, L 111/9.
36 *Acuerdo de Cooperación del Estado Español con la Comisión Islámica de España*, approved by Law 26/1992, of 10 November 1992, *Boletín Oficial del Estado de 12 de noviembre de 1999*, www.mju.es/asuntos_religiosos/ar_n08_e.htm.
37 On these issues see Alex P. Schmid, "Terrorism and democracy", in Alex P. Schmid and Ronald D. Crelinsten (1993), *Western Responses to Terrorism*. London: Frank Cass, pp. 14–25; and Alex Schmid, "Towards joint political strategies for de-legitimising the use of terrorism", in *Countering Terrorism through International Cooperation*. ISPAC, International Scientific and Professional Advisory Council of the United nations Crime Prevention and Criminal Justice Programme, Proceedings of the International Conference on "Countering Terrorism through Enhanced International Cooperation", Courmayeur, Mont Blanc, Italy, 22–24 September 2000, pp. 260–265.
38 See for example *Muslim Youth in Europe: Addressing Alienation and Extremism. Report on Wilton Park Conference, WPSO5/3*, 7–10 February 2005.
39 Author's interviews with Spanish intelligence and military personnel based in Morocco at the time.
40 Alex Schmid, "Terrorism and the media: the ethics of publicity", *Terrorism and Political Violence*, 1, 1989, pp. 539–565, p. 545.
41 J.A. Rodríguez, "La comunidad musulmana en España se siente adaptada y rechaza la violencia", *El País*, 24 November 2006.
42 "Europe's Muslims More Moderate. The Great Divide: How Westerners and Muslims view each other". Nation Pew Global Attitudes Survey, June 2006, pp. 4, 25, 26.
43 Metroscopia, Estudios Sociales y de Opinión, *Estudio de Opinión en 2007, entre la Comunidad Musulmana de Origen Inmigrante en España para el Gobierno de España (Ministerio del Interior, Ministerio de Justicia, Ministerio de Trabajo y Asuntos Sociales)*, Madrid, 11 December 2007, pp. 36–39.
44 José María Irujo, "El 'caballo de Troya' de Al Qaeda", *El País*, 17 December 2006.

10 Salafi–Jihadi terrorism in Italy

Carl Björkman

Introduction

In the last ten to 15 years Italy has emerged as a hotbed of activity for militant Salafi–Jihadists. The chapter charts the emergence of this phenomenon – from the early years associated with the "Milan cell" and its radical mosque environment in Via Quaranta and Viale Jenner to the present day activism of diffused Salafi–Jihadi terrorist networks that operate throughout the country. Italy's geographical position as a bridge between Europe and North Africa, the ease with which Italian documents could be forged and the already existing market for weaponry were key factors in transforming the country from a logistics centre to an active base of operations. Today, Salafi–Jihadi networks in Italy engage in the full spectrum of terrorist activities, from raising funds, procuring weapons and explosives, to equipping operatives both mentally (indoctrination) and physically (high-quality identity and travel documents) and dispatching them to take part in military jihad. Italy has also emerged as an important platform for recruitment and radicalisation, and the chapter will attempt to shed some light on the dynamic relationship of these processes in Italian prisons, mosques and through cyber-space.

Italy's involvement in Afghanistan and Iraq has also transformed Italian interests both abroad and at home to justifiable targets, and after the Madrid and London bombings there is a gloomy perception amongst experts, politicians and the Italian public that Italy is next in line. However, despite repeated attempts, Italy has, to date, avoided any major attacks by Salafi–Jihadi groups on home soil. This is not only due to luck but also to the efficiency and effectiveness of its counter-terrorism tools. The chapter will attempt to provide a critical overview of these tools and show how Italian authorities are trying to balance the aggressive short-term pursuit of terrorists with the longer-term strategy of preventing radicalisation and long-term recruitment.

Muslims in Italy

In the past ten to 20 years, Italy has been transformed from an emigrant country into an immigrant country. Foreign labour has proven indispensable for accelerating and sustaining the rate of economic development – resulting in the appearance of new minority groups, including a substantial number of Muslims. Muslims now constitute the second largest religious community in Italy.

Muslims in Italy come from different ethnic groups and different parts of the world, speak different languages, and have different social backgrounds and legal status. Indeed, Islam is frequently the sole common denominator among these diverse communities[1] who are spread out throughout Italy with pockets of concentration in the regions of Lazio, Lombardia, Campania, Sicilia, Veneto and Emilia-Romagna.

At present, the total Muslim population numbers approximately 700,000. About 40,000–50,000 (among them, about 10,000 Christians who converted to Islam) are Italian citizens[2] whose rights and obligations are protected and regulated by the same legal provisions that apply to other Italian citizens. However, the majority of Muslims are immigrants who arrived within the past ten to twenty years, and have not obtained Italian citizenship.

Of these, approximately 600,000 persons have obtained "regular status", and have the legal right to reside and work in Italy. In addition, 80,000–85,000 persons are "illegal migrants" without residency or work permits. According to current estimates, persons coming from traditionally Muslim countries are the fastest growing immigrant group.

Mosques and cultural centres

There are some 300 mosques spread throughout Italy, but predominantly in the main cities and urban areas. Financing for these mosques and cultural and religious centres has come primarily from Saudi Arabia.[3] This has resulted in a determined and expensive effort to spread a community that adheres to a Wahhabi/Salafi[4] interpretation of Islam. Within this large community, several groups have formed – the majority meant to strengthen the sense of community and social support among the immigrants. A very small minority of these groups, however, espouse a Salafi–Jihadi agenda, and others are full-blown militant cells.

Mosques, particularly those with militant imams, were until recently the nexus of the recruiting operation for Salafi–Jihadi terrorism networks and were particularly seen as an important first step in the personal process of radicalisation. The Salafi–Jiahdi mosque movement throughout Italy attracted a growing crowd of followers by playing on their feelings, sending clear and simple messages, and making extensive use of conspiracy theories.

In recent years Italian authorities have increased the surveillance and monitoring of the mosque environment and the associated cultural areas traditionally associated with recruitment and radicalisation. This has shifted these activities towards other areas and as Guido Olimpio argues, extremists now visit mosques less frequently, preferring instead to establish small communities in provincial towns that do not have as strong a police presence as the larger cities such as Milan, Turin and Naples.[5]

Discrimination and anti-Muslim attitudes in Italy

Although the Italian Constitution stipulates equality under the law[6] and Italian courts have proven willing to apply anti-discrimination provisions, there is significant evidence that such discrimination is being directed at Muslims throughout Italy. For instance, research has shown that those of Moroccan heritage face substantial discrimination in employment. Muslims are typically clustered in low-skilled positions and reportedly experience difficulties in obtaining skilled positions despite sufficient professional and linguistic qualifications.[7] In Italy, a number of small-scale surveys were conducted in the late 1990s. These tend to show that Muslims often live in overcrowded conditions in substandard housing (ECRI Report on Italy, 2001). Research also indicates that people of immigrant origin are charged higher average rents than native Italians.

Studies have also shown that there are substantial anti-Muslim attitudes in Italy, with half of Italians believing Muslims are fanatic fundamentalists who support terrorism. Fifty-six per cent of Italians believe that Muslims have "cruel and barbaric laws", 47 per cent consider them "religious fundamentalists and fanatics" and 33 per cent are convinced that they are invading.[8]

These beliefs are fuelled by a number of notable anti-Muslim intellectuals, including Oriana Fallaci, a respected writer and famous political interviewer. After 9/11, she made a series of criticisms of Islam, culminating in a book *La Rabbia e l'Orgoglio*[9] (The Rage and the Pride). In this book she claimed that the West was superior to Islam, used phrases such as "multiplied like rats" to describe Muslims immigrants, and called Muslims "vile creatures, who urinate in baptisteries". Although she was tried for incitement to hatred in Italy, her book sold a staggering 1.5 million copies.[10]

In Italy, a ban on the building of new mosques was proposed in 2005 by a member of the right-leaning governing coalition. The European Commission against Racism and Intolerance (ECRI) has expressed concern especially about the rhetoric of Umberto Bossi and the Northern League, which was until recently a member of the governing coalition. Issues such as the building of mosques and the wearing of the burka have been publicly associated with concerns about terrorism.

Italian immigration law and the effects of 9/11

The events of 9/11, the Madrid and London train bombings had a profound impact on Italian legislation by forcing the enactment of a number of new laws intended to make it easier to confront the threat of terrorism (see section on counter-measures). These laws[11] were criticised by various Muslim organisations for their focus on after-the-fact remedies rather than action oriented towards preventing the problems from arising. There are reports that the discrimination and intolerance against Muslims is on the increase throughout Italy. This growing distrust and hostility with a concern over polarisation and the growth of the far-right is a worrying aspect, particularly as this dynamic is merely fuelling a problem that might potentially lead to the radicalisation of a new generation.[12] More studies are needed to understand how the dual process of recruitment and radicalisation occurs, although some interesting insights can certainly be gleaned from Social Movement Theory and the excellent work by Quintan Wiktorowicz[13] who poses interesting questions such as "why individuals would engage in radical Islamic activism"[14] even if the risks and costs are high, and more specifically "what explains their initial interests? How are they persuaded that a radical group (...) is a credible source of Islamic interpretation? How are they convinced to engage in risky activism?"[15]

It should be pointed out that it is still unclear that these failures by the Italian state to integrate Muslims actually lead to the emergence of Islamist terrorism. Indeed there is very little evidence to suggest that this is the case. It does, however, seem plausible that the social pre-conditions in Italy – such as an identity crisis, widespread racism and Muslim stigmatisation within the Italian society coupled with pre-existing social ties[16] and external triggers such as the perceived injustices in Bosnia, Chechnya, Afghanistan and Iraq – can provide at least a *partial* explanation of why some individuals are initially attracted by radical and distorted Islamic doctrines.

The Salafi–Jihadi presence in Italy: establishing a foothold

In 1996, soon after Algerians planted bombs in the Paris Metro,[17] Italian authorities began discovering that Salafi–Jihadi terrorist networks had a foothold in their country too. Particular focus was directed at Milan, which was found to be an important link in the broader terrorist matrix. At this early stage, the Milanese cell was made up primarily of Egyptians who had fled their home countries after the government crackdown of Salafists in the 1980s and early 1990s. The networks, which were in contact with prominent individuals such as Ayman al-Zawahiri, rapidly expanded and amalgamated Algerians and other North Africans and their presence proved that Italy – with its geographical position as a bridge between Europe and North Africa, lax immigration laws, the ability to work there without credentials and its proximity to places like Bosnia – was becoming an attractive place to operate. During this period Italy was established as a key node and Milan was frequently used to dispatch jihadists to fight in the conflict in Bosnia. Even at this early stage, the Milan cell, revolving around the mosque and cultural centres of Viale Jenner and Via Quaranta, was important to Salafi–Jihadists for the procurement of false documents and as a logistics base.[18]

In 1999, the situation in Milan changed with the arrival of Abdelkader Mahmoud Es Sayed. According to intelligence sources the pace of recruitment and the quality of false documents that were being produced rose remarkably under Es Sayed. Es Sayed hired Ben Khemais ("Saber") as his main recruiter. Italian authorities recognised the threat early and began wiretapping both of these men, and in so doing discovered that the Milan cell was connected to other cells in Europe, and in particular to the Frankfurt cell,[19] the London cell and Abu Doha – the Algerian who oversaw the Millennium bombing attempt at Los

Angeles Airport in 1999. The Milan cell was also connected to the UK-based radical imam Abu Qatada.

In the spring of 2001, Italian police arrested Ben Khemais and a small number of his associates for planning a terrorist attack – he got a five-year sentence. Es Sayed disappeared from Milan in the summer of 2001 and was later killed by US forces in Tora Bora.

After 9/11, the focus of the jihadists changed in Milan. With the disappearance of the camps in Afghanistan, organisations such as Ansar al-Islam began recruiting people for the terrorist camps in Northern Iraq to fight coalition forces. A series of arrests carried out by authorities in Milan and Madrid effectively dismantled the network. Then, in 2004, Rabei Osman el-Sayed Ahmed, "Mohammed the Egyptian", surfaced in Milan. He was placed under surveillance for three months and arrested after having made incriminating remarks about his role in the Madrid bombings.

From the Salafi–Jihadist viewpoint, Italy remains an attractive target. An attack would not only spread fear but also force Italy to reconsider its foreign policy and help to drive a wedge between the US and Europe. Italy has frequently been warned by Salafi–Jihadi networks owing to their involvement in both Afghanistan and Iraq and the comments of its politicians during the recent "Mohammed Cartoon scandal". This has prompted the Interior Ministry to appeal to members of the public all over the country to be vigilant. Counter-terrorism officials are on high alert especially around sensitive US institutions, such as embassies, consulates, military bases and universities as well as historic and Christian landmarks. In total, some 13,000 potential targets are guarded permanently by 23,000 police and soldiers, between 5,000 and 6,000 of these in Rome.

Salafi–Jihadi cells in Italy: composure, structure, recruitment and financing

The arrest of Abdelkader Mahmoud Es Sayed and other operatives which led to the dismantlement of the first "Milan cell" did not eliminate the Salafi–Jihadi terrorist threat in Italy. New networks had already started to emerge, and a number of different organisations had firmly dug their roots into the peninsula.

Although there is no typical "terrorist cell" in Italy, there are some interesting similarities and generalisations that can be made that help shed some light on the phenomenon. One recurring characteristic is that the cells appear to be loosely organised and are perhaps better described as a network[20] with a core of three to ten friends who in turn are linked to other individuals in Italy and abroad. Typically, they are associated to larger terrorist organisations and, unlike many other European countries, are made up of immigrants[21] from the MENA region and are predominantly Tunisian or Moroccan and occasionally Egyptian, Algerian or Iraqi Kurds. They are exclusively male, entering Italy as legal and illegal immigrants or political refugees, are usually without families and in their mid-20s to mid-30s – although some of the more high-ranking operatives appear to be somewhat older. The majority appear to have entered Italy from the 1990s due to

Italy's strategic location in Europe, traditionally more laissez-faire policies (compared with the UK, for instance) and the tightening of immigration laws in France. Other aspects seem to conform to the threat picture in other European countries and agree with the excellent research carried out by Petter Nasser,[22] Michael Taarnby[23] and others. There is, however, one notable difference compared with other countries, such as France, in that there have been very few reported cases involving second- or third-generation operatives of ethnic Italians.[24] This is likely to change in the coming years as more deliberate efforts are made to attract younger members, and specifically those with authentic Italian passports.[25] Transcripts of Italian wiretaps indicate that a determined effort has already been made to "(…) recruit individuals with Italian papers (…) that are intelligent and highly educated and firm believers of the cause".[26]

The lives of operatives in Italy have always been governed by Spartan principles, putting security before all else. In some districts where they have safe houses, they have created "fortress" zones with a trusted network of look-outs.[27] One of these was in the Porta Venezia district of Milan:

> a member of the cell spending hours in a little Arabic restaurant posing as a customer, the Tunisian barber keeping an eye on a junction, the Algerian seller watching over a possible escape route; they were like sentries with eyes and ears everywhere. They noted the faces of all "suspect" persons: Italian law enforcement agents, as well as "spies" from Arabic intelligence agencies.[28]

There have been important changes in the funding methods of radical Islamist networks in Italy before and after 9/11. Before 9/11 money came largely from *zakat* (alms) and donations from Middle Eastern countries such as Saudi Arabia and the United Arab Emirates.[29] This was usually routed through charities or Middle Eastern banks, but since 9/11 these donations have been coming in the form of small amounts of cash brought by couriers. Cells in Italy have also increasingly started to become fund-raisers and are now seen as the ones funnelling cash to other countries. Although many cell members have regular jobs, working as waiters, painters, in fruit stands or in hotels, it is apparent that crime and illegal activities plays a pivotal role. Investigations have shown that Salafi–Jihadists operating in Italy have resorted to all kinds of crimes to finance their operations, including robberies, petty crime, drug dealing,[30] fraud and the sale of counterfeit goods. According to the testimony of Lorenzo Vidino before the House Committee on International Relations Subcommittee,[31] Islamic terrorists and in particular the GSPC have also been actively involved in the extremely profitable business of smuggling large groups of Sub-Saharan migrants across the desert and then into Italy (and other European countries), where the group can count on an extensive network of cells that provides the illegal immigrants with false documents and safe houses.

It is widely believed that Italian recruits have been involved in a host of terrorist attacks around the world. For instance, Islamists recruited and dispatched from Italy were involved in the suicide bombing of the United Nations' headquarters in Baghdad in August 2003 and intelligence sources also cite evidence that an Italian recruit was involved in the October 2003 rocket attack on the Al-Rashid Hotel in Baghdad while Paul Wolfowitz, the US Deputy Secretary of Defense at the time, was staying there.

Another important source of financing, and even the raison d'être of some Italian-based cells, has been the production and distribution of high-quality forged documents such as ID cards, passports[32] and visas which have been supplied to operatives throughout Europe and beyond. Indeed, it is in large part due to its state-of-the-art document-forging industry that Italy in general, and Milan in particular, has become known as one of the main launch-pads for dispatching Salafi–Jihadi volunteers to places such as Bosnia, Chechnya, Afghanistan and most recently, Iraq. Most of the recruits, stocked with fake documents, go through Syria, where many claim they are going to study Arabic and Islam. Others are said to have gone through Turkey and Iran, with another route reputedly operating from Britain – a major way station in the 1990s – and Saudi Arabia. One particular airline transported so many Islamist fighters that it became known to Italian intelligence officers as "Jihad Air".[33]

It is hardly surprising therefore that a number of fake "made in Italy" documents have been recovered in Iraq and Afghanistan suggesting that recruits from Italy have been killed there. For instance, in 2003, fake Italian-made passports were recovered in Iraq from killed or captured terrorists suggesting that operatives were recruited and supplied with documents and fake identity cards in Italy. Forged "Italian" documents have also ended up in the possession of the network involved in the killing of Afghan Northern Alliance leader, Ahmad Shah Massoud. Others have found their way to an organisation in Morocco and some were found to have been sent to Al-Qaeda leaders arrested in Malaysia in 2002.[34]

The major Salafi–Jihadi networks in Italy

A number of radical Islamic groups have a foothold in Italy, and are actively recruiting and radicalising operatives in many of the major urban areas. Amongst these are the Moroccan Islamic Combatant Group, Ansar al-Islam, the Armed Islamic Group, al Qaeda in the Maghreb, the Egyptian Gamaa, the Egyptian Jihad, Hizb ut-Tahir,[35] Algeria's Salafist Group for Preaching and Combat and the Algerian Islamic Liberation Front. These loosely organised networks, connected to cells in other countries, have proved remarkably resilient and frequent arrests, raids and deportations have not proved effective in eliminating the threat.

Algeria's Salafist Group for Preaching and Combat (GSPC)

Algeria's Salafist Group for Preaching and Combat has a deep and wide network of cells operating throughout Italy. It is engaged primarily in supporting terrorist operations in Algeria by providing recruits and funds in Italy. However the group also places emphasis on "out-of-Algeria" terrorist operations, and is arguably the most cohesive and dangerous Salafi–Jihadi organisation in Italy.[36]

There have been a number of investigations showing the interconnected nature of terrorist cells within Italy,[37] and according to press reports,[38] there have been a number of arrests of Algerian GSPC operatives on suspicion of planning terrorist operations in Italy, and of providing financial, weapons and logistical assistance to other Salafi–Jihadi cells in Europe. Like many other investigations, the fulcrum of the activities leads back to Milan and its mosques.

GSPC cells in Italy employ a dual-track approach to planning terrorist attacks and provide support infrastructure – safe houses, communications, weapons procurement and documentation – to GSPC networks in other countries.[39]

An interesting discovery arising out of recent arrests is the connections between the GSPC cells in Italy and other Salafi–Jihadi operatives in Europe. The relationship is based on logistical support, weapons procurement, communications venues and propaganda mechanisms that enable GSPC and Salafi–Jihadi cells in Europe to plan terrorist activities in the countries in which they reside.[40] Although the GSPC cells in Italy appear to be composed exclusively of Algerian nationals, their interaction with mixed Moroccan and Algerian cells in other countries such as Spain and Norway illustrates that the desire for global military jihad has overcome the historical animosity between these two national groups.[41]

Moroccan Islamic Combatant Group

The Moroccan Islamic Combatant Group (GICM) is a loosely connected network that is an active member of the international Salafi–Jihadi movement, with a strong presence in Italy. Investigations have revealed that GICM had transferred money from Italy to individuals involved in the Casablanca bombings. After the Casablanca bombings, Moroccan authorities passed information to their Italian counterparts about a number of GICM operatives living in Italy. Since then DIGOS, the Italian special police, has been monitoring suspected cells in the northern Italian cities and in particular Turin, Varese, Vercelli, Udine and Vicenza.[42]

GICM appears to have a particular interest in Cremona, where the draft of a document about the formation of the group was found in 1998. Several GICM-orchestrated attacks against Cremona Cathedral have also been foiled. In another case the US Treasury Department, on 1 August 2005, also designated three Italian residents of North African origin as terrorists due to their involvement with a GICM cell in the city. According to reports, the organisation has contacts with Al-Qaeda and Ansar Al-Islam cells operating in Italy and abroad and the three arrested men – Ahmed El Bouhali, Faycal Boughanemi and Abdelkader Laagoub – recruited volunteers for paramilitary training, collected funds and planned terrorist attacks in Morocco, Tunisia and Italy – including one involving Milan's underground in response to "Italy's foreign policy".[43]

During raids of suspected GICM members, instruction manuals on paramilitary activities, information on constructing weapons, bombs and instruments for detecting government communications have been found as well as leaflets on clandestine Islamic organisations and videotapes containing Osama bin Laden's and other terrorist leaders' messages inciting violence. This material was likely used as an integral part of GICM's recruitment and radicalisation drive.

Abu Hafs al-Masri Brigades

Although the precise nature of the Abu Hafs al-Masri Brigades remains unknown, the group seems to have taken a particular interest in Italy. The group has often posted warnings to the Italian state on web sites urging Italian troops to leave Iraq otherwise Italy would be attacked. These include an August 2004 threat pointing out that the deadline for withdrawing troops from Iraq had expired and Berlusconi would pay the price, and another threat later that month promising to spare the Vatican but turn Italy into an inferno. However, it is unclear how credible these threats really are given previous claims by the same group which were then discredited. The al-Masri Brigades claimed responsibility for the March 2004 Madrid bombings, the November 2004 Istanbul bombings and the US blackout, although they took no part in any of these incidents.

Ansar al-Islam

Ansar al-Islam (Supporters of Islam), the Kurdish separatist and Islamic fundamentalist group seeking to transform Iraq into an Islamic state has been shown to have a long history of activities in Italy. Ansar al-Islam's founder,[44] Mullah Krekar (Faraj Ahmad Najmuddin), has been active in Italy and court documents have shown that the organisation has recruited members in Italy, and assisted in providing a route for foreign fighters to enter Iraq. On 23 October 2003, the Pentagon declared that Ansar al-Islam had become the principal "terrorist adversary" of US forces in Iraq.

Investigations of Mullah Fouad (Mohammed Majid), the Iraqi Kurd who was Ansar al-Islam's organiser in Italy, have revealed interesting insights into how the organisation operates. Fouad fled from his base in Parma to Syria in 2003 when Italian authorities began closing in. Phone interceptions show how he continued to maintain active contacts with Italian-based counterparts and took over the reception of European volunteers to Syria – through Damascus and the northern city of Aleppo – playing a key role in infiltrating them across the porous border with Iraq. Chise Mohammed, a Somali and an important Al-Qaeda emissary in Europe, referred to Mullah Fouad as "the gatekeeper to Iraq" in bugged conversations he had in Italian police custody with another Islamic radical known as "Merai".[45] In a telephone conversation recorded in March 2003, just after the US-led invasion of Iraq had begun, Fouad ordered one of his men in Milan to send suicide bombers to him, according to transcripts. He asked for "people who could strike the ground and bring up iron" and stressed he was looking for "people who were in Japan", which Stefano Dambruoso, the Milan-based prosecutor interpreted as a reference to kamikazes.[46] In the spring of 2003, investigators say, Fouad met Mahdjoub in Italy to co-ordinate the recruitment programme and to set up a visit by Chise.

These investigations indicate the extent of Ansar al-Islam's recruitment drive and how they used clandestine routes running from Italy to Syria to smuggle operatives into northeastern Iraq for training at Ansar al-Islam camps. There they were allegedly readied for operations in the "Sunni Triangle" north and west of Baghdad, the main battleground between US troops and insurgent forces. Italian authorities believe that a satellite phone used by Abu Musab al-Zarqawi was used by Ansar operatives to contact recruiters in Italy.[47] Italian authorities claim that Ansar operatives frequently met Al-Qaeda representatives in Europe, such as the aforementioned Chise Mohammed, whose main mission was to provide operatives in Europe with funds sent from Arab countries through the UK. Mohammed was arrested in Milan in April 2003 a few days after he flew there from London, where he had fled months earlier to evade Italian investigators. The Italians suspect he financed the terrorist cell behind the November 2002 Mombasa bombings. According to Italian court documents, he allegedly transferred money from the UK to Somalia through Dubai.[48]

Salafi–Jihadists and organised criminal networks

Unlike the well-documented links between the Camorra and secular terrorist organisations such as the Red Brigades in the 1960s and 1970s, there are few links between the Salafi–Jihadi movement in Italy and organised criminal networks. The notable exception is the indication that weapons from the mafia have ended up in the hands of known terrorists. However, as the Mafia is the de facto supplier of small arms and explosives in Italy, these links should be seen more as "links of convenience" than as indications of strategic operational cooperation.

Italian prisons: a ripe breeding ground

The cases of Richard Reid, Jose Padilla and José Emilio Suárez Trashorras[49] have brought attention to the prospect of recruitment and radicalisation in Italian prisons. The Italian police have stated that it is closely monitoring the activities of Islamic fundamentalists, aware of the dangers associated with the radicalisation of their jail population.

The need to counter Muslim radicalisation in prisons is underscored by recent population statistics and incarceration rates. Combined with the well documented studies that indicate the usefulness of prisons as universities for terrorists, this certainly constitutes an alarming prospect for Italian authorities. Official statistics show that foreigners account for 30 per cent of the Italian prison population, far in excess of the foreign component of the general population. Although precise figures are hard to come by, anecdotal evidence strongly suggests that a large percentage of these foreign prisoners are Muslims. For instance, Tracey Wilkinson's study of the inmates in Bollate, the large prison just outside Milan, show that around 30 per cent of the inmates are Muslim. She argues that their burgeoning numbers in prison are a reproach to Italy's efforts to integrate immigrants, and "(...) provide potential recruiting grounds for radical imams and hard-core militants who could use cellblocks to attract followers and spread radical interpretations of Islam".[50] Further, numerous press reports state that there are clear indications that Al-Qaeda is looking for low-level operatives among the often disparate prison population.[51] This needs to be monitored carefully as terrorist networks in other Western countries have shown their sophistication in developing operational methods, and especially in devising ways of recruiting and training those who spearhead their recruitment and radicalisation drive in prisons. Indeed studies have shown that prisons offer ideal conditions for both the initial recruitment and radicalisation of new members and for the further indoctrination and training of existing cadres.

Italian prison authorities have stated their intent to ensure that their institutions are not used to recruit and indoctrinate extremists – and there have been bans against imams from outside the prison – but in reality, enforcing this is difficult as language barriers hinder the authorities from understanding what the imams are preaching. These fears are expressed by Lucia Castellano, the warden at Bollate Prison, who says "they don't speak Italian, we can't understand them, and in Milan that can be quite dangerous".[52]

Worries have also been expressed over the fact that only a small percentage of those arrested for involvement in terrorist activities – a group made up almost entirely of Muslim men – have actually been charged and convicted of "terrorist offences". It is precisely Muslims such as these, men imprisoned then released for lack of evidence or detained on lesser charges, who according to Ian Cuthbertson, are ripe for radicalisation.[53]

Italy's "virtual madrasas": the Salafi–Jihadi exploitation of Internet resources

Similar to other countries, Salafi–Jihadi terrorists in Italy make extensive use of Internet sites and forums as a vehicle for indoctrination, proselytising and the spreading of propaganda. The size and scope of web resources being developed by technically savvy Salafi–Jihadi sympathisers is enormous and there is ample evidence proving that operatives based in Italy are tapping into these resources. Investigations illustrating the habits of Rabei Osman Sayed Ahmed[54] (Mohammed the Egyptian), is a case in point.

According to police reports, Ahmed was "addicted to the Internet". He used it extensively to download files, participate in forum discussions and communicate with other members of his network. He turned his living room into a "virtual madrasa", and invited prospective members such as Yahia Ragheh to his house. The reports show Mohammed downloaded hundreds of audio and video files – of sermons, communiqués, poetry, songs, martyrs' testimonies, Koranic readings and scenes of battle and suicide bombings from Chechnya, Afghanistan, the Israeli-occupied territories, Lebanon, Bosnia, Kashmir and Iraq. This material was then used for recruitment and radicalisation purposes.

Files downloaded include the "complete story" compiled by a Saudi opposition group of the 1996 terrorist attack on the Khobar Towers in Saudi Arabia, to plaintive recitations by children to their fathers imprisoned in places like Guantánamo, Cuba and Pakistan, videos of battles in Chechnya and speeches by Osama bin Laden.[55] One audio file attacked Jews and Christians and all who collaborate with them, another invited followers to wage holy war against infidels who follow the "laws of the devil". A young girl on one audio file asked if she could have a kamikaze belt so that she could "blow up" her body; a man on another declared, "one day's resistance for the holy war is worth 1,000 years of life". Among the "poems for jihadists" was one that repeated over and over, "I am a terrorist; I am a terrorist", a song proudly proclaimed "(...) we are terrorists, we want to make it known to the world, from West to East that we are terrorists, because terrorism, as a verse of the Koran says, is a thing approved by God".[56]

Sites that Ahmed visited were filled not only with calls for the destruction of Israel but also raw anti-Semitism. In one question-and-answer session with a Saudi sheik who is asked if suicide operations against Jews are allowed under Islamic law, the sheik responds that Jews are "vile and despicable beings, full of defects and wickedness". God, he added, "has ordered us to wage war against them".[57]

Ahmed also created a vast library, wrote posts on Jihadi forums, downloaded and uploaded files, watched movies, engaged in debates and constantly educated himself and radicalised others. Ahmed also installed and demonstrated a computer program that allowed the simultaneous setting of alarms on multiple cell phones, by using a system which masked the country of origin of the caller.[58]

He erased potentially incriminating files, which were later recovered by Italian police, including photographs and precise diagrams of explosive suitcases that could be triggered by a cell phone and vests modified for suicide attacks.

The police report also shows how Ahmed said he would use his computer to create an appropriate martyr's portrait of Ragheh, who he was recruiting for a suicide operation. I will create a portrait "with the light behind you, with your angelic face (...) I will put a green background behind you and the moon above you."[59] He promised to send the image by email to Ragheh's family and to other young martyrs. There would also be a martyrs' video that would be taped the night before the attack.

Ahmed used many difference personas across Europe and he was a focal point in recruiting for the ever-expanding Salafi–Jihadi cell networks across the continent. His extensive use of computer skills was a key element in the co-ordination of the activities of various units throughout Europe and the recruitment operations he organised can be seen to have a longer-term objective than simply providing cannon fodder for the Iraqi insurgency.

Salafi–Jihadi documents found in Italy

Versions of the military manual, from "Military Studies in the Jihad Against Tyrants" and "Muslim Rebels Stationed in America" along with strategic Salafi–Jihadi documents from prominent thinkers such as Al-Suri and Naji, have been spread throughout Italy, on CD-ROMs, videos and audio-cassettes. This material downloaded from the Internet or brought into Italy through couriers reveals information about the Salafi–Jihadi "playbook"; how they are to operate, structure their organisation, conceal their activities, avoid surveillance and detection and resist interrogation in the event of capture.

Raids on Abu Omar's (Nasr Osama Mostafa Hassan) house in Milan[60] revealed a treasure trove of bomb-making manuals, radical Islamic propaganda[61] and proselytising material that lay out the justification for jihad, encouraged Muslims to seek out combat groups that were "actively fighting", and to provide support and encouragement to "brothers" who are unjustly held in Italian prisons.[62] Amongst these documents was *Military Jihad* with three main subsections: *Mujahadeen Preparation, The Jihad – individuals and finance,* and *The creation of the Jihadist Fabric.* The document includes sections that urged operatives to "study all aspects of the foreign territory where you reside; learn how to hide and be discreet, be disciplined and obedient; learn everything about your enemy, its customs and culture, what it fears and how it operates, for *this will become the battlefront of the future*".[63] It encourages the mujahideen to spread terror and, more specifically, to "train the Islamic army and dispatch suicide bombers to fight the near and far enemy wherever he may be".[64]

Another noteworthy document that was found was *Jihad in the name of Allah – Introduction and definition* that included long virulent passages written by Ibn Taymiyya.[65] The twelfth-century Muslim scholar is traditionally one of the main textual sources read by Salafi–Jihadi terrorists because they find in his writings a response to what they see as closer parallels to the modern political situation in Muslim countries. Further, Ibn Taymiyya's writing,[66] unlike many of the theological works favoured by the mainstream, encourage direct action.

Arms, explosives and bomb-making material

Small arms, explosives and bomb-making material[67] is relatively easy and cheap to acquire in Italy. The "going price for a kilo of plastic explosives is about USD 1,500, whereas civil-use explosives cost USD 1,000 per kilo and a machine gun can be bought for just a few hundred dollars".[68] In 2005, SISMI (the Italian Military Security and Information Service) uncovered weapons and C4 explosives which were being smuggled from the Balkans into Italy to be used to attack the funeral of Pope John Paul II.[69] In another instance, a Tunisian detainee who agreed to cooperate with Italian authorities spoke of a cell, active from 2000 to 2001, that had looked into ways of fabricating bombs from substances freely available on the market: the ingredients, and formula were the same as those used in the London bombings.[70]

Italy's counter-terrorism tools

Italy has a long history of combating domestic terrorism and organised crime that will be of great benefit as it seeks to counter the new threat posed by

Salafi–Jihadi terrorism. It is working hard to counter terrorism within its borders, cooperate bilaterally and internationally and is participating in "coalition activities". Its law enforcement authorities maintain an initiative against locally based terrorist networks through investigations, detentions, prosecutions and deportations. It has sought to empower its police forces and prosecutors by adapting more effective anti-terrorism laws and is also amassing considerable intelligence on recruitment operations through the use of surveillance and innovative technology tools. Large-scale pre-emptive raids, a tougher stance against radical mosques and imams, as well as improved bilateral and international cooperation are other elements of Italy's counter-terrorism toolbox.

In addition to operational measures in specific sectors, increasing recognition is being given to the importance of wide-ranging prevention based on the "softer" approach – in particular increasing dialogue between cultures and religions in order to promote reciprocal knowledge and understanding and thereby also denying space for Salafi–Jihadi propaganda and the recruitment of terrorists.

The Italian government has however come under criticism from both national and international Human Rights groups who have labelled the Italian Authorities' methods as draconian and undemocratic. Further, there are also accusations that the Italian regime has taken a short-term approach, clamping down in a heavy-handed way, arresting thousands of suspects, but failing to address the underlying causes of discontent. Clearly, the Italian government faces a difficult balancing act in order to maintain security without infringing too heavily on civil liberties.

Technology

Much of the intelligence about Salafi–Jihadi recruiting and dispatching operations has been assembled from lengthy surveillance operations which Italian authorities have been particularly adept at. Taps on mobiles and satellite phones, GSM tracking of suspect individuals and voice recognition to identify suspects, as well as strategically placed cameras remain key counter-terrorism tools available to the Italian authorities. This continues to be a cornerstone of the Italian security, Interior Minister Pisanu recently saying that "we will continue to prioritise action to monitor the length and breadth of the country, without ever underestimating reasonably reliable reports of specific threats", he also called for developing sophisticated technology to combat terror on Italian soil by stating "(...) there is no doubt that, to achieve maximum efficiency, we need the support of the best technological applications".[71] However, these methods have not been uncontroversial and there have been calls from civil liberties groups who claim that the widespread use of these technologies is transforming Italy into a police state.

Pre-emptive raids

Italy has also continued to launch massive pre-emptive raids. For instance in July 2005 a two-day anti-terrorism campaign in and around Milan led to the arrest of 142 people, including 84 non-EU citizens, and the seizure of explosives. Scores of similar raids were carried out throughout the country after the Madrid and London bombings and particularly in the build up to the Turin Winter Olympics and the 2006 General Elections.

Reforming the Mosque environment: a dual-pronged approach

Italy is enforcing a tougher stance against mosques and imams stating, "either mosques respect the law or they close ... We will not permit Italian mosques to transform into centres of occult finance and of recruitment for Islamist combatants."[72] This was clearly illustrated in the more aggressive approach towards Abu Omar, the ex-imam of via Quaranta, which is emblematic of the increasing effort to monitor and restrict imams. In July 2005, courts convicted Moroccan Mohamed Rafik, a former Florence imam, of belonging to an extremist cell alleged to have planned terrorist attacks in Italy.[73] He was convicted and received a prison term of four years.[74]

Similarly, Sheikh Abdul Qader Fadlallah Mamour was controversially deported from Italy in November 2003 to his native Senegal for security concerns and his vocal support of Osama bin Laden. In an interview in *As-Sharq Al-Awsat*, a London Arabic daily, an infuriated Mamour claimed he commands a formidable army and would seek revenge, promising new terrorist attacks against European targets.[75] Likewise, the Carmagnola-based Abdoul Mamour and Bouiriqi Bouchta, the imam of Turin were deported to their native countries. In total, 12 imams have been deported from Italy since 9/11.

Others such as the Moroccan Mohamed Rafik, who preached in Cremona, Sorgane and Florence, was jailed in 2003 in Italy for raising funds for "attacks in Chechnya and inciting violence". The same fate befell Rachid Maamri, from Florence's Sorgane Mosque, Majid Zergout the immam in Varese, Milan-based Anwar Shaaban El Sayed, Cremona-based Najib Rouass, who were all tried and found guilty in Italy. Others such as Mouard Trabelsi, who is not an imam but frequently held sermons in the mosque in Cremon, have also been put to trial. Interestingly it appears as if most, if not all, of these imams and preachers maintained close ties with each other and were, according to authorities, part of a loose network that sought to raise funds, recruit individuals and spread a radical Salafi ideology.

The Italian government, determined to fight the radicalisation of their burgeoning Muslim populations, is also starting to explore the possibility of training local imams in order to ensure and encourage moderate Islamic teachings. Following similar initiatives in Holland, Britain and Spain, the Italian government announced[76] its intention to finance the creation of an institute that will train and accredit imams. The expectation is that this should help in the determined fight against radicalisation throughout these centres and will also help indirectly control what is preached inside mosques. In addition, Italy is playing a leading role[77] in setting up a European and Western partnership with moderate Islam, both in the countries of origin and in the Muslim communities residing in Italy.

Efforts have also been made to reach out to mosques and religious centres to encourage liaising with the local police and cooperation in dealing with any criminal activity including terrorist threats. It remains to be seen how successful this initiative will be.

Anti-terrorism drills

In order to test and fine-tune its terrorism response, Italy recently undertook several anti-terrorism drills, involving the staging of multiple, simulated attacks in several cities including Rome, Turin, Milan and Naples. The drills – which included the involvement of several thousand people – included simultaneous fake train blasts, simulated attacks on an airport bus, attacks against a tourist attraction and hostage-taking. They were seen as an important exercise in gauging the preparedness and response of emergency services.

Document security

Improved document security is another prominent counter-terrorism tool which is being pursued in Italy. In order to guarantee adequate protection against the possible forging of passports and other travel documents, Italy has sought to promote the insertion of biometric data into such documents. The EU is also preparing to apply new technologies to travel documents so as to establish a reliable link between the citizen and the document. Agreements on joint approaches and standards in this area of considerable operational importance are being discussed within the ICAO (International Civil Aviation Organization). Proposals have also been put forward to promote Italy's system of checking IDs online and thus create a partnership with the public who can check these to detect and report stolen or lost documents.

Data retention

After the London bombings, new anti-terror laws were passed that oblige Internet cafes and public telephone shops with at least three terminals to seek a licence permit. They are now forced to store traffic data for at least six months. WIFI hotspots and locations that do not store traffic data have to secure ID information from users before allowing them to log on. For example, users may be required to enter a number from an ID card or driving licence. Software also needs to be installed that saves a list of all sites visited by clients, and Internet cafe operators should periodically turn this list into their local police headquarters. Although these security measures were rigorously enforced immediately after the laws were passed, this is no longer always the case.

Persons who want to activate a new mobile phone account must identify themselves before service activation, or before a "SIM card" may be obtained, and resellers of mobile subscriptions or pre-paid cards must verify the identity of purchasers and retain a photocopy of identity cards. These new provisions also extend to telephony data including location data, on fixed line and mobile telephony which must be retained for 29 months. There is no requirement to store the content of calls but telephone operators must retain a record of all unsuccessful dial attempts. These measures have been hailed as effective counter-terrorism tools, but there appear to be indications here too that persons of ill intent can circumvent these measures by, for instance, purchasing stolen SIM cards through black markets.

Deportations

A prevalent trend in Italy in recent years has been the use of deportations. In 2006, Italian officials detained several Moroccans allegedly belonging to the Salafist Group for Preaching and Combat cell, which was allegedly plotting to attack targets in northern Italy. The suspects were deported to Morocco rather than tried in Italy. In another case, Italian authorities claim they foiled attacks against the Milan subway system and Bologna's Basilica of San Petronio, home of a 1415 fresco by Giovanni da Modena that depicts the Prophet Mohammed being tormented in hell, by deporting seven people linked to the ALF and GSPC. The suspects, who were returned to Morocco and Tunisia without a trial following a six-month investigation, purportedly planned the Milan attack for around the time of 9 April 2006, Italian parliamentary elections.

The reason for this trend stems largely from the fact that the Italian legal process could have taken years and even ended up in acquittals – illustrated by a 2005 case, where Iraqi-bound operatives were released as the judge ruled that they were "guerrilla fighters" rather than terrorists. Deportations without trials have also been the preferred strategy to avoid increasing the militant populations in Italian jails. Italian authorities also argue that this reduces the risk of militants taking hostages or committing attacks to secure their comrades' release.[78]

Much to the dismay of Human Rights groups, the Italian Government coordinates expulsions with, for instance, the Moroccan and Tunisian governments, which take a hard-line stance against militants and have less stringent requirements for the burden of proof. This practically ensures that the suspects will be detained without trials in those countries as soon as they arrive.[79] The government has been criticised for its willingness to collaborate and unquestioningly deport (and sometimes back) regimes that commit gross human rights abuses.

International cooperation and legislative instruments

Italy responded promptly to the terrorist threat emerging after 9/11, in keeping with the resolutions and regulatory instruments adopted by the United Nations[80] the EU,[81] NATO[82] and the G8 Action Plan: SAFTI – Secure and Facilitated International Travel Initiative.[83] Urgent measures were adopted, through Law No. 438/2001, for the prevention and prosecution of crimes committed for the purposes of international terrorism, along with the introduction of a new category of criminal collusion for the purposes of international terrorism (art. 270

bis of the Penal Code).[84] Legislation was also passed to prevent terrorist organisations from using the Italian financial system by coordination of Italy's efforts to halt the financing of terrorism by authorising the freezing of assets[85] of individuals or organisations associated with terrorist organisations.

In the aftermath of the 7 July 2005 attacks on London's public transport system, Act 155 was passed into law on the 31 July 2005. The counter-terrorism Act has both an incentive and a punitive side. The introduction of the granting of residence permits for investigative purposes to aliens who turn prosecution's evidence in judicial or police probes into international terrorism aims to break the hold of communities often distrustful of the state authorities. The limit for police detention has been extended from 12 to 24 hours, and taking hair or saliva samples with a view to tracing the suspect's DNA is now permitted. Legislation allowing "investigative interviews" conducted without the defence lawyer present is already in force against the Mafia, and Act 155 extended this to terrorist suspects.[86]

The Act also provides extra investigative powers, allowing the intelligence services to conduct wiretaps, hitherto the exclusive responsibility of the crime police, although a magistrate must authorise the wiretaps. It also requires Internet point operators to demand identification of all customers and to be licensed by the provincial police chief.

Bilateral cooperation

Another cornerstone in the Italian counter-terrorism effort has been the strengthening of bilateral cooperation. This has yielded positive results and, for instance, the improved cooperation with Lebanese and Syrian security services helped to thwart the 21 September 2004 attacks on the Italian embassy in Beirut when 300 kg of explosives were discovered. The incident illustrated the potential for Italian "soft targets" – embassies, aircraft, businesses – to be attacked by Islamist extremists and showed the importance of bilateral cooperation in thwarting attacks.

Conclusion: assessing Italian counter-terrorism tools and plotting the challenge ahead

The Italian Government realised that there is a great need for sharing as much information as national security will allow and this has led to several success stories of collaboration and teamwork between national police and intelligence institutions, as well as with supra-national agencies, such as Interpol, Europol and the United Nations. For instance, Italian authorities have sought to improve cooperation with European governments such as Germany (in retracing communications of the Hamburg cell in the build up to 9/11), Norway (where cooperation in the Mullah Krekkar case is illustrative), Spain (in cooperating to arrest "Mohammed the Egyptian") and the United Kingdom (with the extradition of Hussain Osman – Hamdi Issac – where the two governments collaborated in tracking the failed London bomber out of the UK, through France and into Italy, where he was eventually arrested in Rome and deported back to London).

Whilst this increased cooperation between national police and intelligence agencies must surely be seen as a positive development, other measures are more controversial. The way that the Italian Government has dealt with deportations of suspected terrorists is one such example. For instance, since the 9/11 attacks, the Italian government has gone along with the American viewpoint that the terrorist threat to countries in this new millennium has "changed the rules of the game". Further, the Berlusconi Government followed up this rhetoric with concrete plans to deal with the threat of terrorism within Italy's own borders and has empowered the police and security services to carry out pre-emptive raids and use monitoring technology with fewer pre-requisites and restrictions.

A clear example of this redesigning of the "rules of the game" can be seen in plans to make it easier for Government to bypass the courts in deporting imams and terrorist suspects to countries in the MENA region. Not to be deterred by objections that this would be contrary to international Human Rights Law, and in particular the 1996 Chahal case where the European Court of Human Rights prevented deportation to a country where there was a risk of death or torture, there have been suggestions that the Italian Government, similar to what is occurring in the United Kingdom, should review the jurisprudence regarding the European Human Rights Convention in the light of this new, twenty-first-century threat from terrorism.

How successful measures such as these will be remains to be seen. The twenty-first-century terrorist is a different animal to similar threats seen in the past, from for example the Red Brigades. The scale of the 9/11 attacks was unforeseen and a shock to the world, and the possibility of Salafi–Jihadi terrorists committing devastating attacks on Italian soil should not be underestimated, and thus there is certainly a case for adopting a different approach to immigration, asylum and individual liberties of citizens. In the jurisprudence of most nations, and in international law, there is, and always has been, scope for derogating from certain commitments of the state in the interests of national security. However, this is a very fine line for the government to tread.

Muslim communities form a large and growing block of the population in Italy and there is an increasing sense of discrimination and victimisation among these communities, most of whom have never fully assimilated to their new country. It is important for the government to recognise that there comes a certain point whereby its actions in coming down tough on terrorist suspects are adding fuel to the fire. Although the link has not been formally established, it is conceivable that this could at least play a part in the future radicalisation and recruitment process of Salafi–Jihadi terrorism in Italy. For every ten terrorist suspects taken out of the country, 20 formerly moderate Muslims may be pushed towards the extremists in dismay and anger over what they may see as a targeted attack on their own. A heavy-handed approach which is perceived as unjust may alienate individuals who may become reluctant to collaborate with authorities and may even harbour extremists in their midst, protecting them because to expose them is to give the faith and community a bad name. Further, there is an argument to say that deportations are inherently illogical. If such suspects are likely terrorists, then deporting them to far away countries is not likely to deter them from plotting attacks, and possibly carrying them out themselves given the porous borders of today's world. On the other hand, if suspicions were wrong, and the deportees were not likely to become terrorists, then deporting them against their will is surely only likely to build up hatred for Italy within them and push them into the hands of the extremists.

These and ongoing efforts represent a response that aims to cut off the spreading of a cause from within, without necessarily addressing the causes themselves. To address the issues such as the cooperation in Iraq or what the terrorists see as Western decadence would be to give credence to some fundamental parts of their ideology, which the Italian government rightly does not consider an option. The only response that immediately eradicated the cause for the attack happened in Spain straight after the Madrid bombings and that was carried out by the electorate, not by the government. So while the Italian Government continues to try to make it harder for Salafi–Jihadi terrorist ideology to spread from within, it will continue to face an uphill battle so long as it is perceived to be providing a just cause for violence.

These are early days, and the Italian government is still trying to fine-tune its way towards that thin line between national security and individual freedom. There are many parts of the machine that need to be adjusted – foreign policy, intelligence services, immigration policy, etc. – to provide a coherent and appropriate response to this new twenty-first-century threat from Salafi–Jihadi terrorism. Whilst it is surely too early to judge how effective the Italian governments' counter-terrorism tools in this area will be, the threat – evidently – is real and time is short.

Notes

1 Just above 1 per cent of the total population and about 36 per cent of the total immigrant community.
2 The network on comparative research on Islam & Muslims in Europe, at http://euro-islam.info/pages/italy.html.
3 This is of course not unique to Italy. Saudi Arabia has supported and contributed to the establishment of hundreds of mosques and Islamic centres throughout Europe. The overall cost of King Fahd's efforts in this field has been astronomical, amounting to many billions of Saudi Riyals. In terms of Islamic institutions, the result is some 210 Islamic centres wholly or partly financed by Saudi Arabia, more than 1,500 mosques and 202 colleges and almost 2,000 schools for educating Muslim children in non-Islamic countries in Europe, North and South America, Australia and Asia. See: http://memri.org/bin/articles.cgi?Page=archives&Area=sd&ID=SP36002.
4 This is not to say that Wahhabism leads to radical Salafism although many point to the fact that Saudi-funded madrasas in Pakistan gave rise to the radicalism of the Taliban in Afghanistan. It is only a minority among their ranks who have embraced violence as a means of winning their way, the so-called "revolutionary" Salafists, of whom al-Qaeda and other terrorist groups are made up. For an illuminating discussion on Wahhabism and Salfism, see Maha Azzam, "Al-Qaeda: the misunderstood Wahhabi connection and the ideology of violence" The Royal Institute of Interna-

tional Affairs, Middle East Programme, Briefing Paper No. 1. February 2003. Available at: www.riia.org/pdf/briefing_papers/Azzaml.pdf.
5 Guido Olimpo, "Italy and Islamic Militancy: From Logistics base to Potential Target", *Terrorism Monitor*, Volume III, Issue 18, 22 September 2005, p. 4.
6 Equal social status without distinction as to sex, race, language, religion, political opinions, and personal or social conditions for all citizens. Italian laws also ban the dissemination of ideas of racial superiority or ideas that are based on hatred on the basis of race or ethnic origin and instigation to discriminatory or violent acts on the basis of race, ethnicity, nationality and religion (Decree No. 205/1993, Art.1).
7 The network on comparative research on Islam & Muslims in Europe, at http://euro-islam.info/pages/italy.html.
8 Ibid.
9 Oriana Fallaci, *La Rabbia E L'Orgoglio*, Distribooks, Rome, February 2002.
10 www.euro-islam.info/pages/italy.html.
11 Italian immigration is mostly governed by the 2002 Bossi-Fini law. This law tightly controls entry and stay of immigrants. Italy also accepts a very small number of refugees due to the vague laws, inefficient administration and the low likelihood of acceptance (International Helsinki Federation for Human Rights – IHF, 2005). An additional law in 2003 increased penalties for illegal immigration, created more temporary detention centres and limited family reunification.
12 Gordon Corera, "Marginalised Muslims cause concern: A year on from the Madrid bombings, fears are growing that the ideological struggle to stop the next generation of militants in Europe is being lost", 11 March 2005, BBC. At: http://news.bbc.co.uk/2/hi/europe/4340315.stm.
13 Quintan Wiktorowicz, *Radical Islam Rising: Muslim Extremism in the West*, (Rowman & Littlefield, Oxford, 2005).
14 Ibid., p. 5.
15 Ibid., p. 6.
16 Ibid., p. 85.
17 For an excellent overview of radical Islamic terrorism in France see Clara Beyler's "The Jihadist Threat in France", in Hillel Fradkin, Husain Haqqani, Eric Brown (eds.) *Current Trends in Islamic Ideology*, Volume III, (Hudson Institute, 2006). Available at: www.hudson.org/files/publications/TRENDS3.pdf.
18 For an interesting documentary on the rise of radical Islamic militancy in Italy and Europe see the joint CBC/Radio Canada production "The fifth estate: War Without Borders" First broadcast on the fifth estate 1 December 2004.
19 The same cell that tried to carry out the Strasbourg bombing in December 2000
20 See Marc Sageman's groundbreaking work, *Understanding Terror Networks*, (University of Pennsylvania Press, Philadelphia, 2004).
21 There have not been any reported instances of homegrown Salafi–Jihadi terrorist groups.
22 Petter Nasser, "Profiles of Jihadist Terrorists in Europe", in Cheryl Benards *A Future for the Young: Options for helping Middle Eastern Youth Escape the Trap of Radicalization*, September 2005, RAND's Initiative on Middle Eastern Youth.
23 Michael Taarnby, "Recruitment of Islamist Terrorist in Europe: Trends and Perspectives" Research Report funded by the Danish Ministry of Justice, 14 May 2005. Available at: www.jm.dk/image.asp?page=image&objno=73027.
24 This has been supported by studies of the GSPC, which have shown that cell members appear to be almost exclusively first-generation Algerian immigrants who immigrated to Italy for the specific purpose of setting up cells in support of the ongoing Islamist insurgency in Algeria.
25 This has been recognised and encouraged by Osama bin Laden in his speeches as an especially potent weapon and wiretaps have indicated that operatives in Italy have also sought out such individuals.

26 Procura della Repubblica presso il Tribunale ordinario di Milano. Procedimento penale N. 5236/02.21.
27 Guido Olimpio, op. cit., p. 5.
28 Ibid., p. 5.
29 Ibid., p. 5.
30 For instance, Zouaoi Chokri, who was arrested for drug dealing was later found to have been associated with the terrorist network revolving around the Milan mosque in Viale Jenner. Information gleaned from his interrogations was later used to build a case against Abu Omar, Mullah Fouad and Mullah Krekar.
31 Lorenzo Vidino, Testimony Before the House Committee on International Relations Subcommittee on Europe and Emerging Threats: "Islamic Extremism in Europe" 27 April 2005.
32 These stolen blank passports or otherwise forged documents, including national ID cards, present a large problem as the sheer quantity makes it difficult to forward all details to the appropriate units in a timely fashion. A number of passports, either Italian or North African (Moroccan in particular) that are believed to have been forged in Italy, have surfaced during raids and arrests across Europe and the Middle East.
33 D.I.G.O.S. Milano, *Procedimento Penale n.5236/02 r.g.n.r. mod. 21.* p. 42. Investigations into Adineh Travel Agency.
34 Guido Olimpio, op. cit., p. 5.
35 Hizb-ut-Tahrir, although considered as non-violent, "aims to achieve the unification of Muslims worldwide under a single caliphate and believes that Western democracy is unacceptable to Muslims. Countries such as the United States, the United Kingdom and Israel are considered to be the work of the devil."
36 Kathryn Haahr-Escolano, "GSPC in Italy The Forward Base of Jihad in Europe", Jamestown Foundation, *Terrorism Monitor*, Volume 4, Issue 3, 9 February, 2006.
37 SISMI (the Italian military intelligence service) have identified and monitored GSPC members in Salerno, Brescia, Napoli, Milan and Venice.
38 *La Repubblica*, 17 November 2005 and *La Repubblica*, 23 December 2005.
39 Kathryn Haahr-Escolano, op. cit.
40 Ibid.
41 Ibid.
42 *Corriere della Sera*, 15 July 2005.
43 US Department of the Treasury, *Treasury Designates Three Individuals Linked to Al-Qaida Terror Cell in Italy*, 1 August 2005, Press release JS-2668.
44 Reportedly founded in December 2001, with funding and logistical support from al-Qaeda and Osama bin Laden. The group continues to target secular Iraqi Kurds – particularly members of the Patriotic Union of Kurdistan (PUK) – and, since the war in Iraq, US officials have accused Ansar al-Islam of training and deploying suicide bombers against US-led coalition troops in Iraq. Ansar was officially designated a Foreign Terrorist Organization (FTO) by the US Department of State on 22 March 2004. Human Rights Watch has accused Ansar of kidnapping and torture. Ansar al Islam is currently led by Abu Abdallah al-Shafii (aka Warba Holiri al-Kurdi) who reportedly took over leadership of Ansar from Mullah Krekar, who, as of August 2004 has been in exile in Norway. The organisation's name may have changed to Ansar al-Sunna (Supporters of Sunni) to broaden its appeal beyond its Kurdish origins (although this has not been confirmed). See the Council on Foreign Relations for more information on Ansar Al Islam, available at: www.cfr.org/publication/9237/ansar_alislam_iraq_islamistskurdish_separatists_.html#1.
45 *Jane's Sentinel Security Assessments, Italy.*
46 See Chapter 1, I "ragazzi dal Giappone", in Stefano Dambruoso, *Milano-Bagdad: Diario di un magistrate in prima linea nella lotta al terrorism islamico in Italia*, (Mondadori, Milan, 2004).

47 Ed Blanche, "Ansar al-Islam bolsters European network", *Jane's Intelligence Review*, Vol. 16, No. 10, 2004, pp. 18–21.
48 Ibid.
49 A principal conspirator in the Madrid bombings, José Emilio Suárez Trashorras, a Spanish mineworker, was not religious or politically aware when he was jailed in 2001 for a drug offence. Incarcerated in the same prison was Jamal Ahmidan, a young Moroccan living in Spain, also convicted of a petty crime. Once in prison, however, both the nominally Christian Trashorras and the non-observant Muslim Ahmidan enthusiastically embraced radical Islamic fundamentalist beliefs and were recruited into an al-Qaeda-linked Moroccan terrorist group, Takfir wa al-Hijra. See Ian M. Cuthbertson, "Prisons and the Education of Terrorists", *World Policy Journal*, Volume XXI, No 3, Fall 2004.
50 Tracy Wilkinson, "In a Prison's Halls, the Call to Islam", *Los Angeles Times*, 4 October 2005.
51 See for instance, Frances Kennedy "Analysis: Italy's terror connection", BBC, 25 February, 2002, at: http://news.bbc.co.uk/2/hi/europe/1840921.stm.
52 Tracy Wilkinson, op. cit.
53 Ian M. Cuthbertson, "Prisons and the Education of Terrorists", *World Policy Journal*, Volume XXI, No 3, Fall 2004.
54 Ahmed, a key figure in the European Salafi–Jihadi network, is a former Egyptian army explosives expert, who allegedly taught courses at Al-Qaeda training camps in Afghanistan. Spanish authorities identified him as one of the masterminds behind the 11 March train bombings in Madrid. Between 2001 and his arrest in 2004, investigators say that Ahmed recruited young Muslims for suicide bombings in Iraq and elsewhere. He was able to move around between Italy, Germany, France and Spain, and possibly other countries as well, without serious hindrance, exploiting gaps in the security defences because of rivalries and bureaucratic barriers between Europe's intelligence and law enforcement agencies and was only arrested when he resurfaced in Milan in June 2004.
55 *New York Times*, 18 November 2005.
56 Ibid.
57 Ibid.
58 Ibid. Then sent by email. Ahmed used a fictitious e-mail address in which he listed the month and the day of the Madrid attacks as his birthday.
59 Ibid.
60 Raids carried out on 14 June 2004 in via Conte Verde n. 18 in Milan outlined in Procura della Repubblica presso il Tribunale ordinario di Milano. Procedimento penale N. 5236/02.21, p. 80.
61 Ibid, p. 80. Note that although all efforts have been taken to translate the documents precisely, quotes may contain errors as the documents have been translated first from Arabic to Italian by the Milan prosecutors' office and then to English by the author.
62 I documenti sequestrati nell'abitazione e nel computer di ABU OMAR, Ordinanza di Applicazione Della Misura Della Custodia Cautelare in Carcere, Tribunale Ordinario di Milano, Ufficio del Giudice per le indagini preliminari, N.5236/02 R.G.N.R, N.1511/02 R.G.GIP. p. 88. Translated by Author.
63 Ibid., pp. 80–82. Emphasis added by author.
64 Procura della Repubblica presso il Tribunale ordinario di Milano. Procedimento penale N. 5236/02.21 Op. cit. pp. 86–87.
65 Ordinanza di Applicazione Della Misura Della Custodia Cautelare in Carcere, Tribunale Ordinario di Milano. op. cit. pp. 81–82.
66 Maha Azzam, op. cit.
67 For instance, ammonium nitrate, the common fertiliser ingredient is much easier to acquire in Italy than in other countries such as the UK or the United States, where there has been a deliberate effort to monitor the sale of these substances.

68 Corriere della Sera, 12/07/2005, quoted in Guido Olimpio, op. cit., p. 5.
69 Federico Bordonaro, "Italian Security and Potential Terrorist Targets", *Terrorism Monitor*, Volume III, Issue 18, 22 September 2005, p. 10. See also SISMI report at: http://cca.analisidifesa.it/servlets/registration?COMMAND=login&lang_code=it&nextPage=http%3A%2F%2Fcca.analisidifesa.it%2Fit%2Fmagazine_8034243544%2Fnumero4%2Farticle_462748525367458880732502148243_4507362016_0.jsp.
70 In the attacks they were to be packed in trucks specially reinforced to carry large quantities of explosives, rucksacks left in station luggage deposits and a police car that was to be stolen, filled with explosives and launched against the Cathedral in Milan. The possible targets considered were the US Embassy in Rome, American Consulates, an international school in Milan and the Police Headquarters. Federico Bordonaro, op. cit, p. 10.
71 Sofia Celeste, *The Christian Science Monitor*, 4 October 2005.
72 "Les mosquees ne respectant pas la loi seront fermees (ministre.)", *Agence France Press*, September 2003, as quoted in Robert S. Leiken, "Bearers of Global Jihad? Immigration and National Security after 9/11", the Nixon Centre, 2004.
73 Convicted along with Tunisian Kamel Hamraoui for plotting to perpetrate terrorist acts against Milan's subway and Cremona's cathedral.
74 Moroccan authorities have asked Italy for his extradition but Italy's highest court rejected the request.
75 For an English summary of the original As-Sharq Al-Awsat article published on 28 January 2004, see the SITE Institute: http://siteinstitute.org/bin/articles.cgi?ID=publications2704&Category=publications&Subcategory=0.
76 See: www.ansamed.info/ansamed/notizie/newshp/ultime/2005–05–16_326806.html.
77 A meeting of the Mediterranean Observatory was held in Rome in October 2004 on the theme "Islam and Peace", aimed at encouraging dialogue and denouncing violence, which saw the participation of the foremost Islamic institutional organisations.
78 Although this gets the suspects out of the country, it sometimes puts them back into circulation in other areas. If the process is properly carried out, however, the accused militants can be tailed or interrogated by authorities in their home countries. For more on this particular process see Stratfor, "The Moroccan-European Militant Connection", 10 May 2006.
79 Stratfor, "Italy's Attraction for Islamist Militants" 4 April 2006.
80 Italy has ratified all 12 international Conventions against terrorism and supports the actions of the Counter Terrorism Committee as well as the Sanctions Committee against Al-Qaeda and the Taliban. Italy has also presented seven proposals for a total of 79 individuals and 14 organisations listed by the Committees. Italy is in second place, after the US, in terms of the number of proposals for additions to the list.
81 Italy actively contributes to the realisation of the Plan of Action against terrorism adopted by the European Council on 28 September 2001 which contains a wide range of measures to be adopted in various sectors in the fight against terrorism including: judicial and police cooperation, transport safety, border controls and document security, blocking financing, political dialogue and external relations and defence against CBRN (Chemical, Biological, Radiological and Nuclear) attacks. Italy has also been a staunch supported of the EU Commission's "Declaration on solidarity against terrorism", which establishes the obligation to assist, "with all the instruments available, including military resources", any Member State struck by a terrorist attack. Italy is also one of the countries that has most insistently pressed the European Parliament to amend its Directive on Protection of Telecommunications Data and Information.
82 Italy is taking part in the naval mission "Active Endeavour" whose objective is to combat terrorism in the Mediterranean. In addition, NATO approved a Declaration on terrorism at the ministerial-level informal Atlantic Council on 2 April 2004. The Declaration reaffirms the principles of cooperation and solidarity between member states and refers to the guidelines established by the UN for collaboration in opposing inter-

Salafi–Jihadi terrorism in Italy 255

national terrorism. Italy is involved in NATO's activities related to the development of cooperation for civil protection and defence in the case of CBRN attacks.
83 The Plan principally concerns air traffic and consists of a short Declaration and a more detailed Action Plan covering a wide series of measures intended to heighten aircraft safety standards, improve airport control procedures and facilitate exchanges of information. One section of the Plan concerns the safety of maritime transport and infrastructures.
84 For more information see www.esteri.it/eng/4_28_63_60.asp.
85 The value of the financial assets frozen by the Italian administrative authorities amounted, as of December 2004, to approximately 500,000 euro; in addition, assets and property worth approximately 4 million euro were seized at the request of the judicial authorities. See: www.esteri.it/eng/4_28_63_60.asp.
86 *Jane's*, op. cit.

Index

9/11 attacks 1, 22, 148–9, 179, 219
11 M attacks *see* Madrid bombings (2004)

Abdallah, Abu 100
Abdel Bary, Adel 148
Abdellah, Samir Ben 218
Abderahman, Abu Yahya 119
Abdurrahman, Kyai Haji 12
Abedin, Moinul 148
Abu Hafs al-Masri Brigades 239
Abu Nidal Organization 191
Ackcha, Rachid Oulad 218
Action Direct 191
activism 16, 88, 108
Advice and Reformation Committee 148
Afghan veterans 33, 152, 153, 171
Afghanistan 22, 29, 34, 89, 150, 152, 186, 205; insurgency 29; Soviet Union and 28, 42, 150, 152, 213
agency 74, 75
Ahmed, Hamed Abderrahaman 227
Ahmed, Rabei Osman al-Sayed ("Mohammed the Egyptian") 235, 241–2, 248, 253n54
Ahmidan, Hamid 217
Ahmidan, Jamal ('the Chinese') 217, 218
aid 33, 40
Al-Andalus 24–5, 26
al-Faisal, Abdallah 108
al-Faraj, Mohammed 27
al-Fathni, Nouredine 172
al-Feisal, Sheikh 156
al-Fizazi, Mohammad 97
al-Ghuraaba 117, 118, 128, 129–31
Al Haramain Islamic Foundation 36
al-Hariri (Cheik Abdallah) 97
al-Issar, Redouan 172
Al-Jazeera 77, 225
al-Muhajiroun 117, 128
al-Mujahir, Abdullah *see* Padilla, Jose

Al-Qaeda 11, 22, 23, 27, 33, 55, 68–86, 89, 90, 95, 97, 100, 123–4, 151, 204; African US embassy attacks 29, 148; funding 36, 42; ideology 1, 8, 71–3, 82–3; Italian cells 237, 238, 241; and London bombings 102, 138; and Pakistan 41, 42, 43; participation 73–4, 77–81; recruitment 81–2; and Spain 214, 215, 226; training 82; as transnational network 54, 57, 178; UK as target for 148–9, 153
Al Rashid Trust 42
al-Suri, Abu Musab 90
al-Tawhid 97
al-Wafa Humanitarian Organization 36
al-Zarqawi, Abu Musab 240
al-Zawahiri, Ayman 27, 72–3, 98, 100, 153, 213
Algemene Inlichtingen en Veiligheidsdienst (AIVD) 3
Algeria 99, 152, 153, 169, 198
Algerian Islamic Liberation Front 237
Ali, Ayaan Hirsi 11, 171, 173
alienation 23, 74, 129, 158
Alonso, Rogelio 8, 207–30
Alouny, Taysir 225
Amsterdam 182–4
anger 75
Ansar al-Islam 235, 237, 238, 239–40, 252n44
Ansari, Humayun 121, 135–6
Anti-Democratic radicals 175, 177, 178
anti-radicalisation 157; *see also* counter-radicalisation
Appleby, Scott 6
AQ Khan network 41
Arab European League 177
Arab Human Development Report 39, 40
ASALA (Armenian Secret Army for the Liberation of Armenia) 192

Atta, Mohammed 30
attitudes: anti-Muslim 233–4; and behaviour 73
Auzmendi, Ekaitz Sirvent 203
Azizi, Amer 210, 227
Azzam, Abdullah 26, 27, 71
Azzouz, Samir 172, 174

B Specials 159
Badaat, Sajid 151, 156
Bakker, Edwin 8, 168–90
Bakri Muhammad, Omar 117, 118, 156
Bali bombings (2002) 29, 44
Barber, Benjamin 25
Barcelona Process 39, 40
Barot, Dhiren 155–6
Basque terrorism *see* ETA
Beghal, Djamel 95, 96, 96–8, 99, 100, 101, 108
Belgium 96, 99
Ben Khemais, Sami 234, 235
Benmerzouga, Brahim 152
Benyaich brothers 216–17, 227
best practices 12–13, 14, 37, 47
bin Laden, Osama 22, 23–4, 27, 28, 68, 100, 123, 148, 210, 213, 224, 226; as hero 70, 105–6; lectures and speeches 75–6, 78–81; and Muslim Brotherhood 71
Bjorgo, Tore 4
Björkman, Carl 8, 231–55
black holes 22
Black Panther movement 47
Blair, Sir Ian 145
"blind-eye bystanders" 23
blowback effect 33
Bonte, Johan 98, 101, 109
book translations 39
born-again Muslims 30, 34, 91
Bosnia 27, 34, 148, 150, 152, 169, 234
Bossi, Umberto 233
Bouchta, Bouiriqi 245
Boughanemi, Faycal 238
Bourgass, Kamel 124, 155
Bouyeri, Mohammed 30, 172, 173–4
Bowyer Bell, J. 159
Brahim, Ahmed 214–15
braindrain 39
Buijs, Frank 9

Carlile, Lord 156
Casablanca bombings 29, 238
Castro, Manex 203
charities 35–7, 40

Chechnya 27, 33, 36, 63, 150, 169, 171, 205
Chedadi brothers 217
Chergi brothers 217
choice, personal 128
CILAT 198
Civil Rights Movement 47
civil society 41, 46
Clan na Gael 146
Clarke, Peter 141–2, 154
clash of civilizations 25
clerics *see* imams
Clutterbuck, Lindsay 8, 90, 144–67
CNN 24, 77
cognitive opening 5, 91
collective action frames 74–7, 82
collective consciousness 81
colonialism 33
Common Foreign and Security Policy (CFSP) 26, 38, 40
communities: radical 50–4, 56, *58*, 59, 60, 62; traditional 52–3
community-based approaches 12–13, 14
community impact assessment 10
Companions of the Prophet Mohammad 193
computer ownership 39
conflict resolution 14
Conseil Français du Culte Musulman (CFCM) 196
CONTEST strategy 1, 160–1, 163
cooperative counter-terrorist measures 22, 182, 202–4, 247, 248–9
Copeland, David 154
counter-insurgency (COIN) 146–7, 160
counter-narratives 15
counter-radicalisation 9–13, 45–8, 109–10, 157, 160; benchmarking 9–10; *see also under* individual countries
counter-terrorism 1, 34; cooperative measures 22, 182, 202–4, 247, 248–9; *see also under* individual countries
Courtallier, David 87, 101, 109
Courtallier, Jerome 101, 109
"Covenant of Security" 117, 119–20, 122
criminals 151, 240
crisis management 11, 14
cultural studies 5

Dabbas, Mouhannad Almallah 210, 217
Dabbas, Moutaz Almallah 209, 217
Dahdah, Abu 214, 216, 217
Dambruoso, Stefano 239
Dannin, Robert 194

Daoudi, Kamel 98–9, 108
dawa 176, 177
de-radicalisation 157
death 78, 208, 216
Declaration of the World Islamic Front for Jihad against the Jews and the Crusaders 24
della Porta, Donatella 61
Demant, Froukje 9
democracy 16, 39–40, 44
Denmark 2, 11, 12, 14
deportations 247, 249, 250
development 39–40
Dhani, Ahmad 12
dialogue 45
Direction Centrale des Renseignements Généraux (DCRG) 193, 198, 199
Direction Centrale du Renseignement Intérieur (DCRI) 191, 193, 198–9
Direction de la surveillance du territoire (DST) 198, 199
discrimination 47, 181, 233
doctrinal development, EU 37–8, 45–8
document-forging 231, 237
document security 246
Doha, Abu 234
drifters 94–5, 109–10
Droukdel, Abdelmalek 203

education 14, 47, 71, 222; *see also* madrasas; Pesantren
Egyptian Gamaa 237
Egyptian Jihad 237
Eidarous, Ibrahim 148
El Bouhali, Ahmed 238
El Sayed, Anwar Shaaban 245
Empowerent project 10
energy resources 28
entrepreneurs 88, 92–3, 108, 109
entry/exit strategies 16
Es Sayed, Abdelkader Mahmoud 234, 235
ETA 202–4, 219, 225–6
ethnic minorities 51–4, 55, 56, 57
Etienne, Bruno 195
European Commission 13, 221
European Commission against Racism and Intolerance (ECRI) 233
European Security and Defence Policy 26
European Union (EU) 247, 254n81; challenges to 28–9; definition of terrorism 21; doctrinal development 37–8, 45–8; foreign and defence policy 11, 26, 31, 32–3, 38, 40, 45, 48; Joint Situation Centre (SITCEN) 3

exclusivism 176, 177, 178

facilitating (or accelerator) causes 4–5
Fakhet, Sarhane Ben Abdelmajid *see* Sarhane "the Tunisian"
Fallaci, Oriana 233
FATAH-RC 191
Fawwaz, Khalid 148
FINTER 198
Fitna (film) 185
Fizazi, Mohamed 217
foreign policy 2, 4, 11, 15, 26, 31, 32–3, 38, 40, 45, 48, 136
Fouad, Mullah 239–40
Foundation for Plurality and Life Together 222–3
France 8, 25, 33, 89, 90, 96, 191–206; *banlieues riots* (2005) 192, 201; counter-terrorism 197–204 (legal framework 200–2); intelligence agencies 191, 198–9; judiciary police 199–200; 9 September Act (1986) 197; prison population 196; terrorist activity 191–2, 193, 195–7, 205–6; Vigipirate plan 197, 198
friendships 215–16
Front Islamique du Salut (FIS) 97, 214
Frontex agency 204
fundamentalism 69; Islamic 25, 26, 28, 68, 69–70, 71
funding of terrorist groups 35–7, 40–1, 42, 198, 236, 248
funnel-and-filter phenomenon 157

G8 Action Plan 247, 255n83
Gamson, W. 74
gangs 16
gatekeepers 32, 34, 35
gateway organizations 2, 15–16
Gaza 186
Geertz, Clifford 69
Germany 33, 248
GIA (Groupe Islamique Armée) 63, 89, 96, 97, 111n9, 192, 195, 214, 237
GICM *see* Moroccon Islamic Combatant Group
globalization 3, 25
good governance 40
Granada 24–5
group dynamics 16
Groupe d'Intervention de la Gendarmerie Nationale (GIGN) 200
Groupe Salafiste pour la Prédication et le Combat (GSPC) 89, 95, 97, 204–5, 236, 237–8, 247

Guantanamo Bay 47

Hadith 42, 70, 125
Hafs al-Masri, Abu 98
Hamas 186, 214
Hamdy, Atef 9
Hamza al-Masri, Abu 97, 123–4, 132, 144, 156
Hanif, Asif 150
Hardy, Roger 11
Hashmi, Syed 151
Hassan, Nasr Osama Mostafa 243
"hearts and minds" campaigns 38, 40, 45, 48, 147, 160, 161, 164n20, 224–5
Heathrow airport plot 148, 153, 162
Hellmich, Christina 8, 68–86
Hezbollah 169, 192
Hijaz 24
Hizb-ut-Tahrir 131, 132, 178, 186, 237, 252n35
Hofstadgroep 172, 174, 178
holy text: interpretation of 31; *see also* Hadith; Quran
Horgan, John 2, 5, 6, 50
Huband, Mark 8, 117–43
human rights 28, 47, 249
Huntington, Samuel 25
Hussain, Hasib 106–7, 108, 138

Ibn Taymiyya 27, 243
idealism 88
identity 23, 45, 117, 118; assertion of 128, 129–31, 132, 136; and collective action frames 74, 75; crisis 5, 6, 31, 55
ideology 26–7, 51, 55, 56, 108, 131, 138; Al-Qaeda 1, 71–3, 82–3
imams 32, 156, 157, 177, 181, 221, 227, 245
immigrants *see* migrants
imperial policing 38
incentives 77–8, 80–1
India 146, 152, 162
Indonesia 12, 44
informatiehuishouding 183
injustice, sense of 74, 75, 158
innovation 11–13
Institute for Migration and Ethnic Studies (IMES) 182, 183
integration 47, 118, 181
intelligence/intelligence agencies 22, 45, 141–2, 161, 198–9, 244; community 147, 161; cooperation 22, 202–4
international counter-terrorist cooperation 22, 182, 202–4, 247, 248–9

Internet 2, 3, 15, 25, 32, 33, 47, 90, 125, 128, 158, 185, 213, 214–15, 227, 241–2; access to 39; monitoring of 48, 200, 201–2, 246
Iran 28, 147, 169
Iraq 90, 147, 150, 169, 171, 213, 239
Iraq war 29, 34, 38, 215
Iraqi insurgency 29, 38
Iraqi Jihad veterans 33–4, 227
Ireland 38, 126, 146, 147, 158–9, 162
Irish Republican Army (IRA) 63, 147, 153, 159, 162
Irish Republican Brotherhood (IRB) 159
Irish Republicanism 158–9
Islam 25, 26, 69, 70
Islam phobia 181
Islamic Commission of Spain 221
Islamic fundamentalism 25, 26, 28, 68, 69–70, 71
Islamic Jihad 27
Islamic Neo-radicalism 176
Islamic World Front 215
isolation 118, 176
Israel 24, 33, 72, 150, 186, 213, 242
Issac, Hamdi 248
Italy 8, 231–55; anti-Muslim attitudes 233–4; counter-radicalisation 245–6; counter-terrorism 243–50 (legislative framework 233, 248); deportations 247, 249, 250; document-forging 231, 237; intelligence 244, 248, 249; mosques and cultural centres 232, 233, 245–6; Muslim population 231–2, 249; police 248, 249; prison population 240–1; terrorist activity 231, 234–40
Izzadeen, Abu 117, 118, 119, 122

Jahiliyya 27
Jaish-e-Mohammed (JeM) 42
Jama-at-al-Tabligh Wal-Dawa 177
Jamaat al-Dawa wa-al-Tabligh 96, 105
Jemaah Islamiyah (JI) 44, 153
Jews 22, 24, 242
jihad 27, 34, 120, 121, 125, 132–3, 176; covert 178; defensive 150, 155; glorification of 32; individualized 90; offensive 149–50
Jongman, Berto 21
Jung, Carl Gustav 81
juvenilization 90

Kaplan sect 63
Kashmir 27, 42, 150, 153, 171
Kashmiri Welfare Association 103

Kelkal, Khaled 195–6
Kenya 29, 146
Kepel, Gilles 3
Khalistan 152
Khan, Mohammed Siddique 87, 95, 102–4, 105, 107, 108, 109, 138, 154
Khattak, Arasiab 42
Khomeiny, Ayatollah 28
Khosrokhavar, Farhad 3
kinship 215–17
knowledge hubs 40
Korteweg, Rem 7, 21–49
Krekar, Mullah 239, 248

Laagoub, Abdelkader 238
Lakhani, Hemant 151
Lamari, Allekama 218
Lashkar-e-Toiba (LeT) 42
Launching a Musical Jihad against Religious Hatred and Terrorism 12
Lawrence, T.E. 9
leadership 6, 16, 211, 227
Lebanon 28, 248
legislation, anti-terrorism 47; France 200–2; Italy 233, 248
Leheny, David 5
LibForAll Foundation 12
Libya 41, 147, 169
Libyan Islamic Fighting Group 97
Lindsay, Jermaine 104, 107–8, 109, 126–7, 138, 156
London bombings (2005) 1, 3, 14, 102–8, 117, 137, 145, 149, 179; official report 124–5, 126–7, 137–8
Lone Actors 154

Maamri, Rachid 245
McRoy, Anthony 136–7
madrasas 41–2
Madrid bombings (2004) 1, 89, 90, 112n11, 179, 207, 209, 217, 218, 219, 239
Mafia 240
Majid, Mohammed (Mullah Fouad) 239–40
Malaya 38, 146
Malthaner, Stefan 7–8, 50–67
Mamour, Sheikh Abdul Qader Fadlallah 245
Mao Zedong 23
Markaz-ud-Dawa-wal-Irshad (MDI) 42
Marret, Jean-Luc 8, 191–206
martyrdom 32, 72–3, 125, 133, 216, 227
Massoud, Ahmad Shah 148, 237
Maymouni, Mustapha 209, 211–12, 216, 217

media 4, 15, 25, 32, 33, 45, 47, 224–5; *see also* Internet
mentoring 12, 47, 125, 157
Mercy International Relief Organization 36
Meziane, Baghdad 152
Miami 7 153
migrants 8, 61–4, 89, 169, 191, 201
military interventions 4, 33, 40
Ministerial Conference on Integration (2004) 47
minorities, ethnic/religious 51–4, 55, 56, 57
Minta, Mohamed 195
misfits 93–4, 108–9, 109–10
moderation 45
modernism/modernization 25, 71, 74
Mohammad, Abdullah 36
Mohammed cartoon crisis 2, 11, 14, 235
Mohammed, Chise 239, 240
Mohammed the Egyptian *see* Ahmed, Rabei Osman al-Sayed
Mohammed, Khalid Sheikh 30
Mohammed VI, king of Morocco 43
Moqua, Sheikh Ibrahim 121
Morocco 43–4
Moroccon Islamic Combatant Group (GICM) 89, 112n11, 205, 237, 238–9
mosques 8, 34, 35, 124, 177, 185, 193, 208, 232, 233, 245–6, 250n3
motivational aspects 4, 5, 8, 87–114, 149–51, 158, 212
Mughen, Abu 216
Mujahideen Services Bureau 27
Muslim Brotherhood 26, 71, 177
Muslim Nationalism 175, 177, 178

Nadhlatul Ulama 12
Najmuddin, Faraj Ahmad *see* Krekar, Mullah
Naseem, Mohammed 121–2
nation state 57, 61
nationalism: Muslim 175, 177, 178; Sikh 147, 152
NATO 247, 254–5n82
Needl, Mohammed 217
neo-conservatism 28
neo-imperialism 33
neo-radicalism 176
neosalafism 208
Nesser, Petter 2, 8, 87–114
Netherlands 3, 8, 9, 33, 34–5, 36, 168–90; counter-terrorism and counter-radicalisation 179–84, 187; Crimes of Terrorism Act 180; Empowerment

project 10; Immigration and Naturalisation Service (IND) 180; Islamism 168–70; Polarisation and Radicalisation Action Plan 2007–2011 180–1; Security Services 168, 169, 170, 175, 180; terrorist activity 172, 173–4; Terrorist Threat Assessment reports 184, 185, 186–7
networks 153–4, 178, 185, 213–14; interpersonal links 215–17; transnational 51, 54–6, 57, *58*, 59, 61, 62, 63–4, 178
news discourse 76–7
newspapers 39
Northern Ireland 38, 126, 146, 147
Norway 248
nuclear programmes, Pakistan 41

obedience 79
oil revenues 25, 26
Olimpio, Guido 232
Omand, Sir David 1, 138–40
Omar, Abu 243, 245
Operation Crevice 104
Operation Enduring Freedom 29, 42, 153
Operation Infinite Reach 29
Operation Iraqi Freedom 29
Operation Muntasir 99–100
Operation Overt 145
Oplan Bojinka plot 145
Osman, Hussain 248
Ottoman Empire 25
Oulad brothers 217

Padilla, Jose 194, 240
Pakistan 41–3, 44, 186; Inter-Services Intelligence Directorate (ISI) 42
Palestine 33, 54, 72, 146, 147, 162, 213
Palestine Liberation Organisation (PLO) 153
parallelism 63, 176, 177, 178
participation 73–4, 77–81
Pearl, Daniel 42, 155
personal responsibility 72, 79
Pesantren 44
PET (Danish Security Service) 12
Piranha group 174
Piscatori, James 69
police 22; cross-border anti-terrorist actions 202–4; France 199–200; Italy 248, 249; Spain 219, 220–1, 223–4
politics 109, 132; religion and 69–70
Post, Jerrold 5
Preventing Extremism Together (PET) project 3, 10, 156, 158

prisons 3, 32, 35, 46, 177; France 196; Italy 240–1; Spain 8, 208, 217–18, 225–6; UK 157; US 194–5
propaganda 96, 125, 212–13, 214
protégés 93, 108
protest, public 16
protest movements 51, 57, 59–61
Provisional IRA (PIRA) 159
psychological approaches 2
public–private partnerships 47–8
Puritan Islamic Missionary 177
Puritanism, Islamic 175, 177, 178

Qatada, Abu 97, 132, 156, 210, 213, 235
Quran 42, 68, 70, 125
Qutb, Muhammad 27
Qutb, Sayyid 26–7

radical communities 50–4, 56, *58*, 59, 60, 62
radical milieu 50
radical networks, transnational 51, 54–6, 57, *58*, 59, 61, 62, 63–4
radical subcultures 51, 57, 59–61
Rafik, Mohamed 245
Rahaman-Alan, Hazil 154
Ramadan, Tariq 97
Ranstorp, Magnus 1–18
reality 69–70
recruitment 34–48; radical communities 51, *58*; radical subcultures 60; of the toughest 8, 81–2; transnational radical networks *58*
regional conflicts 4, 15
Reid, John 148
Reid, Richard 30, 35, 124, 149, 151, 155, 156, 240
Reinares, Fernando 3
religion 2, 28, 55, 109; and politics 69–70
religious minorities 51–4, 55, 56, 57
religious seeking 5–6, 74
rendition of suspects 47
research agenda 13–17, 37–8, 46
resource mobilization theory 77
responsibility, personal 72, 79
Reynald of Chatillon 24
Ricin trial 144
Riyadh 29
Rouass, Najib 245
Rowe, Andrew 151, 155, 156
Roy, Olivier 54
Royal Ulster Constabulary 159
Rushdie, Salman 168

SAFTI (Secure and Facilitated International Travel Initiative) 247
Sageman, Marc 5, 82, 110, 151
Sahraoui, Imam 195
Salafists/Salafism 8, 68, 120, 131, 136, 172, 175, 186, 193, 208, 250n4
Salafiyya Jihadiyya 178
Sarhane "the Tunisian" 209, 210, 211, 215, 216, 217, 218
Saudi Arabia 24, 29, 41, 44, 72, 169, 212, 213, 232, 250n3; charities 35–7
Schmidt, Alex 21
schools 41–2, 177
Schwartz, Stephen 68
security impact assessment 40
Setmariam, Mustapha 227
Shabiba Islamiya 205
shared grievances 75, 85n33
Sharif, Omar 150
Sheikh, Ahmed Omar Saeed 155
Shiite Muslims 28
"shoe bomber" *see* Reid, Richard
Sikh nationalism 147, 152
Single Narrative 3, 11, 15
Sirseloudi, Matenia 7–8, 50–67
Skirmishers 146
social movement theory 2, 5, 8, 234
social movements 57, 59
social network analysis 6
social resistance 184–5, 186–7
social-revolutionaries 60
socio-economic background 73, 89, 92, 93, 158, 193–4, 195, 227
socio-economic lag 29, 32, 45, 47
Somalia 28
Soviet Union 28, 42, 150, 152, 213
Spain 8, 202–4, 207–30, 248; Civil Guard 219; counter-radicalisation 221–4, 225–6, 228; counter-terrorism 202–4, 219–26, 228; education initiatives 222–3; Foundation for Plurality and Life Together 222–3; intelligence capabilities 219, 220–1, 228; Office of Religious Affairs 221, 222, 224, 226; police force 219, 220–1, 223–4; prison population 8, 208, 217–18, 225–6; public diplomacy 224–5; terrorist activity 207, 219; *see also* Madrid bombings
splinter groups 59, 63
Squarcini, Bernard 198
stigmatization 31–2, 47
Strasbourg Christmas market attack 46
structural causes 4–5
students 156

subcultures 51, 57, 59–61
Submission (film) 11, 171
Sudan 29
suicide/suicide attacks 72–3, 125, 134–5, 150, 153, 196–7, 227
Suleiman, Abu 119–20
Sykes–Picot agreement (1915) 25
sympathy 73, 82
Syria 248

Takfir wal Hijra 172, 173, 178
Taliban 22, 36, 42, 124, 153
Talibi, Moulay El-Hassan El-Alaoui 196
Tanweer, Shehzad 87, 102, 104–6, 108, 138
Tanzania 29
Taylor, Charles Holland 12
technology: extremists use of 25; intelligence 244
telephones 196, 244, 246–7
Templar, Sir Gerald 38
Tensamani, Hicham 209, 210
territory, defence of 52, 55
terrorism 1, 89–91; anti-systemic 21–3; background and contributing factors 29, 30, 31–48; catastrophic 22; causes of 23–6, 29, 30; cultural or religious 22; homegrown 1–2; ideological roots 26–7; justification for 125, 212, 213, 226; pyramid structure 23; state-sponsorhip 147, 169; transnational 54, 55, 56, 178; *see also under* individual countries
terrorist groups 61; documents and propaganda 96, 125, 212–13, 214, 242–3; *see also* Internet; funding 35–7, 40–1, 42, 198, 236, 248; organisation and structure 153–4, 235; radical communities and 53–4, 56; typology of members 88, 91–5; *see also* names of individual groups
Tilly, Charles 57
Tönnies, F. 53
Trabelsi, Mouard 245
Trabelsi, Nizar 98, 99–101, 108
traditional communities 52–3
training, Al-Qaeda 82
transnational radical networks 51, 54–6, 57, *58*, 59, 61, 62, 63–4, 178
Trashorras, José Emilio Suárez 240
triggering causes 4
Trotsky, Leon 74
Tunisian islamic Fighting Group 97
typology of terrorist cell members 88, 91–5

umma 79, 175–6
underdevelopment 39–40
unemployment 32, 192, 193
Unité de coordination de la lutte anti-terroriste (UCLAT) 198
United Kingdom (UK) 8, 25, 38, 89, 117–43, 144–67; counter-insurgency (COIN) doctrine 146–7, 160; counter-terrorism 1, 10, 121, 122–3, 135–42, 146–7, 160–3, 248–9; foreign policy 136; House of Commons Intelligence and Security Committee 3; Preventing Extremism Together (PET) project 3, 10, 156, 158; prisons 157; terrorist activity 145–9, 151, 152–3, 154, 162; *see also* London bombings
United Nations Development Program (UNDP) 39
United Nations (UN) 72, 247
United States 24, 33, 40, 72, 90, 121, 157; Civil Rights Movement 47; and Iraq 38; neo-conservatism 28; 9/11 attacks 1, 22, 148–9, 179, 219; prison population 194–5
universities 156
urbanization 25–6
USS Cole, attack on 29

van Gogh, Theo 11, 14, 21, 30, 171, 172, 173–4, 179
veterans 171; Afghan 152, 153, 171; Iraqi Jihad 33–4, 227
Victoroff, Jeff 2
Vidino, Lorenzo 236

Vigipirate plan 197, 198
violence 134
Vlahos, Michael 5

Wahhabism 42, 68, 172, 175, 193, 250–1n4
Waldmann, Peter 7–8, 50–67, 88
war 22
War on Terrorism 29
weapons 151, 240, 243; chemical/biological 151, 155, 205–6; radiological-based 151, 155, 205
weapons of mass destruction (WMD) 22, 41, 151
Wij Amsterdammers programme 182, 183
Wiktorowicz, Quintan 5, 68, 77–8, 110, 234
Wilders, Geert 185
Wilkinson, Tracey 240–1
Wolfowitz, Paul 237
World Assembly of Muslim Youth 36–7

Yarkas, Imad Eddin Barakat *see* Dahdah, Abu
Yousef, Ramzi 145

Zergout, Majid 245
"Zionist–Crusader Alliance" 22, 24, 28, 40, 75
Zitouni, Djamel 195
Zougam, Jamal 216
Zubair, Abu 173
Zubaydah, Abu 98, 100

eBooks – at www.eBookstore.tandf.co.uk

A library at your fingertips!

eBooks are electronic versions of printed books. You can store them on your PC/laptop or browse them online.

They have advantages for anyone needing rapid access to a wide variety of published, copyright information.

eBooks can help your research by enabling you to bookmark chapters, annotate text and use instant searches to find specific words or phrases. Several eBook files would fit on even a small laptop or PDA.

NEW: Save money by eSubscribing: cheap, online access to any eBook for as long as you need it.

Annual subscription packages

We now offer special low-cost bulk subscriptions to packages of eBooks in certain subject areas. These are available to libraries or to individuals.

For more information please contact webmaster.ebooks@tandf.co.uk

We're continually developing the eBook concept, so keep up to date by visiting the website.

www.eBookstore.tandf.co.uk

Printed in Great Britain
by Amazon.co.uk, Ltd.,
Marston Gate.